Bribery and Corruption

Navigating the Global Risks

BRIAN LOUGHMAN
RICHARD SIBERY
ERNST & YOUNG LLP

WILEY

John Wiley & Sons, Inc.

Published by John Wiley & Sons, Inc., Hoboken, New Jersey.
Published simultaneously in Canada.

For general information on our other products and services or for technical support, please contact our Customer Care Department within the United States at (800) 762-2974, outside the United States at (317) 572-3993 or fax (317) 572-4002.

Wiley also publishes its books in a variety of electronic formats. Some content that appears in print may not be available in electronic books. For more information about Wiley products, visit our web site at www.wiley.com.

Library of Congress Cataloging-in-Publication Data

Loughman, Brian P.
  Bribery and corruption: navigating the global risks/Brian P. Loughman, Richard A. Sibery.
    p. cm. – (Wiley corporate F & A series; 568)
  Published simultaneously in Canada.
  Includes index.
  ISBN 978-1-118-01136-2 (hardback); ISBN 978-1-118-16618-5 (ebk);
ISBN 978-1-118-16619-2 (ebk); ISBN 978-1-118-16620-8 (ebk)
    1. International business enterprises–Law and legislation–Criminal provisions.
    2. Bribery.   3. Corporations, Foreign–Corrupt practice. I.   Sibery, Richard A. II.   Title.
  K5216.L68 2011
  345'.02323–dc23

                                                                                    2011025471

Printed in the United States of America
10 9 8 7 6 5 4 3 2

To David Stulb, the Global Leader of Ernst & Young's Fraud Investigation and Dispute Services practice. David is a long-time mentor, colleague, and friend. His support has been instrumental in the creation of this book and the success of Ernst & Young's anti-corruption team.

Contents

Foreword

Brian Loughman, Rick Sibery, and the professionals from Ernst & Young's Fraud Investigation & Dispute Services (FIDS) practice have done a fine job in putting together a highly practical, comprehensive guide on the global risks of bribery and corruption. This is a topic that has grown in complexity and risk—and this guide is helpful to all of us who must navigate this road in challenging jurisdictions throughout the world.

It is no secret that bribery and corruption continue, for good and welcome reasons, to be an increasing focus of governments and public institutions around the world. New laws continue to be passed, and enforcement outside the United States is increasing, though many jurisdictions remain woefully behind in enforcing anticorruption laws. The United States continues to be a leader in aggressively enforcing the Foreign Corrupt Practices Act (FCPA). During 2010 and 2011, we have seen heavy fines, many individual prosecutions, and even an FCPA sting. The Department of Justice and the Securities and Exchange Commission are working with their counterparts throughout the world to ensure an even playing field for companies as they compete for contracts and expand business in far-reaching corners of the world.

The most significant recent change has been in the United Kingdom. The U.K. Bribery Act of 2010, which came into force in July 2011, is a significant step forward in anticorruption legislation. Comments from the U.K.'s Serious Fraud Office indicate that enforcement is also likely to be aggressive.

This guide capably walks through the U.S. and U.K. laws, providing a helpful outline of the major legal principles—including the sometimes-overlooked books and records provision of the FCPA and the important and new concept in the U.K. law of an "adequate procedures" defense—in effect, a defense where a company has a robust compliance program.

The book gives readers a clear and thorough picture of the key elements of who should form an anticorruption compliance program. Brian and Rick hit all the key elements and in doing so provide sound, practical explanations and guidance: from setting the overall tone for an organization through anticorruption policies and procedures; to establishing proactive steps to identify and monitor bribery and corruption risks throughout the organization; to being prepared to respond when an issue is identified through an investigative protocol/ombudsman process. At GE, we think of these elements as "prevention, detection and response." Each element is discussed in a realistic and understandable manner. Brian and Rick also illustrate how bribery and corruption issues may change over time and provide examples of how a company's anticorruption program should continuously evolve to maintain its effectiveness—including "learning from misses," since there is no such thing as a perfect program.

I have had the pleasure of working with Brian, Rick, and Ernst & Young's FIDS practice. This book makes the considerable experience of the Ernst & Young professionals very clear. I especially like the chapter on the regions of the world that highlights the importance of understanding the local environment when expanding into new geographies. It underscores the value of having local knowledge and perspective in helping to identify and address bribery and corruption risks. Likewise, the chapter on industries contextualizes the rest of the book across a broad spectrum of diverse business areas. While certain industries have been a focus for enforcement activity (e.g., pharmaceuticals and energy), it is helpful to see bribery and corruption risks considered across a wide range of industries.

Many thanks to my friends at Ernst & Young for helping us all increase our understanding and awareness of what should be done to effectively navigate global bribery and corruption risks. I am sure you will find this a rewarding book to consult.

Brackett Denniston
Senior Vice President and General Counsel
General Electric Company

Preface

The risk of bribery and corruption continues to be an area of concern for companies around the world. As businesses continue to expand globally into new and emerging markets, bribery and corruption risks have increased exponentially due to increased awareness and enforcement.

Bribery and Corruption: Navigating the Global Risks offers a comprehensive picture of this growing problem and what companies should be doing to mitigate their risks. The book provides background on the Foreign Corrupt Practices Act, the U.K. Bribery Act, and international anti-bribery and corruption conventions, highlighting recent enforcement trends and regulatory expectation. Practical considerations and solutions are offered to help companies develop and refine their response to bribery and corruption through an anti-corruption compliance program.

The book includes an overview of several regions of the world as well as further detail on a number of countries. Regional commonalities and "red flags" are highlighted, and country-specific laws and enforcement information are included. Insights from an industry perspective are provided on trends and potential areas of focus for players in a number of industries.

This book was written by a group of experienced professionals from Ernst & Young's Fraud Investigation & Dispute Services (FIDS) practices worldwide. Ernst & Young firms have FIDS practices is in over 50 countries, including over 1,000 dedicated professionals focused on assisting companies with fraud issues. We have drawn upon the collective experience of this group to share our views and experience in a way that we hope will provide practical guidance with real-world issues.

CHAPTER ONE

Introduction

B RIBERY AND CORRUPTION HAS an impact on everyone, and while the impact is not immediately recognizable to most of us, the global impact cannot be underestimated. From developing countries in Africa, Latin America, and Asia to the United States, Western Europe, and the United Kingdom, bribery and corruption continues to create an uneven playing field in international trade, commerce, and the process of government. Problems range from the small payment demanded by a customs official to inappropriately process an import package, to multimillion-dollar payments to secure a large government contract. These are just two examples of the myriad of scenarios that businesses face in the international market place.

"A part of the culture." "The cost of doing business." "Our competitors are doing it." "Not a big deal." These refrains are just a few of the reasons given to make corrupt payments. Only in recent years have we begun to see a change. One would be very hard-pressed to identify a country that has not banned corruption within its own borders. Even the most remote, undeveloped, totalitarian regime has laws on the books against bribery (albeit selectively enforced). However, it was only just over 30 years ago that the United States took a strong stand against corruption outside its borders. The Foreign Corrupt Practices Act of 1977 (FCPA) was an attempt to level the playing field by preventing corrupt payments to foreign government officials for the purposes of gaining new business.

For many, many years the FCPA was the only game in town. Even then, most businesses either hadn't heard of it or didn't see it as a significant deterrent. Enforcement was rare, and when heard about, usually involved exotic locales and large payments to government insiders. And so was the case of the FCPA for many years. Bribery and corruption remained global scourges, and there were additional attempts to level the playing field and reduce their effects. The Organization for Economic Cooperation and Development (OECD) Convention on Combating Bribery of Foreign Public Officials in International Business Transactions (OECD Anti-Bribery Convention) in 1997 was a significant step forward and at least notionally gained worldwide support.

As the new century arrived, the tide began to change. The FCPA had always had teeth—too many teeth, argued some. But it was enforcement and the advent of modern corporate compliance programs that began to turn the tide and start a wave of focus on bribery and corruption that still surges forward. Billions of dollars in fines, penalties, disgorgement of profits, and professional fees signal that we are in a world that has bribery and corruption firmly in the center of any international company's radar. The United Kingdom passed a law that many believe surpasses the FCPA in its breadth and limitations. Whether viewed as the beginning of a new era of shrinking bribery and corruption or simply as regulatory enforcement stepping over the line, the current regulatory environment demands attention.

The objective of this book is to help businesspeople understand the relevant bribery and corruption legislation, enforcement environment, and how to effectively manage the associated risks. First, we lay the groundwork by discussing bribery and corruption legislation both in the United States and around the world. We focus on laws limiting foreign bribery and corruption as the area of domestic bribery and its enforcement is much more mature and outside the scope of this book. We then discuss bribery and corruption policies, procedures, and monitoring. These chapters focus on establishing an anti-corruption compliance program. Understanding and establishing an effective anti-corruption environment through focused internal controls, training, risk assessment and monitoring is the goal. We discuss how to respond to common corruption challenges, appropriately investigate issues, and mitigate corruption concerns. We have also supplemented the book with geographic and industry profiles of corruption challenges.

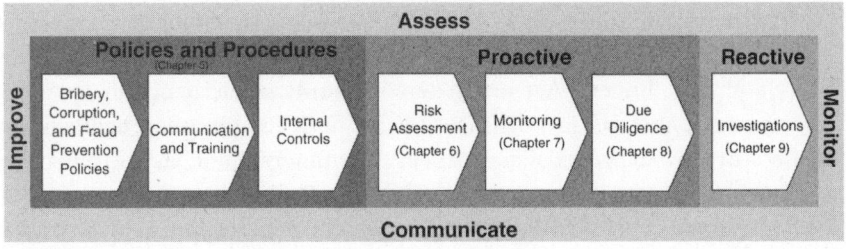

FIGURE 1.1 Anti-Corruption Compliance Program

Figure 1.1 shows the elements of an Anti-Corruption Compliance Program and is the framework of this book. Each of the elements are described in detail throughout the book.

A casual search of the Internet for bribery and corruption guidance results in an ever-expanding number of articles, books, blogs, courses, seminars, and software products that are there to assist businesses respond to bribery and corruption risks. This book was written to be a practical guide to businesspeople who are trying to understand their company's risks and how to respond. There are other resources that will provide much more legal analysis on the statutes and the implications of resulting cases.

Bribery and corruption has a very detrimental effect on an economy. The World Bank has estimated that 0.5 percent of gross domestic product (GDP) is lost through corruption each year.[1] Engaging in corrupt practices also creates a very unfavorable business environment by encouraging unfair advantage and anti-competitive practices. In addition to allowing organized crime to flourish, corruption is one of the primary obstacles to the economic development of a country; it undermines the rule of law, weakens trust in public institutions, and challenges democratic principles.[2] For example, Transparency International, a nonprofit international organization that tracks global corruption, estimates that former Indonesian leader Suharto embezzled anywhere between $15 and $35 billion from his country and that Ferdinand Marcos in the Philippines, Joseph-Désiré Mobutu in Zaire, and Sani Abacha in Nigeria may have embezzled up to $5 billion each.[3]

Saddam Hussein's regime engaged in very widespread corruption highlighted by corrupt payments it received as a result of the United Nations' "oil-for-food program" that was designed to alleviate the economic sanctions against Iraq for the benefit of its people. Well-known companies from around the world were involved in this program, and there have been a string of prosecutions and settlements in the years since it ended.

The impact of bribery and corruption can't be understated.

Although anti-corruption laws have been enacted by many countries, the FCPA and U.K. Bribery Act are generally the most expansive in terms of proscribed activities and jurisdictional reach. The FCPA is the most aggressively enforced by several orders of magnitude. Accordingly, these are the laws that most global companies use as the standards for their anti-corruption compliance programs. Consult with your legal counsel concerning local bribery laws that might apply to the jurisdictions where you do business, but know and understand the FCPA and U.K. Bribery Act and use them as the foundation for your global anti-corruption compliance program, including anti-corruption policies, procedures, controls, and training activities.

The FCPA makes it unlawful for U.S. persons and companies to pay bribes to foreign government officials (non-U.S.) for the purpose of obtaining or retaining business or for any improper advantage. The FCPA prohibits direct and indirect bribe paying through intermediaries. The FCPA also requires U.S. and non-U.S. companies with securities listed in the United States (issuers) to adhere to its books and records provisions. These provisions, which were designed to operate in tandem with the anti-bribery provisions of the FCPA, require issuers to make and keep detailed books and records that accurately and fairly reflect the transactions of the corporation and to devise and maintain an adequate system of internal accounting controls.[4] In practice, the accounting provisions have been interpreted very broadly to include false accounting or record keeping for any illegal act, including commercial bribes paid both within and outside the United States.

We discuss the U.K. Bribery Act, which came into effect on July 1, 2011, at length in the book. It remains to be seen whether the act will be enforced in a similar way as the FCPA. Serious Fraud Office (SFO) officials have painted a picture of strong enforcement using a practical approach. The question of jurisdiction and how it will be enforced is of particular concern. Some say the U.K. authorities will try to start off with a bang and bring a big case. What will happen remains to be seen, but our expectation is that the U.K. Bribery Act has further changed the landscape of anti-corruption enforcement and will continue in the vein of FCPA enforcement.

 ENFORCEMENT TRENDS

For many years the FCPA was not a statute that the U.S. Department of Justice (DOJ) aggressively or significantly utilized to prosecute international bribery. In fact, there are few reported decisions of such prosecutions in the first 20 to 25 years in the life of the statute. In the past few years, however, the number of DOJ prosecutions and Securities and Exchange Commission (SEC) enforcement actions has steadily increased from a few in 2004 to over 70 in 2010. More important, DOJ officials have steadily warned that this trend will only continue.

For example, in a November 2010 FCPA conference, Deputy Attorney General Lanny Breuer indicated that we were in a "new era" of FCPA enforcement and warned that those worried about more aggressive anti-bribery enforcement "are right to be more concerned." Mr. Breuer added that "[o]ur FCPA enforcement is stronger than it's ever been—and getting stronger." He noted figures indicating that the DOJ had recently imposed more than US$1 billion in criminal penalties in FCPA-related cases in any single 12-month period and that more individuals were going to jail.

At other recent conferences, Mr. Breuer and other DOJ officials have indicated the importance of companies having effective FCPA compliance programs that prevent fraud and corruption. The importance of effective FCPA compliance programs is highlighted by the recent enactment of the U.K. Bribery Act of 2010, wherein a defense to a prosecution under that act is having "adequate procedures."[5] Such procedures refer to a company having an effective anti-corruption/bribery compliance program in place.

Global companies are challenged on how to compete for business in countries where the norm is to demand/seek/make (bribe) payments to obtain and retain business, yet seek to be compliant with the FCPA and other broad-based laws. U.S. regulators have focused on industries, and a central theme of these agreements has been building or strengthening anti-corruption compliance programs. Industries investigated have included oil and gas, medical devices, tobacco, telecommunications, and aerospace and defense. In addition to comments by DOJ officials outlined earlier, Cheryl J. Scarboro, chief of the SEC's newly formed FCPA Unit, said that the SEC "will continue to focus on industry-wide sweeps, and no industry is immune from investigation."[6]

The 2008 Siemens corruption investigation, which led to the largest fine (US$1.6 billion) so far imposed by regulators from different countries, is a recent example of international cooperation among governments in attacking global corruption. The OECD's Anti-Bribery Convention, which sets forth standards for anti-corruption legislation, explains confronting conflicting jurisdictions, "when more than one Party has jurisdiction over an alleged offense described in this Convention, the Parties involved shall, at the request of one of them, consult with a view to determining the most appropriate jurisdiction for prosecution."[7]

ANTI-CORRUPTION COMPLIANCE PROGRAMS

A well-thought-out and comprehensive anti-corruption compliance program is the benchmark that leading companies are utilizing to manage their corruption risks. It can be a challenge to reach this benchmark in the current tumultuous business and regulatory environment. Companies are facing significant economic challenges with shrinking margins and more expectations of growth. International markets and developing economies continue to be the focus for increasing revenues and profits. All the while, the expectation is that overhead (and associated head count) will be kept low. When considering these economic challenges and constraints and adding the unprecedented level of bribery and corruption enforcement, it is no wonder that many are daunted. The chapters that follow are meant to be a guide to understand and meet the challenges of building an effective anti-corruption compliance program. Credence is also given to the necessity of accomplishing these challenges with limited resources. A one-size-fits-all approach is not the answer. Balancing risk with available resources is a key point to implementing a strong anti-corruption compliance program.

REMEMBER THE PURPOSE

As you read through the book, we encourage you to remember the original reason for dealing with bribery and corruption problems: promoting transparency and a level playing field for all businesses. At the end of the day, most international businesses benefit significantly from less corruption. They can focus their efforts on selling a good product or service and not on greasing the right palm. Many companies and even entire industries have made significant strides over the past decade in cleaning up businesses that at one time was thought impossible, and in many instances with little or no impact on their bottom line. That's not to say there are not locations or industries that still need significant help. It also doesn't mean there aren't difficult business decisions to be made. We have tried to pull together our experiences in a way that will assist you when these situations arise. We hope we have been successful.

NOTES

1. "Explanatory Memorandum on the UN Convention against Corruption." United Nations Convention against Corruption, September 30, 2009; www.fco.gov.uk/en/publications-and-documents/treaty-command-papers-ems/explanatory-memoranda/explanatory-memoranda-2005/corruption.
2. "What Effect Does Bribery and Corruption Have on Business Transactions?" Tackling Bribery and Corruption; www.anticorruption.ie/en/ACJS/Pages/FQ08000019.
3. "The Costs of Corruption." World Bank News & Broadcast, April 8, 2004; http://web.worldbank.org/WBSITE/EXTERNAL/NEWS/0,,contentMDK:20190187~menuPK:34457~pagePK:34370~piPK:34424~theSitePK:4607,00.html.
4. "Foreign Corrupt Practices Act: An Overview." DOJ; www.justice.gov/criminal/fraud/fcpa/.
5. The U.K. Bribery Act of 2010 and the adequate procedures guidance are discussed further in Chapters 3 and 4.
6. "SEC Charges Seven Oil Services and Freight Forwarding Companies for Widespread Bribery of Customs Officials." SEC, November 4, 2010; www.sec.gov/news/press/2010/2010-214.htm.
7. "Expert Meeting of the OECD Anti-Bribery Convention." OECD, November 21, 2007; www.oecd.org/dataoecd/18/56/39691044.pdf.

CHAPTER TWO

Overview of FCPA

THE U.S. FOREIGN CORRUPT Practices Act of 1977 (FCPA), containing criminal and civil sanctions, prohibits U.S. citizens, domestic or foreign companies, and persons acting on behalf of such companies to make use of any means or instrumentalities of interstate commerce to corruptly pay or offer to pay directly or indirectly, money or anything of value to a foreign official in order to obtain or retain business.[1] The FCPA also requires "issuers," including foreign companies with securities traded on a U.S. exchange or required to file reports with the Securities and Exchange Commission (SEC), to keep accounting records that accurately reflect business transactions, and maintain effective internal controls.[2]

In sum, the FCPA provides the following:

- **Anti-bribery provisions:**
  - Makes it a criminal offense for U.S. companies or persons to bribe foreign officials for business purposes.
- **Books and records and internal control provisions:**
  - Requires U.S. issuers (SEC registrants) to make and keep detailed and accurate financial records.

- Prohibits the falsifying of corporate records to conceal bribes to foreign officials and other improper payments that reflect value provided to the foreign official.
- Issuers must devise and maintain a system of internal accounting controls to ensure accurate reporting of transactions, safeguarding of assets, and that financial statements are prepared in accordance with generally accepted accounting principles (GAAP).

This chapter provides the essential statutory elements in order to understand the FCPA. Before discussing these elements, some contextual and legislative history is helpful in order to understand the statutory requirements. The FCPA was passed as a result of SEC investigations in the mid-1970s, where over 400 U.S. companies admitted to making questionable or illegal payments in excess of US$300 million to foreign government officials, politicians, and political parties in return for favorable actions.[3]

> The abuses ran the gamut from bribery of high foreign officials to secure some type of favorable action by a foreign government to so-called facilitating payments that were allegedly made to ensure that government functionaries discharged certain ministerial or clerical duties. Congress enacted the FCPA to bring a halt to the bribery of foreign officials and to restore public confidence in the integrity of the American business system.[4]

In response to these and other investigations and scandals, the FCPA was enacted. Since its enactment, the FCPA has been amended on a number of occasions, significantly in 1998 where the Act was amended to conform to the Organization for Economic Cooperation and Development (OECD) Convention of 1997.

Despite the reasons for its enactment in 1977 and amendments, as well as broad jurisdictional reach, initially the FCPA was not a statute that the U.S. Department of Justice (DOJ) aggressively or significantly utilized to prosecute international bribery. In fact, there are few reported prosecutions in the early years of the life of the statute. In the past few years, however, the number of DOJ and SEC investigations has increased from a few in 2005 to over 200 in 2010.[5]

Today, in an era of increasing FCPA investigations and government scrutiny, a challenge for global companies is how to fairly compete for business in countries where the culture is to demand/seek/make (bribe) payments to obtain and retain business, yet seek to be compliant with the FCPA and other broad-based international laws, and strive for sufficient due diligence to improve and/or maintain an effective compliance program.[6] Chapter 4 discusses anti-corruption compliance programs in detail.

 ## LEGISLATIVE HISTORY

After two-and-a-half years of hearings investigating international business corruption as noted earlier, Congress enacted the FCPA intending to bring a halt to the bribery of foreign officials and to restore public confidence in the integrity of the American business system.

In signing the FCPA into law on December 20, 1977, President Jimmy Carter stated, in part:

> I share Congress' belief that bribery is ethically repugnant and competitively unnecessary. Corrupt practices between corporations and public officials overseas undermine the integrity and stability of governments and harm our relations with other countries. Recent revelations of widespread overseas bribery have eroded public confidence in our basic institutions.[7]

However, over the years that followed, American companies were found to be at a disadvantage in conducting business abroad, particularly in competition with foreign businesses. In introducing legislation to amend the FCPA in 1998 and seeking consistency of law to international standards,[8] the Senate Committee on Banking, Housing, and Urban Affairs stated:

> Since the passage of the FCPA, American businesses have operated at a disadvantage relative to foreign competitors who have continued to pay bribes without fear of penalty. Such bribery is estimated to affect overseas procurements valued in the billions of dollars each year. [...]
>
> This legislation, coupled with implementation of the OECD Convention by our major trading partners, will go a long way towards leveling the playing field for U.S. businesses in international contracts.
>
> In 1988, Congress directed the Executive Branch actively to seek to level the playing field by encouraging our trading partners to enact legislation similar to the FCPA. These efforts eventually culminated in the Organization for Economic Cooperation and Development

Convention on Combating Bribery of Foreign Public Officials in International Business Transactions (the "OECD Convention"). Thirty-three countries, comprising most of the significant trading countries in the world, signed this Convention in Paris in December 1997.[9]

On November 10, 1998, President Bill Clinton signed into law the International Anti-Bribery and Fair Competition Act of 1998 (amending the FCPA of 1977), in order to implement the OECD Convention into the existing law. (The OECD Convention is further explained in Chapter 3.) In his signing statement, President Clinton added:

> The United States has led the effort to curb international bribery. We have long believed bribery is inconsistent with democratic values, such as good governance and the rule of law. It is also contrary to basic principles of fair competition and harmful to efforts to promote economic development. Since the enactment in 1977 of the Foreign Corrupt Practices Act, U.S. businesses have faced criminal penalties if they engaged in business-related bribery of foreign public officials. Foreign competitors, however, did not have similar restrictions and could engage in this corrupt activity without fear of penalty. ...
>
> The OECD Convention ... is designed to change all that. ... The United States intends to work diligently, through the monitoring-process to be established under the OECD, to ensure that the Convention is widely ratified and fully implemented. We will continue our leadership in the international fight against corruption.[10]

OVERVIEW AND KEY FCPA STATUTORY ELEMENTS

The FCPA contains criminal anti-bribery/corruption provisions, which are investigated by the DOJ. As reflected earlier, the statute also contains books and records and internal controls provisions, which are normally civil violations and investigated by the SEC. The DOJ and the SEC tend to work together when necessary to enforce the provisions of the FCPA.[11]

Anti-Bribery Provisions

The anti-bribery provisions make it unlawful for a U.S. person, corporation, and certain foreign issuers of securities, to make a payment to a foreign official for the purpose of obtaining or retaining business.[12]

The Statute

The FCPA provisions are detailed. Later in this chapter, we set forth the relevant provisions of the statute and thereafter attempt to simplify the understanding by indicating practical considerations and how courts have interpreted the requirements of the statute. Before doing so, however, it's important to provide some definitional perspective.

Who Does the Statute Apply To?

The FCPA has broad application. It applies to what it refers to as a "domestic concern." It defines a "domestic concern" as

> (A) any individual who is a citizen, national, or resident of the United States; and (B) any corporation, partnership, association, joint-stock company, business trust, unincorporated organization, or sole proprietorship which has its principal place of business in the United States, or which is organized under the laws of a State of the United States or a territory, possession, or commonwealth of the United States.[13]

The statute also applies to any issuer that has a class of securities registered pursuant to Section 78 of Title 15, United States Code, or that is required to file reports under Section 78o(d) of Title 15, or for any officer, director, employee, or agent of such issuer or any stockholder thereof acting on behalf of such issuer.[14]

Thus, the act can apply to an individual; business, regardless of whether it is a public corporation or private business; or for that matter a sole proprietorship, and even a foreign company that has a class of securities registered within the United States. Because of the law of conspiracy (i.e., two or more persons agreeing to commit a crime with one conspirator committing an overt act as defined in 18 U.S.C. 371), foreign firms and individuals can be criminally liable under the FCPA.

What Is a Foreign Official?

In the legislative history discussed earlier and, as we see in the following language of the statute, the FCPA refers to the phrase *foreign official* in the context of bribery to retain or obtain business. The term *foreign official* means any officer or employee of a foreign government or any department, agency, or instrumentality thereof, or of a public international organization, or any person acting in an official capacity for or on behalf of any such government or department, agency, or instrumentality, or for or on behalf of any such public international organization.[15]

Instances of the broad definition and application of a *foreign official* can include judges, legislators, doctors, or administrators at government-controlled hospitals; officials from government-controlled universities; United Nations officials and persons working for international organizations; private persons acting in an official capacity; and a spouse, dependent, or sibling of an official.[16]

What Do the Criminal FCPA Bribery Statutory Provisions Prohibit?

The criminal anti-bribery statutory provisions of the FCPA provide as follows:

(a) It shall be unlawful for any domestic concern, other than an issuer which is subject to section 78dd-1 of this title, or for any officer, director, employee, or agent of such domestic concern or any stock-holder thereof acting on behalf of such domestic concern, to make use of the mails or any means or instrumentality of interstate commerce corruptly in furtherance of an offer, payment, promise to pay, or authorization of the payment of any money, or offer, gift, promise to give, or authorization of the giving of anything of value to—

1. any foreign official for purposes of—
   A. (i) influencing any act or decision of such foreign official in his official capacity, (ii) inducing such foreign official to do or omit to do any act in violation of the lawful duty of such official, or (iii) securing any improper advantage; or
   B. inducing such foreign official to use his influence with a foreign government or instrumentality thereof to affect or influence any act or decision of such government or instrumentality, in order to assist such domestic concern in obtaining or retaining business for or with, or directing business to, any person;
2. any foreign political party or official thereof or any candidate for foreign political office for purposes of—
   A. (i) influencing any act or decision of such party, official, or candidate in its or his official capacity, (ii) inducing such party, official, or candidate to do or omit to do an act in violation of the lawful duty of such party, official, or candidate, or (iii) securing any improper advantage; or
   B. inducing such party, official, or candidate to use its or his influence with a foreign government or instrumentality

thereof to affect or influence any act or decision of such government or instrumentality, in order to assist such domestic concern in obtaining or retaining business for or with, or directing business to, any person;

3. any person, while knowing[17] that all or a portion of such money or thing of value will be offered, given, or promised, directly or indirectly, to any foreign official, to any foreign political party or official thereof, or to any candidate for foreign political office, for purposes of—

A. (i) influencing any act or decision of such foreign official, political party, party official, or candidate in his or its official capacity, (ii) inducing such foreign official, political party, party official, or candidate to do or omit to do any act in violation of the lawful duty of such foreign official, political party, party official, or candidate, or (iii) securing any improper advantage; or

B. inducing such foreign official, political party, party official, or candidate to use his or its influence with a foreign government or instrumentality thereof to affect or influence any act or decision of such government or instrumentality, in order to assist such domestic concern in obtaining or retaining business for or with, or directing business to, any person.[18]

The Elements of the Statute

While the number of FCPA cases prosecuted is not large, a recent case provides guidance that, in effect, simplifies the understanding of what constitutes a violation of the FCPA. In the prosecution of Congressman William J. Jefferson, for a violation of the FCPA, among other violations,[19] a Virginia district court case indicated that in order to obtain a criminal conviction under the FCPA, the government must prove beyond a reasonable doubt that the defendant is a

1. domestic concern, corporate issuer, individual, firm, officer, director, employee, agent/stockholder of a firm;
2. that made use of a means or instrumentality of interstate commerce;
3. corruptly;
4. in furtherance of an offer or payment of anything of value to any person;

5. while knowing that the money or item of value would be offered or given directly or indirectly to any foreign official; and

6. for purposes of influencing any act or decision of such foreign official in his or her official capacity.[20]

Interpretation and Practical Considerations

As a practical matter, anything of value can include cash, lavish gifts or entertainment, improper campaign contributions, scholarships, travel for families, and overpayment for services or underpricing of assets.

"Obtaining or retaining business or improper advantage" can mean receiving increased profits, preventing government action, getting regulatory approvals, retaining/renewing a contract, and avoiding duties or taxes.

The corruption element can mean the following: seeking to obtain some *quid pro quo*, intending to influence someone improperly, acting contrary to law, or doing an act secretively or surreptitiously. In some instances, acting corruptly can be inferred by law enforcement given the circumstances.

The "in furtherance" element can include approving a payment of some sort, relaying e-mail instructions to make a payment, discussing a payment by phone or in a meeting, acquiescing in payment, knowingly cooperating regarding a payment, covering up a payment, or creating or accepting a false invoice.

The "directly or indirectly" element can mean a payment while knowing there is a high probability that payment will pass through an official, intermediary, or third parties agreeing to a demand for a payment. This includes making a payment through a third party, agents, business partners, or joint venture, where knowledge exists or can be inferred that the payment, in whole or in part, will go directly or indirectly to a foreign official. For example, in *U.S. v. Kay*,[21] the federal court said that Congress intended the FCPA to apply broadly to direct and indirect payments to assist the payor in obtaining reduced customs and tax liabilities. In *Kay*, the court said that the FCPA did not prohibit every payment to a foreign official, but rather payments that were intended to influence a foreign official to act in his/her official capacity, to act or refraining from acting in violation of his/her duty, or to secure an improper or wrongful benefit or advantage to the payor or beneficiary.[22]

In May 2011, two executives of a company were convicted of conspiracy and FCPA violations. An individual from a Mexican company, hired to serve as a representative for the U.S. company, was convicted of conspiracy to commit money laundering.[23] According to the DOJ, the executives of a U.S. company hired a Mexican company as its sales representative to obtain contracts from a Mexican state-owned utility company. The government's evidence showed that the sales representative's company received a 30 percent commission where a percentage of the commission was used to pay Mexican government officials in exchange for contract awards. The evidence further showed that the executives understood that all or part of the commissions would be used to bribe government utility officials in exchange for obtaining contracts. The evidence also showed that the representative submitted invoices to the U.S. company for commissions where the executives then caused monies to be wired to the representative, knowing that the invoices were fraudulent and commission payments were being used to pay bribes.[24]

Exceptions and Affirmative Defenses

The FCPA provides exceptions to the statue if the conduct is for a routine government action, and it provides affirmative defenses to prohibited conduct.

The statute provides that the prohibited conduct previously stated "shall not apply to any facilitating or expediting payment to a foreign official, political party, or party official the purpose of which is to expedite or to secure the performance of a routine governmental action by a foreign official, political party, or party official."[25] This, for example, means that:

> ... only an action which is ordinarily and commonly performed by a foreign official in—obtaining permits, licenses, or other official documents to qualify a person to do business in a foreign country; processing governmental papers, such as visas and work orders; providing police protection, mail pick-up and delivery, or scheduling inspections associated with contract performance or inspections related to transit of goods across country; providing phone service, power and water supply, loading and unloading cargo, or protecting perishable products or commodities from deterioration; or actions of a similar nature.[26]

Routine governmental action, however, "does not include any decision by a foreign official whether, or on what terms, to award new business to or to continue business with a particular party, or any action taken by a foreign official involved in the decision-making process to encourage a decision to award new business to or continue business with a particular party."[27]

The statute provides for affirmative defense if the "the payment, gift, offer, or promise of anything of value that was made was lawful under the written laws and regulations of the foreign official's, political party's, party official's, or candidate's country."[28]

It is also an affirmative defense if "the payment, gift, offer, or promise of anything of value that was made was a reasonable and bona fide expenditure, such as travel and lodging expenses, incurred by or on behalf of a foreign official, party, party official, or candidate and was directly related to the promotion, demonstration, or explanation of products or services; or the execution or performance of a contract with a foreign government or agency thereof."[29]

Other Instructive Aspects of the Criminal Provisions and FCPA Generally

The FCPA contains provision that can assist the public in determining whether certain conduct might be a violation of the statute. The DOJ has established procedures wherein an individual or entity can request guidance and an opinion from the attorney general on a particular or contemplated matter or transaction. Section 78dd-2(f) of Title 15 provides that:

> The Attorney General shall, within 30 days after receiving such a request, issue an opinion in response to that request. The opinion shall state whether or not certain specified prospective conduct would, for purposes of the Department of Justice's present enforcement policy, violate the preceding provisions of this section. Additional requests for opinions may be filed with the Attorney General regarding other specified prospective conduct that is beyond the scope of conduct specified in previous requests.

There is a further benefit from seeking such an opinion. Should the DOJ file a criminal action based on the facts and information provided in the request for opinion, the procedures permit for a rebuttable presumption—somewhat of a defense—that the alleged misconduct is in conformity with enforcement policy. Section 78dd-(2)(f) provides:

> In any action brought under the applicable provisions of this section, there shall be a rebuttable presumption that conduct, which is specified in a request by a domestic concern and for which the Attorney General has issued an opinion that such conduct is in conformity with the Department of Justice's present enforcement policy, is in compliance with the preceding provisions of this section.

Such a presumption may be rebutted by a preponderance of the evidence. In considering the presumption for purposes of this paragraph, a court shall weigh all relevant factors, including but not limited to whether the information submitted to the Attorney General was accurate and complete and whether it was within the scope of the conduct specified in any request received by the Attorney General.

As the statute indicates, one must be careful and accurate in the information provided in seeking such an opinion, for inaccuracy can rebut the presumption in favor of conformity with enforcement policy. The procedures for seeking guidance or a statement from the DOJ on potential enforcement actions can be obtained at www.justice.gov/criminal/fraud/fcpa/. (For further guidance, Chapter 8, "Anti-Corruption Due Diligence," contains an example of an opinion.)

By omission, it should be noted that there is no materiality element on value in the statute. Therefore, it can be illegal to offer anything of value as a bribe, including cash or noncash items.[30] The government focuses on the intent of the bribery rather than on the amount.[31]

Because of its broad application and the application of conspiracy law, jurisdiction under the FCPA can reach conduct or activity that takes place entirely outside of the United States.[32]

Penalties

The foregoing criminal statute provides for imprisonment and fines. For an individual, imprisonment can be up to five years and a US$100,000 fine. Depending on the circumstances, entities can be fined up to US$2 million per occurrence.

The Books and Records and Internal Control Provisions of the FCPA

The FCPA requires companies whose securities are listed in the United States (thus, it can include foreign companies) to meet its accounting and internal controls provisions. These provisions, which complement enforcement of the anti-bribery provisions, require corporations to make and keep books and records that accurately and fairly reflect the transactions of the corporation and to devise and maintain an adequate system of internal accounting controls.[33]

These provisions are normally enforced by the SEC, meaning they are civil in nature. However, the internal controls provisions can sometimes lead to criminal violations, which are investigated by the DOJ.

The Statute

Like the anti-bribery provisions, the books and records and internal control provisions are detailed and contain directives, as is the case with other securities regulations. In this section, we focus on the key aspects of these provisions in terms of anti-corruption. These provisions apply to issuers and provide as follows:[34]

(b) Form of report; books, records, and internal accounting; directives

    (2) Every issuer which has a class of securities registered pursuant to section 78*l* of this title and every issuer which is required to file reports pursuant to section 78*o*(d) of this title shall–

        A. make and keep books, records, and accounts, which, in reasonable detail, accurately and fairly reflect the transactions and dispositions of the assets of the issuer;

        B. devise and maintain a system of internal accounting controls sufficient to provide reasonable assurances that—

            i. transactions are executed in accordance with management's general or specific authorization;

            ii. transactions are recorded as necessary (I) to permit preparation of financial statements in conformity with generally accepted accounting principles or any other criteria applicable to such statements, and (II) to maintain accountability for assets;

            iii. access to assets is permitted only in accordance with management's general or specific authorization; and

            iv. the recorded accountability for assets is compared with the existing assets at reasonable intervals and appropriate action is taken with respect to any differences . . . [35]

As indicated, the books and records and internal controls provisions are very detailed, and only the basic or key statutory provisions are provided. To better understand these provisions, some definition and interpretation is helpful.

Interpretation and Practical Considerations of These Provisions

The statute does not permit an entity to effectively ignore its responsibilities regarding these provisions. The statute provides that "[n]o person shall knowingly circumvent or knowingly fail to implement a system of internal accounting controls or knowingly falsify any book, record, or account described in" the above provisions under paragraph (2).[36] Thus, the statute requires affirmative action on the part of companies and its board and officers. But there are some limitations on this point. For example, section 78(b)(6) provides that if corporation holds 50 percent or less of the voting power with respect to a domestic or foreign subsidiary or affiliate, it must only attempt in good faith to use its influence to cause the firm's compliance with this section.[37]

Practically speaking, the purpose behind the record keeping and internal accounting controls standards and rules is to prevent the hiding of bribery through misrepresentation in accounting records. The books and records provisions require covered companies to make and keep books and records "which, in reasonable detail, accurately and fairly reflect the transactions and dispositions of the assets of the issuer."[38] Further, the internal controls provisions require companies to devise and maintain a system that provides "reasonable assurances that ... transactions are executed in accordance with the management's general or specific authorization."[39] According to the statute, these terms mean "such level and degree of assurance that would satisfy prudent officials in the conduct of their own affairs."[40]

With respect to civil/administrative liability, there is no materiality threshold. These provisions cover all transactions, not just those directly related to a corrupt payment. Moreover, civil books and records and internal controls charges do not require a corrupt intent. They instead require that the books and records be accurate and effective internal controls be in place.

Mischaracterizing the nature of a bribe or facilitating payment as a normal operational expense may be considered a books and records violation. The books and records provisions have been interpreted to require indication of the character of a payment—that is, bribes should be recorded as such, and facilitation payments should be recorded as such. Recording a bribe, for instance, as a "logistics expense" or "customs duties" or in any other category may be deemed a violation.

The following hypothetical scenario highlights the issue, which can lead to false accounting or inaccurate entries: an agent for the American company bribes an entity in Asia to obtain or retain business on behalf of the American company; how the company reflects that transaction in its ledger and other accounting records can have FCPA consequences.

Moreover, consider the following example of a violation of the books and records or internal controls provisions. In a civil matter, an SEC cease-and-desist order indicated that the recording of a payment to Argentinian customs officials in accounting records as "Amortization—Fixed Costs" was improper and thus a violation of the books and records provisions.[41]

Keep in mind that improper payments to a foreign official to obtain or retain business that results in a books and records or internal controls violation can also result in criminal anti-bribery charges. This is so given that improper payments falsely characterized on a company's books and records also forms the basis of facts that constitute a criminal bribery violation. Thus, the risk of books and records or internal controls violation cannot be underestimated.

Penalties

Penalties for the books and records and internal control provisions can be fines of up to US$25 million for companies. For individuals, the penalties include up to 20 years in prison and a fine of up to US$5 million.

 ## ANCILLARY STATUTES

Other statutes that criminalize conduct similar or related to criminal acts under the FCPA include the following laws.

Conspiracy—18 USC 371

By its nature, an FCPA violation includes conduct of two or more individuals or entities. Conspiracy generally involves an agreement or plan between two or more persons to commit at least one crime. The defendant must know of the object of the crime—that is, what the agreement seeks to accomplish (the specific crime) and that a person who is part of the conspiracy accomplishes at least one overt act. In other words, a conspiracy is a kind of criminal partnership to do something unlawful, and the agreed-upon crime does not have to be committed. The agreement is the crime. Further, it is not necessary that the conspirators made a formal agreement, but rather that there was an agreed-upon plan to commit a crime. The conspirators need not have agreed on every detail of the conspiracy.

Bribery of a Public Official—18 USC 201

In some instances and depending on who was bribed (usually here an American official), the government may decide not to charge an FCPA violation, but rather the substantive offense of bribery of a public official. There are various forms of bribery, including kickback schemes, but generally the elements to these types of criminal offenses are similar to those for an FCPA anti-bribery violation. The elements to bribery of a public official are that: (1) the defendant gave, offered, or promised something of value to a public official; and (2) the defendant acted corruptly, that is, with the intent to influence an official act by the public official to influence the public official to commit or allow a fraud on the United States, or to induce the public official to do or to omit to do an act in violation of his or her lawful duty.

Mail or Wire Fraud—18 USC 1341 or 1343

In many instances, to constitute a federal crime it must involve an element of interstate commerce. Otherwise, the criminal misconduct may fall to the states to prosecute. The concept of interstate commerce or foreign commerce provides the federal government with a broad jurisdictional basis upon which to attack criminal activity. Two such crimes include the use of the mails or any use of a wire communication (e.g., telephone, radio, television, or Internet) in any scheme, including bribery and kickback schemes, or the making of false statements/promises to obtain money or a thing of value. As one can imagine, the criminal conduct can be broad and extend beyond U.S. borders.

The elements for both crimes are similar. They involve: (1) knowingly participating or devising or intending to devise a scheme or plan to defraud for obtaining money or property by means of false or fraudulent pretenses, representations, or promises; (2) the statements made or facts omitted as part of the scheme were material; that is, they had a natural tendency to influence, or were capable of influencing, a person to part with money or property; (3) the individual acted with the intent to defraud (e.g., intent to deceive or cheat); and (4) the scheme or plan to defraud included the use of the mails or wire communications.

As indicated, the difference between mail and wire fraud is the use of the mails or wire communications in interstate or foreign commerce.

False Statement to Federal Agency or Official—18 USC 1001

Invariably, witnesses or potential targets of an FCPA or any investigation may be interviewed by a federal law enforcement agent. Lying to that agent is a federal offense (e.g., misrepresenting an accounting entry in connection with a bribe payment). This offense is different than perjury, where a false material statement was made under oath. The elements to an offense under Section 1001 include the knowingly and willfully making a false statement or using a document containing a false statement in a matter within the jurisdiction of a governmental agency, wherein the untrue statement dealt with a material matter in the activities or decisions of the particular agency.

The Travel Act—18 USC 1952

This statute is entitled Interstate and Foreign Travel or Transportation in Aid of Racketeering Enterprises, but it is commonly known as the Travel Act. That act prohibits interstate travel or using the mails or any facility in interstate or foreign commerce with intent to, among other acts, otherwise promote, manage, establish, carry on, or facilitate the promotion, management, establishment, or carrying on of any unlawful activity. Given the language of the statute, it is conceivable that someone who engages in conduct tantamount to an FCPA violation can also be in violation of this statute.

The Exchange Act—Section 20 Control Person

Section 20 of the Securities and Exchange Act of 1934 (Exchange Act) provides liability of controlling persons and persons who aid and abet violations under such act. The effect of this statute is that it substantially broadens the ability of the SEC to seek civil penalties. Specifically, Section 20(a) provides that:

> Every person who, directly or indirectly, controls any person liable under any provision of this title or of any rule or regulation thereunder shall also be liable jointly and severally with and to the same extent as such controlled person to any person to whom such controlled person is liable, unless the controlling person acted in good faith and did not directly or indirectly induce the act or acts constituting the violation or cause of action.

Money Laundering—18 USC 1956 or 1957

As a result of some of the aforementioned crimes, such misconduct can lead to charges of money laundering. Money laundering generally involves conducting other financial transactions to promote the scheme and/or otherwise disguise the source or nature of proceeds of illegal conduct. There are various forms in which one can commit money laundering. Generally, the elements involve an individual (1) conducting or intending to conduct a financial transaction involving property that represented the proceeds of a specific prior crime; (2) knowing that the property represented the proceeds of the specific crime; (3) acting with the intent to promote or disguising the specified crime; and doing something that was a substantial step toward committing the crime.

Another form of money laundering occurs where the individual (1) knowingly engaged or attempted to engage in a monetary transaction; (2) knew the transaction involved criminally derived property; (3) the property had a value greater than US$10,000; (4) the property was, in fact, derived from a specific crime, and the transaction occurred in the United States or maritime or territorial jurisdiction of the United States.

SUMMARY

As reflected in this chapter, the FCPA's jurisdictional reach is broad. While the numbers of investigations and prosecutions has been limited over the history of the statute, the DOJ and the SEC have made it clear in the past few years that enforcement of the FCPA is a priority. And while it may be the culture in other countries to pay a bribe in order to obtain or retain business, regulators are not sympathetic of U.S. companies and individuals engaging in such behavior. Companies will have to improve their due diligence in how and who they engaged in business aboard. The chapters that follow will provide guidance on how to enhance your due diligence procedures, internal controls and accounting procedures, and anti-corruption compliance programs.

NOTES

1. See 15 U.S.C. Section 78dd-2 and 78m (quotations omitted). The information in this chapter is for informational/education purposes only and should not be construed as legal advice.
2. See 15 U.S.C Section 78 (quotations omitted).
3. See www.justice.gov/criminal/fraud/fcpa/docs/lay-persons-guide.pdf.
4. Id.
5. See Response of the United States Questions Concerning Phase 3 OECD Working Group on Bribery, May 3, 2010, (Part II) at www.justice.gov/criminal/fraud/fcpa/docs/response3.pdf.
6. See United States Sentencing Guidelines for Organizations, as amended (November 1, 2010), Chapter 8 at Section 8B2.1 (Part B—Remedying Harm from Criminal Conduct, and Effective Compliance and Ethics Program). See also Chapter 4 for more information on compliance programs.
7. John T. Woolley and Gerhard Peters, The American Presidency Project, Santa Barbara, CA, at www.presidency.ucsb.edu/ws/?pid=7036.
8. See Senate Report No. 105-277.

9. Id. (quotations omitted).

10. William J. Clinton, Statement by the President, November 10, 1998; www .justice.gov/criminal/fraud/fcpa/docs/signing.pdf.

11. Other relevant authority in the anti-corruption area includes The U.N. Convention Against Corruption (2005), European Union Convention on Corruption (1997), Council of Europe Criminal Law Convention on Corruption (2002), Inter-American Convention Against Corruption (1996), and the African Union Convention (2006). The Transparency International Corruption Index provides an index that measures the level of corruption by country. See www.transparency.org.

12. See Notes 1 and 2.

13. See 15 USC 78dd-2(h)(1).

14. See 15 U.S.C. 78dd-1.

15. See 15 U.S.C. 78dd-2(h)(1).

16. See www.justice.gov/criminal/fraud/fcpa/docs/lay-persons-guide.pdf for other examples.

17. The state of mind or knowledge requirement occurs where "such person is aware that such person is engaging in such conduct, that such circumstance exists, or that such result is substantially certain to occur; or such person has a firm belief that such circumstance exists or that such result is substantially certain to occur. When knowledge of the existence of a particular circumstance is required for an offense, such knowledge is established if a person is aware of a high probability of the existence of such circumstance, unless the person actually believes that such circumstance does not exist." 15 U.S.C. 78dd-2(h) (3) (section numbering omitted; footnote added in quote).

18. See 15 U.S.C.78dd-2.

19. The federal court in Virginia relied on a 2003 FCPA higher court appellate decision from New York. See *Stichting Ter Behartiging Van Oudaandeelhouders in Het Kapitaal Van Saybolt Int'l B.V. v. Schreiber*, 327 F.3d 173 (2d Cir. 2003).

20. See U.S. v. Jefferson, 594 F. Supp. 2d 655 (E.D. Va. 2009). That decision was affirmed by the appellate court (see 546 F.3d 300 (4th Cir. 2008)) and further review upon request of Congressman Jefferson was denied by the Supreme Court. See 129 S.Ct. 2383 (2009).

21. Reported at 359 F.3d 738 (5th Cir. 2004); rehearing and rehearing en banc denied, 513 F.3d 461; *certiorari denied*, 129 S.Ct. 42 (2008).

22. Id.

23. See www.justice.gov/opa/pr/2011/May/11-crm-596.html.

24. Id.

25. 15 U.S.C. 78dd-2(b).

26. 15 U.S.C. 78dd-2(h)(4)(A).

27. 15 U.S.C. 78dd-2(h)(4)(B).

28. 15 U.S.C. 78dd-2(b).

29. 15 U.S.C. 78dd-2(c).
30. See, for example, 15 U.S.C. 78dd-1, 78dd-2, and 78dd-3.
31. See U.S. Department of Justice Lay-Person's Guide to FCPA at www.justice .gov/criminal/fraud/fcpa/.
32. See 15 U.S.C. 78dd-1(a), -1(g), -2(a), -2(i).
33. See 15 U.S.C. 78m(b) (quotations omitted).
34. See 15 U.S.C. 78m.
35. 15 U.S.C. 78m(b).
36. 15 U.S.C. 78m(b)(5).
37. See Section 78m(b)(6).
38. 15 U.S.C. 78m(b)(2)(A).
39. 15 U.S.C. 78m(b)(2)(B)(i).
40. 15 U.S.C. 78m(b)(7).
41. See SEC Securities Exchange Act of 1934 Release No. 49390, SEC Accounting and Auditing Enforcement Release No. 1972, SEC Admin. Proceeding File No. 3-11427 (March 10, 2004), available at www.sec.gov/litigation/admin/34-49390.htm. In this instance, it should be noted that the company conducted an internal investigation, undertook remedial action, and reported the matter to the SEC.

CHAPTER THREE

The U.K. Bribery Act and International Bribery and Corruption Initiatives

T HE NEGATIVE IMPACT OF bribery and corruption has long been recognized, and in the 1990s a number of international organizations made up of various member states began working to address this problem. These efforts underline the determination of more and more countries to eradicate bribery and corruption. The key early initiatives include the Organization for Economic Cooperation and Development (OECD) Convention on Combating Bribery of Foreign Officials (1997) and The Inter-American Convention against Corruption of the Organization of American States (1996). Later initiatives include the United Nations Convention against Corruption (2005) and efforts in Africa, Asia, and Europe. The objectives of these initiatives are to pressure member states to enact comprehensive legislation to criminalize global corruption and to increase enforcement of these laws. These efforts have been fruitful from a legislation perspective; however, the laws are not consistently enforced. The enforcement landscape is changing as more countries increase enforcement and work together to stop corruption.

One of the most significant recent legislative anti-corruption developments is the U.K. Bribery Act of 2010, which was passed in April 2010. The act addresses a wide array of bribery related crimes and rivals the Foreign Corrupt

Practices Act of 1977 (FCPA) in being the most comprehensive anti-bribery statute in the world.

 ## U.K. BRIBERY ACT OF 2010

The United Kingdom's Bribery Act 2010 (U.K. Bribery Act), which came into force on July 1, 2011, represents a strengthening of the U.K. position on bribery and corruption and an important development in global anti-bribery legislation. In keeping with the FCPA, the current global benchmark, the U.K. Bribery Act makes bribery of foreign public officials an offense and extends beyond company employees to include the behavior of third parties acting on behalf of a company. However, in certain respects, the U.K. Bribery Act goes further than the FCPA. The act:

- Covers all bribery, both commercial and public officials.
- Makes no exception for facilitation payments made to expedite routine governmental actions.[1]
- Makes it a corporate offense to fail to prevent bribery.
- Makes it an offense not only to give but also to receive a bribe.

With such wide-ranging scope, the U.K. Bribery Act is an important development in global anti-corruption efforts, especially because the United Kingdom's Serious Fraud Office (SFO), the main body currently tasked with enforcement, has expressed a determination to enforce the U.K. Bribery Act internationally. Richard Alderman, director of the SFO, stated in an interview, "I have made it clear that the new extended jurisdiction in respect of foreign corporates is very important to the SFO. This creates a level playing field and enables us to support ethical U.K. corporates who have been undermined by foreign corporates who use bribery to obtain a business advantage."[2] Additionally, Chris Walker, head of policy of SFO, stated, "We intend to adopt an aggressive interpretation of the Act's jurisdictional reach."[3]

The extent to which it will be possible to use the U.K. Bribery Act to take action against overseas companies has not yet been legally tested, but the SFO's position is consistent with the recent aggressive cross-border enforcement of the FCPA and growing international coordination between regulators.

Legislative History

Prior to the U.K. Bribery Act, the United Kingdom's bribery and corruption regulations dated back to early 1900s. After ratifying the OECD Anti-Bribery Convention in 1998, the United Kingdom nonetheless faced criticism from the OECD and others for a lack of enforcement resources and actual prosecutions under the laws. In particular, the OECD disapproved of the SFO's handling of BAE Systems investigation and its decision to discontinue the investigation. In its *2008 Progress Report on Enforcement of the OECD Convention on Combating Bribery of Foreign Public Officials in International Business Transactions*, Transparency International stated:

> The UK's termination of the investigation of Al Yamamah–related bribery allegations against BAE Systems (BAE) in December 2006 was a damaging setback for the Convention. The assertion that national security concerns overrode the obligation to enforce the Convention, created a dangerous precedent that other governments could readily follow. The termination of the BAE investigation compounded prior concerns about lack of UK commitment, including the failure to correct deficiencies in UK corruption legislation called for in OECD reviews, and the failure to bring any prosecutions, notwithstanding numerous UK investigations of foreign bribery.

This investigation was subsequently pursued by the U.S. Department of Justice (DOJ), with the SFO remaining involved. The ultimate settlement with the DOJ was for $400 million.[4] BAE also agreed to pay a £30 million fine (approximately US$45 million) to resolve a related, long-running investigation by the SFO concerning BAE's alleged failure to maintain adequate accounting records.[5] The continuing negative publicity of the case helped overcome the opposition from the conservative lawmakers, who were concerned such law would put U.K. businesses at a competitive disadvantage.

The Provisions of the U.K. Bribery Act

The U.K. Bribery Act specifies the following four major offenses:

The general offense of offering, promising, or giving a bribe.
This offense provides a broad-spectrum coverage of the act of bribery from the standpoint of a bribe giver. The action is divided into two types of cases, in the first case, the advantage (financial or other) is offered to a

person for improper performance, either as a reward or to induce. The person would still be guilty of this offense even if the actual bribe were given to a person, other than the one performing improperly. In the second case, the advantage is offered, and the person knows or believes that the acceptance of the advantage itself would constitute an improper performance. Additionally, the law specifically states that there is no difference between the methods of giving a bribe: even if the bribe were given through an intermediary, the person would still be liable.

The general offense of requesting or agreeing to receive a bribe.

The offense of receiving a bribe spells out several scenarios under which the person receiving a bribe would be liable. The offense of receiving a bribe is divided into several cases, all of which deal with requesting, accepting, or agreeing to receive a financial or other advantage in exchange for improper performance. As in the offense of giving a bribe, the involvement of a third-party intermediary does not absolve the receiver from the guilt, and the advantage gained does not have to benefit the receiver. The act further states that the receiver does not have to know or believe that the performance of the function or activity is improper. The same is applicable to cases where a third party is performing the activity.

A separate offense of bribery of a foreign public official.

The act lists bribery of a foreign public official as an offense separate from just giving a bribe. The person would be guilty if he or she specifically influences another person in that person's capacity as a foreign public official. Additionally, intent to obtain or retain business or business advantage needs to be present.

A corporate offense for failing to prevent bribery.

Failure of a commercial organization to prevent bribery is a new corporate offense that would spur the corporate prosecutions under the act. Failure to prevent bribery can be triggered by employees, agents, subsidiaries, or anyone who performs services on the business's behalf meaning that schemes commonly seen in the past where third parties may have been used to distance a corporation from a bribe are caught in the scope of the act. However, the act specifically provides for a defense of the organization, if it can prove it had adequate procedures designed to prevent bribery.

The corporation itself and its senior officers may be found guilty of paying or receiving bribes if it is found that a senior officer has consented or connived in the offence.

Unlike the FCPA, no exemption is made for facilitating payments and such payments are therefore illegal under the U.K. Bribery Act. Prosecution guidance released in March 2011 set out the list of public interest factors for and against that would need to be considered when deciding whether to pursue a prosecution. This means that in practice, although illegal, it is unlikely that a corporation would face prosecution for a one-off facilitation payment where it has good policies and procedures to try to prevent them.

The act is designed to have the maximum deterrent effect. The definition of what constitutes a bribe is extremely broad and covers any financial or other advantage offered (not just given) to someone to induce him or her to act improperly. Similarly, the penalties for those found guilty of an offense under the act can be severe, including unlimited fines and up to 10 years' imprisonment.

The corporate offense of failing to prevent bribery also allows for unlimited fines and extends to include the activities of third parties acting on behalf of a company. This new offense is noteworthy because it expands the scope of the act beyond an individual transaction or event, to consider the corporate environment in which the bribery took place.

The defense available to an organization is one of having "adequate procedures" in place to prevent bribery. What constitutes "adequate procedures" is a matter of opinion and has been the subject of extensive discussion and further guidance issued by the U.K. Ministry of Justice in March 2011. The guidance issued is principles based and laid out six key principles.

- Proportionate procedures
- Top level commitment
- Risk assessment
- Due diligence
- Communication
- Monitoring and review

The adequate procedures guidance is discussed further in Chapter 4, "Compliance Programs."

The U.K. Bribery Act has put companies on notice that they need to evaluate their procedures for preventing and detecting bribery and corruption. Ultimately, the enforcement of the U.K. Bribery Act will determine its success in the eyes of organizations like the OECD and based on the commentary by the SFO and other regulators it is clear that significant activity should be expected.

GLOBAL ANTI-CORRUPTION INITIATIVES

Bribery and corruption is recognized throughout the world as an impediment to fair business practice and a leading cause of income imbalances. In recognition of this and to demonstrate political commitment to reduce bribery and corruption groups of countries have banded together to draft anti-corruption conventions. These conventions lay out the group's objectives and a framework of requirements that signatories must implement to meet these objectives. All regions of the world are covered through the various anti-corruption conventions whose scopes can vary significantly.

The signatories are responsible for ensuring local laws are sufficient to meet the requirements of the convention and passing new laws if needed. Local enforcement remains the blocking point to greater success of these conventions; however, significant advances are being made.

Joint Cooperation

With the growing body of significant legislation and the aggressive jurisdictional enforcement activity, the potential for inquiry from many governments exists. Fortunately, recent enforcement activity shows an increase in the cooperation between various agencies tasked with anti-bribery enforcement around the world. In a speech by Assistant Attorney General Lanny Breuer, he states, "[The DOJ] will continue to work with the Departments of State and Commerce and the SEC. With them, we will press for ever-increasing vigilance by our foreign counterparts to prosecute companies and executives in their own countries for foreign bribery—both through the OECD and less formal means."[6] In addition to the BAE Systems case other examples include:

- In 2008, Siemens AG settled with both U.S. DOJ and German authorities. Due to the coordinated enforcement actions "brought by the Department [of Justice], the SEC and the Munich Public Prosecutor's Office, Siemens AG will pay a combined total of more than $1.6 billion in fines, penalties, and disgorgement of profits, including $800 million to U.S. authorities, making the combined U.S. penalties the largest monetary sanction ever imposed in an FCPA case since the act was passed by Congress in 1977."[7]
- In 2009, two citizens of the United Kingdom were charged by the United States with bribing Nigerian government officials for their part in the KBR joint venture scheme. "In a related criminal case, KBR's successor company, Kellogg Brown & Root LLC, pleaded guilty in February 2009 to

charges related to the FCPA for its participation in the scheme to bribe Nigerian government officials. Kellogg Brown & Root LLC was ordered to pay a $402 million fine and to retain an independent compliance monitor for a three-year period."[8] In February 2011, the SFO announced a civil settlement with M. W. Kellogg Limited, a U.K. subsidiary of KBR, in which M.W. Kellogg Limited agreed to pay £7 million in recognition of funds it was due to receive.[9]

■ In 2009, due to the cooperation between the U.S. and Danish authorities, AGCO Corporation agreed to "pay a combined total of more than $20 million in fines, penalties, and disgorgement of profits in connection with the cases brought by the Department of Justice, the SEC and the Danish State Prosecutor's Office."[10]

As the number of anti-corruption enforcement initiatives becomes increasingly common and widespread, it facilitates further growth of such cross border cooperation.

Former deputy chief of the Fraud Section of the DOJ, Mark Mendelsohn, illustrated this increase in joint cooperation in his August 2010 interview with the Metropolitan Corporate Counsel:

> Through work on the Siemens case, [the] DOJ developed a very close relationship with the Munich Public Prosecutors Office. Over the course of many years and many matters, the Fraud Section has developed an excellent relationship with the Serious Fraud Office in the UK, as well as with other prosecutors in many other jurisdictions. Building these international relationships was a very important part of [. . .] the DOJ's efforts to level the playing field. Prosecutors and regulators in one jurisdiction, especially once they know each other, will notify their counterparts in other jurisdictions in which a target company does business of the opening of an investigation and arrange for exchanges of information.

The Inter-American Convention against Corruption of the Organization of American States (www.oas.org)

The Inter-American Convention against Corruption (IACAC) of the Organization of American States (OAS), adopted in March 1996, was the first international anti-corruption treaty. The Convention requires member states to reform their judicial systems and public policies to implement and promote prevention and detection of corruption as well as facilitate cooperation between member states to prosecute and eradicate corruption cases. Thirty-four member countries have ratified the OAS Charter and are participating members of the Organization.[11]

The IACAC consists of two key elements: preventing and repressing corruption.

The preventive measures consider items aimed at creating, maintaining, and strengthening their own institutional systems. Examples of these preventative measures are creating standards of conduct for public functions, mechanisms to enforce the standards of conduct, instructions to government personnel about their responsibilities and ethical rules, as well as a system to register the income, assets, and liabilities of those government personnel, systems that protect both public and private citizens who report acts of corruption, creating oversight bodies, having a mechanism to encourage participation in anti-corruption efforts by the civil society as well as nongovernmental organizations, and to continue to further the study of anti-corruption preventative measures. Aside from these examples, the governments of the member states should also focus on creating systems for government hiring, procurement of goods and services, collection and control of government revenue, laws denying favorable tax treatment for expenditures made in violation of anti-corruption laws, and measures to deter bribery of both domestic and foreign government officials.

To effectively repress corruption IACAC member states must criminalize certain activities in their country's legal system. These include requesting or receiving a bribe and offering or paying a bribe both domestically and internationally. Other required areas include conspiracy to commit bribery, illicit enrichment, and improper use of state information or property.

Additionally, the IACAC treaty states that member countries shall provide mutual assistance and cooperation in taking necessary actions to facilitate investigations or prosecutions of acts of corruption.

United Nations Convention Against Corruption (www.unodc.org/unodc/en/treaties/CAC/index.html)

The United Nations Convention Against Corruption (UNCAC), which became effective December 15, 2005, requires its members to establish anti-corruption legislation into their country's laws, institutions, and practices. The UNCAC's resolution is extensive in its coverage of public and private sector corruption with a wide definition of corruption covering bribery, embezzlement, and money laundering. The UNCAC was signed by 140 countries[12] and is the only legally binding global anti-corruption initiative.

During the UNCAC Convention, the member states agreed upon various requirements that should be met, also at this time a broad definition of the term public official was formulated. These requirements are preventive measures, criminalization, international cooperation, asset recovery framework, technical cooperation, information exchange, and an implementation mechanism. Each requirement has unique features and backgrounds. For preventative measures, member states shall develop, implement, and maintain anti-corruption policies as well as have anti-corruption enforcement bodies with increased transparency for both public and private sectors. With regard to criminalization, member states are required to establish offenses that broadly cover acts of corruption. The international cooperation framework is to be provided by the UNCAC.

A fundamental principle of the Convention is its detailed framework on asset recovery. The provisions on technical cooperation and information exchange provide for the need of financial, material, and technical assistance to developing countries to help enforce the resolutions of the Convention. Finally, for the implementation mechanism, the UNCAC provides guidance that includes reviewing the implementation of the Convention by State Parties, developing technical assistance needs, incorporating other global and regional anti-corruption measures and establishing a review body to assess initiatives by member states to implement the UNCAC's policies.

In 2009, the State Parties agreed to a mechanism for the peer review of member states to assist in the effective implementation of the Convention. This mechanism is meant to exchange ideas and leading practices in preventing and fighting corruption.

Due to its broad scope and international acceptance, the UNCAC is a key global anti-corruption initiative.

OECD Convention on Combating Bribery of Foreign Officials in International Business Transactions (www.oecd.org/dataoecd/4/18/38028044.pdf)

The OECD Convention on Bribery of Foreign Public Officials in International Business Transactions (OECD Convention), which was signed in December 1997, concentrates on addressing bribery in international business transactions including global exports and foreign investment as it raises moral and political concerns and can distort international competitiveness. 38 states (31 OECD and 7 non-OECD) have ratified the OECD Convention.[13]

During the OECD Convention the members decided on obligations that need to be completed. These obligations include themes of anti-money laundering, criminalization, international cooperation, accounting specifics, and monitoring. Anti-money laundering consists of requiring member states to treat bribery of a foreign official, whether active or passive in form, as subject to money laundering legislation. There are limited exceptions to anti-money laundering. For criminalization, each member of the OECD should take measures in defining a criminal offense for any individual who intentionally bribes, directly or through intermediaries, a foreign official or third party to gain an improper advantage in the conduct of international business. For international cooperation, the Convention describes how there should be mutual legal assistance between countries as well as making extraditions easier.

There is also a focus on exchanging information between countries, which can assist in cases against offenders. With accounting, the member states shall take measures regarding the maintenance of books and records, disclosures in the financial statements, and to prohibit the establishment of off-the-book accounts to assist in combating bribery of foreign officials. Finally, for monitoring, member states are required to cooperate in monitoring and promote the full implementation of being compliant with the rules set forth during the Convention.

On November 26, 2009, the OECD released "Recommendation for Further Combating Bribery of Foreign Public Officials." The Recommendation includes the "Good Practice Guidance on Internal Controls, Ethics and Compliance," which is discussed further in Chapter 4, "Compliance Programs."

For the period from 1999 through 2010, a total of 164 convictions of individuals (and 35 other sanctions), and 59 convictions of business entities (and 32 deferred and non prosecutions agreements) have been obtained in foreign bribery cases by the signatories of the OECD Convention. While the United States is generally viewed as the leader in enforcement, other counties such as Germany, Hungary, Italy, and Korea are actively prosecuting corruption cases; collectively, their efforts account for roughly 30 percent of the individual convictions and approximately 45 percent of convictions of entities (65 percent including the deferred prosecution agreements [DPAs] and non-prosecution agreements [NPAs]). Additionally, 41 individuals and 46 legal persons were subject to civil and administrative penalties in the states subject to the OECD Convention.[14]

The signatories to the OECD have either modified or drafted local laws specific to the OECD Convention obligations. The OECD monitors the implementation of the laws by reviewing legislation implemented with the goal of evaluating the adequacy of the law and by assessing the effectiveness with which the legislation is applied. The country-specific legislations are discussed in Chapter 10 "Regional Considerations for Bribery and Corruption Risks".

African Union Convention on Preventing and Combating Corruption (www.africa-union.org/official_documents/ Treaties_%20Conventions_%20Protocols/Convention% 20on%20Combating%20Corruption.pdf)

The AU Convention on Preventing and Combating Corruption was adopted on July 11, 2003. The objective of the AU Convention is the development in Africa of policies and legislation to prevent, detect, punish, and eradicate corruption. A unique feature to the AU Convention is its call for transparency for public officials. This requirement calls for designated public officials to declare their assets before and after public service as well as puts restrictions on immunity for these public officials. The Convention also requires member states to create an environment that provides a high level of transparency and accountability. The AU Convention consists of 53 African states.[15]

The obligations of the member states include preventative measures, criminalization, and cooperation with the international community. The preventative measures include and are not limited to the requirement of public officials to declare their assets as discussed above, create an internal committee to establish a code of conduct that assists in training public officials on matters of ethics, and have access to any information that is needed to assist in the fight against corruption. The AU Convention requires members to criminalize offenses, which include illicit enrichment and concealing proceeds that were received from bribes. The AU Convention also seeks that member states cooperate in dealing with requests from authorities empowered by national laws to help prevent, detect, investigate, and punish acts of corruption and related offenses.

The AU Convention established the Advisory Board on Corruption within the African Union. The advisory board's is responsible for various functions, which include, but are not limited to, promoting and encouraging adoption and application of anti-corruption measures, collect and document information, creating new methodologies for analyzing the data and sharing with the public in an effort to educate the public, advising governments on how to deal with corruption, and working to harmonize codes of conduct for public officials by developing and promoting them.

South African Development Community Protocol Against Corruption (www.sadc.int/index/browse/page/122)

The South African Development Community Protocol against Corruption (SADC Protocol) was adopted in August 2001. The Protocol was signed by 14 SADC member states[16].

The SADC Protocol preamble discusses the adverse and destabilizing effects of corruption throughout the region and acknowledges that corruption undermines good governance, which includes the principles of accountability and transparency. The SADC Protocol provides both preventive and enforcement guidance.

The Protocol has three main purposes, which affect both the public and private sectors:

1. To promote and strengthen the development [. . .] of mechanisms needed to prevent, detect, punish, and eradicate corruption [. . .]
2. To promote, facilitate, and regulate cooperation among the State Parties to ensure the effectiveness of measures and actions to prevent, detect, punish, and eradicate corruption.
3. To foster the development and harmonization of policies and domestic legislation of the State Parties relating to the prevention, detection, punishment, and eradication of corruption.[17]

The Protocol provides for categories of obligations, which include preventive measures, confiscation, and an implementation mechanism. The preventive measures include, but are not limited to, standards of conduct for the proper fulfillment of public functions, systems for protecting individuals who report acts of corruption, laws that punish those who make false claims against innocent individuals, and creating institutions responsible for implementing mechanisms for preventing, detecting, punishing, and eradicating corruption. For confiscation, the Protocol allows for the confiscation of assets. For implementation, the Protocol will implement a committee consisting of State Parties to oversee the implementation of the Protocol. The committee's responsibility is to gather and disseminate information, organize training programs, and report on a regular basis on the progress made by each member state.

The Protocol states that all participating countries shall afford one another with mutual assistance and technical cooperation by processing requests from authorities that have the power to investigate or prosecute the acts of corruption.

Criminal and Civil Law Conventions on Corruption of the Council of Europe (http://conventions.coe.int/Treaty/EN/Treaties/Html/173.htm; http://conventions.coe.int/treaty/en/treaties/html/174.htm)

The Criminal Law Convention on Corruption was negotiated by the 47 member states of the Council of Europe, along with the participation of a number of observers, including Belarus, Canada, Japan, Mexico, and the United States.[18]

Some requirements for member states of the Council of Europe Conventions include criminalization, international cooperation, and monitoring. The Convention establishes that member states should take measures for active and passive bribery of both the public and private sectors. Criminalization is also extended to cover foreign public officials, public assemblies, and international organizations. With regard to monitoring, the Group of States against Corruption (GRECO) will monitor the implementation of the Convention by the member states. For international cooperation, the member states shall cooperate with each other for the purpose of investigations and proceedings concerning criminal offenses established in accordance with this Convention. Additionally, members shall mutually assist each other by promptly processing requests from authorities, in conformity with their domestic laws.

The Criminal Law Convention on Corruption includes regional agreements on the importance of addressing corruption with the intention of setting common standards for criminalization. Additionally, the Criminal Law Convention on Corruption has a cooperation framework for improved law enforcement assistance.

The Civil Law Convention on Corruption was an initial attempt to define consistent international rules related to civil law and corruption. Each party shall provide in its internal law for effective remedies for persons who have suffered damage as a result of acts of corruption, to enable them to defend their rights and interests, including the possibility of obtaining compensation for damage. Material damage, loss of profits, and nonpecuniary loss are also covered by the compensation.[19]

Asia Development Bank/OECD Anti-Corruption Action Plan (www.oedc.org)

In 1999, the Asian Development Bank (ADB) and the OECD launched an anti-corruption initiative for Asia-Pacific, and in 2001, they adopted an action plan, which defines objectives in building sustainable legal frameworks to fight corruption. Currently, there are 28 participating country members.[20]

The action plan includes goals and standards for sustainable safeguards against corruption in the region. The initiative, which includes (1) fostering policy dialogue, (2) providing policy analysis, and (3) capacity building, helps support member governments.

The action plan includes promoting preventive measures through educating and raising awareness to the general public, media, and civil society about preventing corruption. The action plan also emphasizes the importance of regional agreement in addressing corruption with a comprehensive framework and agreement to strive toward international standards.

Guidelines on Preventing and Combating Fraud and Corruption in Projects Financed by IBRD Loans and IDA Credits and Grants

On October 15, 2006 the World Bank issued "Guidelines: On Preventing and Combating Fraud and Corruption in Projects Financed by IBRD Loans and IDA Credits and Grants." These Guidelines broadly apply to the borrower as well as all "recipients of Loan proceeds."

The Guidelines state that the borrower is to take all appropriate measures to prevent corrupt, fraudulent, coercive, and obstructive practices with the use of loan proceeds. The borrower should immediately report to the bank and take timely action to address any allegations of fraud and corruption. The borrower should cooperate fully with the bank in the investigation into the allegations and cease transactions with any recipient of loan proceeds deemed ineligible by the bank.

The Guidelines state that the recipient of loan proceeds should comply with its agreement with the borrower and report to the bank any allegations of fraud and corruption with the use of the loan proceeds. The recipient should take timely action and cooperate fully with the bank in the investigation into the allegations.

 SUMMARY

International initiatives targeting bribery and corruption are encouraging countries to pass anti-corruption laws and regulations, and while businesses continue to look to expand worldwide, they will increasingly need to evaluate their operations under a variety of criteria.

As demonstrated by the passage of the U.K. Bribery Act, the international initiatives have had success. Many countries recognize that they have to strengthen their anti-bribery legislation and enforcement activities to level the playing field for international business. While there is still a long way to go, the recent increases in corruption investigations and prosecutions signify a new business environment where unfair, unethical, and unlawful behavior is no longer tolerated.

 NOTES

1. The FCPA contains an explicit exception to the bribery prohibition for "facilitating payments" for "routine governmental action."
2. Barry & Richard "Prosecuting Overseas Corporates Will be a Top Priority for the SFO." TheBriberyAct.Com, March 1, 2011; http://thebriberyact .com/2011/03/01/prosecuting-overseas-corporates-will-be-a-top-priority-for-the-sfo/.
3. Chris Walker, "Best Practices in Fighting Bribery and Corruption: The Bribery Act 2010; Enforcing the Bribery Act." February 15, 2011; www.sfo.gov.uk/ about-us/our-views/other-speeches/speeches-2011/icc-conference-hosted-by-herbert-smith.aspx.
4. "BAE Systems PLC Pleads Guilty and Ordered to Pay $400 Million Criminal Fine." Department of Justice, March 1, 2010; www.justice.gov/opa/pr/2010/ March/10-crm-209.html.
5. "BAE Systems plc." Serious Fraud Office, February 5, 2010; www.sfo.gov.uk/ press-room/latest-press-releases/press-releases-2010/bae-systems-plc.aspx.
6. Lanny A. Breuer, www.justice.gov/criminal/pr/speeches-testimony/documents/ 11-17-09 aagbreuer-remarks-fcpa.pdf. Speech, The 22nd National Forum on the Foreign Corrupt Practices Act, November 17th, 2009.
7. "Siemens AG and Three Subsidiaries Plead Guilty to Foreign Corrupt Practices Act Violations and Agree to Pay $450 Million in Combined Criminal Fines." Department of Justice, December 15, 2008; www.justice.gov/opa/pr/2008/ December/08-crm-1105.html.
8. "Two UK Citizens Charged by United States with Bribing Nigerian Government Officials to Obtain Lucrative Contracts as Part of KBR Joint Venture Scheme." Department of Justice, March 5, 2009; www.justice.gov/opa/pr/2009/March/ 09-crm-192.html.
9. www.sfo.gov.uk/press-room/latest-press-releases/press-releases-2011/mw-kellogg-ltd-to-pay-7-million-pounds-in-sfo-high-court-action.aspx
10. "AGCO Corp. to Pay $1.6 Million in Connection with Payments to the Former Iraqi Government Under the U.N. Oil-For-Food Program." Department of

Justice, September 30, 2009; www.justice.gov/opa/pr/2009/September/ 09-crm-1056.html.

11. The 34 member countries include: Antigua and Barbuda, Argentina, Barbados, Belize, Bolivia, Brazil, Canada, Chile, Colombia, Costa Rica, Dominica (Commonwealth of), Dominican Republic, Ecuador, El Salvador, Grenada, Guatemala, Guyana, Haiti, Honduras, Jamaica, Mexico, Nicaragua, Panama, Paraguay, Peru, Saint Kitts and Nevis, Saint Lucia, Saint Vincent and the Grenadines, Suriname, Bahamas (Commonwealth of), Trinidad and Tobago, United States, Uruguay, and Venezuela (Bolivarian Republic of).

12. The member countries that have signed and ratified the UNCAC include: Afghanistan, Albania, Algeria, Angola, Antigua and Barbuda, Argentina, Armenia, Australia, Austria, Azerbaijan, Bahamas, Bahrain, Bangladesh, Belarus, Belgium, Benin, Bolivia, Bosnia and Herzegovina, Brazil, Brunei Darussalam, Bulgaria, Burkina Faso, Burundi, Cambodia, Cameroon, Canada, Cape Verde, Central African Republic, Chile, China, Colombia, Congo, Costa Rica, Croatia, Cuba, Cyprus, Republic, Democratic Republic of Congo, Denmark, Djibouti, Dominica, Dominican Republic, Ecuador, Egypt, El Salvador, Estonia, Ethiopia, European Union, Fiji, Finland, France, Gabon, Georgia, Ghana, Greece, Guatemala, Guinea-Bissau, Guyana, Haiti, Honduras, Hungary, Indonesia, Iran, Iraq, Israel, Italy, Jamaica, Jordan, Kazakhstan, Kenya, Kuwait, Kyrgyzstan, Lao People's Democratic Republic, Latvia, Lebanon, Lesotho, Liberia, Libyan Arab Jamahiriya, Liechtenstein, Lithuania, Luxembourg, Macedonia, Madagascar, Malawi, Malaysia, Maldives, Mali, Malta, Mauritania, Mauritius, Mexico, Moldova, Mongolia, Montenegro, Morocco, Mozambique, Namibia, Netherlands, Nicaragua, Niger, Nigeria, Norway, Pakistan, Palau, Panama, Papua New Guinea, Paraguay, Peru, Philippines, Poland, Portugal, Qatar, Republic of Korea, Romania, Russian Federation, Rwanda, Sao Tome and Principe, Senegal, Serbia, Seychelles, Sierra Leone, Singapore, Slovakia, Slovenia, South Africa, Spain, Sri Lanka, Sweden, Switzerland, Tajikistan, Tanzania, Timor-Leste, Togo, Trinidad and Tobago, Tunisia, Turkey, Turkmenistan, Uganda, Ukraine, United Arab Emirates, United Kingdom, United States of America, Uruguay, Uzbekistan, Venezuela, Vietnam, Yemen, Zambia, and Zimbabwe.

The countries that have signed, but not yet ratified the UNCAC include: Barbados, Bhutan, Comoros, Côte d'Ivoire, Czech Republic, Germany, Guinea, India, Ireland, Japan, Myanmar, Nepal, New Zealand, Saudi Arabia, Sudan, Swaziland, Syria, and Thailand.

13. The 38 member countries include: Argentina, Australia, Austria, Belgium, Brazil, Bulgaria, Canada, Chile, Czech Republic, Denmark, Estonia, Finland, France, Germany, Greece, Hungary, Iceland, Ireland, Israel, Italy, Japan, Luxembourg, Mexico, Netherlands, New Zealand, Norway, Poland, Portugal, Slovakia, Slovenia, South Africa, Spain, South Korea, Sweden, Switzerland, Turkey, United Kingdom, and United States.

14. "Working Group on Bribery: 2010 Data on Enforcement of the Anti-Bribery Convention." OECD, April 2011; www.oecd.org/dataoecd/47/39/47637707 .pdf. Also, "The UK Bribery Act—Developing an Anti-Corruption Compliance Framework," Ernst & Young LLP, 2011; – EYG no. DQ0029.

15. The 53 member countries include: Algeria, Angola, Benin, Botswana, Burkina Faso, Burundi, Cameroon, Cape Verde, Central African Republic, Chad, Comoros, Democratic Republic of the Congo, Republic of the Congo, Côte d'Ivoire, Djibouti, Egypt, Equatorial Guinea, Eritrea, Ethiopia, Gabon, Gambia, Ghana, Guinea-Bissau, Guinea, Kenya, Lesotho, Liberia, Libya, Malawi, Mali, Mauritania, Mauritius, Mozambique, Namibia, Niger, Nigeria, Rwanda, São Tomé and Príncipe, Senegal, Seychelles, Sierra Leone, Somalia, South Africa, Sudan, Swaziland, Tanzania, Togo, Tunisia, Uganda, Sahrawi Arab Democratic Republic, Zambia, and Zimbabwe.

16. The 14 member countries include: Angola, Botswana, Democratic Republic of Congo (DRC), Lesotho, Malawi, Mauritius, Mozambique, Namibia, Seychelles, South Africa, Swaziland, United Republic of Tanzania, Zambia, and Zimbabwe.

17. www.sadc.int/key-documents/protocols/protocol-against-corruption/.

18. The 47 member states of the Council of Europe include: Albania, Andorra, Armenia, Austria, Azerbaijan, Bosnia and Herzegovina, Bulgaria, Croatia, Cyprus, Czech Republic, Czechoslovakia, Denmark, Estonia, Finland, France, Georgia, Germany, Greece, Hungary, Iceland, Ireland, Italy, Latvia, Liechtenstein, Lithuania, Luxembourg, Macedonia, Malta, Moldova, Monaco, Montenegro, Netherlands, Norway, Poland, Portugal, Romania, Russia, San Marino, Serbia, Slovakia, Slovenia, Spain, Sweden, Switzerland, Turkey, Ukraine, and United Kingdom.

19. http://conventions.coe.int/Treaty/en/Treaties/Html/174.htm.

20. The 28 participating member countries include: Australia, Bangladesh, Bhutan, Cambodia, People's Republic of China, Cook Islands, Fiji Islands, Hong Kong, China, India, Indonesia, Japan, Republic of Kazakhstan, Republic of Korea, Kyrgyz Republic, Macao, China, Malaysia, Mongolia, Nepal, Pakistan, Republic of Palau, Papua New Guinea, the Philippines, Samoa, Singapore, Sri Lanka, Thailand, Vanuatu, and Vietnam.

CHAPTER FOUR

Compliance Programs

CORPORATE COMPLIANCE PROGRAMS GENERALLY came into being for large companies in the United States in the early 1990s and have been evolving since that time. For example, compliance programs emerged in the health care industry in the 1990s as a systematic way for companies to detect and prevent misconduct. In 1991, the Federal Sentencing Guidelines defined the components of a compliance program allowing courts to consider the adoption of one as a mitigating factor in sentencing. The Sarbanes-Oxley (SOX) legislation in 2002, which set new and enhanced regulations of corporate governance and financial practice for all U.S. public company boards, management, and public accounting firms, continued this trend.

Business leaders, regulators, and commentators generally agree with the proposition that companies need to be proactive in their efforts to combat corruption and bribery. Bribery and corruption are widely viewed as significant problems and a barrier to economic and social stability in developing societies. Developed nations, led by the United States, have made bribery of foreign government officials an enforcement priority, and companies caught paying bribes have had to pay dearly. This has incentivized larger companies to create structures to mitigate the risk of noncompliance with the Foreign Corrupt Practices Act of 1977 (FCPA) and other anti-corruption laws.

These have evolved into what is now referred to as an anti-corruption compliance program.

Anti-corruption compliance programs have become an important element of most companies' overall compliance program given the increase in enforcement by the U.S. Department of Justice (DOJ) and Securities and Exchange Commission (SEC) in the mid-2000s. This has become especially true, due to the impact of voluntary disclosures and the fact that the vast majority of cases end up being settled with the U.S. government. Anti-corruption compliance programs or the lack thereof have become a major consideration in these settlement negotiations.

 ## GOALS OF AN EFFECTIVE ANTI-CORRUPTION COMPLIANCE PROGRAM

Anti-corruption compliance programs vary widely from company to company. However, over the past decade, a consensus of leading practices has emerged. The goals of such programs are fairly straightforward: to deter, detect, and prevent bribery and corrupt payments. This is done through a compliance structure that includes people, processes, and technology.

People focuses on the individuals tasked with developing, implementing, and monitoring a company's anti-corruption compliance program.

Processes are the elements of the anti-corruption compliance program and include conducting anti-corruption risk assessments; the adoption of policies and enhanced financial controls; anti-corruption training, audits, and monitoring mechanisms; and continuous review and improvement. These leading practices are described below.

Technology includes the tools used to assist in carrying out the overall compliance mandate and can include the accounting system, the company's web site where the code of conduct and other policies are posted, the company's online training system, online travel and entertainment, and vendor payment and approval controls, as well as technology tools used to monitor the ongoing activities, which are further described in Chapter 7, "Monitoring."

 ## ACCEPTED STANDARDS AND GUIDANCE

Much has been published about building corporate compliance programs in general and anti-corruption compliance programs in particular. There are, however, four documents with the most significant impact and influence in the development of compliance programs. These four documents are "must reads" before designing an anti-corruption compliance program:

- "Internal Control–Integrated Framework," issued by the Committee of Sponsoring Organizations of the Treadway Commission (COSO) in 1992.[1]
- The U.S. Federal Sentencing Guidelines for Organizations.[2]
- "Good Practice Guidance on Internal Controls, Ethics and Compliance," Annex II to the Recommendation of the Council for the Organization for Economic Cooperation and Development (OECD) for Further Combating Bribery of Foreign Public Officials in International Business Transactions (OECD Anti-Corruption Compliance Framework), February 18, 2010.[3]
- "The Bribery Act 2010 Guidance about procedures which relevant commercial organisations can put into place to prevent persons associated with them from bribing" (The Bribery Act Adequate Procedures Guidance) issued by the U.K. Ministry of Justice, March 30, 2011.[4]

COSO Framework

The 1992 COSO report, "Internal Control–Integrated Framework," is the most commonly used and understood framework for evaluating internal controls over financial reporting. Since anti-corruption compliance programs are a form of an internal control program, understanding the COSO framework is useful for gaining perspective on what an anti-corruption compliance program should seek to achieve and how to define success.

COSO is a voluntary private-sector organization that is dedicated to guiding executive management and governance entities toward the establishment of more effective, efficient, and ethical business operations globally. COSO was formed in 1985 to sponsor the National Commission on Fraudulent Financial Reporting, an independent private-sector initiative that studied the causal factors that can lead to fraudulent financial reporting. It sponsors and publishes frameworks and guidance based on in-depth research, analysis, and best practices. COSO also developed recommendations for public companies and their independent auditors, for the SEC and other regulators, and for educational institutions.[5]

The COSO report defines internal control as a process—effected by an entity's board of directors, management, and other personnel—designed to provide reasonable assurance regarding the achievement of objectives in the following three categories of control: (1) effectiveness and efficiency of operations; (2) reliability of financial reporting; and (3) compliance with laws and regulations. It also identifies five essential components that must be present and functioning to have an effective internal control system.[6]

The five elements from the COSO framework for effective internal control systems:

1. Control environment

    The control environment establishes the foundation for the internal control system by providing fundamental discipline and structure. It also sets the tone of the organization, influencing the control consciousness of its people.

2. Risk assessment

    The process of identifying, analyzing, and managing risks is a critical component of an effective internal control system; acknowledging that change is always present, identifying changed conditions, and taking actions as necessary to respond to those changes are fundamental to an effective risk assessment process.

    The purpose of a company's risk assessment process is to identify, analyze, and manage risks that affect the ability to achieve its objectives. Risks can exist at both a company level and at a process/application level. Risks at the company level can arise from external factors (e.g., competition can alter marketing or service activities; changing customer needs or expectations can affect product development, production processes, pricing) or internal factors (e.g., disruption in information systems processing can adversely affect operations; a change in management responsibilities can alter the operation of certain controls).

    Once risks are identified, management considers their significance, the likelihood of their occurrence, and how they should be managed. Management may initiate plans, programs, or actions to address specific risks, or it may decide to accept a risk because of cost or other considerations. Risks can arise or change due to circumstances such as changes in operating environment; new personnel; new or revamped information systems; rapid growth; new technology, new business models, products, or activities; corporate restructurings; expanded foreign operations; and new accounting pronouncements.

3. Control activities

    Control activities are the policies, procedures, and practices that ensure management objectives are achieved and that risk mitigation strategies are carried out. Control activities, whether automated or manual, have various objectives and are generally applied at various organizational and functional levels. Control activities include reviews, approvals, authorizations, verifications, reconciliations, security over assets, and segregation of duties.

4. Information and communication

Information and communications is the process of capturing and exchanging the information needed to conduct, manage, and control the company operations. The quality of the company's information and communications affects management's ability to make appropriate decisions in controlling the business activities and to prepare reliable financial reports.

An information system consists of infrastructure (physical and hardware components), software, people, procedures (manual and automated), and data. The information system relevant to financial reporting objectives, which includes the accounting system, consists of the procedures, whether automated or manual, and records established to initiate, record, process, and report company transactions, (as well as events and conditions) and to maintain accountability for the related assets, liabilities, and equity.

Communication involves providing an understanding of individual roles and responsibilities pertaining to internal controls over financial reporting. Consideration should be given to the methods utilized. Methods of communication include staff meetings, training, newsletters, policy updates, management reports, accounting systems, and so on.

Information and communication supports all other control components by communicating control responsibilities to employees and by providing information in a form and time frame that allows people to carry out their duties

5. Monitoring

Monitoring is the continuous process that assesses the quality of the performance of internal control over time. An important management responsibility is to establish and maintain internal control. Management monitors controls to consider whether they are operating as intended and whether they are modified as appropriate for changes in conditions.[7]

An anti-corruption compliance program is part of the overall internal control system of a company, and the logic of the COSO framework is fully applicable in designing an effective anti-corruption compliance program. The COSO report specifies that an effective internal control system should provide "reasonable assurance" to management and the board that applicable laws are being complied with. This does not mean absolute assurance, as all instances of poor judgment cannot be anticipated, and management override or collusion can overcome any compliance program or individual control. COSO also recognizes that a limiting factor in the design of any internal control system is that there are resource constraints, and the benefits of the program must be considered relative to costs. This is why risk assessment is such an important part of the COSO model. Conducting a risk assessment is crucial to establishing an effective anti-corruption compliance program because, if done properly, it best ensures that limited resources will be aligned with the most pressing risks.

The COSO report also provides a foundation for all parties to speak a common language and communicate effectively on internal control issues. This yields a better understanding of the benefits and limitations of internal controls, where legislators and regulators can better assess their objectives and the costs and benefits necessary to achieve them.

The Federal Sentencing Guidelines

The Federal Sentencing Guidelines (Sentencing Guidelines) are rules that attempt to provide a uniform sentencing policy for criminal convictions in the U.S. federal court system. The Sentencing Guidelines are promulgated by the United States Sentencing Commission, which is an independent agency within the judicial branch of the U.S. government. The commission was created by the Sentencing Reform Act of 1984 to reduce inconsistencies in the sentencing systems across the United States.

Because federal criminal law applies to companies, the U.S. Sentencing Commission publishes standards related to sentencing of companies and provides standards for leniency if companies have effective corporate compliance programs. Accordingly, the Sentencing Guidelines provide an accepted framework for U.S. corporations to organize their corporate compliance programs. It states that an effective compliance program is one that is reasonably designed, implemented, and enforced so that it generally will be effective in preventing and detecting criminal conduct. At the most basic level, to be considered effective, a compliance program must contain the following seven elements[8]:

1. Established standards and procedures

   This element is often the easiest to prove as the policies and procedures may be set forth in various documents, including a code of conduct, code of ethics, employee handbook, personnel policies, travel and entertainment policies, anti-corruption policy, health and safety guidelines, and overall documentation of the corporate compliance program. Law enforcement agencies are often critical of corporate compliance materials that "just sit on the shelf." Accordingly, it is equally important to demonstrate the operational aspect of the program as well, which may be more difficult to show. It is important to demonstrate that the compliance program functions on a day-to-day basis. Sources of relevant documentation may include internal audit plans, hotline logs, records of internal investigations, disciplinary records, training materials, training attendance lists, and correspondence or e-mails addressing compliance matters.

2. High-level oversight

The compliance program must be run by senior company officials and must have oversight at the highest levels of the company. While it is relatively easy to identify those charged with corporate compliance responsibilities, showing their commitment to the process can be tricky. This commitment may be prevalent from their involvement in revisions to the corporate compliance program; correspondence with employees emphasizing the need for compliance; participation in supervision of the compliance program; investigation of complaints; and inappropriate behavior reports to management, the audit committee, or the board of directors.

3. Led by competent and ethical employees

A company should use reasonable efforts and due diligence not to place any individual in a position of substantial authority who the organization knew, or should have known, had a history of engaging in violations of law. Discretionary authority is frequently exercised at all levels of senior and middle management, and sometimes at lower levels of management as well. Accordingly, this measure would apply broadly to a company's management team. Most companies perform some level of background check prior to extending an offer of employment to an individual; however, few companies perform similar checks when employees are promoted to positions of authority or given significant increases in authority. Alternative sources of support may come from a history of positive performance evaluations, support and recommendations of fellow employees who know the individual, or a lack of past disciplinary action.

4. Effective communication and training

Education is the hallmark of meeting this standard. Companies frequently rely on training programs, seminars, wall posters, e-mail notifications, and periodic signed certifications from employees to make sure that employees fully understand the program. Many companies periodically notify their agents of the need to observe the company's policies, include clauses in agency agreements that require compliance with stated policies, or invite agents to participate in company-sponsored training programs.

5. Effective auditing and monitoring systems

    Effective compliance programs also include mechanisms to monitor the ongoing compliance functions and to encourage employees to report violations, often anonymously, and to reassure that such reports are confidential and will be processed without repercussion. The corporate compliance officer, internal audit, or other senior management are often tasked with the monitoring function. Internal audit may include procedures to test compliance. Compliance officers may interview employees or review hotline logs to see that employees understand their obligations under the program. Internal audit reports, employee interviews, hotline logs, and employee certifications that all known violations have been reported serve as documentation of these processes.

6. Appropriate disciplinary measures

    When a violation of law is detected, effectiveness requires that the organization take reasonable steps to respond appropriately to the violation. Law enforcement officials frequently inquire about disciplinary action taken as a result of the violation. The failure to take meaningful disciplinary action, which may include suspension, reassignment, termination, or forfeiture of a bonus, may be viewed as condoning the inappropriate behavior. Evidence of these actions is usually documented in personnel files.

7. Appropriate response to incidents and modification of prevention measures

    Reasonable steps include taking action to prevent and detect recurrences of similar conduct. This responsibility is often demonstrated through timely, thorough internal investigations; expanded auditing procedures and modifications to the compliance program; relevant internal controls; or oversight responsibilities. These steps should be followed up with the processes discussed about regarding communication of policies and procedures.[9]

As many companies already have corporate compliance programs that address other legal and reputational risk issues, it is important to leverage what your company already has in place in addressing corruption risk. For example, compliance with the FCPA should be included in your overall company code of conduct, as well as be addressed in a separate and more detailed stand-alone policy. Generally, corporate compliance programs include professionals and processes to oversee compliance activities and for conducting internal investigations. These resources could also be used to oversee your anti-corruption compliance program. The Federal Sentencing Guidelines are also instructive as many of the "leading practices" in anti-corruption compliance follow a similar outline (i.e., anti-corruption standards, communication and training, and auditing and monitoring). This is no coincidence as companies that run afoul of the law will be judged by DOJ prosecutors and the federal courts in accordance with these standards. Therefore, an effective, continually updated, robust, and well-documented compliance program that allows company-wide understanding of and adherence to the many legal and regulatory compliance requirements will remain the first line of defense in this era of increased scrutiny well into the foreseeable future.

The OECD Good Practice Guidelines

The OECD's mission is to promote policies that will improve the economic and social well-being of people around the world by providing a forum in which governments can share experiences to work together and seek solutions to common problems. Its predecessor, the Organization for European Economic Cooperation (OEEC), was established shortly after World War II to administer the Marshall Plan, which funded postwar reconstruction. After its involvement in the Marshall Plan, the focus of OEEC shifted to economic issues and economic cooperation within Europe. The United States and Canada joined the OEEC in establishing the OECD in 1961. Over the years the membership has grown to 34 countries, and the OECD serves as a forum where countries openly identify, analyze, and discuss problems and develop policies to address them.

The OECD has been instrumental in promoting anti-corruption efforts globally by pressing member countries to pass anti-corruption legislation similar to the FCPA and to intensify their enforcement efforts. Recently, it has recognized the need to more directly address the private sector and, similar to the U.S. Sentencing Commission, it has issued its own global guidelines for companies to ensure "the effectiveness of internal controls, ethics, and compliance programmes or measures for preventing and detecting the bribery of foreign public officials in their international business transactions." The OECD "Good Practice Guidance on Internal Controls, Ethics and Compliance" is more specific than the Federal Sentencing Guidelines. It directly addresses anti-corruption programs for global companies and calls for companies to identify foreign bribery risks (through a risk assessment process) and to adopt many of the leading practices based on these risks, including:

- Strong tone at the top

  Effective compliance starts with effective communication. Words matter when designing and implementing a compliance program. The corporate anti-corruption policy should be approved by your board of directors, distributed to your company management, and posted on your internal web site with other compliance-related policies.

- A clearly articulated and visible corporate policy prohibiting bribery

  Develop a company-wide policy requiring compliance with the FCPA, the U.K. Bribery Act and other anti-corruption laws. The overall compliance policy should detail how compliance will be achieved and address such issues as facilitating payments, due diligence in mergers and acquisitions, joint ventures, contracting with agents and consultants, commercial bribery, accuracy of financial reporting, and audits of internal controls.[10]

- Emphasis on individual employee responsibility for compliance

  References to your anti-corruption policy should be included in a written code of conduct issued to all company employees. Make a short and simple statement of employees' duty to comply with bribery and corruption laws. Compliance with the anti-corruption policy should have a prominent place in your company's overall compliance regime.

- Board of directors and senior management oversight of the program

  Many companies have formal programs to certify and recertify senior employees regularly on compliance. Certifications will not stop the deliberate wrongdoer, but the requirement serves as a continuing reminder of the manager's compliance responsibility. Certification processes may also identify issues that otherwise might not have surfaced, which can then be brought to the attention of the board of directors and senior management.

- Specific guidance on areas that should be covered, including gifts; hospitality, entertainment and expenses; customer travel; political contributions; charitable donations and sponsorships; facilitating payments; and solicitation and extortion.

  Giving gifts or providing meals, entertainment, or travel to government employees could, under certain circumstances, violate the FCPA or U.K. Bribery Act. Such payments, or even offers, need to be monitored carefully to avoid even the appearance of impropriety. This is an area of special concern in certain Asian countries, where the culture of gift giving and business entertainment is firmly ingrained and government and private-sector officials at various levels are known to frequently request and expect such courtesies.

- Specific guidance related to retaining agents, consultants, and other risky intermediaries

    Create policies to govern the retention of agents, consultants, commercial sales representatives, and other third parties to address the risk that such third parties may pay or offer to pay bribes on the company's behalf. The policies could include mandates that the company perform FCPA due diligence, require a written contract with anti-bribery representations and warranties, dictate periodic compliance certifications from the vendor and demand in the contract—and exercise—the right to audit the vendor for compliance.

- Strong internal controls in place to ensure accurate record keeping and prevention of concealment of bribery

    Consider implementing specific anti-corruption financial controls around high-risk operations and processes. Focus these controls on high-corruption-risk areas such as transactions with government customers, procure-to-pay, cash, petty cash, gifts, customs and cross-border shipping, executive travel, meals, and entertainment. Such heightened financial controls are focused on deterring and detecting illicit payments and can be a critical firewall in avoiding FCPA books and records violations.[11]

- Communication and anti-corruption training

    At a minimum, every person in a position to obtain business through bribery or other improper means should receive anti-corruption compliance training. Also consider training all accounting and financial employees. Consider a mixture of live training for targeted and senior employees and Web-based training for all employees.

- Support for whistle-blowing activity

    Responding to fraud or corruption allegations can create further difficulties. Companies need to react swiftly—often within 24 hours—to gauge the impact of the allegations, to establish an effective crisis management approach, and to identify and secure the relevant evidence. Careful consideration needs to be given as to how to handle a whistle-blower and what immediate steps to take to substantiate the allegations.

- A confidential process for seeking compliance guidance and whistle-blowing

Clearly delineated roles for internal audit, legal, compliance, and finance are increasingly important. For example, who assesses a tip from a whistle-blower hotline and decides on what action? Who should investigate? Who should impose disciplinary procedures? Who informs the board (and when)? Who should maintain a record of proceedings?[12]

- Appropriate disciplinary measures

Internal audits have a powerful deterrent effect: They send a message that the senior management is committed to compliance. Appropriate follow-up and disciplinary action are crucial to creating an anti-corruption culture.

- Periodic reviews and action to update and improve the program

For example, training should be reviewed and approved by legal counsel and tailored to meet the company's FCPA risk profile. Continually update the training and provide it to new or transitioning employees.

The Bribery Act 2010—Adequate Procedures Guidance

As discussed earlier in Chapter 3, the U.K. Bribery Act provides for a defense for companies that have in place "adequate procedure" even if bribery takes place. The question remained: What are "adequate procedures"? Additionally, when the U.K. Bribery Act was issued and received Royal Assent during 2010, many companies were concerned that the act was so broad and lacked bright-line rules and guidance that the impact on business practices such as corporate entertainment would put U.K. companies at a disadvantage on the world stage.

In response, the Ministry of Justice issued draft guidance in September 2010 that outlined their initial views on "adequate procedures," the comment period ran for eight weeks and they received over 175 comment letters from companies across the spectrum, including companies, law firms, professional organizations, public-sector organizations, and nongovernmental organizations.

In March 2011, the final "adequate procedures" guidance was issued, with Kenneth Clarke (Secretary of State for Justice) stating:

> ... I hope this guidance shows, combating the risks of bribery is largely about common sense, not burdensome procedures. The core principle it sets out is proportionality. It also offers case study examples that help illuminate the application of the Act. Rest assured – no one wants to stop firms getting to know their clients by taking them to events like Wimbledon or the Grand Prix.

The guidance sets out six guiding principles to help a company establish an anti-corruption program that is adequate to mitigate its corruption risks. The guidance was not intended to be prescriptive and clearly stated:

> ... commercial organisations should adopt a risk-based approach to managing bribery risks. Procedures should be proportionate to the risks faced by an organisation. No policies or procedures are capable of detecting and preventing all bribery. A risk-based approach will, however, serve to focus the effort where it is needed and will have most impact. A risk-based approach recognises that the bribery threat to organisations varies across jurisdictions, business sectors, business partners and transactions.[13]

The six guiding principles for a company to develop adequate procedures to prevent bribery and corruption are:

1. Proportionate procedures

The guidance is clear in that the approach taken should be proportionate to the risk that the entity faces and it is not a "one-size fits all"[14] guide. "Procedures" is meant to encompass both the anti-corruption prevention policies and the related implementation procedures. These procedures set the tone at the company that bribery and corruption are not tolerated. The acknowledged key first step is a risk assessment, which is the third guiding principle. Therefore, a small company that faces significant risk would need to have strong tone but place reliance on verbal communications rather than volumes of written communication.

The policies and procedures of an organization should be intertwined with the five other guiding principles that are discussed more fully below.

The following areas are listed as potential policies and procedures that may be considered based on the risks faced.

Involve top level management	Employment relationships	Decision making:
Risk assessment	Business relationships	Delegation of authority
Due diligence	Financial controls:	Segregation of duties
Policies on:	Bookkeeping	Conflicts of interest
Gifts	Auditing	Implementation plan
Hospitality	Approval	Communication and training
Promotional expense	Transparency and disclosure	
Donations	Enforcement and discipline	Monitoring, review, and evaluation of policies and procedures
Facilitation payments	Whistle-blower process	

2. Top-level commitment

The leaders of an organization are best situated to set the tone of nontolerance of bribery and corruption. The guidance encourages involvement of the most senior people in an organization in establishing and maintaining a culture where bribery and corruption are not tolerated as well as their involvement in addressing bribery risk.

Communication both internally and externally by the leaders of the organization of the stance on bribery and corruption is critical to demonstrating the commitment to operating in an ethical manner. This will establish a strong foundation where all employees understand the right thing to do when it comes to bribery and corruption.

The expected senior-level involvement includes a broad involvement in a number of areas, some as a leader and others as a sponsor.

- Leadership in the key anti-corruption measures including the code of conduct and the anti-corruption policy and the training and dissemination of these policies.
- Leadership with external parties on the company's anti-corruption stance.
- Leadership in high-profile decision making.
- Sponsorship of the team tasked with leading the company's anti-corruption efforts including endorsing messages related to bribery and corruption and the risk assessment process.
- High-level oversight on the investigation and reporting of potential breaches.

3. Risk assessment

The purpose of a risk assessment is to understand the bribery and corruption risks that an organization faces both internally and externally. The risk assessment must be proportionate to the size, scale, nature, structure, and geographic diversity of a company. The bribery and corruption risk assessment can be done as a standalone project or embedded into other risk assessments carried out by the organization.

Basic characteristics identified for conducting a risk assessment include: management oversight, empowered resources, consideration of internal and external factors, due diligence enquiries and documentation of procedures and the basis for conclusion. The risk assessment should be regularly updated as the risk profile of the company changes over time.

The guidance identified five broad categories of external risk that should be considered in identifying bribery and corruption risks:

Country	Sector	Transactional	Business Opportunity	Business Partnership
Certain countries have a higher perceived risk of corruption stemming from a lack of anti-corruption legislation and overall lack of transparency.	Some types business sectors are inherently more risky. Examples provided were the extractive industries, such as mining and oil and gas, and large-scale infrastructure, such as telecommunications, hydroelectric, and rail.	Transactions such as charitable and political contributions, licensing and permitting and public tenders carry a higher level of risk than a routine transaction.	High value and nonstandard projects and transactions carry more risk as do projects with multiple third parties involved.	Entering into business relationships such as joint ventures, consortia, or the use of a third party tied to a public official carries a higher risk level than direct dealings.

After the external risks are identified, the next logical step is to see how these risks are mitigated by internal procedures. It is noted that some internal factors can increase the bribery and corruption risk, this can include a lack of clear policies and procedures, lack of controls, lack of executive sponsorship of the anti-bribery tone, lack of training, and a compensation structure that rewards disproportionate risk.

4. Due diligence

Due diligence in the adequate procedures guidance focuses on individuals or organizations performing business on behalf of an entity and should be applied in a proportionate and risk based fashion. It can serve both as a form of risk assessment or a way to mitigate risk.

With the broad definition of an "associated" person under the U.K. Bribery Act, the level of risk associated with a business relationship can vary significantly. The due diligence procedures may even be considered for certain employees or candidates for employment as they are considered an "associated" person.

Due diligence procedures can be performed internally or by consultants (such as Ernst & Young) and depending on the risk level associated can range from no procedures to general internet searches to very detailed investigation of a person's background and relationships.

5. Communication

The principle of communication focuses on raising consciousness and comprehension of the policies and procedures in place to address the bribery and corruption risk of an organization. This includes internal and external communications and training.

Internal communications set the organizational tone as described previously in top-level commitment and are all the more powerful if coming from senior level individuals in the company. This can also include more detailed communications on the implementation of policies and procedures and the impact that a violation could have on the company and the individual. Another important element is establishing a confidential mechanism to raise bribery and corruption concerns within the company and to get advice on how to handle these concerns.

External communications of the bribery and corruption policies and the code of conduct can deter an associated person from making a bribe on behalf of a company. Consideration can be given to the distribution of a company's bribery and corruption policies to a wider audience such as suppliers, third-party intermediaries, and customers.

Training helps to solidify the organizational tone and stance on bribery and corruption. Training can be used to raise awareness of bribery in general, specific risks faced by an entity, and the specific policies and procedures in place to address these risks. When determining who should be trained and how to train them, a company should establish a plan that is proportional to the risks it has identified. Training can take the form of e-learning, live training, and seminars. It can extend to all employees or be focused on high-risk areas within the business such as marketing and sales professional in high-risk locations or can even be extended to high-risk associated persons outside the organization such as agents.

6. Monitoring and review

A company needs to monitor the effectiveness of its anti-corruption compliance program and make adjustments based on its ever-changing risk profile. A variety of methods can be used to monitor an anti-corruption compliance program, including monitoring/testing of the controls in place and soliciting feedback internally through surveys or questionnaires. External verification and review is another potential method of monitoring. The results of monitoring should be presented to senior management.

The following table summarizes high-level considerations that an entity should consider when contemplating if they have "adequate procedures."

Proportionate Procedures	Top-Level Commitment	Risk Assessment	Due Diligence	Communication	Monitoring and Review
Bribery prevention procedures should be:	*Top-level management should:*	*The risk assessment should:*	*Due diligence should be:*	*Communication and training:*	*Regular monitoring and review should:*
■ Proportionate to the risks faced and the size and complexity of the business ■ Clear, practical, accessible, properly implemented and enforced	■ Take responsibility at board level for bribery prevention ■ Foster a zero tolerance culture toward bribery	■ Consider both internal and external risks ■ Be performed periodically and documented	■ Conducted on parties performing services for or on behalf of a business ■ Proportionate and risk based	■ Should ensure bribery prevention policies and procedures are embedded and understood throughout the business ■ May include external communication and a secure, confidential, and accessible "speak-up" procedure	■ Evaluate the effectiveness of current bribery prevention procedures ■ Identify and implement necessary improvements

The COSO report, Federal Sentencing Guidelines, OECD Good Practices Guidelines, and the Bribery Act 2010–Adequate Procedures Guidance are certainly key reference points to understand when beginning the process of building an anti-corruption compliance program. However, there are many other sources for guidance on anti-corruption programs. In settlement and deferred prosecution agreements, the DOJ regularly sets out its expectations of the minimum elements required in a corporate compliance program that is consistent with the following discussion.

Anti-corruption compliance continues to be a top priority for boards of directors, audit committees, and senior management at many multinational companies. In fact, a recent Ernst & Young Global Fraud Survey found that 40 percent of boards have recently asked chief financial officers for a review of their anti-fraud, anti-bribery, and anti-corruption internal controls. These organizations are facing increased pressure to integrate reasonable compliance programs and procedures to prevent and detect actions that may violate the FCPA. Furthermore, increased FCPA enforcement and penalties in the United States in recent years are expected to be compounded by growing enforcement in OECD countries and the U.K. Bribery Act. Therefore, understanding the preceding referenced laws and compliance guidelines provides the necessary framework to begin the process of building your anti-corruption compliance program.

WHAT SHOULD AN ANTI-CORRUPTION PROGRAM INCLUDE?

An anti-corruption program should be developed to incorporate the elements of an effective program. Global policies should include a code of conduct and policies regarding gifts, training, political and charitable contributions, and delegation of authority, as well as accounting policies regarding the proper recording of transactions. Rigorous training on these policies, particularly at the executive levels, should be conducted with department-specific training provided at the business unit level on a periodic basis.[15]

An anti-corruption program should focus on the specific risks of corruption and bribery facing a company. These risks are derived from the nature of its operations, the degree of business with government entities, business locations and company size, and the regulatory environment it operates in. The first step in building an effective anti-corruption program is to conduct a corruption risk assessment to identify and prioritize these and other risks faced. Then develop a

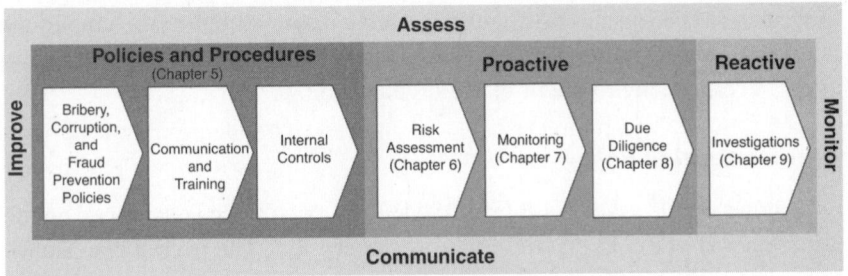

FIGURE 4.1 Anti-Corruption Compliance Program

program to design and implement strategies and allocate resources to manage such risks. Additional risk assessments should be undertaken periodically to ensure that the program in place is meeting new risks and challenges as the business and regulatory environments change.

As shown in Figure 4.1, the three aspects of a holistic anti-corruption program include:

1. Setting the proper tone at the top within the organization through policies and procedures.
2. Proactively identifying corruption risks and monitoring internal controls to prevent or detect the fraud risks.
3. Developing reactive protocols in the event that corruption is suspected.

Policies and Procedures

Policies and procedures establish an overall tone for an organization and impact the day-to-day operations. Adopting a code of conduct, formalizing policies and procedures, widely disseminating these policies, conducting awareness training, and establishing the overall internal control systems and the controls focused on bribery and corruption are key elements to successful tone setting.

A company sets the overall tone through broad policies such as a code of conduct, which should set forth the business rules of the organization, and it can provide a framework to guide the response of the organization in the challenging and sometimes difficult choices that are presented to members of the organization. While the code of conduct is a broad policy that helps focus an organization's behavior, to address bribery and corruption is it necessary to have more detailed policies and procedures such as the anti-corruption policy that address the specific risks and are widely disseminated to the employees who also receive training on the key policies. These policies help form the internal control environment of the organization.

Anti-Corruption Policy

Companies should develop a company-wide anti-corruption policy based on the requirements of the FCPA and the U.K. Bribery Act. The overall compliance policy should be a clear and unambiguous statement of the company's position that both governmental and commercial bribery on any scale or level will not be tolerated. It also should discuss the company's commitment to accuracy in reporting and recording transactions and having in place internal controls to ensure proper control, accountability, and safeguarding of shareholder assets. The policy should also provide operational guidance on how compliance will be achieved in certain high-risk areas.

Communication and Training

The code of conduct, anti-corruption policy, and other policies need to be disseminated widely within an organization. Training reinforces management's message and provides stakeholders with information regarding the latest issues, challenges, and concerns of the company. Lack of understanding and reinforcement of a company's policies, procedures, reporting protocols, and corruption risks exposes a company to employees, vendors, customers, and other stakeholders not knowing what is considered acceptable behavior or how to effectively report suspected improper activities.

Anti-corruption training is imperative. This is especially true for global organizations employing nationals in countries with a high history of corruption. For employees in these countries, training is crucial. At a minimum, every person in a position to obtain business through bribery or other improper means should receive anti-corruption compliance training. Training should highlight the company's position that it does not tolerate corruption, its anti-corruption policies to ensure compliance with the requirements of the FCPA and U.K. Bribery Act, potential "red flags" or problem situations, and guidance for employees to get help. Consider a mixture of live training for certain targeted and senior employees and Web-based training for all employees. Along with senior management, employees in sales, marketing, finance, legal, and internal audit should receive enhanced training. Continually update the training and provide it to new or transitioning employees. Many companies complement their training with a certification program, whereby the employee certifies that he or she has taken the training, understands his or her responsibility, and is not aware of or has reported any and all incidents of corruption.

Anti-Corruption Financial Controls

Good controllership is the first line of defense against corrupt payments. For example, strict enforcement of travel and entertainment rules related to meals and entertainment and the detailed reporting of the business purpose and people entertained supports anti-corruption compliance. Reconciling bank accounts on a monthly basis is a key cash control that also protects against misappropriation and possible off-books payments.

Increased financial controls in high-risk areas can be a critical firewall in avoiding FCPA books and records violations. Often, this means enhancing financial controls beyond what might normally be considered adequate to ensure accurate financial reporting under SOX. This is because there is the additional purpose of deterring and detecting illicit or improper payments for which there is no materiality standard. Such controls include enhanced transaction review, approval and accounting procedures, controls around bank accounts and petty cash, enhanced vendor approval and payment processes, and increased scrutiny of high-risk transactions. Companies should focus on high-corruption-risk areas such as:

- Bank accounts.
- Petty cash.
- Procurement and contracting.
- Consultants, agents, and other high-risk intermediaries.
- Customs and cross-border shipping.
- Gifts, meals, and entertainment of customers and government officials.
- Charitable giving and offset commitments

Heightened controls should be put in place in high-risk locations to mitigate the risk of an improper payment.

Proactive Measures

The proactive elements of an anti-corruption compliance program are critical to the overall operational effectiveness of the program. The risk assessment is key to understanding bribery and corruption risk and where to allocate resources to mitigate these risks. Monitoring measures the effectiveness of the anti-corruption compliance program. Anti-corruption due diligence is vital to understanding bribery and corruption risks in the context of a merger or joint venture.

Corruption Risk Assessment

Taking the time to thoughtfully identify and analyze risk is essential to developing an effective anti-corruption compliance program. As stated earlier in the chapter, COSO, the OECD, and the U.K. Ministry of Justice recognize the importance of risk assessment in developing any internal control framework: resources are limited, and a company needs to allocate its scarce compliance resources as efficiently as possible. A thorough and complete risk assessment process also puts a company in a position, should issues arise that were not foreseen, to demonstrate that it used due care in assessing its risk. In short, a thorough risk assessment adds both efficiency and credibility to your anti-corruption compliance efforts.

The first stage of the corruption risk assessment should focus on actual risks posed by the nature of a company's operations, the revenue generation process, the degree of business with governmental entities, its use of agents and other intermediaries, the countries where it does business, the regulatory environment, and other factors. The second stage should identify what policies and controls the company has in place to mitigate its corruption risk and analyze the effectiveness or gaps in such policies and controls, (i.e., the residual corruption risk still facing the company). The third stage is to produce a plan to build an effective and efficient anti-corruption compliance program based on the present risk, the current controls in place and additional resources available to provide reasonable assurance of compliance.

The actual procedures to be conducted and the intensity of the risk assessment will vary by company. Generally, the more thorough the risk assessment, the more confident one can be that the corruption risks have been sufficiently identified and analyzed. There is, however, a point of diminishing returns. The actual procedures involve information collection and analysis, generally through document collection, interviews, and financial analysis. More robust risk assessments also involve transaction testing that can be performed at the corporate level and in high-risk locations. The output of the risk assessment is often a detailed report on the company's anti-corruption risks and gaps in its current anti-corruption compliance regime. Most important, the output should consist of detailed recommendations for modifications to the design and implementation of the anti-corruption compliance program elements needed to effectively meet the company's needs. Refer to Chapter 6, "Risk Assessments," for further details.

Monitoring

Monitoring is crucial. Programs that are not monitored are generally not very effective. Monitoring means anti-corruption compliance audits. It also can include data mining and analytics.

The purpose of anti-corruption compliance audits should be both to audit for compliance with the various elements of the anti-corruption compliance program and to test for substantive compliance by seeking to identify potential violations or "red flags." Audits also often uncover new risks not previously seen or fully appreciated. In this way, they act as part of an ongoing corruption risk assessment process.

Creating an effective anti-corruption compliance monitoring program requires having the right people, processes, and resources. Anti-corruption compliance audit programs should be designed based on risk, address the areas of elevated corruption risk faced by the company, and test the controls in place to mitigate the risk. Audits should be conducted at the various business units based on a periodic anti-corruption risk assessment that ranks the business units and locations by risk and ensures adequate audit coverage of those locations over a defined time period.

The auditors need to be trained in the particulars of FCPA and the U.K. Bribery Act. The most effective audits are conducted by professionals with legal and forensic accounting backgrounds. Core skill sets to have on the audit team include good interviewing skills, the knowledge and experience to select high-risk transactions for testing, and the experience to recognize red flags for potential violations. Some companies choose to have their internal audit department conduct these audits. Others employ different strategies—pairing legal or compliance department personnel with internal auditors or using outside forensic accountants (such as Ernst &Young's Fraud Investigation & Dispute Services Practice discussed in the "Introduction").

Anti-corruption audits have a powerful deterrent effect. They send a message that the senior management is committed to compliance and that they are checking to make sure compliance is achieved. Appropriate follow-up and disciplinary action are crucial to creating an anti-corruption culture. However, the audit is not an investigation. It is a business process like other internal audits a company might undertake—a predetermined set of procedures designed to test for compliance with company policies. Potential FCPA violations or red flags uncovered in the audits are reported to the legal or compliance department for further investigation.

As financial systems become more automated, companies are turning more and more to analytics as a tool for compliance monitoring. Analytics can be a very useful tool to complement a robust anti-corruption compliance audit program. Vendor analytics can be used to identify various risk traits associated with high-risk vendors, including high-risk locations, different bank account locations, offshore banking, politically exposed persons (PEP) or possible association with government officials, and vendors with similar addresses. As with audits, the key is to deploy the right tools but also to have trained personnel who can interpret and recognize trends and anomalies in the data.

An emerging practice is invoking the audit rights that are often embedded in contracts with supplier as a means to address specific vendors with high corruption risk. These audits generally focus on vendor payments.

Refer to Chapter 7, "Monitoring," for further details.

Due Diligence

Companies should develop a policy and specific procedures for anti-corruption due diligence in any contemplated merger, acquisition, or joint venture. Conducting anti-corruption due diligence makes good business sense, as the risk includes:

- Inheriting liability for past corrupt activities.
- Becoming liable for continuing corrupt activities that you failed to identify and stop.
- Overpaying for a business that was built on corruption.
- Inheriting corrupt employees from the acquired company.
- Becoming saddled with significant increased compliance costs required to change the new business that were not anticipated.

In the United States, many FCPA prosecutions have arisen in the context of mergers and acquisitions where past actions of corruption came to light in the due diligence. The DOJ has taken the position that companies must conduct thorough due diligence on the issue of past corruption to avoid inheriting liability for such actions.

The amount of anti-corruption due diligence that can be performed in the context of a merger or acquisition is subject to negotiation between the buyer and the seller and is often conducted under intense time constraints. If the situation permits, anti-corruption due diligence should include some or all of the following activities:

- Background investigation and public database searches of key executives.
- Interviews of key executives relating to past corruption and risks of corruption in the business.
- Review of documents related to acquired company's anti-corruption compliance program, past incidents of corruption, and risks of corruption in the business.
- Forensic accounting and transaction testing procedures related to high-corruption-risk transactions.

Statements accurately disclosing any past corrupt actions or FCPA violations should be included in the seller's representations and warranties related to the transaction or as part of the merger or joint venture contract. The contract also should address future compliance with the FCPA, U.K. Bribery Act, and other anti-corruption laws.

Following the closing of the transaction, the acquiring company should put anti-corruption compliance high on its integration plan and conduct further risk assessment procedures as necessary to ensure it has a good grasp of and is addressing the corruption risks posed by the new organization. Refer to Chapter 8, "Anti-Corruption Due Diligence," for further details.

Reactive Measures

Incident Response Plan and Investigations

The final step in a cohesive anti-corruption program is the establishment of reactive elements. Therefore, management should establish protocols to react to those situations in which inappropriate behavior is suspected. An incident response plan (see Figure 4.2) should be established that encompasses investigations, remediation, and uniform disciplinary processes. The incident response plan can be a basic document, but it is important to have to ensure consistent treatment of red flags and allegations of impropriety.

FIGURE 4.2 Incident Response Plan

Investigation protocols should be established so that management has a framework from which to operate if corruption is suspected. The protocols should state that all suspected activity, regardless of source, will be investigated and the results of the investigations will be communicated to the audit committee in a timely manner.

The setup of policies and procedures that establish the uniform practice of disciplining any individual, regardless of position, who commits bribery or fails to comply with the organization's code of conduct or ethics is considered a best practice. Additionally, any disciplinary action that is taken against an employee, vendor, or customer should to be communicated to the audit committee.

Results of the investigations should be reviewed to determine what remediation, if any, is required to eliminate the potential for reoccurrence (e.g., changes in policies, procedures, or processes). Management should be required to report the status of the remediation plans to the audit committee.

In order for the incident response plan to be effective, upon identification through the whistle-blower hotline, a tip, or otherwise, the response process should allow for this alleged potential complaint to escalate properly and enable an appropriate investigation of the facts.[16]

Refer to Chapter 9, "Investigations," for further details.

Periodic Reassessment of Program

As risks change over time, comprehensive corruption risk assessments should be conducted periodically to ensure that the anti-corruption compliance program is evolving to meet new risks posed by the changing business and external environment. Assuming a robust monitoring structure is already in place that offers the company continual feedback on its risks, we would suggest a process that provides an extensive review of corruption risk every three to five years. If the business changes significantly, such a process should be accelerated.

 SUMMARY

No compliance program, no matter how expensive or extensive, can provide absolute assurance of compliance. An effective anti-corruption compliance program will positively affect a company's culture and deter wrongdoing, make noncompliance far less likely, and, in the unhappy event of a violation, better position a company for potential dealings with regulatory authorities. Be mindful that one by-product of the increased rate of corporate prosecutions and settlements has been a dramatic increase in criminal prosecutions of executives. For executives, the risks are real—they are not just about money.

 NOTES

1. See www.coso.org.
2. 2007 Federal Sentencing Guidelines Manual, Chapter 8, Sentencing of Organizations (can be found at www.ussc.gov).
3. The OECD Guidelines can be found at www.oecd.org/dataoecd/11/40/44176910.pdf.
4. www.justice.gov.uk/guidance/docs/bribery-act-2010-guidance.pdf.
5. www.coso.org/aboutus.htm.
6. "Preparing for Internal Control Reporting: A Guide for Management's Assessment under Section 404 of the Sarbanes-Oxley Act." Ernst & Young publication, 2002. SCORE Retrieval File No. EE0677.
7. Id.
8. Bill Foale, Paul Harris, and Jeff Taylor, "How Do You Demonstrate the Effectiveness of Your Corporate Compliance Program?" Compliance Week, October 2009.
9. Id.
10. William Henderson, "Staying Out of Trouble: The Role of a Global Anti-Corruption Program." March 11, 2008; www.oceg.org/view/20796.
11. Id.
12. Ernst & Young, "Driving Ethical Growth—New Markets, New Challenges." 11th Global Fraud Survey.
13. www.justice.gov.uk/guidance/docs/bribery-act-2010-guidance.pdf, paragraph 6.
14. Id., paragraph 4.
15. Richard Sibery and Charles Owens, "Best Practices for a Global FCPA Compliance Program." Compliance Week, November 2009.
16. Ernst & Young, "The Guide to Investigating Business Fraud," p. 283. Also, Bill Henderson, "Building a Robust Anti-Corruption Compliance Program—Seven Steps to Help You Evaluate and Address Corruption Risks," Ernst & Young LLP, 2010. SCORE No. WW0203.

CHAPTER FIVE

Policies and Procedures

T O CREATE A CULTURE of integrity, management must embed ethical practices into the company's day-to-day operations. Policies and procedures form the backbone of this culture and help to set the overall tone for an organization (see Figure 5.1).

An entity's policies and procedures are a set of documents that describe its philosophy and practices as set out by management. They can include guidance covering compliance, finance and accounting, human resources, operations, information technology, risk management, and business development. This chapter discusses the policies and procedures necessary for an effective anti-corruption program focusing on bribery, corruption, and fraud prevention policies; communication and training; and internal controls. These are key elements to successfully setting the tone for the organization and provide the foundation of an anti-corruption compliance program.

Bribery, corruption, and fraud prevention policies include items such as the code of conduct, whistle-blower process and anti-corruption policy. For an anti-corruption program to function effectively, communication of these policies and reinforcement through training makes the employees understand the importance of anti-corruption compliance and where to go for help when an issue arises. Internal controls serve as a defense against corrupt payments.

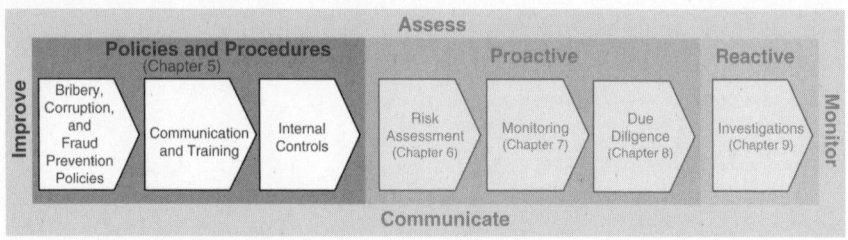

FIGURE 5.1   Anti-Corruption Compliance Program

Controls help to ensure that financial activities are properly authorized and recorded accurately in the books and records.

BRIBERY, CORRUPTION, AND FRAUD PREVENTION POLICIES

A company's bribery, corruption, and fraud prevention policies include an array of guidance with varying degrees of focus. This includes broad documents that are part of the company's overall compliance program such as the code of conduct and whistle-blower programs to specific policies that have been developed to address identified bribery and corruption risks such as an anti-corruption policy and related certification program (see Figure 5.2).

The sections below cover a number of the key anti-corruption policies in greater detail.

Code of Conduct

The code of conduct is the clear set of business rules put forth by an organization and provides a general framework to guide the response of the organization in the challenging and sometimes difficult choices that are presented to members of the organization. Many companies encapsulate the message of their code to broad statements of corporate values to guide the behavior of employees, while other companies prepare a detailed code that embodies the company's business philosophy.

The code of conduct is typically approved by the board of directors and reviewed on a periodic basis. The code of conduct should be incorporated into new-hire orientation (that is, all new employees must read and sign the code as part of their condition of employment) and periodically reaffirmed by all employees.[1]

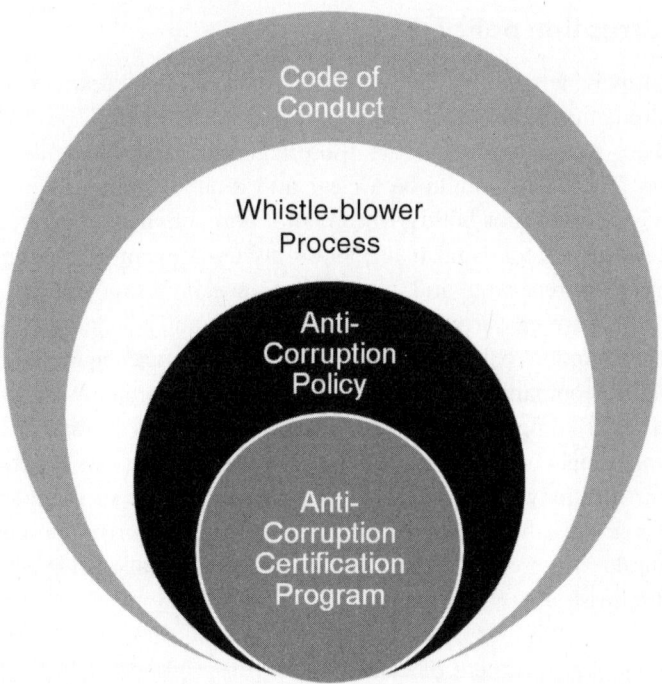

FIGURE 5.2 Bribery, Corruption, and Fraud Prevention Policies

Whistle-Blower Process

In the United States, the Sarbanes-Oxley Act (SOX) requires that all public companies set up a mechanism for the confidential, anonymous submission by employees of the issuer of concerns regarding questionable accounting or auditing matters. This mechanism is known as a "whistle-blower process", "ombudsman" or "tip line." As part of this process, a company must have procedures to handle the receipt, retention, and treatment of concerns and complaints received. SOX also protects whistle-blowers from retaliation.

The Dodd-Frank Wall Street Reform and Consumer Protection Act of 2010 set up significant financial incentives for a whistle-blower. A recent Ernst & Young fraud survey found that 66 percent of respondents indicated that the Dodd-Frank Act would encourage employees to report cases of fraud, bribery, or corruption.[2] As a result of this, whistle-blower activity is expected to increase and companies should reevaluate their processes to make sure that they can handle the additional activity.

Anti-Corruption policy

Every company needs to develop a company-wide anti-corruption policy using the requirements of the Foreign Corrupt Practices Act of 1977 (FCPA) and the U.K. Bribery Act as a guideline, as those are comprehensive anti-corruption legislation. The policy should be a clear and unambiguous statement of the company's position that both governmental and commercial bribery on any scale or level are not tolerated. It also should discuss the company's commitment to accuracy in reporting and recording transactions and having internal controls to ensure proper control, accountability, and safeguarding of assets. The anti-corruption policy should be approved by the board of directors, distributed to company management, posted on the company's internal web site with other compliance-related policies, and be the central focus of anti-corruption compliance training (discussed further later in this chapter).

Companies may choose to address corruption issues in more detail in a series of policies or have one overriding company anti-corruption policy. The policy should also provide operational guidance on unallowable activity and certain high-risk areas, including:

- Bribery of government officials.
- Commercial bribery and other corrupt activities undertaken for the financial gain of the company.
- Misreporting and concealment in the accounting records of bribery and other improper acts.
- Use of third-party agents, consultants, and other intermediaries in potential bribe schemes.
- Facilitating payments.
- Travel, entertaining, and gift giving to customers.
- Charitable giving and community payments.
- Controls around cash, petty cash, and certain vendor disbursements.
- Other high-risk transactions.
- Corruption risk in mergers and acquisitions.
- Other areas of high risk such as customs and offset commitments.

The policy should encourage employees to report violations or seek guidance, as well as offer examples of "red flags" for employees to recognize or avoid problem situations. References to the anti-corruption policy should be included in the written code of conduct issued to all company employees. The code of conduct should contain a short and simple statement of the requirements and of employees' duty to comply. Compliance with the anti-corruption policy should have a prominent place in the overall corporate compliance program.

Facilitating Payments

The anti-corruption policy should take a position on facilitating payments. Facilitating payments to government officials are legal under the FCPA in limited contexts for routine and nondiscretionary actions. These are commonly thought of as "grease payments," and generally provided to low-level government employees. There is no exception for facilitating payments in the U.K. Bribery Act so such payments are presumably illegal under that legislation. Many payments that meet the FCPA's narrow definition of facilitating payments may be illegal in the local country where payment is made. Given the different legal treatment by the various authorities and the inherent difficulties in enforcing a policy that prohibits bribery but allows facilitating payments, many companies ban facilitating payments altogether, with limited exceptions for situations involving imminent harm to life or property. If a company decides that it will permit facilitating payments, it should develop a process to ensure appropriate review and preapproval of all such payments, including analysis of their legality under local law, the U.K. Bribery Act, and the FCPA.

BOOKS AND RECORDS CONSIDERATION

If the company allows **facilitating payments**—is the accounting system set up so that these payments can be properly recorded and tracked?

As stated earlier, there is no exception for facilitating payments in the U.K. Bribery Act; however, the U.K. Serious Fraud Office (SFO), the governmental body responsible for enforcement of the U.K. Bribery Act, recognizes that an immediate ban is impractical. Therefore, companies need a plan to phase out facilitation payments. In a speech by Richard Alderman, the director of the SFO, he stated, "I acknowledge that these payments will not cease as from the date when the Bribery Act comes into force. [...] companies within my jurisdiction should be working towards zero tolerance within a reasonable period of time." He went on to state, "if [the SFO] find a company that is continuing to use facilitation payments as a normal part of its business, particularly if it thinks that it can get an advantage over other companies by doing this, then that company will receive attention from the SFO that it will not welcome."[3]

The SFO encourages open dialogue about facilitating payments, with Richard Alderman stating, "corporates should come and talk to the SFO about [facilitation] issues so that we can understand that their commitment is real. This also gives the corporate the opportunity to talk to us about the problems that they face in carrying on business in the areas in which they trade."[4]

Anti-Corruption Certification Program

Many companies have formal programs requiring senior employees to regularly certify compliance with the FCPA and other anti-corruption laws. While certifications will not stop the deliberate wrongdoer, the requirement serves as a continuing reminder of a manager's compliance responsibility. Certification processes also may identify issues that might not have surfaced otherwise. An anti-corruption certification could be incorporated into an existing business conduct certification program such as an annual certification around the code of conduct or SOX certifications related to internal control.

When considering implementation of an anti-corruption certification program, an organization should be prepared if an employee refuses to certify. Generally speaking, an anti-corruption certification program would not be rolled out prior to a significant training effort and risk assessment.

 ## COMMUNICATION AND TRAINING

Communication

The code of conduct, anti-corruption policy, and other policies must be disseminated widely within an organization. Anti-corruption legislation is complex, and employees need an appropriately qualified resource to turn to for support and guidance. Organizations that fail to provide this support face an increased likelihood that incidents will go unreported and misunderstandings of the policy requirements will continue. Formal and informal communications, along with training, reinforce management's message. A lack of reinforcement of a company's policies, procedures, reporting protocols, and corruption risks exposes a company to employees, vendors, customers, and other stakeholders not knowing what is considered acceptable behavior or how to effectively report suspected improper activities. These communications can include messages from senior management (such as the CEO, chief financial officer, general counsel, or chief compliance officer) to all employees that officially role out or remind the employees of the importance of adhering to the policy. Additional communications can be made at internal meetings; sales or finance meetings are excellent opportunities to raise awareness of a company's policy on bribery and corruption. The development of a strategy for communicating anti-corruption requirements to key financial reporting and accounting personnel, highlighting the books and records requirements, is a key area. These communications should be part of a controller's manual or other accounting policies and should be discussed at meetings and in training sessions.

Training

Training is a critical component of an effective anti-corruption compliance program. Knowledge and awareness of the risks by employees is any organization's first line of defense against potential problems. Training is an effective tool to educate employees on identifying potential red flags. This will aid in the detection and prevention of potential violations of the FCPA and other bribery and corruption legislation. Training is especially important for organizations with a significant global workforce, particularly in countries with a high risk of corruption. Often, employees in foreign locations may not be well-versed on the intricacies of the FCPA and how it relates to the companies policies and procedures and their particular responsibilities.

For employees in foreign countries, training is crucial. At a minimum, every person in a position to obtain business or a business advantage through bribery or other improper means should receive anti-corruption compliance training. Training should highlight the company's position that it does not tolerate corruption, its anti-corruption policies to ensure compliance with the requirements of the FCPA and U.K. Bribery Act, potential "red flags" or problem situations, and guidance for employees to seek help. Consider a mixture of live training for certain targeted and senior employees and Web-based training for all employees. Many companies complement training with a certification program, whereby the employee certifies that he or she has taken the training, understands his or her responsibility, and is not aware of or has reported any and all incidents of corruption.

What Should Be Covered?

Typical training would include an overview of the company's code of conduct and anti-corruption policy and an overview of the relevant laws such as the

FCPA and U.K. Bribery Act. Examples of recent enforcement and the company's bribery and corruptions risks highlight the real impact on the company and the individual and help the employee better understand the implications.

First, it is important to explain the laws, their importance, and potential implications, both for the organization as a whole and for individuals. Recent FCPA enforcement actions and trends provide real-life examples to the trainees, including fines and penalties associated with prohibited actions. The anti-bribery and books and records components of the FCPA should also be addressed, demonstrating its complexity and its various elements requiring compliance.

Another critical training topic is the definition of a government official. This definition can change, depending on the industry and country where business is done. For example, in certain countries, a medical doctor is considered to be a government official because hospitals are government owned. This nuance is particularly relevant for an organization in the pharmaceutical or medical device manufacturing industries, which often solicit products to medical doctors. For example, China has many state-owned or state-controlled enterprises (SOEs) and the U.S. Department of Justice (DOJ) and the Securities and Exchange Commission (SEC) view their employees as being "foreign officials" regardless of position. Also, employees of sovereign wealth funds, for example, are generally considered to be government officials, which is a risk factor for private equity firms or banks raising capital overseas.

Doing business with third-party sales intermediaries should also be included as a training topic. Organizations might not realize they can be held accountable for the actions of agents or other third parties acting on their behalf. A common corruption scheme involves foreign suppliers or distributors that pay bribes to local officials to accelerate projects. Furthermore, organizations might not be aware of all relationships with third-party intermediaries, such as consultants, agents, sales representatives, distributors, and teaming partners. These relationships can take many forms, and these vendors can be compensated in various ways. It is important that all such relationships are defined in agreements that contain anti-bribery provisions and that all parties are vetted through a due diligence process. Perhaps more important is for the sales force to received education on this subject so that the risk of dealing with unethical third-party sales intermediaries can be mitigated at the outset.

Reporting channels and escalation of issues should also be addressed in training. Company ethics hotline or ombudsman information should be communicated to participants as well as protocol for reporting potential incidents, questions, and concerns. Contact information for the anti-corruption compliance officer, designated legal/compliance officer, ombudsman, or responsible party should also be provided to training participants.

Other topics to be addressed in training include policies and procedures around gifts and entertainment, including rules around cash gifts, charitable contributions, donations, and sponsorships. Training should provide real-life examples relative to the company's business and practical instruction on how to handle those issues.

Companies should also consider providing training to targeted departments based on areas of responsibility (e.g., finance/accounting and sales/business development). For example, employees in finance or accounting responsible for reviewing expense reports of employees who travel internationally should be trained to identify potential corruption red flags as well as to enforce adherence with anti-corruption policies and procedures. Finance and accounting employees should be trained to verify that name, business affiliation, and business purpose are documented for any individual to whom gifts, meals, or entertainment is provided. Similarly, payments for travel and hospitality for government customers to promote company products (e.g., a factory tour) should be closely monitored and verified by accounting and finance to verify compliance with established policies. Red flags to be aware of include providing business-class flights, luxury hotel accommodations, or side trips to cities where the company does not have offices.

Who Should Be Trained?

The training should be extended not only to sales professionals, but also to members of management who may interact with local government officials for regulatory matters such as business permits. Finance and accounting professionals responsible for recording transactions in the books and records should also receive training. It also may be necessary to develop training materials for, or to present training to, third parties to ensure that they understand their obligations when working on behalf of the company. Others to consider include personnel from compliance, logistics, legal departments, and employees who travel internationally, interact with foreign officials, engage intermediaries involved with government business, or develop business in general. Some organizations require any employee who travels internationally to complete anti-corruption training prior to travel.

What Is the Appropriate Format?

Due to the importance of the subject, training is often most effective when it is conducted in-person. Typically, training is given by individuals from the legal and compliance departments, such as the anti-corruption compliance coordinator if appointed. Training should be provided on a regular basis and supplemented by written materials such as a training manual or online training modules. Employees who attend training should sign certificates of completion and their attendance should be documented. In addition, the company should follow-up with employees to make sure policies are understood and being followed.

Also, for organizations with employees or business units around the world, training should be conducted in multiple languages, and anti-corruption policies should be made available in local languages accordingly. It is important that employees in countries with high levels of perceived corruption, specifically employees with responsibilities for anti-corruption compliance, receive training in the local language and are provided with real-life scenarios in the local context. For example, employees in China should be educated on potential corruption red flags that arise in the local culture, including gifts linked to holidays and festivals, travel, gifts or donations made in cash. A real-life example to drive this home is Lucent Technologies, who allegedly spent more than US$10 million to pay expenses (including per diems) for 315 trips to the United States for employees of Chinese state–owned or state–controlled telecom enterprises from 2000–2003. Trips were to Hawaii, Las Vegas, the Grand Canyon, Disneyland, Niagara Falls, Universal Studios, and other popular U.S. tourist destinations.[5]

Training Third-Party Intermediaries

In certain instances a company should consider training third-party sales intermediaries on its bribery and corruption policy. Third parties that interact with the government customers, including sales representatives, consultants, agents, distributors, brokers, and other service providers are among the third parties that are likely to be included in a company's training program. The content of the training should be similar to that provided to employees, or can be similar to a targeted training offered to business development or sales executives. Some companies might invite all sales agents to their annual sales conference, which includes a briefing on the company's anti-corruption policy, enforcement trends, and refresher on bribery and corruption red flags.

Effective Training Guidelines

Most companies have developed training regarding their policies or codes of conduct. However, findings from compliance assessments often indicate that the policies and the spirit in which they were created are often not understood by individuals in local markets. To increase the effectiveness of training, efforts should be made to ensure that the training:

- Is presented in the local language.
- Includes the support of local management.
- Presents realistic case studies or examples.
- Creates opportunities to interact or ask questions.
- Includes practice aids for sales professionals and others to improve understanding.
- Is offered on a regular basis and is part of the new employee training.
- Attendance is tracked.
- Is regularly reviewed and updated.

An overall anti-corruption training program example follows:

Training	Audience	Contents
General Ethics Annual All locations Online and live	All employees	Focus on the code of conduct and its impact on business practices Whistle-blower process High-level information related to anti-corruption policy and the bribery and corruption risks faced by the organization Provide a means for employees to ask questions and raise concerns Other topics covered include other general compliance topics and policies
Live Anti-Corruption Annual All international locations In local language	Sales Business development Management Procurement Finance/Accounting Human resources	Anti-corruption policy Overall risks faced by organization Customized for local business environment Books and records requirements Case studies to encourage discussion and understanding of potential issues
Online Anti-Corruption Annual	All employees Key third parties	Anti-corruption policy Overall risks faced by organization Books and records requirements Case studies Includes electronic certification

INTERNAL FINANCIAL CONTROLS

Internal controls are designed to help a company accomplish specific goals or objectives and serves as a means in which the company's resources are directed, monitored, and measured. Internal controls are important because they help prevent and detect fraud and thereby protect the company's resources.

At the company level, internal controls are necessary to produce reliable financial reports, accurate results of operational or strategic goals, and compliance with laws and regulations. At the transactional level, internal controls relate to achieving detailed objectives (e.g., how to ensure the company has received the goods or services purchased). Internal controls are a key element of the FCPA and SOX.

The FCPA's books and records provision requires companies to make and keep accurate books and records in reasonable detail that accurately and fairly reflect the company's transactions and disposition of assets. The FCPA's internal controls provision requires companies to devise and maintain reasonable internal accounting controls focused on preventing and detecting FCPA violations. While these requirements extend only to "issuers" (i.e., SEC registrants), awareness of the requirements is important.

Section 404 of SOX requires the company's external auditor and management to report on the adequacy of the company's internal control over financial reporting on an annual basis. The internal control report must affirm "the responsibility of management for establishing and maintaining an adequate internal control structure and procedures for financial reporting"[6] and contain an assessment of the effectiveness of the internal control structure and procedures at the end of the fiscal year. The external auditor attests to management's assessment of the effectiveness of internal control over financial reporting.

Internal controls are generally designed to provide reasonable assurance that operations are effective, financial reporting is reliable, and the entity is compliant with laws and regulations. The following are examples of internal control activities:

- Segregation of duties—includes separating the following roles from one individual: authorization, custody, and record keeping.
- Authorization of transactions—requires appropriate approvals for transactions.
- Records retention—requires adequate documentation to be maintained in order to substantiate transactions.

- Supervision of operations—includes monitoring or reviewing ongoing operational activity.
- Physical safeguards—requires using cameras, locks, and other physical barriers to protect company assets.
- Information technology (IT) security—includes using passwords and implementing access rights into company programs to ensure access is allowed only for authorized personnel.
- Information processing—includes a review of data entered and accounting for transactions in numerical sequences.

Anti-Corruption Financial Controls

Strong controllership is the first deterrent against corrupt payments. Anti-corruption controls should focus on deterring and detecting illicit payments. For example, strict enforcement of travel and entertainment rules related to meals and entertainment and detailed reporting of the business purpose and people entertained supports anti-corruption compliance. Reconciling bank accounts on a monthly basis is a key cash control that also protects against misappropriation and possible off-book accounts or payments.

Although there is no formal definition of FCPA internal controls, there are certainly key areas where internal controls are critical in addressing bribery and corruption risks. Depending on a company's risks, specific anti-corruption internal controls should be implemented around those high-risk operations and processes. An example is implementing strict account posting requirements for high-risk transactions to promote transparency and accountability.

Increased financial controls in high-risk areas can be a critical firewall in avoiding FCPA books and records violations. Often, this means enhancing financial controls beyond what might normally be considered adequate to ensure accurate financial reporting under SOX. This is because of the additional purpose of deterring and detecting illicit or improper payments with no materiality standard. Such controls include enhanced transaction review, approval and accounting procedures, controls around bank accounts and petty cash, enhanced vendor approval and payment processes, and increased scrutiny of high-risk transactions. Companies should focus on high-corruption-risk areas such as:

- Bank accounts.
- Petty cash.
- Procurement (including contracting and third-party due diligence).

- Consultants, agents, and other high-risk intermediaries.
- Customs and cross-border shipping.
- Gifts, travel, and entertainment of customers and government officials.
- Charitable giving and offset commitments.

As previously discussed, a company must communicate the importance of compliance with bribery and corruption laws to business unit controllers, accounts payable, and other accounting professionals. These communications should provide specific guidance to ensure accounting professionals are watching for "red flags" and be clear about how certain expenses should be recorded.

Bank Accounts

A company should have a clear policy on the opening, operation, maintenance, and closing of bank accounts. Bank accounts should be used for valid business purposes, and payments made are legitimate and comply with the FCPA. Internal controls are critical in the establishment of bank accounts, and access to these accounts must be controlled.

The following internal controls should be implemented to mitigate the potential unauthorized use of funds:

- Limit the number of bank accounts.
- Review and close inactive accounts.
- Limit access and establish signatory approvals around check writing and the issuance of wire transfers.
- Limit off shore payments.
- Endorse checks "For Deposit Only" upon receipt and make frequent deposits.
- Perform timely bank reconciliations—monthly reconciliations are important in ensuring accurate company financial reporting because it identifies errors and inconsistencies which will require employees to verify the accuracy of each account.
- Periodically, perform additional analyses of bank statements and related disbursement activity. Follow up on any disbursements that appear questionable or unusual in nature.

Because off-balance-sheet accounts are often used to make improper payments, which can include bribes and corrupt payments, it is important that all accounts are properly reflected in the accounting system and are within the company's control environment.

Petty Cash

BOOKS AND RECORDS CONSIDERATION

Are the petty cash records detailed enough to ensure that the activity is properly reflected in the accounting system? If an improper payment is made out of petty cash, will it ultimately be recorded appropriately?

Petty cash funds are an extremely high-risk area with regard to bribery and corruption. Often, petty cash is used for low-dollar items that are generally incidental in nature and occur in the normal course of business. It is important that any petty accounts are properly controlled. A key control includes a petty cash policy that covers the following areas:

- Account owner
- Custodian
- Record keeping
- Accounting in the general ledger
- Voucher system
- Minimal balance
- Petty cash counts and reviews

A petty cash policy should establish and address the controls, purpose, limit amounts, and procedures for obtaining petty cash. This policy will help ensure that consistent practices are applied to petty cash across business units and geographies. Clear accountability for the petty cash fund should be established, and this can be done by identifying an owner of the petty cash fund. The owner is ultimately responsible for the fund, petty cash expenditures, and recording of fund activity in the accounting records. The actual maintenance of the fund should be assigned to a custodian who is different than the owner and has physical custody of the cash, controls disbursements out of the fund, and maintains the records related to the fund use and replenishment.

Any activity in the petty cash fund should require supporting documentation for all requests of funds, and this activity should be recorded in the petty cash log. Receipts should be required for all petty cash disbursements. The receipt should include the payee date, amount received, purpose for the funds, and name of the employee receiving the funds. The log should provide sufficient detail so that the activity can be accurately reflected in the general ledger. A voucher system should be used to document and approve any use of the petty cash fund. The petty cash balance maintained should be minimized and reflect the operating purpose of the account. Additionally, the overall number of petty cash accounts should be kept at a minimum level.

Periodic petty cash counts are key to maintaining the integrity of the account and its record keeping. A custodian will maintain better documentation if they are held accountable for the balance. Surprise counts of the petty cash to verify the amount should be conducted by an individual who does not report to the owner or the custodian. Surprise counts help ensure that the records are prepared on a timely basis. The count should also include a detailed review of the petty cash account to look for unusual patterns, round sum amounts, large amounts, nonemployee payee beneficiaries, transactions that should have been procured via normal purchasing or processing, and unusual descriptions. Additional controls could include restricting the permitted uses of petty cash, rigorous documentation standards, and a heightened review process for petty cash reimbursement.

If a division operates in a cash-based economy, special policies, and procedures should be designed to meet the operating requirements of the entity as well as the overall control environment of the company.

Procurement

Companies should take a proactive approach in implementing a vendor selection and approval process to prevent payments to unauthorized vendors as well as mitigate the risk that a distributor or reseller will engage in an illegal act. For example, illicit payments may be channeled through local resellers and distributors, who, then pay bribes to government officials to gain access to markets. In addition, procurement controls should focus on high bribery and corruption risk areas, such as consultants, agents, and other local service providers. Accounts payable functions within a company should ensure complete adequate background check procedures prior to set-up in the vendor master files.

Internal controls related to the vendor master files include the following:

- Enhance vendor approval and authorization processes:
  - All vendors require proper documentation of identity (such as W-9 in the United States) prior to setup on the vendor master file.
  - Any required licenses are validated.
  - Screen all vendors against Office of Foreign Asset Control and other government watch lists.
- Heighten access controls around vendor master databases:
  - Inactive vendors are identified on a periodic basis.
  - Duplicate vendor addresses are identified.
- Require additional vendor authorization sign-off procedures for sales representatives, agents, and consultants.
- Identify suppliers that are government entities or have relationships with government-controlled entities, political parties, or similar relationships and examine payment histories for irregularities.
- Sample and review supporting documentation to assess reasonableness of the payment, whether the payment was properly approved, and whether such payments were reviewed for compliance with the anti-corruption policy.

A company should pay particular attention to internal controls related to disbursements. Strong internal controls processes will assist in detecting and preventing problematic transactions within a timely manner.

Contracting Considerations   In many developing economies, a company is required to partner with a local entity in order to operate commercially. Through these partnerships, companies may become involved with corrupt activity through the actions of its third-party partners or even the relationship itself is a de-facto bribe. As such, it is important that the company prepares contracts with third parties to limit the company's involvement in corruption and to mitigate the loss or damage caused by such involvement. The inclusion of anti-corruption provisions in its contracts shows a company's outside suppliers that the company is committed to integrity and complying with laws. If the company intends to change contracting procedures, the company needs to decide how to qualify existing vendors. Additional acceptance procedures may include requiring the vendor to complete a questionnaire and the business unit to prepare a business justification memorandum that details the business purpose for hiring the vendor. A leading practice is to have senior legal or compliance offers that are removed from the business operations to approve hiring of vendors.

BOOKS AND RECORDS CONSIDERATION

Exercising audit rights on vendors provides support to ensure that the activities presented in invoices represent the underlying services performed and do not mask improper payments and demonstrates a commitment to compliance.

Anti-corruption provisions often included in contracts with third parties, particularly with agents and consultants, could include:

- Requirement of compliance with the company's anti-corruption policy at the time of signing the contract.
- Requirement of compliance with local laws, the FCPA, and the U.K. Bribery Act and specific language that the vendor will not make any prohibited payments.
- Disclosures of all foreign government officials who are directors, officers, or employees and any relatives of such that may be foreign government officials.
- Certifications of compliance with the FCPA, U.K. Bribery Act, and the company's anti-corruption compliance program on an annual or periodic basis.
- Right of the company to terminate the contract and withhold payment if the vendor pays bribes or violates any of the contract terms.
- Requirement that payments to the vendors must be in the vendor's name and in the country where the vendor is located and not offshore or in a tax haven jurisdiction.
- Requirement that the vendor maintain detailed and accurate books and records and internal controls as required by the FCPA.
- Right to audit the vendor's books and records at the company's discretion to assure that no improper payments have been made.

It is also important that the contract includes the responsibilities of the third party and specifies the scope of services to be provided.

Third-Party Due Diligence Many global corporations are taking a closer look at how they manage their vendor and customer compliance. Specific instructions from U.S. regulators in settlement agreements address the expectations on conducting thorough background checks for a company's third-party relationships. In Europe, guidance from the U.K. Bribery Act and other sources specifically address the need for an effective third-party due diligence program as part of an effective corporate compliance/anti-fraud program. Third-party risk management is still in the process of being developed, but the convergence of government regulations and increased enforcement has raised the bar for many companies as it relates to the due diligence necessary for third-party acceptance.

Key Components of an Effective Due Diligence Program   When evaluating the effectiveness of a company's third-party due diligence program relative to the existing guidance, four key principles become apparent that serve as a strong frame of reference for incorporating the multiple guidelines and legal rulings into an effective third-party due diligence program. These guidelines are consistency, management oversight, objectivity, and reasonableness.

Consistency. Automating the process and developing standard templates for vetting third parties, especially overseas, will help drive consistency across the company. A robust platform allows a company to effectively and efficiently manage a decentralized program. The goal should be to have one system that everyone uses.

Management Oversight. In this context, management's oversight incorporates management's intent and actions to provide for a robust third-party due diligence process. Is management doing the best they can based on their perceived risk, or are they choosing to look the other way.

Objectivity. Are the due diligence procedures objective and performed separately from the requestor, which could contain inherent conflicts of interest? Each due diligence investigation should be independently performed with its own case file, notifications, investigative findings, remediation actions, educations, and representations between the company and its agent, partner, distributor, third parties, and others. Having a defined case management workflow integrating people, process, and technology can be particularly useful to ensure an objective process.

Reasonableness. Given limited company resources, taking a risk-based, tiered approach to third-party due diligence helps management to allocate resources accordingly. Reasonableness addresses the question, "How much is enough?" In efforts to avoid doing business with the wrong people, a prudent and well-thought-out process is important. A thoughtful and reasonable compliance program that is risk based is the best preventive strategy for making sure that compliance is practical, thorough, and defensible.

Taking a Risk-Based Approach   The four principles described earlier are predicated on a critical first step—a credible, risk-based assessment of a company's third parties. Many corporate compliance departments conduct their due diligence programs based on deploying up to three levels of investigation on the third party. The first two levels focus on background while the third level is an in-depth analysis of the third party.

Level I: Open-Source Background Checks

Level I analysis includes a comprehensive check of available sanctions, embargos, and watch lists. A Level I check also includes Internet and media search inquires. These searches use open-source databases and public information to search a wide range of business journals, web sites, industry publications, and mainstream media. The review of these publicly available resources should include reviewing of any negative news, and government affiliation of the intermediary and its owners/shareholders. Examples of media resources include the Internet, social networking web sites, Factiva, LexisNexis, WorldCheck, and WorldCompliance.

When these processes are streamlined through the use of case management software, online databases and internet searching, a Level I analysis can be accomplished by an investigator in a few hours. Level I analysis, given its streamlined, repeatable nature, is ideal for centralization and perhaps even outsourcing.

Level II: Enhanced Due Diligence

Based on an elevated risk profile as identified in a Level I analysis, Level II analysis involves additional public database searches with a specific focus on localized public records databases, such as court filings. A Level II analysis may also incorporate research into potentially vulnerable corporate relationships and a deeper dive into public records and media searches, with a focused inquiry on a particular risk area (as identified in the Level I analysis). A Level II analysis often requires local country presence to gain access to local records and contacts and typically requires significantly more hours of local, in-country investigator time to research and report.

Level III: Deep Dive

As the risk level dictates, a Level III analysis may be further warranted. This may include detailed questionnaires, on-site inspections; interviewing associates in political, business, and social circles to uncover reputation; reviewing corporate, civil, and criminal documents; and validating financial records. Times when Level III might be required include the use of an unfamiliar agent to secure a large contract in a region of the world new to a company or in the context of an acquisition or joint venture.

Today's global companies should evaluate their current third-party due diligence program in the context of a risk-based framework that incorporates attributes of consistency, management oversight, objectivity, and reasonableness. Key consideration should be given to determining if the best option is to insource or outsource key processes such as Level I and Level II analyses. Companies should develop categorization and decision rules as part of the data-gathering process and, when needed, be willing to seek assistance from outside advisers and legal resources who are specialists in the areas of third-party due diligence and bribery and corruption.

While corporations are still grappling with what processes represent an effective due diligence program, incorporating the preceding attributes can go a long way in demonstrating an effective, risk-based vetting program.

EVALUATING YOUR THIRD-PARTY DUE DILIGENCE PROGRAM— QUESTIONS TO ASK

Consider your current anti-corruption vendor on-boarding process and ask tough questions around consistency, management oversight, objectivity, and reasonableness.

Consistency. Is the process followed consistently? Can you audit or tie back vendor request forms to each vendor in the vendor master? Is there training around the process? Is it globally deployed? Is the process repeatable—that is, would you arrive at the same conclusion if you were to run a selection of new vendor setup forms through the same process? Are the rules and contract language around FCPA and anti-corruption consistent from country to country?

Management Oversight. Does your company use software tools for case management to manage and document the vendor setup process? What database and due diligence steps does accounts payable take to categorize new vendor submissions received from the requestor? Is the right person making the decision? During the escalation process, who is responsible for making the tough calls? How robust is the vendor "vetting report"? Who is made aware of a new vendor once approved—is it communicated to the corporate office and centrally managed, or is it handled and decided by the local office?

Objectivity. Given so many decision makers at the country or subsidiary level, can the current process stand up to independent scrutiny from an outside (or DOJ) perspective? For example, can the accounts payable clerk processing the original new vendor setup form be forced to designate a form as "low risk" from the requestor in order to avoid additional scrutiny from upper management?

Reasonableness. Is the process reasonable? Does the process generate too much paperwork that may not get reviewed or too little paperwork where rogue third parties or necessary contract terms might be missed? Does the process incorporate leading practices?

Consultants, Agents, and Other High-Risk Intermediaries

More than 90 percent of reported FCPA cases involve the use of third-party intermediaries such as agents or consultants.[7] Accordingly, this is a significant area and the central focus of many companies' anti-corruption compliance programs. A company should thoughtfully consider the level of oversight required to effectively manage the risk from third-party vendors as these procedures are likely to be expensive. The company should identify the different types and numbers of vendors with which the company does business. The company then needs to categorize its vendors, analyze the risks posed by each vendor type and determine if any vendors warrant enhanced treatment to mitigate corruption risks and third-party due diligence procedures.

In addition to the third-party due diligence procedures discussed earlier, prior to entering into a written contract with a third-party intermediary, a company should consider performing procedures directly with the intermediary. These additional procedures may include:

- Requiring the intermediary to complete a questionnaire about:
  - Its business.
  - Owners.
  - Operations.
  - Countries in which it operates.
  - Expertise.

- Any relationship or affiliation of the intermediary or its employees (and their close families) with government.
- Its compliance structure.
- Conducting interviews of the key personnel of the third party.
- Requiring the company employee who identified the intermediary to complete a questionnaire justifying the reasons this specific intermediary should be hired and the reasons behind the proposed compensation structure.
- The above-described information should be documented, and approved by the relevant individuals (e.g., business unit director, finance director, and legal). During this process, red flags may arise that will need to be resolved in a timely manner, depending on their significance. Examples of red flags associated with third-party intermediaries include:
  - Request for an excessive commission by the intermediary.
  - Use of the intermediary as per recommendation or requirement by the government.
  - Intermediary that is related to a government official.
  - Suggestions by the intermediary that money is needed to "get the business."
  - Refusal by the intermediary to promise not to violate the FCPA or other anti-corruption laws.
  - Refusal by the intermediary to sign the language involving compliance with the FCPA or other anti-corruption laws.
  - Request by the intermediary for false invoices or other documents.
  - Invoice or request for payment that is unusual or departs from normal practice.
  - Requests by the intermediary to have its compensation be paid to an offshore account or to a country in which the services are not provided.
  - Request for an advance payment.

Consideration should be given to implement transaction monitoring controls to assess potential high-risk transactions, which are discussed further in Chapter 7, "Monitoring." When red flags are identified through these monitoring controls, additional follow-up should be performed.

Customs and Cross-Border Shipping

The customs clearance process is especially exposed to bribery and corruption risk. As demonstrated in Table 5.1, FCPA cases involving customs clearance

TABLE 5.1   FCPA Cases Involving Customs

Company	Year	Fine Amount
Chiquita Brands International Inc.	2002	$0.1 MM
BJ Services Company	2004	N/A
Vetco International Ltd.	2007	$26MM
Aibel Group Ltd.	2008	$4.2MM
Con-Way Inc.	2008	$0.3MM (SEC)
Helmerich & Payne Inc.	2009	$1.4MM
Nature's Sunshine Products, Inc.	2009	$0.6MM/$0.025MM (SEC)
Panalpina, Inc.	2010	$81.9MM
Pride International	2010	$56.2MM
Royal Dutch Shell plc	2010	$48.1MM
Transocean, Inc.	2010	$20.7MM
Tidewater, Inc.	2010	$15.7MM
Noble Corp.	2010	$8.2MM
Global Santa Fe Corp.	2010	$5.9MM
Ball Corp.	2011	$0.3MM (SEC)

Source: Related DOJ and/or SEC settlements

have dramatically increased in number and penalty size. Other international trade regulations have also featured prominently in recent FCPA settlements, including economic sanctions (numerous companies have resolved FCPA matters related to the former Iraq Oil-for-Food program) and export controls (such as the BAE Systems plc resolutions). While most customs-related cases have involved the energy sector, the same issues may apply to every industry, especially those that actively ship tools of the trade (such as construction) or are subject to import registration and permitting (such as pharmaceuticals, medical devices, food, and information technology).

The November 4, 2010 Panalpina settlement highlights this risk as six companies in the Oil & Gas industry settled related charges at the same time. Panalpina, a forwarding and logistics company, settled foreign bribery charges by the DOJ and SEC for paying bribes to foreign officials to speed clearance of drilling rigs and other equipment through customs. The alleged bribes occurred in a number of countries including Nigeria, Angola, Brazil, Russia, and Kazakhstan. Panalpina paid $81.9M in penalties and all seven companies paid over $230 million.

One of the key drivers of this risk is the complexity of the regulatory requirements across the globe. Each country has its own laws and regulations that are often onerous to navigate, and many government employees and outside agents may be involved in managing the process. It is vital that a company understand the nature of the work of its customs clearance agents and brokers and be aware of local laws and behaviors. For instance, relatively minor documentation discrepancies may lead to significant customs clearance delays, and in some countries the fines for minor discrepancies may exceed the value of the goods. This provides custom officials with potential leverage for soliciting a bribe. In industries where the delivery of materials and services is especially time sensitive, unscrupulous customs and government officials may also take advantage of their position.

In many cross-border shipping arrangements, companies utilize the services of an outside customs clearance company to provide expedited clearance. It is important to clearly understand the nature and components of this service. In some countries, it is a distinct possibility that customs clearance companies may make illegal payments in order to expedite shipments. If a company becomes aware that its customs clearance company may be engaged in improper activity, then the company is at risk of breaching anti-corruption laws, particularly if the company directly or indirectly provided funds for those activities.

The manner in which freight forwarder, customs agent, and visa processing agent invoices are generated and paid makes them much more susceptible to inadvertent books and records violations. While commercial sales agents may be paid with a small number of high-value invoices which are scrutinized in detail and comparatively easy to audit, the reverse holds true for invoices from freight and immigration service providers. A single facility may pay hundreds or even thousands of customs broker invoices per year, each financially minimal, and supported by pages of vague descriptions for services rendered.

When a freight forwarder or customs broker invoice is received, it typically includes backup and a detailed listing of services rendered and monies advanced by the intermediary. The support may span dozens of pages. Particularly with respect to "risky" countries, companies may strongly wish to scrutinize this backup line by line prior to payment. If among its many line items the invoice describes a corrupt payment, paying the invoice may arguably be considered ratification or reimbursement of the corrupt payment. Such failure may also be considered a books and records violation. Typically, in accounts payable workflows, logistics costs are categorically coded to specific accounts—such as logistics expense, customs duties, and similar accounts. A failure to identify and segregate a facilitating payment, bribe, or extortion payment described as a line item within an invoice may mean it is characterized as a routine expense under the normal (and often automated) accounts payable workflow. If the routine accounts payable workflow is not modified, then the corrupt payments may be automatically recorded in the normal accounts, and this may be deemed a books and records violation for failing to capture the corrupt character of the payment.

For example, government authorities have alleged that requests for reimbursement of corrupt payments have been described by freight agents using terms like:

- Local processing fee
- Special handling
- Intervention
- Evacuation
- Expedited customs clearance

On their face, such terms are ambiguous and may describe enhanced services and not corruption, but in this context ambiguity poses risk.

Problems with Facilitating Payments in Customs Clearance and Immigration As discussed earlier in this chapter, the FCPA provides a statutory exception for facilitating payments related to "routine governmental action." Per the FCPA, the term *routine governmental action* does not include any decision by a foreign official whether, or on what terms, to award new business to, or to continue business with, a particular party, or any action taken by a foreign official involved in the decision-making process to encourage a decision to award new business to or continue business with a particular party.[8] Thus, the facilitating payments exception is ordinarily understood to apply only to nondiscretionary acts that an official performs as part of his normal job responsibilities.[9]

This "nondiscretionary" distinction is of critical importance when examining payments made in connection with customs clearance, because it is often remarkably hard to prove that the action taken was nondiscretionary. For example, assume that a broker calls and indicates that goods are languishing in customs, but for 100 Euros he can expedite the process. If the importation is completely compliant, and the customs official is merely slow to act, then a payment for him to perform the nondiscretionary act of examining the customs entry and releasing a compliant shipment may arguably be entitled to the exception (mindful of the need for proper recordation in the books and records). But what if the delay is caused by some error—no matter how small—in the paperwork? Then the payment may have induced the official to release a noncompliant shipment, something that arguably is not within his discretion. Therefore, slight changes in the facts create remarkably different outcomes—an allowed facilitating payment or a forbidden bribe. It is remarkably difficult to tell the difference in the real world, particularly when payments are made through intermediaries. In an environment where companies invariably settle FCPA cases rather than bring them to trial, as stated earlier, the ambiguity creates risk.

Other problems are caused by the limited acceptance of a facilitating payments exception in other jurisdictions. Most countries do not explicitly allow facilitation payments in their extraterritorial anti-bribery laws, and the Organization for Economic Co-operation and Development (OECD) has called on the countries that do to eliminate this exception. An entity subject to extraterritorial jurisdiction under more than one country's rules may find that facilitating payments are allowed by one but not the other (such as allowed under U.S. law but precluded under Japanese or U.K. law). More important, there is generally no exception under most domestic anti-bribery laws; a facilitating payment to a Nigerian customs official may be lawful under U.S. rules but unlawful under Nigerian rules.

Local Customs and Immigration Rules and Practices   In some jurisdictions, any paperwork error in a customs entry or visa application is an excuse for unscrupulous officials to solicit a bribe. One of the best ways to avoid corruption risk in the international movement of goods or people is to know the local customs and immigration laws and institute customs and immigration compliance policies and procedures. While there is a tendency to focus on a small handful of regions—West Africa, for example—the reality is that corruption in the customs and immigration process is widespread.

Mitigating Corruption Risk in Customs Clearance and Immigration Processing   There are a number of techniques that can meaningfully reduce bribery and corruption risk with respect to customs and immigration. Which techniques work best varies considerably by industry and company.

Revise Anti-Corruption Compliance Tools to Reflect Different Risks Posed by Customs Clearance and Immigration   Many companies have long-established policies and procedures designed to reduce the risk of FCPA violations. These tools are used to govern the internal sales function as well as commercial sales agents, bidding consultants, and similar entities that may be engaged in representative services. Common tools include due diligence, offshore payment restrictions, cash payment restrictions, meals, gifts and entertainment policies, and so on.

At most companies, these tools were created to minimize bribery and corruption risks posed by internal sales efforts, commercial sales agents/representatives, or consultants assisting with the bidding process, but they may fail to adequately address foreign customs clearance risks. The bribery and corruption risks posed by commercial sales agents or bidding consultants are entirely different than the bribery risks posed by freight forwarders and customs brokers. As a consequence, tools utilized to address sales, commercial sales agents, and bidding representatives are generally not effective to reduce logistics bribery and corruption risk without modification.

Policies may require complex background checks into the nature of the services supplied by the representatives, and their connections with government officials. All of these tools are fairly meaningless in reducing bribery risk in logistics or immigration operations (except in situations where a commercial sales representative is also performing logistics or visa processing functions and is, therefore, already subject to extensive scrutiny as a sales representative).

Additionally, traditional red flags are not particularly helpful in spotting risk when using other kinds of intermediaries such as freight forwarders, customs brokers, visa processors, or dangerous goods licensing consultants.

Bribery by freight forwarders, customs brokers, and visa processors typically involves comparatively smaller payments, situations where there is only a transitory relationship with the representative and the government official, and circumstances where there are a number of plausible reasons why a number of payments may be made to various parties.

For example, if a customs broker paid a $500 bribe to release goods seized by customs:

- Would audit rights over the general books and records of the freight forwarder be likely to reveal the bribe? No, because the payment would likely be hidden by the numerous other payments associated with each shipping transaction by any number of shippers. The bribe may not be paid by the customs broker itself, but may be paid by a subcontractor, and therefore may appear to be a subcontractor expense. It would be very difficult to track payments to government actors, let alone ascribe them to the import files of any particular importer. Moreover, most freight forwarders would not grant access to their books and records.

■ Would analysis of the relationship between the customs broker and government officials reveal the bribe? No, because the bribe is fairly transactional in nature; it is not based on any special relationship.

■ Would lack of qualifications be a red flag? While this may be a useful factor when evaluating commercial sales agents, it would not be particularly relevant in this context. Customs agents require licensing in most countries.

Similarly, commissions (unusually high or otherwise) are not typical in these situations, and financial arrangements might not seem unusual because the relatively small amount would likely be buried as an expense in the broker or forwarder's routine invoicing.

There are, of course, different tools for spotting and reducing bribery risk in logistics operations. For example, while an overly slow customs clearance time may be a negative factor in logistics key performance indicators, an unusually fast customs clearance may be a red flag in an anti-bribery context. Companies that have anti-bribery procedures that are general in nature should reassess them to see if they are effective for customs and immigration clearance.

Establish Customs Compliance Procedures to Manage Shipments from Origin through Delivery Bribe requests in an import country are often caused by paperwork errors created in the export country. For example, an invoice created in Miami may cause a critical shipment to be detained when clearing customs in Brazil.

Customs declarations in the receiving country are generally prepared based on commercial invoices, packing lists, certificates of origin, bills of lading, and other documents created in the exporting country. If a bad description or the wrong customs tariff classification or an inaccurate price is placed on the invoice, it is possible that the customs officials in the receiving country will seize or detain the merchandise or initiate penalty demands or assess additional duties. Seizure or penalties also may occur where the documents meet industry norms, but do not meet special requirements of the importing country.

Recognize that a payment made to solve a problem with a shipment will be considered a bribe and not a facilitating payment. The best way to minimize bribe solicitations when importing is to make sure that the customs paperwork is accurate, complete, and satisfies local import laws. And the best time to do this is *prior* to export. Once a shipment has been seized, the only lawful recourse may be to pursue administrative or judicial remedies that take time. Business pressures caused by such delays may themselves increase the risk of an unlawful act's occurring.

To lessen bribery risk, one should establish policies and procedures that increase customs compliance in advance of shipment. This may include detailed shipping procedures that guide export logistics operations on how to create shipment documents that comply with the import laws of the receiving country. Personnel should be appropriately and adequately trained to understand the risks involved and the importance of adhering to the procedures.

Reduce the Quantity of Logistics and Immigration Vendors   The actions of freight forwarders, customs brokers, and visa processors can lead to FCPA or similar exposure. A leading practice to reduce risk is to minimize the number of vendors used and manage them properly. Each separate vendor is a separate process and a separate opportunity for a defective process. Each separate process drains the internal resources spent policing anti-bribery efforts (e.g., management, diligence, and auditing). Reducing the number of logistics and immigration vendors reduces risk and decreases internal compliance costs. Logistics vendor reduction may also lead to operational cost savings through volume discounts and a more predictable and transparent supply chain.

Align with Vendors that Have Their Own Compliance Programs   Rather than micromanaging a vendor's operations, consider aligning with vendors that already have their own compliance programs in place. Logistics and immigration companies often subcontract to local service providers themselves; when examining service providers, ask how they "push" compliance expectations down to their own vendors. Given the recent enforcement activity, this topic will be top of mind of the players in this industry.

Inform Your Vendors about Compliance Expectations   Does the service provider know your anti-bribery policies? If it makes a mistake, do you have documents in your files memorializing communication of your expectations?

There are a number of ways that companies communicate compliance expectations to their logistics and immigration vendors. These include:

- Communicating compliance expectations as part of any vendor due diligence or vendor selection process.
- Institutionalizing compliance expectations as part of vendor contracts.

- Providing periodic reminders.
- Asking vendors to communicate these expectations to their employees and subcontractors.
- Merging operational and compliance requirements into the same vendor instructions or agreements.

Establish an Effective Logistics Organization It is difficult to manage logistics anti-bribery risk without a competent logistics organization. Anti-bribery compliance for logistics operations requires consistent adherence to procedures, proper management of freight forwarders and customs brokers, and an ability to spot warning signs. These tasks will be complicated by an unstructured environment, particularly where shipping is handled by personnel for whom logistics is only one of their many responsibilities.

Review Freight Forwarder, Customs Broker, and Visa Processor Invoices for Red Flags Companies that pay freight forwarder, customs broker, or visa processor invoices without review expose themselves to risk. Ambiguous services such as "intervention," "special handling," "expedited customs clearance," and the like may describe wholly lawful services or may instead be a euphemism for facilitation payments or bribes paid to customs or immigration officials by the vendor. Companies do not want to find themselves in a position where they have paid for a particular "service" for years only to learn that they have been reimbursing customs bribes or failing to characterize facilitation payments in the books and records properly.

Companies should consider:

- Requiring invoice reviewers to know the language for the invoices they review.
- Establishing special invoice review protocols for customs broker, freight forwarder, and visa processor invoices (at least for "risky" jurisdictions).
- Requiring invoice reviewers to read each invoice line item and to be aware of what described services entail before they authorize payment.
- Having contractual agreements with logistics and immigration vendors requiring sufficient invoice detail and invoice formats and backup.
- Modifying their accounts payable process, if appropriate, to provide independent review of invoices in high-risk countries.
- Providing relevant training to logistics, human resources, and finance personnel.

- Publishing a list of customs-specific red flags for logistics personnel.
- Implementing defined and documented escalation protocols.

Provide Function-Specific Training and Auditing While many companies offer training and have internal audit programs addressing anti-corruption in general terms, leading companies supplement their programs with content for specific functions such as logistics.

Give Local Operations a Way to Seek Outside Guidance When Appropriate Understanding the local customs and immigration laws is an essential part of planning and compliance. For example, if a customs broker offers "expedited" customs clearance programs, is such a legitimate government pre-release program[10] or a euphemism for bribes? Are "fees" paid to use the program going to the government—or to a customs official? Determining the answer may require local expertise, and a mechanism should exist for operations to obtain such expertise on a timely basis.

Utilize Electronic Customs Declarations When Possible Many countries have recently begun deploying online systems to process customs declarations and release online. Systems, like the United Nations Conference on Trade and Development's ASYCUDA World,[11] are powerful anti-bribery tools because they supply transparency. They track when goods arrive, when they are declared, what data elements are declared, which officials are involved, and changes that occur during liquidation of the customs entry. These systems make it harder for corrupt customs officials to extort. In some countries, these systems have been piloted in some ports but not others. When operating in a country where some ports are using electronic declaration and some are not, choose the electronic-file ports to make entry when possible.

Gifts, Travel, and Entertainment

Gifts, meals, and entertainment provided to customers including government officials may be used to facilitate or give the appearance of corruption. Gifts may include cash or material goods given as presents. Entertainment may include meals, hotel accommodations, flights, and tickets to sporting events. A company may choose to mitigate its bribery risks associated with gifts, meals, and entertainment of customers by instituting a complete ban on such hospitality; however, this is impractical in most contexts. A comprehensive control structure can allow the reasonable and customary activities to take place while not exposing the company to significant bribery and corruption risks.

The FCPA and the U.K. Bribery Act can be implicated when companies give gifts or provide travel and entertainment (T&E) to government officials. Such payments, or even offers, need to be monitored carefully to avoid even the appearance of impropriety. This is an area of special concern in certain Asian countries, where the culture of business gift giving and business entertainment is firmly ingrained and government and private-sector officials at various levels are known to frequently request and expect such courtesies.

BOOKS AND RECORDS CONSIDERATION

Do the T&E records include enough information to allow for the accurate recording of the expenses?

Is there a "gift" account in the general ledger?

Recall that the U.K. Bribery Act is similar to the FCPA, but in some respects significantly more aggressive because it covers all bribery, regardless of whether it involves a public official. In terms of T&E, the authorities responsible for enforcing the U.K. Bribery Act have issued a "prosecution guidance" stating that "hospitality or promotional expenditure which is reasonable, proportionate, and made in good faith is an established and important part of doing business. The [U.K. Bribery] Act does not seek to penalize such activity." As such, lavishness is "just one factor that may be taken into account in determining whether an offence has been committed," and prosecutors will evaluate each incident.

As a result of the new legislation and enhanced enforcement regime, businesses urgently need to examine their existing internal controls related to T&E and assess what improvements should be made as a priority.

Compliance is greatly enhanced where additional communications and controls are established related to the employee T&E expense reimbursement process. Many companies have detailed rules for employee submission of T&E expenses for reimbursement including T&E policies and paper or electronic forms to be completed. These policies and forms provide additional control processes to ensure the proper review and approval of gifts, meals, and entertainment of government officials. For example, an automated T&E submittal process may be customized to identify government officials and to provide for preapprovals of gifts or meals and entertainment that the employee must initiate in advance if he or she wishes to be reimbursed for such expenses. The following additional procedures within the T&E controls may strengthen compliance and serve as useful reminders to employees that they need to manage relations with governments and customers carefully to avoid even the appearance of impropriety:

- Review T&E supporting documentation and business purpose to determine if it is valid.
- Assess whether T&E was reasonable and/or lavish and assess whether the attendees included nonessential individuals (spouses or children of customers or government officials).
- Determine whether the T&E report was approved in accordance with the company approval authority policy.
- Determine whether the payments were properly recorded and classified in the accounting records.
- Assess whether anything was expected or received in exchange.
- Review records to determine whether there are reimbursements to government agencies or officials for visits either directly to the office or through employees. For each reimbursement, assess whether the payments were properly documented and were for legitimate business purposes and were reasonable amounts.
- Assess whether anything was expected or received in exchange. Review whether the payments or gifts assisted the operation in obtaining or retaining business or favorable treatment or in referring business to others.
- Analyze data to spot unusual activity or trends over time.
- Follow up on any payments that appear questionable or unusual or payments that appear to be excessive.

Payments for travel and related expenses for government officials are permitted under the FCPA in limited circumstances, when related to the demonstration of a product or performing a contractual obligation. For example, it is permissible to pay a government official's travel expenses to visit a factory in the United States so the official is able to ascertain the quality control processes involved in a product to be purchased by a foreign government. Many government officials are aware of this exception and often request trips of this nature.

There are also a number of reported cases highlighting abuses in this area. If the company believes it is in its interest to pay for such trips, it must be careful to pay only expenses and meals and entertainment that are linked directly to the business purpose of the trip. Companies should have written policies in addressing such trips to ensure that all payments are valid business expenses and that there is no appearance of impropriety. Any travel or lodging provided to government officials should be subjected to a heightened approval process, preapproved in advance, and expenses reconciled thereafter. The DOJ has provided some guidance through the opinion release procedures on these situations that should be considered carefully. The FPCA provides for an affirmative defense stating that it is permissible for companies to pay for travel expenses of government officials under specific criteria such as "the promotion, demonstration or explanation of products or services or the execution or performance of a contract with a government or agency."

Red flags related to T&E include:

- Business purpose is, or seems, incidental to entertainment purpose.
- Official is strategically located to grant business or improper business advantage to company.
- Expenses are lavish or out of line with company guidelines and local customs.
- Spouse or children are invited.
- Expenses are paid to official personally.
- Official is unwilling or unable to get written approval for trip from her own agency.

In addition to enhanced T&E controls, some companies have enhanced procedures directly related to gifts. A clearly stated approval process for gifts and a gift log are effective components of internal controls over gifts.

Charitable Giving and Offset Commitments

Charitable giving policies should be designed to ensure that bribes are not disguised as charitable donations. All charitable giving should be subject to an approval process that includes specific documentation related to the purpose of the gift, the legitimacy of the organization and whether the donation is consistent with the company's charitable giving. In addition, due diligence should be performed on the charitable organization to better understand the purpose of the organization and the directors and officers. The company's level of scrutiny of charitable giving is likely to be proportionally higher in countries where there are higher incidences of corruption.

In one case, the SEC fined a company $500,000 (Schering Plough Poland) for making improper payments to a legitimate charitable organization.[12] The organization was headed by a government official who had the power to influence the business of the company. While on the surface, the donation may not have been suspect, it is critical to ensure that a company's policies are designed so that donations go through a proper vetting process prior to payment.

Similar to charitable giving, many government contracts require companies to make other investments or offset commitments to obtain or retain business from a foreign government. The purpose of these offset commitments is to benefit the local economy, but the risks of corruption can be significant. Offset obligations are common in defense and infrastructure contracts with foreign governments. An offset is an obligation in which the company performs certain services that are for the general well-being or development of the local economy as a condition of the contract with the foreign government.

Offset obligations may be direct or indirect. Direct offsets relate to the underlying transaction, such as the requirement for the company to invest in and purchase components from local manufacturers. Indirect offsets are not related to the contract and may include building schools or hospitals in the foreign country or providing foreign investment in a certain technology or industry. Offsets carry a number of corruption risks, including (1) offset boards and officials; (2) sole-source third parties; and (3) offset service providers/consultants. Foreign offset programs generally have local offset laws or policies that are overseen by governing bodies. If a company is attempting to receive offset credit for certain activities to reduce its offset obligations, there is a threat of providing bribes in order to influence local offset officials. Companies need to be wary of direct offset agreements that require sole sourcing or exclusivity with a subcontractor or manufacturer in the local economy. The third party may have those exclusivity rights because of familial or other ties to government officials. In addition, indirect offsets may be completely unrelated to the company's line of business. Performing activities outside of the company's business acumen may require significant use of offset service providers and consultants, which also exposes the company to corruption risks.

Companies involved in offsets should institute a strict due diligence, approval, and transaction monitoring process for offset partners similar to internal controls dealing with very high-risk agents. Internal controls to consider are:

- Obtain certifications by the organization that it will comply with the requirements of the FCPA.
- Perform due diligence to confirm that none of the organization's officers or directors are affiliated with the foreign government at issue.
- Require that the organization provide audited financial statements.
- Obtain a written agreement with the organization restricting the use of funds to humanitarian or charitable purposes only.
- Make certain funds were transferred to a valid bank account.
- Confirm that humanitarian or charitable activities had occurred before funds were disbursed.
- Perform ongoing reviews to monitor the performance of the organization.

 ## SUMMARY

Setting the tone of an organization through policies and procedures is an important part of an anti-corruption compliance program. Enhanced internal controls in high-risk areas can serve as a critical firewall in avoiding bribery and corruption issues. Companies should focus on high-risk areas such as bank accounts; procure-to-pay; customs and cross-border shipping; contracting; transactions with consultants, agents, and high-risk vendors including government officials; gifts, meals, travel, and entertainment of customers; charitable giving; and petty cash. Accordingly, companies should implement additional financial controls in high-risk countries and for high-risk operations.

It is critical to communicate the importance of bribery and corruption compliance to business-unit controllers, accounts payable, and other accounting professionals. Anti-corruption internal controls serve as a defense to mitigate compliance risks.

 ## NOTES

1. Ernst & Young, "The Guide to Investigating Business Fraud," p. 284.
2. Ernst & Young, "European Fraud Survey 2011," p. 21.
3. Richard Alderman, "Strengthening of Anti-Corruption Mechanisms in Business Activities: Impact of the UK Bribery Act on Businesses Working in and with the UK." March 17, 2011.

4. Richard Alderman, "Managing Corruption Risk in the Real World." *Salans–Bribery Act 2010,* April 7, 2011.

5. www.justice.gov/opa/pr/2007/December/07_crm_1028.html.

6. 15 U.S.C. § 7262(a).

7. Ernst & Young, "Building a Robust Anti-Corruption Program: Seven Steps to Help You Evaluate and Address Corruption Risks."

8. 15 U.S.C 78dd-3(b).

9. There are competing theories on how this operates with respect to customs. Some believe that facilitating payments cause customs entries to "jump queue" and thus are not really discretionary. Others disagree, and point out that in many countries there is not a "queue" but rather a stack of open customs entries that will be processed in any reasonable order within the discretion of the customs official. Another question is whether systemic facilitation payments, when aggregated, can effectively be considered a bribe. Thoughts on such matters should be informed by discussions with counsel.

10. Many countries have programs for lawfully "pre-releasing" goods or otherwise expediting customs clearance. When such programs are mentioned by a forwarder or broker, one should assure oneself as to their bona fides.

11. For details on ASYCUDA World, see www.asycuda.org/aboutas.asp.

12. www.sec.gov/litigation/admin/34-49838.htm.

CHAPTER SIX

Risk Assessments

A N EFFECTIVE ANTI-CORRUPTION COMPLIANCE program needs to be risk based to ensure that it is properly designed to implement strategies and allocate resources to mitigate the specific and most substantial risks of corruption and bribery facing the organization. The corruption risk assessment is the cornerstone and essential first step in building an effective anti-corruption compliance program and, as shown in Figure 6.1, is a proactive element. Conducting a corruption risk assessment helps the organization identify and prioritize its corruption risks. These risks are derived from the nature of the organization's operations, the degree of business with government entities, its business locations, the organization's size, the regulatory environment in which it operates, and other factors.

The value of conducting a risk assessment for any internal control system is discussed in the Treadway Commission's seminal paper on internal control, "Internal Controls–Integrated Framework" issued by the Committee of Sponsoring Organizations of the Treadway Commission (COSO).[1] The 1992 COSO report includes risk assessment as one of the five elements for an effective internal control system. COSO provides that identification and analysis of risks is essential for determining a basis for how risks should be managed. COSO also underscored the point that businesses operate in a dynamic environment and

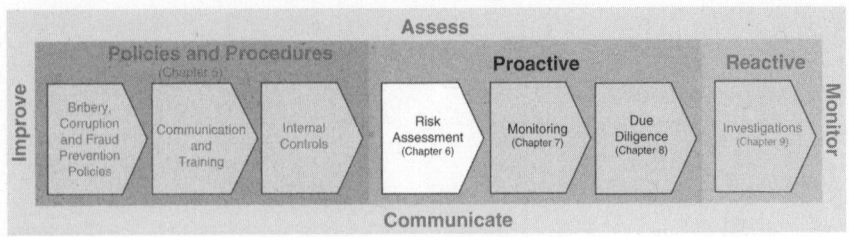

FIGURE 6.1 Anti-Corruption Compliance Program

as business conditions change, risks associated with the business also change over time.

The "Adequate Procedures Guidance" issued for the U.K. Bribery Act (Guidance) follows on the logic of COSO in stressing the importance of conducting a risk assessment in connection with an effective anti-corruption program. It includes risk assessment as "Principle 3" of the six principles that should inform commercial organizations wishing to put procedures in place to prevent bribery. As stated in the Guidance: "The commercial organization assesses the nature and extent of its exposure to potential external and internal risks of bribery on its behalf by persons associated with it. The assessment is periodic, informed and documented." The Guidance goes on to state: "the fuller the understanding of the bribery risks an organization faces the more effective its efforts to prevent bribery are likely to be."

The "Adequate Procedures Guidance" describes the basic characteristics of an appropriate anti-corruption risk assessment process:

- Oversight of the risk assessment by top-level management.
- Appropriate resourcing—this should reflect the scale of the organization's business and the need to identify and prioritize all relevant risks.
- Identification of internal and external information sources that will enable risk to be assessed and reviewed.
- Due diligence inquiries (or transaction testing).
- Accurate and appropriate documentation of the risk assessment and its conclusions.[2]

Commonly encountered risks are categorized by the Guidance as country risk, business-sector risk, transactional risk, business opportunity risks, and business partnership risks. The Guidance also provides that in addition to looking at procedures to mitigate risk, the risk assessment should assess

CASE**STUDY: STEEL COMPANY INC.**

To illustrate the process undertaken to perform a risk assessment, a case study is included in this chapter. It involves a company that has retained an outside accounting firm to evaluate the company's anti-corruption program and identify corruption risks.

weaknesses in current procedures that might be contributing to or increasing the level of risk, for example, lack of employee anti-corruption training or a bonus culture that rewards excessive risk taking. Both the COSO framework and the Guidance are discussed further in Chapter 4, "Compliance Programs."

Consistent with the "Adequate Procedures Guidance," this chapter presents an anti-corruption compliance program risk assessment containing four basic elements:

1. A review of the organization's business to identify and understand its most significant corruption risks.
2. A review of the current state of the organization's current anti-corruption program.
3. A "gap analysis" of the current program versus the anti-corruption risks identified.
4. Recommendations for improvement to the program based on common and leading practices but also what is most practicable for the particular organization in terms of achieving compliance.

The focus is on corruption risk. It is therefore essential to understand the organization's business drivers, its products and/or services, how it goes to market, how it sells, where it sells, to whom it sells, the competitiveness of the industry, the history of corruption in the industry, past events of corruption involving the organization, and other factors. Factors bearing on risk will include whether the organization sells to governments or government-affiliated entities; whether it is heavily regulated or licensed; whether it extensively utilizes agents, consultants, and other intermediaries; whether it does business in high-risk jurisdictions; existing practices related to facilitating payments, gift giving, and travel and entertainment; whether there are existing anti-corruption policies procedures and controls in place; and the strength of those controls and how they operate in practice.

Two important goals of a thorough and complete risk assessment are (1) to educate executives about corruption issues and risks, and (2) to obtain organization buy-in for the anti-corruption program; that is, the risk assessment provides the data or proof for doubters within the organization that its anti-corruption risks are real and need to be appropriately addressed. Accordingly, it is strongly recommended that senior decision makers be either included or informed about the process and provided the risk assessment report, and that the person who sponsors the process at a senior executive level has the influence and independence required to facilitate the process.

In the United States, anti-corruption risk assessments are often performed at the direction of counsel to aid counsel in providing legal advice to the organization relating to its anti-corruption compliance efforts and to attempt to maintain privilege in the event that an issue is identified. They are also often performed without counsel involvement. The risk does exist that improper activity may be disclosed in the risk assessment process.

CASESTUDY: STEEL COMPANY INC.

Steel Company Inc. is a midsize U.S.-based company specializing in providing steel solutions and construction materials to major commercial and government customers in North America, the Far East, and eastern Europe. Steel Company's shares are listed on NASDAQ. The company has a manufacturing facility in the United States, where it designs the steel solution systems customized for the requirements of its specific projects. The systems and other construction materials are then shipped to the project's location using a network of freight forwarders and customs brokers.

The company has regional hubs in the Far East and eastern Europe that oversee the company's business and operations in these regions and report to Steel Company Corporate. The two hubs have U.S. expatriates responsible for sales pursuits and business development. For government projects, Steel Company may use agents or third-party intermediaries to interact with the officials of foreign governments.

Since 2009, Steel Company has been experiencing exponential growth in revenue primarily due to the increase in infrastructure projects funded by the government of the fast-growing economies in the Far East and eastern Europe. In 2010, the company was awarded a large contract from the Ministry of Transportation in Country A related to making improvements to a local railway system. A year later, the company successfully bid on a proposal for a renovation project of an airport with the Civil Aviation Administration of Country B.

In 2007, Steel Company conducted an internal investigation of the company's operations in Country C triggered by a whistle-blower, alleging that a company's agent in Country C had been improperly influencing high-ranking foreign officials from the national transportation authority in that country. The whistle-blower claimed that the agent had been providing extravagant meals and entertainment to the officials using the company's funds in order to win a project for the procurement of materials for a road project. Steel Company's general counsel, assisted by external counsel, launched a thorough investigation, which concluded that the allegations were unfounded. However, the investigation revealed numerous gaps in the company's internal controls surrounding agent due diligence and approvals of meals and entertainment expenses. As a result, the company embarked on an effort to formulate a strong anti-corruption compliance program and foster a "no-to-bribery" culture across its international operations. The effort was spearheaded by a core team consisting of general counsel and the director of internal audit.

In light of the company's expansion of international operations and the resulting increasing corruption risk from close dealings with foreign government entities and officials, Steel Company's general counsel decided to evaluate the strength and efficacy of the company's anti-corruption program and turned for independent advice to an outside forensic accounting firm experienced in conducting anti-bribery and anti-corruption risk assessments. The firm was retained to review the company's new anti-corruption program and assess the adequacy of the company's anti-corruption internal controls in identifying corruption risks.

 ## SCOPING THE RISK ASSESSMENT

A large element of a risk assessment is fact gathering and analysis of that information. It is a process of obtaining relevant information about risk, analyzing the information, and providing recommendations for improvement. The principal activities in the risk assessment are:

- Conducting interviews of selected company officers and employees.
- Obtaining and reviewing documents, financial and other evidentiary matter.

- Reviewing or testing transactions to further understand or clarify issues.
- Reporting the results to the organization, usually by a written findings and recommendations report.

A common question concerns the appropriate level of activity required to conduct a thorough anti-corruption risk assessment. There is no right answer. The level of activity required will vary, depending on the size and complexity of the organization and the corruption risks it faces. Generally, the more thorough the risk assessment, the greater confidence the organization will have that it has identified and understands the nature of the corruption risks it faces. There is, however, a point of diminishing returns.

The anti-corruption risk assessment process is a business process and not an investigation. The risk assessment is not designed to uncover all corrupt activity that may be occurring but to assess corruption risk. The process is more akin to an audit than an investigation.

An anti-corruption risk assessment should be carefully planned. Procedures should be determined in advance with a budget in mind related to time, cost, and activity. The budget should allow for flexibility in extraordinary circumstances. Any specific improper activity should be discussed immediately and a response coordinated carefully with the organization's legal advisers. Thorough planning of the corruption risk assessment is achieved through meetings with executives in the organization, review of previous investigations or issues, and the preparation of a work plan that is thoroughly vetted by the senior executives in the organization.

Kickoff Meeting

It is generally recommended that the risk assessment start off with a formal kickoff meeting with the executive sponsors of the assessment. The following matters, among others, should be accomplished at the kickoff meeting or shortly thereafter:

- Level-set expectations by discussing the scope and timing of the project and anticipated procedures to be performed.
- Provide/discuss a preliminary interview list.
- Provide/discuss a first document request.
- Discuss logistics, points of contact, and desired communication protocols and channels.

- Discuss past events that might bear on the risk assessment. Also take the opportunity to explore whether any executives have any specific concerns (not previously disclosed) about past or current corruption in the organization.

CASESTUDY: STEEL COMPANY INC.

Continuing with our Steel Company example, representatives from the forensic accounting firm met with Steel Company's core team to discuss the scope and timing of the project, details of procedures to be performed, other project logistics, and the company's expectations.

At their request, the forensic accountants were provided with a listing of all contracts and proposals for the past three years, with details such as contract value, country, customer, agent/intermediary used and commission paid, and employee responsible for the account. They were also provided with other descriptive information about the company's operations, chart of accounts and financial documentation, and the company's corporate anti-corruption policies, among other documents.

At the meeting, Steel Company shared details from the past allegations of corruption in Kuwait and the results of the investigation. The scope of work was reviewed in light of the results of this investigation.

Preparing a Detailed Work Plan

Because risk assessments are generally based on a fixed or budgeted number of hours of work, it is imperative that a detailed work plan be put together prior to starting the work. Some general areas that should be covered in a work plan include:

- Coverage of the business—in what areas of the business will inquiries be made and procedures be conducted in order to get a good and full understanding of its corruption risks; for example, will the risk assessment activities be confined to the corporate level or will interviews also be conducted and transaction tested at the subsidiary level?
- Executives to be interviewed to understand the business, the business development process, and specific high-risk business operations.

- Customer review with particular focus on government customers.
- Review of other interactions with government officials and in what capacity, for example, government as a customer, as a business regulator, or related to licenses, customs, taxes, and so on.
- Review of use of agents, consultants, and business partners, particularly in dealings with governments, new customers, large contracts, and the company's controls around these parties.
- Practices related to facilitating payments, gift giving, travel and entertainment of government officials, charitable giving, and so on.
- Anti-corruption policies, procedures, and controls as well as general compliance culture and program framework.
- Financial analyses to be performed.
- Plans for selection and testing of transactions.
- Protocols for communication, feedback, and reviewing the preliminary results with the executive sponsors.

CONDUCTING THE RISK ASSESSMENT

Interviews

The preliminary interview list may start with persons in the legal, compliance, and internal audit and finance functions at the corporate level and expand from there as more is learned about the organization.

Conducting effective interviews is the most important fact-gathering technique to be employed in the assessment. The interviewer should be prepared with a list of subject areas that he or she wishes to address with the interviewee. The preferred format is to have two persons present at all interviews, with the more junior person assigned to take detailed notes. Notes should be typed up as soon as possible at the conclusion of the interview and reviewed by both persons present at the interview.

In starting the interview, always explain the purpose of the interview. As the subject is corruption, it is helpful to explain the context of the interview, the purpose of conducting the risk assessment, that there have been no specific allegations related to the company (if that is true), and, most important, that there have been no allegations or concerns related to the interviewee. Ask the interviewee if he or she has any questions prior to beginning the interview process.

CASE**STUDY: STEEL COMPANY INC.**

In the Steel Company example, the forensic accounting team interviewed key personnel at Steel Company Corporate and the managing directors of Steel Company's regional hub locations in the Far East and eastern Europe. The team wanted to gather as much insight as possible into the company's international operations and business development process, with an emphasis on the company's interactions with foreign government officials, use of third parties, and Steel Company's existing practices to address corruption risk.

As a result of these preliminary interviews, the forensic accounting team identified four areas carrying potential corruption risks: (1) interactions with foreign government customers, (2) interactions with foreign regulatory bodies, (3) interactions with customs officials, and (4) interactions with agents and representatives who interact with foreign government officials.

The forensic accounting team also had discussions with finance personnel to inquire about existing accounting systems and how and where transactions are recorded in an effort to identify the pool of transactions to be tested. All transactional activity related to non-U.S. countries in the Far East and eastern Europe is maintained by the respective regional hubs and rolls up to corporate on a monthly basis.

Document Review and Financial Analysis

Review of company documents and financial information is part of the fact-gathering process. The process begins with the preparation of a preliminary document request list and continues throughout the risk assessment. Documents mentioned in interviews should be added as the risk assessment continues, as well as important documents surfaced in transaction testing. All information, interviews, documents, and results of testing will need to be analyzed at the conclusion of the fieldwork and preparatory to writing the report.

The following is an illustrative list of the types of documents that might be included in a preliminary document request list:

- Organizational charts.
- Lists of offices, plants, warehouses, and other locations.

- Presentations or other internal descriptive information about the company's operations.
- List of recent acquisitions or joint ventures entered into outside the United States and related due diligence files.
- Descriptive information about the company's corporate compliance program, including:
  - Code of conduct.
  - Any and all compliance policies, guidelines, or manuals.
  - Descriptive information about the corporate compliance program, including program charter, reporting lines, infrastructure, personnel, business conduct certification, education and training programs, communications, audits and monitoring, and so on.
- Copies of all current policies, procedures, and programs related to anti-corruption compliance.
- Corporate chart of accounts.
- Corporate financial policies related to corruption.
- Copies of any past internal audit reports related to operations to be reviewed or related to the topic of bribery/corruption/improper payments.
- Copies of any hotline or whistle-blower complaints or reports of investigations of prior allegations related to corruption.

CASESTUDY: STEEL COMPANY INC.

Taking into account the four risk areas identified, the team obtained vendor disbursement files, general ledger detail for commissions, customs payments, gifts, meals and entertainment, and travel and expense reports submitted by the employees working on the five contracts. The team selected a judgmental sample of financial information and requested supporting documentation and selected transactions for further testing based on that review.

Financial information that may bear on corruption risk should also be requested, for example, summaries of vendor spending by vendor; detail of commissions paid to sales agents; samples of travel and expense reports; selected general ledger account information related to such areas as commissions, facilitating payments, gifts, charitable contributions, and political donations; and so on.

Transaction Testing

Transaction testing is an important part of the risk assessment process. Transaction testing could expose a corrupt payment or "red flag" indicating high-risk activity or reveal a weakness in certain anti-corruption controls or the overall control environment, or failure to follow policies. The purpose of testing in the context of an anti-corruption risk assessment is information gathering. Testing provides information that might not be obtained through interviews or document review, either because the persons interviewed did not know about certain risks or, perhaps, because they did not want to mention the risk. Generally, testing in this context is very limited. Samples are selected on a judgmental basis. It should be made clear to the organization that not finding evidence of any corrupt payments or red flags in the test samples, while good news, does not provide any measure of assurance that no such violations have or have not occurred.

Common areas of testing in anti-corruption risk assessments may include:

- Payments to agents and consultants
- Gifts
- Travel, meals, and entertainment expenses
- Petty cash
- Charitable contributions
- Facilitating payments
- Payments to customs agents
- Licenses, inspections, and other government fees
- Security payments

CASE**STUDY: STEEL COMPANY INC.**

Based on this information and the knowledge gained during the kickoff meeting, the forensic accounting team decided to focus on five international contracts representing 65 percent of Steel Company's international sales. These contracts or proposals were executed in high-risk locations, involved foreign governments as either end customer or regulatory authority that issues permits or licenses, were facilitated by an intermediary, and constituted a high percentage of sales. A summary of the selected contracts follows:

Project Description	Date Awarded	Contract Type	Country	Agent Used?	Value (USD, millions)
Railway system improvements	5/1/2010	Government	A	Yes	$78M
Airport renovation	2/1/2009	Government	B	Yes	$85M
Parking facilities construction	1/1/2011	Commercial	E	No	$45M
Shopping mall renovation	3/1/2009	Commercial	D	No	$115M
Bus station terminal	Pending (proposal)	Government	C	Yes	$106M
					$429M

Looking at the contract data allowed the forensic accounting team to focus their risk assessment on the locations with the highest corruption risk. As part of the assessment, the team planned to do transactional testing and conduct preliminary and follow-up interviews to determine whether the contracts and proposals were genuinely and legitimately pursued, procured, and fulfilled.

In testing transactions, look for:

- Compliance with establish policies or controls, especially and including anti-corruption controls.
- Sufficient supporting documentation and appropriate sign-offs in place to support the transaction.
- Proper coding into the general ledger for the transaction.
- No corrupt payments, "red flags," or indications of unusual or improper activity.

In reviewing the testing, analyze the results in terms of what they say about the organization's risks or effectiveness of controls in place to mitigate risk. Any potential Foreign Corrupt Practices Act of 1977 (FCPA) "red flags" or indications of unusual or improper activity should immediately be elevated to the organization's legal counsel. Consideration should also be given to increasing the scope of testing where warranted by the results.

GAP ANALYSIS

The fieldwork is the gathering of information. Once that process has been completed, the information needs to be analyzed. The analysis should be focused on corruption risk and the potential impact and likelihood of the occurrence of a risk event. The risks should be prioritized in terms of likelihood/frequency of occurrence and potential harm that could ensue to the organization.

After assessing the inherent corruption risks or areas of corruption risk, the analysis should turn to the mitigating controls in place and the residual risk to the organization. Do the controls—that is, the various facets of the existing anti-corruption program—significantly mitigate the risk? If not, what recommendations should be made to the organization to strengthen anti-corruption compliance?

The gap analysis should be fully vetted with the organization and potential remedies or controls to increase compliance fully discussed prior to preparation of the written report. Getting input from senior executives and reviewing the results of the gap analysis is crucial to the process. Having a session with senior executives to review the results of the risk analysis is a great way to educate senior executives and get buy-in for recommendations coming out of the risk assessment.

CASESTUDY: STEEL COMPANY INC.

In the case of Steel Company Inc., the transactional testing identified wide gaps in supporting documentation, most noticeable in the following areas: instances of gifts, travel, and entertainment to foreign government officials without documentation showing the business purpose of the expense; commission payments to certain agents without detail of the agents' activity or with missing due diligence files; and seemingly high payments to customs brokers without customs declaration forms. When the team made inquiries to employees about the insufficient supporting documentation, it became evident that the employees were neither aware of the policy documentation requirements nor familiar with the FCPA and anti-corruption risk areas. Further, the team identified what appeared to be an excessive commission to an agent in Country D that merited additional review. The transaction was brought to the attention of Steel Company's general counsel.

REPORTING

The report should be organized as follows:

- Executive summary.
- Procedures performed.
- Locations covered.
- Summary of the business and significant corruption risks uncovered.
- Current state of mitigating controls.
- Recommendations for improvement to increase anti-corruption compliance.

The report should be summary in format and be designed to convey the most important information coming out of the risk assessment. It is generally recommended that a report be provided first in draft for the organization's comments before being issued in final format. The final report, along with the work papers should be retained as documentation of the process and work performed, should it be needed in the future.

CASESTUDY: STEEL COMPANY INC.

Here is how Steel Company approached their analysis and presented their findings. The team amassed the results of their findings from transactional testing and employee interviews in a draft report, which was presented to Steel Company's core team for discussion. The findings were categorized by issue and priority in such a way that items requiring highest immediate remediation by the company were distinctly isolated. Concrete examples of remediation steps were provided, and suggestions were made for designated company employees who would take the lead on the proposed action steps.

All findings were discussed first with the core team to ensure that the forensic accountants' recommendations are applicable, implementable, and nonduplicative. The company's general counsel proceeded to probe further into the questionable transaction brought to the company's attention in due time by the forensic accounting firm.

DOCUMENTING THE RISK ASSESSMENT

Retaining documentation of the risk assessment is very important as it serves as evidence of the risk assessment process, and, more generally, of the soundness of an anti-corruption program. A thorough risk assessment adds both efficiency and credibility to the anti-corruption program. The documentation is accordingly partial proof of the bona fides of the anti-corruption program. This is very important, should questions be raised at a later date as to the soundness or apparent gaps in the anti-corruption program. The documentation should include work papers of all procedures performed, interview memoranda for interviews conducted, data and documents reviewed, risk analyses performed, and the final report. Documentation of communications and interactions with senior executives in the risk assessment process should also be retained.

 SUMMARY

For an anti-corruption compliance program to operate effectively, a sound risk assessment process is key. The anti-corruption risk assessment helps to focus the efforts and resources on the areas that warrant the most attention. A company's anti-corruption risk profile changes over time, and as such it is important to review and update the risk assessment on a regular basis.

 NOTES

1. See www.coso.org.
2. See www.justice.gov.uk/guidance/docs/bribery-act-2010-guidance.pdf, paragraph 3.3.

CHAPTER SEVEN

Monitoring

NTI-CORRUPTION MONITORING IS A critical component of an effective anti-corruption compliance program. The U.S. Department of Justice (DOJ) has consistently stated that one of the minimum requirements of an effective anti-corruption compliance program is having a system monitoring the effectiveness of the compliance program, including anti-corruption compliance audits, to identify any potential "red flags" in the business operations.

At the Compliance Week 2010 Annual Conference, Assistant Attorney General Lanny Breuer, for the Criminal Division of the DOJ, stated that "an effective compliance and ethics program is one that prevents fraud and corruption in the first place and, when it can't, has in place clear policies to quickly detect, fix, and report the violations."[1] Monitoring enables a company to understand the effectiveness of its anti-corruption compliance program and where future efforts should focus in order to minimize risks. It can, however, be a challenge to determine what to measure, how to do it, and how to report the results in a way that stimulates action rather than fosters bureaucracy. Compliance programs that are not monitored are generally not very effective. Monitoring means anti-corruption compliance audits and can also include data mining and analytics.

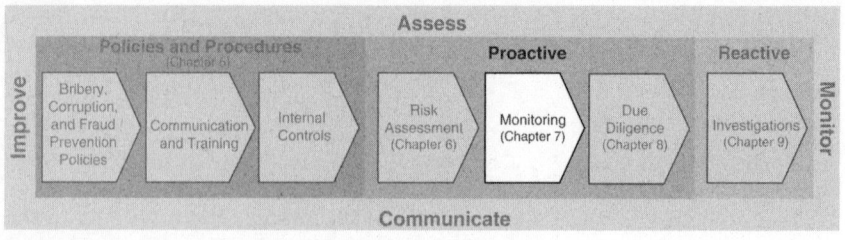

FIGURE 7.1 Anti-Corruption Compliance Program

The purpose of anti-corruption compliance audits should be both to audit for compliance with the various elements of the anti-corruption compliance program and to test for substantive compliance by seeking to identify potential violations or "red flags." Audits often uncover new risks not previously seen or fully appreciated. In this way, they act as part of an ongoing corruption risk assessment process. Anti-corruption audits should be stand-alone audits that are not integrated with a larger set of procedures. Generally, integrating anti-corruption audit procedures into larger audit programs is ineffective and, inevitably, leads to situations where the auditor doing the testing lacks the necessary training, focus, or supervision to do the work properly. Anti-corruption audits have a powerful deterrent effect. They send a message that the senior management is committed to compliance and that they are testing to make sure compliance is achieved. Appropriate follow-up and disciplinary action are crucial to creating an anti-corruption culture.

BUILDING AN ANTI-CORRUPTION MONITORING PROGRAM

Monitoring Plan

An organization's existing corporate compliance program should be leveraged and used as a starting point to develop an anti-corruption monitoring program. Primarily, an anti-corruption risk assessment should be performed to determine the best approach to monitoring. Conducting a risk assessment allows an organization to rank its business units and locations by relative risk and assists in planning adequate audit coverage of those locations over a defined time period. In addition, a risk assessment adds efficiency and credibility to the anti-corruption compliance efforts.

The risk assessment can be conducted in part by requiring each location or business unit to complete a self-assessment questionnaire. The questionnaire would typically solicit information regarding volume of sales to government customers, identification of significant government customers, and requirements related to anti-corruption training. One other aspect that a questionnaire could solicit a response to is the specifications of anti-corruption policies and procedures in place. The level of such policies and procedures can sometimes provide an indication of an organization's awareness and attention to this topic. Finally, consideration should be given on the timing of conducting anti-corruption compliance audits. Anti-corruption compliance audits should be performed on a periodic and rotational basis across business units and locations, depending on the relative risk inherent in those operations.

Roles and Responsibilities

Organizations tailor the roles and responsibilities for the anti-corruption monitoring program based on the structure, resources, size, and particular risks where the companies operate. The Federal Sentencing Guidelines and other leading practices suggest that the program should have high-level oversight and be administered by competent and ethical employees. A leading practice established by some organizations is the appointment of an anti-corruption compliance officer or coordinator. This individual can be a part of the compliance, legal, or another department, but should have defined roles and responsibilities and be seen as the primary point of contact for anti-corruption compliance. Primary responsibilities include overseeing and assisting the organization in implementing, administering, monitoring, and improving the program. The anti-corruption coordinator can provide oversight of ethics and compliance at the corporate level or at a business-unit level. The role of anti-corruption coordinator can be a full- or part-time position, depending on the size and complexity of the organization, and often coordinates with other departments, including legal, ethics, human resources, finance, internal audit, and local management to administer the anti-corruption monitoring program.

A common approach is tasking the compliance department with enforcing the program, and tasking the internal audit department to perform periodic audits of the program.

Planning the Anti-Corruption Compliance Audit

The primary objectives of the audit include testing the effectiveness of the current anti-corruption compliance program and uncovering potential bribery and corruption risks to the organization. An anti-corruption compliance audit is not an investigation, and caution should be taken by the audit team to emphasize this to the business unit or organization undergoing the audit. Accordingly, any red flags identified during the audit should be treated and dealt with according to the organization's anti-corruption compliance program in place. To most effectively perform an audit, the right team should be in place. Also, sufficient planning should be carried out to ensure efficient use of time in the field.

The FCPA/Anti-Corruption Audit Team

The desired skills for persons performing the audit include:

- In-depth knowledge of the Foreign Corrupt Practices Act of 1977 (FCPA), U.K. Bribery Act, and other relevant anti-corruption regulation.
- Extensive experience in conducting interviews.
- Knowledge and experience to select high-risk transactions for testing.
- Knowledge and experience in using data analytics tools.
- Experience to recognize red flags for potential violations.
- Experience in conducting FCPA, anti-corruption, and/or fraud investigations.
- Knowledge of internal control systems and generally accepted accounting principles (GAAP).
- Analytical skills.

If a company conducts anti-corruption audits with internal resources, the team members typically include individuals from the internal audit, compliance, and legal departments. Often, companies hire external forensic accountants to conduct anti-corruption audits. Forensic accounting firms have a large network of global resources with relevant experience and knowledge of local cultures and business practices that may be extremely beneficial to conducting the audit. Consideration should be given to ensuring that there is access to local legal advice if required.

Review of Prior Incidents

Prior to commencing the audit, the team should familiarize themselves with any prior risk assessments and audits performed, noting any known or suspected anti-corruption issues. The team should also work with the entity under audit to obtain information and documentation related to all areas considered to be in scope for the audit. For example, a general understanding of the operations should be obtained, including locations of operations, significant customers (noting those that are government owned or affiliated), use of third-party sales intermediaries, recent acquisitions, and major business partners or joint ventures. The audit team should inquire with the legal and compliance departments or anti-corruption compliance officer regarding any prior issues or issues that occurred since the previous audit that should be considered in preparing for the audit. In addition, the audit team should inquire with the internal audit department regarding any previous audits in this area.

Further, any current or prior anti-corruption self-assessments performed by the location or business unit should be reviewed by the audit team during the planning process.

Data Requests

A data request list should be prepared and submitted to the entity undergoing the audit including requests for:

- Anti-corruption policies and procedures.
- Organizational charts of key departments, including management, finance, legal, business development, compliance/ethics, and so on.
- Revenues/sales orders by country, by customer.
- Volume of interaction with third-party sales intermediaries, including names and sales associated with each.
- Financial data related to specific areas of transaction testing.

Consideration should be given to performing data analytics on the financial data obtained, depending on the volume and format of the data (data analytics will be discussed in greater detail later in this chapter). For each area of focus, obtain financial information (summary and transaction-level detail, as applicable) for the period under review to understand the population of relevant transactions. Either through manual analysis or utilizing the results of the data analytics, select a sample of transactions to test accounting controls and compliance with policies and procedures for each area. The audit team should provide selections to the business unit to initiate the compiling of supporting documentation prior to fieldwork. Finally, the audit team should arrange interviews to be conducted during the audit prior to commencing fieldwork.

CONDUCTING THE ANTI-CORRUPTION COMPLIANCE AUDIT

When conducting an anti-corruption compliance audit, activities focus around the review of policies and procedures, the general ledger and accounting system, detailed testing on certain areas such as cash disbursements, and third-party intermediaries. Often, the most critical part of the audit is the interview. These areas are discussed further.

Anti-Corruption Policies and Procedures

Given that a large part of conducting the audit relates to testing compliance with policies and procedures in place, it is important that the audit team obtain all anti-corruption-related policies and procedures in advance to familiarize themselves prior to commencing fieldwork. It is necessary to obtain policies and procedures specific to the business unit that is being audited as well as any corporate policies that could apply. The audit is an opportunity to identify areas where policies are not being followed, but also serves as an opportunity for identification of areas where policies and procedures are not currently in place or not effective but could be warranted. For example, organizations might overlook the risks associated with third-party vendor due diligence. A robust and defensible vendor vetting process is a key part of any anti-corruption program. Having policies and procedures in place to address vendor due diligence, specifically as related to third-party sales intermediaries, and testing compliance with this process is important.

General Ledger Account Review

Also, financial data relevant to performing transaction testing should be obtained. First, the chart of accounts and trial balance for the business unit under review should be obtained. The audit team should scan the general ledger (G/L) account headings on the trial balance and note any unusual G/L account headings or items otherwise warranting further scrutiny (e.g., accounts related to gifts, meals, or entertainment with government officials; "special" marketing expenses; or "other" expenses). Next, the team should request transaction-level detail of selected G/L accounts and, on a judgmental basis, select a sample of transactions for testing and request supporting documentation. Accounts selected could include:

- Gifts, travel, and entertainment
- Donations/charitable contributions

- Agents/consultants/commission fees
- Miscellaneous/other
- Consulting/professional fees
- Licenses/permits
- Marketing/advertising

Cash Disbursements

Another important area of focus for the audit team is testing cash disbursements to selected vendors. The audit team should obtain a summary disbursements schedule by vendor with total dollar amounts spent by vendor for the year under review. Next, review the vendor names and dollar volume by vendor, and select a sample of vendors from the vendor disbursement summary. The selection of vendors should be made on a judgmental basis to bring into account the volume of business, type of vendor, and potential bribery and corruption risks associated with the vendor and other factors, and obtain disbursement detail for selected vendors.

Payments to Third-Party Sales Intermediaries

An area of special focus for the audit team is testing payments to third-party intermediaries, sales representatives, agents, and consultants, if applicable to the business. The audit team should review a summary of payments for the period under review and use their judgment to select several vendors to perform further testing. Documents requested should include the documents supporting due diligence of the intermediaries, contracts, and transaction information and supporting documentation relevant to each vendor. Payments and reimbursements to third parties can be requested on a sample basis, depending on the level and number of payments.

Further Testing

Additional areas of testing during the review could include the following areas, depending on the risk profile:

- Cash accounts (active bank accounts), including review of bank reconciliations and accounts not specifically covered by cash disbursements testing.

- Petty cash accounts (including cash advances from petty cash).
- Employee travel and entertainment expenditures (T&E).
- Employee credit cards (if separate from T&E reimbursements).
- Gifts, meals, and entertainment activities (with government officials).
- Offset activities (accounts receivable).
- Government oversight (licenses and permits, fines, and settlements).
- Charitable or political donations or contributions.
- International logistics providers/freight forwarders and dealings with customs.
- Facilitating payments as defined in the FCPA.
- Payroll records.
- Credit notes process.

Transaction Testing

During an anti-corruption compliance audit, transaction-level testing typically is performed on a judgmental sample basis. The audit team should obtain and analyze supporting documentation for selected transactions for relevant areas of testing. This review should test for adequate documentation as to the nature and purpose of the transactions, payment approvals, agreement with the underlying contracts, and proper recording of the transaction in the company's books and records. Supporting documentation for payments could include the invoice, evidence of payment, and other supporting documentation. For payments to third-party sales intermediaries, the audit team should also test compliance with the contracts with these vendors and if due diligence was performed on a sample basis.

Interviews

One of the most important aspects of performing an anti-corruption audit is conducting interviews with individuals in key roles related to anti-corruption compliance. The target group for these interviews at each location or business unit should include compliance, business development, legal, ethics, finance/accounting, sales agents/representatives, and certain areas of operations, including logistics/international shipping. The primary purpose of the interviews is to assess employee knowledge of and understanding of the anti-corruption compliance program and requirement to comply with company policy.

SAMPLE INTERVIEW OUTLINE

Business Development/Sales:

- Background/current position.
- General roles and responsibilities, including territories/regions covered.
- Business development process.
- Customer base, including percentage of government customers or potential customers.
- Interactions with and identification of all third-party sales intermediaries.
- Gifts, meals, and entertainment with government officials.
- Promotional expenses/customer visits.
- Sponsorships/donations/charitable contributions.
- Knowledge of any improper payments or solicitation for improper payments.
- General corruption environment in territories covered.
- General concerns/risk areas related to bribery and corruption compliance.

Who Should Be Interviewed?

Based on discussions with the anti-corruption compliance officer or legal or compliance representative responsible for anti-corruption compliance at the business unit and on a review of organizational charts, the audit team should identify appropriate individuals to interview. Depending on the size of the organization, the number of individuals interviewed can vary but, typically include:

- Anti-corruption compliance officer or legal or compliance representative responsible for anti-corruption compliance at business unit or location (discuss overall responsibilities related to anti-corruption compliance program, including training, anti-corruption policies and procedures, gifts and hospitality to government officials, reporting hotline/queries, and instances of noncompliance).
- Individuals in the business development or sales organization responsible for international sales (see sample interview outline for discussion topics).
- Legal (discuss prior incidents related to anti-corruption compliance).

- Ethics/Compliance (discuss reporting hotline, gift log).
- Finance (discuss financial controls related to anti-corruption compliance).
- Logistics (discuss international shipments and responsibilities for customs clearance).
- Agents, consultants, sales representatives.

General topics such as roles and responsibilities related to anti-corruption compliance should be covered. Some pointed questions should be asked of all interviewees, including knowledge of solicitation for improper payments. Other important topics to be covered during interviews include interactions with government customers and suppliers, interactions with and identification of all third-party sales intermediaries, direct interactions with government authorities, and knowledge of competitors' business practices.

Also, asking if the interviewee has had any training on the FCPA and the format of that training is helpful to determine FCPA knowledge and compliance. This perspective can vary, depending on the individual's department, level, responsibilities, and other factors. One additional important question to ask is the interviewee's views on the primary risk areas related to anti-corruption compliance to the organization.

Anti-Corruption Training Compliance

In Chapter 5, "Policies and Procedures," the importance of training and leading practices is discussed. However, similar to other activities, if the training participation is not documented in the correct manner, then the audit trail for the training completeness could be compromised. Therefore, an additional area of focus during the audit should be testing compliance with required anti-corruption training. The audit team should perform testing to confirm that individuals identified to take the training have completed the training, as follows:

- Request and review the business unit's anti-corruption training material.
- Determine if training is conducted only in English or in another native language and whether some training is provided in person by legal representatives.
- Review history of anti-corruption compliance training, including when and how training was delivered and persons attending. If live training was conducted, determine the name and position of the trainer conducting the class.

- Review control list of all persons required to take training and determine if there are any omissions from the listing that should potentially be included, such as accounting personnel, sales associates, and senior management. Ascertain whether anyone on the list did not take the training.
- Confirm that training material incorporates U.S., U.K., and local laws and regulations.

Tracking to ensure that all employees received the appropriate level of training is important. In the event of an investigation, establishing whether the appropriate training was provided to certain employees may be an important factor in settling the case—and deciding on the potential disciplinary actions for the employees involved. Also, it may impact an organization's ability to pursue legal action against third parties who were provided with training by the company.

REPORTING THE RESULTS

The results of an anti-corruption audit should be documented in a report. There are no established standards for anti-corruption audit reports, but certainly there are a number of items that should be included. Often, reports include the background of the audit that details the scope of work performed, time frame of the testing, interviews conducted, and so on. More important, the report should detail incidents of noncompliance with the organization's anti-corruption compliance program and recommendations for improvements. The incidents of noncompliance should be sufficiently described to include the basis of noncompliance (i.e., contractual clauses, company policy). In addition, any policy violations or deficiencies in anti-corruption-related policies and procedures should be identified. It is also important that recommendations for strengthening anti-corruption internal financial controls should be included in the report. For example, recommendations could include:

- Requiring a gift log to be maintained for all items of a certain value provided to government officials.
- Establishing thresholds upon which gift, meal, and entertainment expenditures with government officials are required.
- Establishing anti-corruption due diligence standards for all third-party vendors involved in international transactions.

- Requiring FCPA or anti-corruption language in all contracts with third-party vendors involved in international transactions.

The anti-corruption audit report will serve as a basis to review deficiencies in policy and procedures and strengthen internal controls. Depending on the company and circumstances of the anti-corruption audit, the reports are often provided to the company's audit committee, legal department, compliance department, and others for their input and consideration.

Company-wide Reporting

Analyzing cumulative anti-corruption audit reported issues, including deficiencies and recommendations, over a period of time for multiple business units or locations could allow an organization to identify potential risk areas from a different perspective, particularly if the audit results have not been considered in the aggregate. Compiling a summary or high-level analysis of all topical risk areas identified over a defined time period could be very helpful to an organization. For example, if a·consistent observation across business units is that dealings with certain international third-party intermediaries (e.g., international logistics providers and freight forwarders) have not been considered for anti-corruption compliance, including limited or no due diligence performed and contracts do not contain anti-bribery language, then there may be a potential issue for the organization to address on a global perspective.

Alternatively, for example, lack of guidance or formal policies and procedures in a particular risk area could be a consistent trend among business units or locations. If specific guidance on a particular topic has not been provided from the headquarters of an organization, there is a strong likelihood that the organization is opening itself up to potential risk areas that might not have been considered in the anti-corruption compliance program. Lack of petty cash and cash advance policies is an area where downfalls are frequently identified.

Furthermore, requiring individual business units or locations to perform self-assessments on a regular basis and report those results back to the anti-corruption compliance coordinator should be part of an ongoing anti-corruption monitoring program. Organizations should provide guidance or establish a framework to each business unit or location, stipulating areas to be evaluated on a yearly basis, including training, policies and procedures, relationships with significant third-party intermediaries, and so on. Requiring locations or business units to consider anti-corruption compliance on a regular basis reinforces awareness and requires regular attention to the topic. Many companies have formal programs requiring senior employees to regularly certify and recertify compliance with the FCPA and other anti-corruption laws.

AUDITS OF AGENTS/INTERMEDIARIES

While not a commonly used anti-corruption monitoring tool, companies are more frequently exercising their contractual rights and performing anti-corruption audits of high-risk vendors and other third parties who interact with government officials on behalf of the company. The importance of exercising such rights is highlighted by a settlement with the DOJ involving bribes paid though agents on behalf of a company. In its 2011 settlement, Johnson & Johnson admitted that "its subsidiaries, employees, and agents paid bribes to publicly-employed health care providers in Greece, Poland, and Romania, and that kickbacks were paid on behalf of Johnson & Johnson subsidiary companies to the former government of Iraq under the United Nations Oil for Food program."[2]

The scope of audits of agents or intermediaries is often defined within the terms of the underlying contracts. Hence, a company must focus on the contract language in establishing the initial scope of the audit. Primarily, audit rights must be included in the terms of the contract. Often, companies may want to expand the scope of the audit, based on factors that may not have been contemplated at the time of the contract execution. Certain other contract provisions may be helpful in the negotiations of audit scope. For example, rights to terminate the vendor contract and withhold payment may be crucial leverage in the ultimate determination of scope. For example, most vendor audits are principally focused on vendor payments. While there often is a need to sign confidentiality agreements in connection with such audits, the company should preserve its right to disclose findings of corrupt activity to authorities if it seems fit to do so.

Efforts to mitigate corruption risks posed by agents, consultants, commercial sales representatives, and other third parties include three separate activities: precontract due diligence and acceptance procedures, contracting provisions with anti-bribery representations, and warranties and other vendor requirements such as certifications and anti-corruption training. Organizations should create policies to govern the retention of agents, consultants, commercial sales representatives, and other third parties to address the risk that such third parties may pay or offer to pay bribes on the company's behalf. Consideration should also be given to requiring agents and other intermediaries to undergo company-sponsored anti-corruption training.

USE OF DATA ANALYTICS IN MONITORING

As financial systems become more automated, companies are turning more to analytics as a tool for compliance monitoring. Analytics can be a very useful tool to complement a robust anti-corruption compliance program, and can be used in several ways as a monitoring tool—including as part of prefieldwork for transaction testing related to an anti-corruption audit, as well as ongoing analysis of certain accounts or payments on a recurring basis.

Where companies have implemented financial software on a global basis, there are many analytical tools that may be used to identify and assess risk areas without leaving the confines of the corporate headquarters. For example, vendor analytics is a particular data analytics tool that is used to identify various risk traits associated with high-risk vendors, including high-risk locations, use of various bank account locations, offshore banking, politically exposed persons or potential associations with government officials, round-dollar payments, vendors with the same or similar addresses, and so on. As with conducting anti-corruption audits, the key is to deploy the right tools, but also to have trained personnel who can interpret and recognize trends and anomalies in the data.

To detect bribery and corruption, new tools need to be integrated into the anti-corruption monitoring program that incorporates model-based statistical and text mining analysis, coupled with visual analytics. In other words, let the data speak for itself in terms of anomalies, rather than trying to identify the anomaly or rule being violated. When integrated with traditional rules-based tests, these sophisticated technologies can be a powerful tool to identify unusual transactions derived from the multidimensional attributes in the data. Model-based data mining shifts the focus to high-risk areas where controls may not necessarily exist or are perhaps even bypassed, while reducing the amount of false-positive transactions often associated with traditional rules-based tests. Collectively, these analytics are known as "Anti-Bribery and Corruption Analytics" or ABC Analytics.

Data analytics can play an important role in assisting organizations with respect to monitoring, auditing, and evaluating the overall effectiveness of the organization's compliance and ethics program. Anti-bribery and -corruption analytics can be highly effective when used in the following contexts:

- **Diagnostic in nature:** ABC Analytics should be used prior to fieldwork or at the beginning of an audit to identify high-risk areas that warrant substantive testing or a deep dive. Analytics won't find corruption; however, it will serve as a smoke detector to guide the auditors where to look.
- **Use of advanced technology:** Leverage text mining of the free text payment descriptions and visualization tools, statistical techniques, and leading anti-fraud research to identify key risk areas to focus on—looking beyond just the dollar amounts and vendors, and into the text field descriptions of the payments or expenses.
- **An interactive and intuitive process:** ABC Analytics should be designed to be simple to navigate, intuitive, highly visual, and require minimal training.
- **More efficient audits:** Tests should be designed to highlight suspicious or potentially improper activity before the on-site visits, leading to time in the field better spent on the risk areas identified, rather than just pulling random samples.
- **Cost effective:** Done properly, ABC Analytics create value and save time in the field—they should not be crippling to the audit and compliance program.
- **Repeatable and transferrable:** The ABC Analytics approach is a learning model for the accountant that incorporates observations from previous projects and continuously improves. Further, many of the tests are designed to be collaborative with the engagement team (including interested parties from management, compliance, and legal).

Anti-Bribery and -Corruption Analytics

Traditional rules-based tests are generally not as effective for identifying high-risk transactions that may indicate the presence of bribery and corruption in the context of an FCPA violation. These schemes often involve the circumvention of existing accounting rules, or perhaps even going where rules do not exist. For bribery and corruption, new approaches to data analytics are needed that integrate statistical analysis, anomaly detection, data visualization, and text mining as discussed later. Some fundamental differences exist between the methodologies used to detect bribery and corruption compared to traditional accounting tests. Notably, the more sophisticated tests typically do not yield as many "false positives" for the anti-corruption audit team as traditional rules based tests, therefore helping to make the ongoing monitoring process more seamless.

Traditional Rules-Based Tests

- The accountant asks questions of the data.
- Questions are based on current risks or what is currently "known."
- Tests often require time and luck to uncover.

Anti-Bribery and -Corruption Analytics

- Utilizes some traditional rules-based tests on a targeted basis, but also incorporates additional statistical and text mining techniques.
- Data is allowed to define itself—based on text frequency, anomaly detection, and predictive modeling.
- Complements controls monitoring.
- Helps look for large and unusual transactions derived from the multi-dimensional attributes in the data, not just one variable.
- Moves focus to high-risk areas where controls don't exist or are perhaps even bypassed.

Following are three examples of more sophisticated data analytics that can be used as part of an anti-corruption monitoring program:

1. Text analytics or text mining in journal entries

   Text analytics, or text data mining, describes a set of analytical tools that identify, classify, and parse words and clusters of words in electronic documents. The software provides for linguistic searches; recognizes and isolates lexical patterns; and provides additional functionality for extracting words by category, theme, or meaning. Moreover, it enables users to tag and structure search results, interpret the data through use of visual tools, and use predictive techniques. Text analytics also describes the process auditors and other professionals use to apply these techniques to solve business problems such as identifying potentially improper payments—especially with respect to identifying areas of "corrupt intent." It can also add to the auditors' understanding of the people, transactions, and dates associated with significant events—including the development and incidence of bribery and corruption—without having to read hundreds of records or free-text field descriptions. The software can help practitioners increase their audit efficiency, gain more meaningful information about high-risk transactions, and support the organization's compliance efforts. Text analytics tools can be used in the context of a risk-based anti-corruption compliance audit, as part of a forensic review of controls or business practices, or during an investigation. See Figure 7.2 for an example of concept analysis for accounts payable.

When combined with traditional keyword searches for high-risk terms (including searches in multiple languages), text mining of free-text fields linked to payment activity is the most effective type of analytics available to auditors in identifying potential anti-corruption risk areas.

2. Statistical analytics using clustering and anomaly detection techniques

As Records A, B, and C in the example in Figure 7.3 demonstrates, anomaly detection identifies unusual cases, or outliers, that do not conform to patterns of "normal" data. With this methodology, it is possible to identify outliers even if they do not fit any previously known patterns. Anomalies are also referred to as outliers, surprise, aberrant, deviation, peculiarity, and so on. There are dozens of mathematical techniques for anomaly detection and clustering in many statistical and data mining software packages that are beyond the scope of this chapter.

3. Data visualization tools

When mining for bribery and corruption, it is often easier to spot patterns and anomalies in the data when looking at it visually, rather than dumped into a spreadsheet output. Many tools are available that allow auditors and accountants to "drill down" into the data in a dashboard interface. When integrated with text mining and statistical analysis, these data visualization dashboards can become very powerful tools to assist with identification of high-risk vendors, transactions, employees, or business units.

Data visualization dashboards can be used to analyze T&E detail, accounts payable, sales, and G/L data. Dashboards can be easy-to-use, interactive tools to identify specific names, countries, payees, and the like. Auditors and accountants can "zoom in" or "zoom out" to spot anomalies, compared to reviewing 10,000 or more records in an XLS spreadsheet. Examples of a T&E dashboard and an accounts payable dashboard are provided in Figures 7.4 and 7.5

Data Gathering

Inappropriate payments can be made through a variety of mediums within financial accounting systems. The data sources for anti-bribery and -corruption analytics typically focus in several risk areas, including procure-to-pay processes

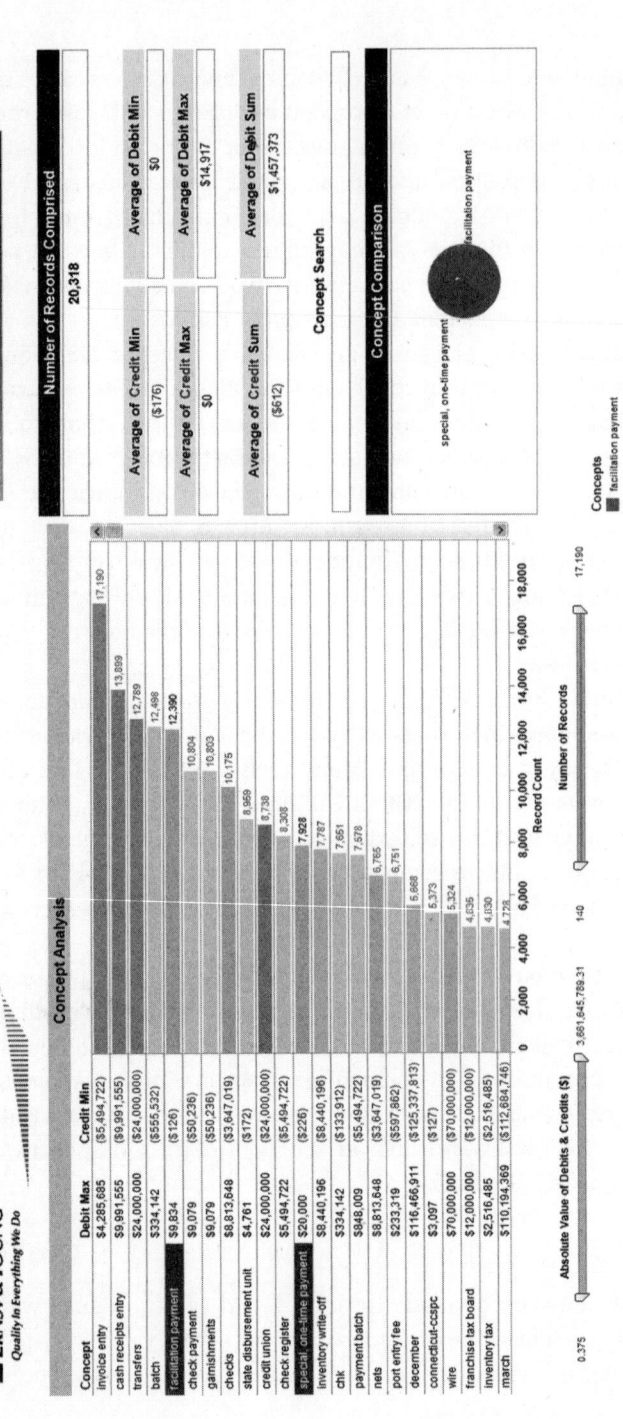

FIGURE 7.2 Concept Analysis

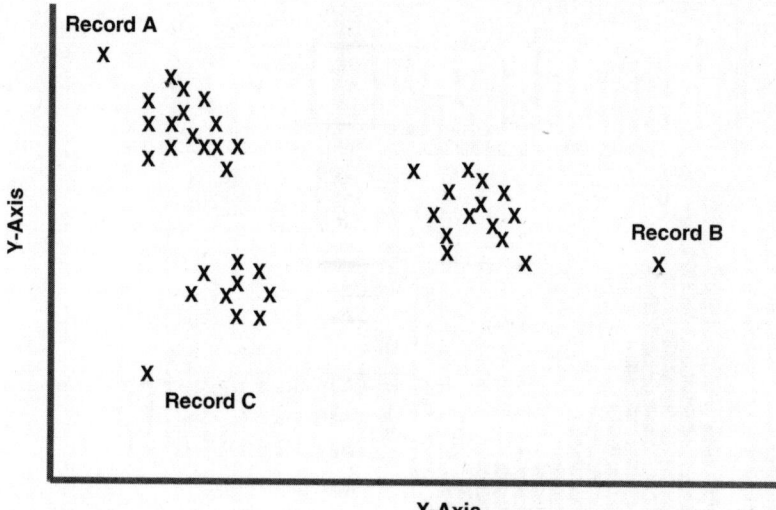

FIGURE 7.3 Anomaly Detection

(purchases and accounts payable), the order-to-cash process (sales process), T&E process, and certain G/L expense accounts. Although these areas could be tested as part of ongoing internal compliance audits, the lens under which these data sources are reviewed is different for anti-bribery and -corruption analytics. The following types of financial data are typically obtained:

- Chart of accounts, along with company codes and/or business-unit numbers.
- Trial balances for relevant period and ledgers, used to verify account totals.
- Sales journal/purchase order subledger.
- Accounts payable subledger and/or cash disbursements detail.
- G/L details—with a focus on select expense accounts, including gifts, entertainment, consultants, commissions, donations, contributions, and miscellaneous.
- T&E line header and line item details.

Also, certain master file data should be obtained, including:

- Vendor master (active and inactive).
- Agent/Broker/Subcontractor master (active and inactive, if different from vendor master).

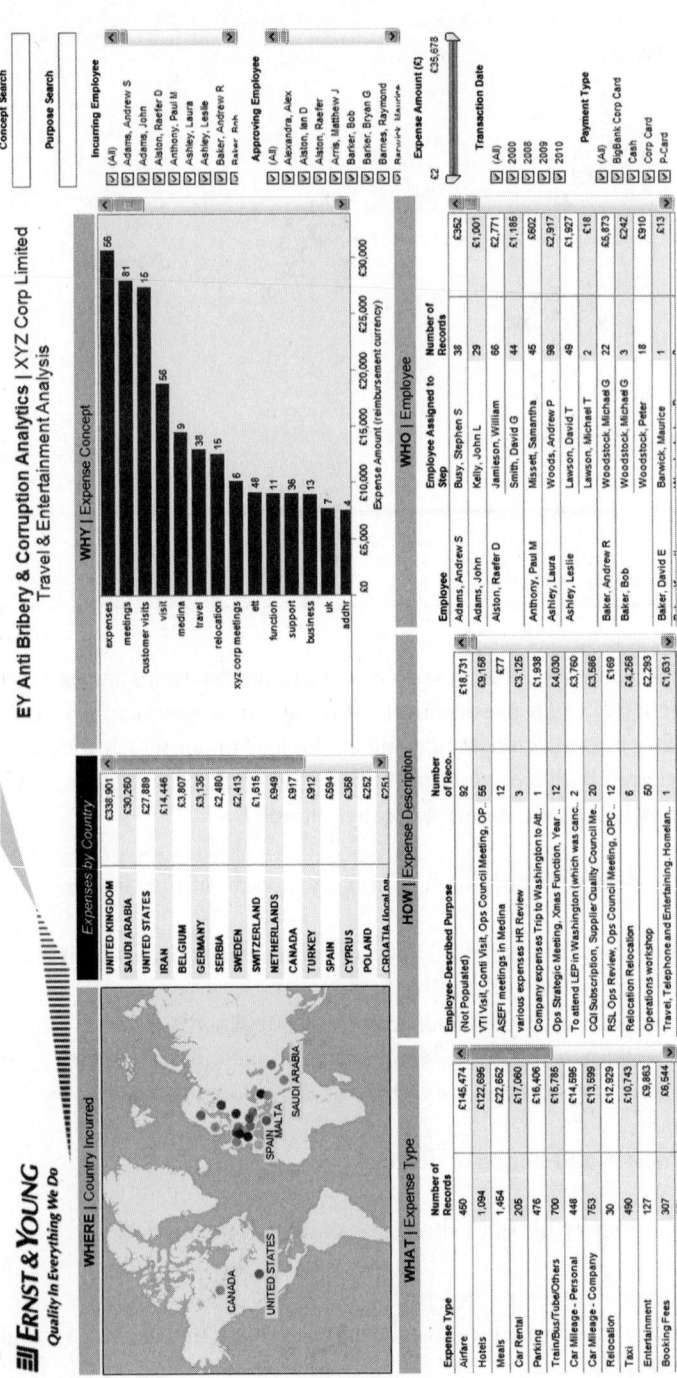

FIGURE 7.4 T&E Review and Drill-Down Dashboard

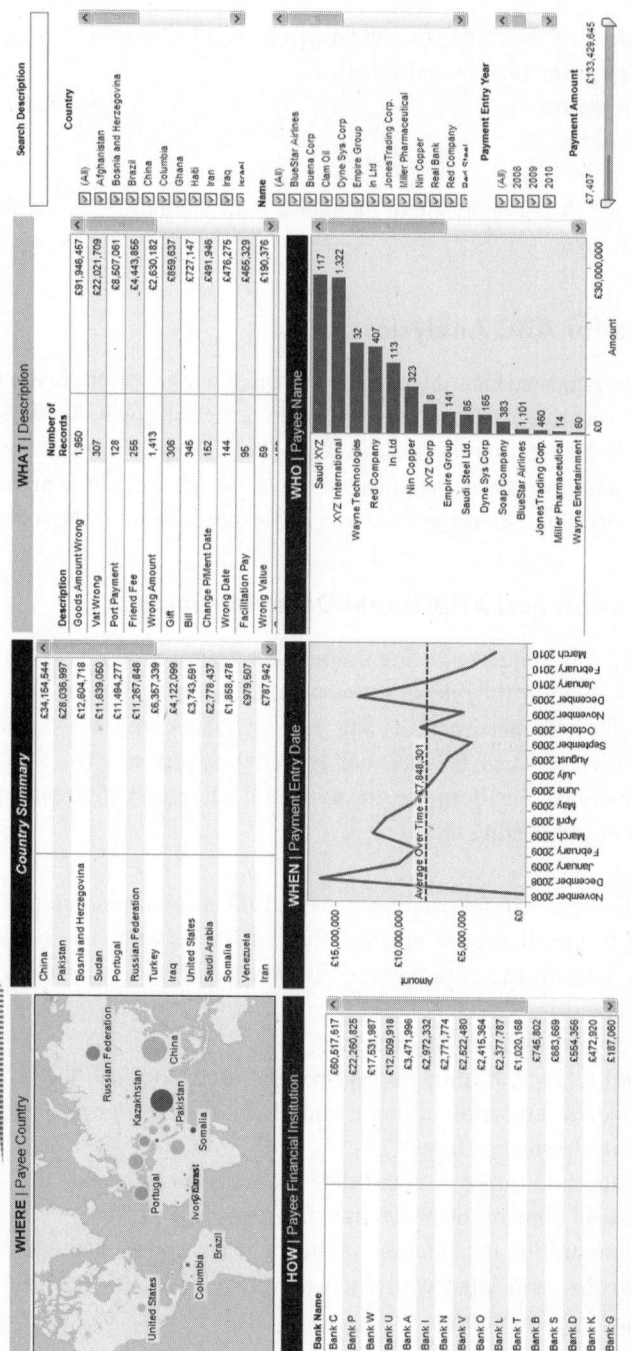

FIGURE 7.5 Accounts Payable Review and Drill-Down Dashboard

149

- Freight forwarders master (if different from vendor master).
- Employee master (active and inactive).
- Customer master.
- Product master file.

For each file, it is important to include a data dictionary, describing the nature of each field.

Date Range for ABC Analytics

The date range requested for analysis will vary based on the specific needs risks of the audit. For proactive assessments, organizations typically include a date range between 6 and 18 months to obtain a reasonable sample of transactions for analysis. If data analytics are performed on a routine basis as part of an ongoing monitoring effort, the date range could be consistent 12-month periods.

Data Validation and Additional Data Requests

It is often helpful to request existing financial or operational reports from the business unit owner for the relevant time periods that may be used to evaluate for completeness and accuracy of data received. This step, which includes referencing back to the trial balance, will prevent any rework if the data export needs to be amended. Furthermore, the following additional information could be helpful when requesting data:

- File format or layout for each file provided. This document would outline the type of file. It should also list the data fields and the sequence of the data fields in the data file and provide a description for each of the data fields.
- File size (bytes) for each file provided.
- File record totals and numeric field control totals for each file provided.
- Return address and contact name and phone number for returning data and the media storage units.
- Appropriate date range or cutoff date for each file provided.
- Numeric field control totals for each file provided.
- Description and/or explanation of the various codes, flags, and other business rules associated with each file provided if not included in the file layout documentation.

Challenges in Obtaining Data

Implementing an anti-corruption data analytics program that sufficiently addresses potential violations and control deficiencies can be complex, and the challenges can be many, including:

- Global coordination between offices or business units.
- Multiple, disparate accounting systems—with different formats of data.
- Personnel constraints, especially around expertise familiar with the intricacies of the FCPA.
- Foreign language and familiarity with the local idioms, subtleties, and nuances often associated with bribery payments.
- Data privacy concerns.
- Identification, collection, and analysis of large data sets.

 SUMMARY

Establishing a program to consistently monitor anti-corruption compliance is an essential part of developing an effective anti-corruption compliance program. The various elements of the monitoring program, including developing the plan, monitoring training, monitoring policies and procedures, conducting the audit, and reporting the results of the audit, are all vital aspects to consider. Incorporating data analytics into ongoing anti-corruption compliance monitoring or as a part of the planning stages for a specific anti-corruption compliance audit can be a valuable tool to enhance the effectiveness of such procedures. Incorporating ABC Analytics and can be a more efficient and cost-effective way to analyze the data set over time. Given the level of risk involved and potentially negative impact on an organization, regular anti-corruption compliance monitoring serves as a strong deterrent to employees, and sends a clear message from the top of the organization that the topic is important.

 NOTES

1. www.justice.gov/criminal/pr/speeches-testimony/2010/05-26-10aag-compliance-week-speech.pdf, Speech, May 26 2010.
2. Principal Deputy Assistant Attorney General Mythili Raman of the Justice Department's Criminal Division, www.justice.gov/opa/pr/2011/April/11-crm-446.html, press release, DOJ, April 8 2011.

CHAPTER EIGHT

Anti-Corruption Due Diligence

A NTI-CORRUPTION DUE DILIGENCE IS an important part of an anti-corruption compliance program (see Figure 8.1). Recent enforcement activity by the U.S. Department of Justice (DOJ) and the Securities and Exchange Commission (SEC) has made it essential for any company considering entering into a business transaction outside of the United States to conduct thorough anti-corruption due diligence procedures.

Bribery and corruption pose significant challenges for companies entering into new markets through business transactions, including mergers, acquisitions, or joint ventures. The Foreign Corrupt Practices Act of 1977 (FCPA) places responsibility on the acquiring company to conduct comprehensive due-diligence procedures on the target companies that are based or operating in foreign markets. The acquiring company may be held liable for any corrupt activity that occurred before the acquisition even took place. This holds true, even if the acquirer did not have direct knowledge of any corrupt activity's taking place. This leads to increased emphasis placed on the need to conduct anti-corruption due diligence procedures. In addition, special importance is placed on what the acquiring company knew at the time of the

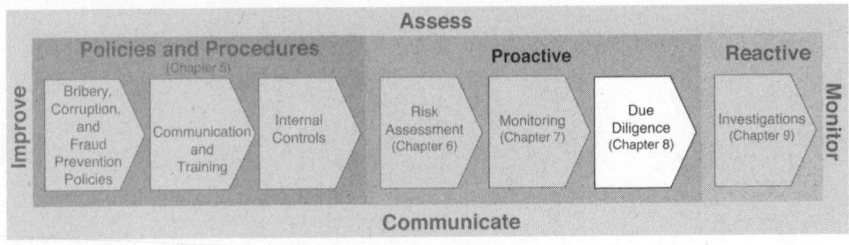

FIGURE 8.1 Anti-Corruption Compliance Program

acquisition versus what it should have known through the procedures it should have conducted.

The question here stands: how much due diligence is sufficient to satisfy the requirements of the FCPA and other anti-corruption legislation? When should a company continue its due diligence procedures and when should it walk away from the deal?

CURRENT TRANSACTION MARKET PERSPECTIVES

Companies enter global markets through a variety of ways, often through mergers, acquisitions, or joint ventures.

One of the aftermaths of the years following the financial crisis of 2008 has been an increase in transaction activity. This increase in activity has not focused on a specific industry, but on a variety of industries, including technology, life sciences and energy. Regulators in the United States and abroad continue to emphasize the importance of anti-corruption due diligence.

Transaction Activity Increasing in High-Risk Emerging Markets and Industry Sectors

Global merger-and-acquisition (M&A) activity in 2010 strongly increased over the continued decline that had been experienced during 2008 and 2009. The strength in 2010 was most apparent in cross-border transactions, especially in emerging markets, such as China and Russia. Global M&A growth in 2011 and forecasts for beyond continues to be strong and is expected to continue to grow rapidly, not only in China and Russia but also with additional anticipated strong growth in South and Central America as

1 in 5 aim to grow aggressively in next 12 months, and 1 in 3 will look out for opportunities, but 1 in 3 are waiting for prospects to improve

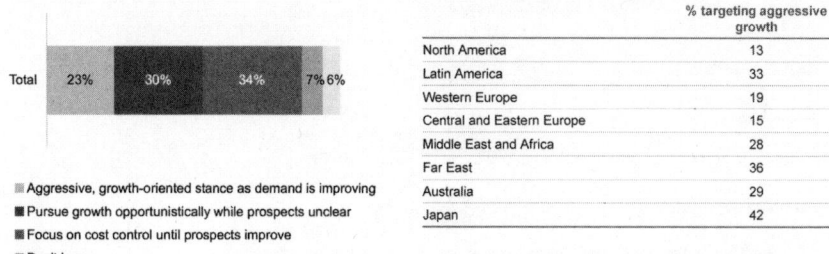

	% targeting aggressive growth
North America	13
Latin America	33
Western Europe	19
Central and Eastern Europe	15
Middle East and Africa	28
Far East	36
Australia	29
Japan	42

Total 23% 30% 34% 7% 6%

■ Aggressive, growth-oriented stance as demand is improving
■ Pursue growth opportunistically while prospects unclear
■ Focus on cost control until prospects improve
■ Don't know
Other

Q: Which of the following best characterizes your company's strategy over the next year?
Base: All respondents (1,409)

FIGURE 8.2 Substantial Proportion of Management Targeting Aggressive Growth

well as Eastern Europe and Africa. Due to their growing consumer demand by an emerging middle class, transactions in these countries are especially appealing to U.S. investors for their significant revenue and profit potential. In fact, Ernst & Young's 11th Fraud Survey, "Driving Ethical Growth—New Markets, New Challenges" (Ernst & Young's Fraud Survey) from 2010 asked executives from around the world about their strategy in the upcoming years. Twenty-three percent of respondents indicated they will be growing aggressively, and 30 percent indicated that they will pursue growth opportunistically. The geographies focused on aggressive growth were Japan, the Far East, and Latin America (see Figure 8.2).

The tendency to conduct due diligence focusing primarily on the financial health of the target company may come quite naturally to many executives around the world. Ernst & Young's Fraud Survey found that about 20 percent of companies conduct no fraud-related preacquisition due diligence procedures, and 42 percent of companies conduct no fraud-related postacquisition due diligence. Also interesting was the fact that nearly 30 percent of companies that acquired a new business in the last two years "never or infrequently" considered bribery or corruption risks in the context of a potential acquisition (see Figure 8.3). This increases the gaps between the expectations of regulators in regard to pre- and postacquisition anti-corruption due diligence procedures, and the reality of how companies are approaching these procedures.

Preacquisition
Total: 37 | 10 | 14 | 11 | 19
10th Global Fraud Survey (2008): 36 | 11 | 11 | 14 | 14
Postacquisition
Total: 23 | 9 | 14 | 15 | 27
10th Global Fraud Survey (2008): 28 | 11 | 12 | 17 | 17

■ % fairly frequently ■ % very frequently ■ % always
■ % not very frequently ■ % never

	% not very frequently/never	
	Pre-acquisition	Post-acquisition
North America	18	41
Latin America	16	27
Western Europe	33	43
Central and Eastern Europe	38	43
Middle East and Africa	29	42
Far East	30	41
Australia	25	54
Japan	40	53
CFO	38	47
Compliance	24	36
Internal Audit	31	41
Legal	24	41

Q: How frequently has your company conducted due diligence into fraud and/or corruption-related risks before acquiring a new business in the last two years?
Q: How frequently has your company conducted fraud and/or corruption-related postacquisition due diligence in the last two years?
Base: All making acquisitions (888)
The "Don't know" percentages have been omitted in order to allow better comparison between the responses given.

FIGURE 8.3 Frequency of Conducting Due Diligence Fraud Risk (Including Bribery and Corruption Risks)

Increased Expectation for Due Diligence from Regulators

The enforcement trends in the United States and overseas have increased the importance associated with proactive approaches in an anti-corruption compliance aspect. For example, in 2010, the DOJ endorsed the "Good Practice Guidance on Internal Controls, Ethics, and Compliance" that was issued by the Organization for Economic Co-operation and Development (OECD), which emphasizes the importance of having a proactive approach toward compliance. Among other areas, this guidance discusses the importance of having documented due diligence, as well as appropriate and regular oversight of business partners.

The U.K. Bribery Act, discussed further in Chapters 3 and 4, also emphasizes the importance of focusing on the third parties, as well as conducting thorough anti-corruption procedures in an acquisition setting.

An acquiring company that does not perform an effective and thorough due diligence review of a proposed merger or acquisition target runs the risk of entering into a business transaction with an entity that may have corrupt practices. In addition, the acquiring company can be held accountable by U.S. authorities for the past or continuing FCPA violations of the merger target or division of another company that is being acquired. This might lead to significant penalties and fines—in addition to the costs associated with the compliance efforts postacquisition.

THE FCPA DUE DILIGENCE REGULATORY ENVIRONMENT

The DOJ has issued several opinion procedure releases in the context of a merger and acquisition or a joint venture.[1] Though all of these releases give an insight into the ways of DOJ, one of the most significant is the DOJ Opinion 08-02, which is also referred to as the Halliburton opinion. More recently, the DOJ included information specific to anti-corruption due diligence activities in an M&A context in the April 2011 deferred prosecution agreement with Johnson & Johnson (J&J).

DOJ Opinion 08-02 (Halliburton Opinion) and Its Impact on FCPA Due Diligence

Even if the acquiring company has the intention of conducting anti-corruption due diligence procedures, there may be situations, for example, due to the privacy laws of the country in which the target is operating, that do not allow for the acquirer to continue with such procedures. Halliburton was in the process of submitting a proposal to purchase a company in the United Kingdom. Due to tender rules in this country, Halliburton was not able to conduct a meaningful preacquisition anti-corruption due diligence. Having been fined for the FCPA previously, Halliburton requested the DOJ's opinion on the following questions:[2]

- Whether the acquisition itself would violate the FCPA.
- Whether Halliburton would be held liable for preacquisition violations of the target company.
- Whether Halliburton would be held liable for postacquisition violations of the target company.

The DOJ determined that if Halliburton was to complete its anti-corruption due diligence within a 180-day period after closing the contemplated transaction, it would not be liable for any prior illegal activity associated with the new acquisition, provided it took appropriate steps to stop those activities, put in place proper controls, and ensured that no violations occurred. In detail, the steps to be taken by Halliburton were:

- Disclose to the DOJ, immediately after closing, any FCPA, corruption or internal controls, and accounting violations it discovered during preacquisition;

- Within 10 days of the closing, present a comprehensive FCPA and anti-corruption due diligence work plan, which addresses areas of risk, including use of agents and other third parties, commercial dealings with state-owned customers, joint ventures, customs and immigration matters, and governmental licenses or permits. The opinion also set priority dates for each risk category, for which Halliburton had to provide progress reports.
- Retain external counsel and third-party consultants, including forensic accountants, to conduct the anti-corruption due diligence work plan. Procedures included review of relevant records, e-mail reviews, review of financial records, and interviews of relevant personnel at the target, as well as other persons of interest.
- Disclose to the DOJ, any FCPA, corruption or internal controls and accounting violations it discovered during the 180-day postacquisition anti-corruption due-diligence plan.

During the postacquisition phase, Halliburton was also required to do the following:

- Impose its own code of conduct, FCPA and anti-corruption policies and procedures upon the target immediately after closing. Train all employees of the target on such policies and procedures within a set timetable.
- Require all agents and other third parties with which Halliburton expects to continue business to sign new contracts, which includes appropriate FCPA, anti-corruption representations and warranties and audit rights.

Although the Halliburton opinion applies only to Halliburton, it illustrates the DOJ's view regarding the significance of conducting thorough FCPA due diligence procedures. It also demonstrates the need for companies making global acquisitions to have a robust FCPA/anti-corruption due diligence process. The provisions of the Halliburton opinion should be carefully considered by all acquisitive companies and incorporated thoughtfully into the overall anti-corruption due diligence plans and procedures.

Johnson & Johnson Deferred Prosecution Agreement: Enhanced Compliance Obligations

In April 2011, J&J entered into a deferred prosecution agreement (DPA) with the DOJ, as it settled FCPA charges regarding improper payments made by J&J subsidiaries to medical professionals in Eastern Europe, and kickbacks paid to government officials in Iraq under the UN Oil for Food Program. As part of this DPA, in regard to acquisitions, J&J agreed to:

- Ensure that all acquisitions are completed after conducting thorough FCPA/anti-corruption due diligence by a team comprised of legal, accounting, and compliance. If such due diligence cannot be conducted due to applicable laws or regulations, J&J will "conduct FCPA and anti-corruption due diligence subsequent to the acquisition and report to the Department any corrupt payments, falsified books and records, or inadequate internal controls."
- Apply J&J's policies and procedures regarding anti-corruption laws to the target entity as soon as possible, no later than one year postclosing, and will:
  - Train directors, officers, employees, agents, consultants, representatives, distributors and joint venture partners on the anti-corruption laws and regulations and J&J's related policies and procedures.
  - Conduct an FCPA-specific audit of all companies acquired within 18 months of the completion of such acquisition.[3]

The timetable for J&J to conduct postclose activities appears to be more realistic than the Halliburton opinion in the context of a significant acquisition. The J&J DPA also sets out clear preclose guidelines around the expectations of the DOJ in an acquisition setting.

WHY IS ANTI-CORRUPTION DUE DILIGENCE SIGNIFICANT?

A merging or acquiring company's due diligence efforts, both before a merger or acquisition agreement is signed, as well as during any due diligence period before a transaction closes, should be structured to inquire whether or not the target company or division has been involved in any corrupt activity involving non-U.S. public officials or private persons. Discovery of fraud or a serious regulatory violation after closing is one of the fastest ways for a transaction to lose value—in some cases, potential losses can even exceed an acquirer's original investment.

Some companies have begun to take proactive steps to fast-track investigations and lay any concerns to rest. The acquirer must show that great effort was expended to ensure that current activity is lawful and that, when violations were identified, actions to address such violations were taken. Ultimately, the new parent bears the responsibility for the people, practices, and activities brought along in an acquisition, irrespective of when and where questionable action occurred.

If comprehensive preacquisition due diligence procedures are not conducted, the acquiring company exposes itself to many risks—from financial penalties, to diminution in value in the underlying investment as well as the significant costs associated with implementation of a stringent compliance program. Acquiring company becomes liable for past FCPA violations of acquired company.

If preacquisition due diligence procedures are not conducted, a company may unknowingly acquire any past violations of the target company. The exposure to risk and liability for the acquiring company is even greater if the target company was already subject to the FCPA prior to the acquisition but failed to comply with it. In transactions where the target was already under the jurisdiction of the FCPA, the U.S. government regulators naturally have higher expectations.

In addition, if preacquisition anti-corruption due diligence is conducted without following up on the questionable practices unveiled during the diligence, the acquiring company is subject to successor liability if these practices are later uncovered or continue unmonitored. During 2010, RAE Systems was ordered to pay approximately $3 million in penalties to the SEC and DOJ as a result of FCPA violations associated with corrupt payments made by two RAE joint ventures in China to Chinese government officials. Before entering into one of the joint ventures, RAE initiated anti-corruption due diligence procedures, as a result of which RAE became aware of kickbacks and undisclosed payments made by local employees. For the second joint venture, RAE did not conduct preacquisition anti-corruption due diligence despite indications of corrupt activity by employees of the entity. Subsequently, RAE voluntarily disclosed its practices.[4]

The RAE case illustrates that pre-acquisition anti-corruption due diligence is not a "check-the-box" item when assessing an acquiring company's FCPA liability. Additional anti-corruption due diligence procedures should be undertaken when red flags are uncovered for the acquiring company to be possibly exempt from liability.

Acquiring Company Becomes Liable for Ongoing FCPA Violations that Continue after Closing

A potential FCPA liability can adversely affect a merger and acquisition. A company may be held criminally liable for any pre- or postacquisition activity of the target and, as a result, endure monetary and nonmonetary repercussions. In addition to the significant fines levied by the SEC and DOJ, the acquiring company may also be prohibited from bidding for U.S. government contracts as well as contracts with international organizations, such as the World Bank, participating in any procurement or nonprocurement activity with federal agencies, or receiving export licenses. The slash to the reputation of the acquiring company associated with a corrupt target is palpable as well.

Acquiring Company Acquires and Overpays for Business Built on Corruption

During postacquisition financial integration of the Latin Node acquisition by eLandia, some irregularities were identified by eLandia in Latin Node's financial records. Following further review and analysis, eLandia determined that Latin Node had been making corrupt payments to public officials in Yemen in order to obtain and retain business. In fact, without making these payments, Latin Node was not able to conduct business in Yemen. In good faith, eLandia disclosed the illegal acts to the DOJ and the SEC, conducted an internal investigation, and took substantial corrective actions, including discontinuing all business within Yemen.[5]

Acquiring Company Inherits Corrupt Employees that May Continue to Engage in Corrupt Practices

During a global internal compliance review triggered by a discovery of improper payments in China, Avery Dennison uncovered numerous other instances in which the employees of an acquired entity, Paxar Corporation, made bribe payments totaling $51,000 to customs and other officials in Indonesia, Pakistan, and China. It was established that the Paxar employees were involved in making illegal petty cash payments to officials prior to the acquisition and continued this practice afterwards. In 2009, Avery made a voluntary disclosure of the corrupt findings, and was charged by the SEC for failing to devise and maintain adequate internal controls to detect and prevent such occurrences.[6]

The Avery case emphasizes the importance of integrating the target company and its employees soon after the acquisition is complete and ensuring that the acquiring company's policies and procedures are implemented thoroughly in the target company.

Cost of Increased Compliance Efforts at the Acquired Organization Changes the Business Case for the Deal

Traditional financial due diligence typically does not consider the impact of any costs relating to post acquisition compliance efforts that may have a significant effect on the valuation of the target. In fact, in the past few years, a number of companies have walked away from a deal or had to adjust the valuation of the target significantly to incorporate the costs relating to the considerable efforts associated with compliance implementation. Such costs don't only relate to expenses incurred, but also relate to the costs relating to the time the employees spent focusing on the implementation of compliance.

Companies contemplating acquisitions are increasingly becoming wary of the implications of the FCPA and factoring in their decision making any costs associated with potential investigation undertakings and compliance monitoring. At times, if the risks associated with an acquisition become unacceptable, including the risks that become apparent after the fact, such was in the case of eLandia's acquisition of Latin Node, the acquiring company ends up with no choice but to close down the related operations to minimize any future risks.

The Joint Venture Partner May Be Participating in Corrupt Activity

Similar to conducting thorough preacquisition anti-corruption due diligence procedures on an acquisition, companies should also consider conducting similar procedures directed toward partners with which they enter into a joint venture agreement. The FCPA and other anti-corruption laws continue to emphasize the importance of getting to know one's partner prior to entering into a business relationship. This is important, as any misconduct done by a company's partner reflects on the company itself, despite the fact the company knew nothing about it. What you should have known is key.

ITT, a U.S.-based manufacturing/engineering company through its joint venture and wholly owned subsidiary in China, NGP, was allegedly making direct and indirect payments to Chinese government officials, generating over $4 million in sales to NGP and over $1 million in improper profits to ITT. NGP allegedly disguised the payments as commissions, which were then consolidated into ITT's financial statements. As a result of an investigation, ITT agreed to pay penalties and to the disgorgement of profits.[7]

Individual Personal Liability for Directors Serving on Boards of Target/Investee Companies

It is important to remember that the directors serving on boards of target companies may be held individually liable for corrupt activity that occurred even before the acquisition of the target. Also as important is the fact that directors can be held liable for ongoing corrupt activity, even if there is no direct evidence that the directors knew about these acts. This is a high-risk area for individuals, which will no doubt receive even more attention going forward.

In summary, there are significant risks—financial, commercial, and personal—in which the acquiring company and/or its officers may find themselves, if they do not conduct thorough preacquisition anti-corruption due diligence procedures.

UNIQUE CONSIDERATIONS OF ANTI-CORRUPTION DUE DILIGENCE

Conducting due diligence procedures in a M&A leads to numerous unique factors that companies should consider. For example, similar to the Halliburton case discussed previously, there may be privacy issues within the country in which the target company is based. In addition, the target company may not be open to sharing information with external consultants. Alternatively, the target may not give access to all the documents needed or access to individuals with whom the anti-corruption due diligence team would like to speak. Each of these situations leads to significant challenges for the team conducting the anti-corruption due diligence procedures.

In connection with joint venture agreements, the anticipated percentage investment may have an effect on the extent of pre or post anti-corruption due diligence procedures that is allowed by the seller or majority partner.

Another consideration that is a unique challenge to preacquisition anti-corruption due diligence efforts relate to any potential resistance that may arise from the target. In a due diligence setting, numerous external advisers are present and request information from the target company, including access to systems, documents, as well as access to target company employees. Requests from a variety of external advisers that focus on a variety of different topics may often cause disruption to routine operations of the target company. In order to minimize such disruptions and the perception that the anti-corruption due diligence procedures are duplicative, the anti-corruption due diligence team should work closely and simultaneously with the other advisers who are focusing on financial due diligence. Working together with other teams also makes the deadlines easier to achieve, as in an acquisition setting, the deadlines are usually tight. In summary, preacquisition anti-corruption procedures should not be an afterthought.

When these factors are present and they prohibit the deal team from conducting a comprehensive and meaningful preacquisition anti-corruption due diligence, thorough due diligence should be conducted immediately post closing. Commonly, the parties to the transaction sign a letter of intent discussing postclosing procedures. These procedures should be carefully devised to follow a written work plan outlining the scope of the postacquisition anti-corruption due diligence and any potential liability that may result from it. In the Halliburton opinion, for example, the DOJ required Halliburton to also disclose if it was aware of any corruption red flags at the target prior to closing. Protocols surrounding disclosure and reporting of issues noted preclosing and postclosing should be stipulated in the letter of intent.

If the target company did not previously have a strong anti-corruption compliance program, the letter of intent should also describe a postclosing compliance policy to be implemented by the target in order to bring it up to par with the compliance control environment of the acquiring company.

Due Diligence Team and Timing of Procedures

The team conducting the preacquisition anti-corruption due diligence should be a multidisciplinary team, comprised of individuals from different backgrounds, including attorneys and forensic accountants (deal team). It is crucial that the team work together in all phases of the process: this enables the focus of the process to be broader versus a purely legal or a purely accounting one.

In order to minimize any disruptions to the target company's operations, the anti-corruption due diligence procedures should be conducted at the same time as financial due diligence procedures. This would reduce duplication of information that will be provided by the target company.

Phases of Anti-Corruption Due Diligence

As each business transaction is unique, a work plan should be tailored to the specific risks of the transaction.

It is important for the acquiring companies not to restrict their anti-corruption due diligence procedures to the obvious areas or targets. At a minimum, companies may conduct the following steps in a phased approach to identify any past FCPA violations and unacceptable conduct or practices by the target company.

Phase 1: Corruption Risk Assessment

A key step in performing anti-corruption due diligence is understanding the corruption risks of the target. This process is similar to the discussion in Chapter 6, "Risk Assessments;" however, there are some unique aspects to performing a risk assessment in a deal setting.

Obtain High-Level Understanding of Target Company's Operations
Gathering an understanding of the target company's operations is the first step in a risk assessment. This includes understanding the industry and the countries in which the target operates. Such an analysis should be focused not only on the physical locations of the target company business, but on the country location of each of their customers.

Some industries are perceived to have inherent risks, mostly due to the locations in which they operate or the levels of interaction companies working in this industry have with public officials. For example, life sciences, energy, financial services, defense contracting, and freight-forwarding industries are perceived to be of higher risk.

If business is conducted in countries with low ratings in the annual Transparency International's Corruption Perceptions Index, the deal team should consider doing a more detailed review, focusing on these countries.

Also focusing on these countries, higher scrutiny should be applied when reviewing certain areas such as gifts, travel and entertainment, charitable contributions, and concessions. Should the business deal allow for flexible timing, the acquiring company should consider in-country interviews, bringing in both local resources who understand the culture and U.S. experts that are familiar with the risks associated with the FCPA and other bribery and corruption laws.

As a result of corrupt activities by a target company the developing nations promise strong growth in several sectors, high costs to clean up or close operations may make a strong case for the acquiring company to walk away from the deal.

Analyze Target's Anti-Corruption Policies/Procedure Gathering an understanding of the target company's approach to anti-corruption as part of its overall compliance program is an important step. Lack of a compliance program, anti-corruption policies or procedures, communication, and training of their employees and agents may increase the risk of misconduct taking place. In addition, lack of a whistle-blower hotline or procedures on how to conduct an investigation of the matters arising from such a hotline also increases the risk of a misconduct occurring without being noticed.

Accordingly, the deal team should obtain and review the sufficiency of anti-corruption policies and procedures and the training activities relating to these policies. An important step in this review is for the deal team to familiarize itself with the local anti-corruption laws and regulations. For example, in countries such as Thailand and Taiwan, gifts to public officials during holidays or for other occasions are acceptable if they do not exceed a certain monetary threshold. In other countries, the local laws are less directive, leaving it up to the companies to set their own standards. Recognition of these nuances and whether they are in the wide reach of the FCPA or U.K. Bribery Act is of essence when concluding on the adequacy of the target's anti-corruption policies and procedures.

Understanding the effectiveness of the whistle-blower hotlines is important to the overall anti-corruption due diligence process. In some companies, management indicates that though there is no anonymous hotline, employees know to reach out to the CEO, should there be a need. This may not give the employees the feeling of anonymity, should they need to report a possible issue. In addition, some companies, though they have a hotline structure in place, these hotlines are either not advertised in local languages, not monitored, or there is no process in place in regard to handling of reports. The potential lack of awareness regarding the reporting structure or the lack of anonymity increase the risks that the misconduct may not be reported, even if noticed.

Similarly important is obtaining an understanding of the overall compliance structure of the target company in regard to other compliance issues, including anti-money laundering, export controls (e.g., conducting business in sanctioned countries).

Conduct Public Searches of Target Company's Foreign Subsidiaries and Third-Party Intermediaries Conducting background searches on the target company, its executives and subsidiaries as well as all third-party intermediaries is an important step of the preacquisition due diligence process, one that should not be overlooked. Similar to the Level I diligence discussed in Chapter 5, the background checks should be conducted on the target itself and its management, key officers and shareholders, from publicly available resources and to include review of any negative news.

Negative findings identified relating to the target company or any persons associated with the target should be considered in the final risk evaluation of the target company.

Special considerations include situations where the target company and its subsidiaries or intermediaries cannot be identified in any of the compliance or news databases. Though this should not automatically raise alarm bells, the deal team should consider conducting additional procedures for the entities that have not been identified. These procedures can include going to the local court or commercial registries to review the registration documents. One item to review in these documents is the nature of the service registered: for example, a travel agency should be registered to perform travel services, and not other types of services.

Conduct Interviews of Key Executives at Target Company's Locations
After gathering a high level understanding of the target company's operations and locations, the next step should be to hold interviews with key executives of the target. Areas to cover during these interviews may include: target's business from state-owned entities; areas in which the target may have high levels of interaction with government officials; the extent with which the target uses third-party intermediaries; compliance structure of the target company, including the existence of anti-corruption policies or procedures and their enforcement; and previous instances of corrupt activity and how they were resolved.

It is important to hold interviews with various departments within the business units. It is also important that these interviews be conducted individually, whenever possible, as opposed to in a group setting, where it is possible that the subject of the interview may be intimidated or hesitant to speak openly. The due diligence team at a minimum should hold interviews with the chief executive officer, chief financial officer, chief operations officer, sales executive, and general counsel of the target company. In some cases, where timing or access to employees of the target is limited, the deal team may be able to conduct only two to three interviews. In these situations, relevant individuals that can provide the most information about the target and its operations should be selected for interviews.

This is different than a traditional financial due diligence in that the interviews are conducted with individuals with a good understanding of the business operations, and interactions with government officials/entities and the extent with which third parties are used. Again, to the extent possible, in order to obtain a more thorough understanding of the operations, the interviews should be conducted in private and separately. Suggested topics to cover and follow-up as appropriate can include:

- Introduction of the interview team and the purpose of the interview.
- Background responsibilities of the interviewee.
- Discussion of business unit operations.
- Overall climate of corruption in the country including dealing with the government.
- Business dealings with government entities, including individuals, institutions, and/or state-owned enterprises.
- Use of third-party intermediaries.
- Culture of gift giving in the country and the company.
- Process and controls surrounding:
    - Accounts payable and expenses
        - Cash and petty cash
        - Employee expense reporting and disbursements
        - Payroll
        - Political and charitable gift giving
    - FCPA and other anti-corruption regulation compliance activities, including code of conduct, training, and so on.

It is important to note that each interview should be tailored according to the industry and the country in which the target company operates, and the responsibilities of the individual being interviewed. For example, if the target company is a pharmaceuticals company, it is most appropriate to discuss the levels of interaction the company has with health care professionals (e.g., doctors, pharmacists, nurses, etc.), whom are considered to be government officials in some countries, if they work for state-owned hospitals or clinics. The goal of the interviews is to understand as much as possible about the target company's operations, business, and levels of interactions with government officials—directly or indirectly through the use of third-party intermediaries. It is also important to obtain an understanding around the compliance structure as well as the financial controls around disbursements.

Understand the Role of Third-Party Intermediaries Utilized by the Target Company Third-party intermediaries are one of the highest bribery and corruption risk areas. Any misconduct by these intermediaries reflects directly on the company, willful ignorance is not considered to be a defense. What it comes down to is: a company needs to know who its associates are and who is representing them in the marketplace. Again, what a company knows is equally important as what a company should have known.

It is very common for companies to work with third-party intermediaries in a variety of areas. These intermediaries represent the company in sales transactions, or assist the company in a variety of circumstances, including obtaining permits, providing logistics services, dealing with customs clearance, handling disputes with government authorities or merely providing consulting services. If the right one is hired, these intermediaries will have knowledge of the industry, local laws, and culture and will assist the company in a variety of situations.

Accordingly, during the preacquisition anti-corruption due diligence phase, the deal team should inquire about:

- The extent of third-party intermediaries used by the target company.
- The nature of services provided by these intermediaries.
- How the third-party intermediaries are identified and retained.
- Types of background checks conducted prior to entering into a contract with them (reference checks? reputational checks?).
- Their interaction with government officials and entities.
- Their compensation structure.
- Existence of written contracts and whether they include the relevant provisions, including anti-corruption provisions, audit rights, and termination clauses.
- Monitoring of these third-party intermediaries.

If thorough third-party due diligence and background checks have not been conducted by the target before entering into contracts with a third party, an acquiring company may unwittingly enter into a partnership with an entity who does not have a good reputation or one with strong ties to the government (or an actual government official or a politically exposed person), which would, of course, increase the risks associated with the FCPA and other bribery and corruption laws. Third-party due diligence is discussed further in Chapter 5, "Policies and Procedures."

Identify Potential "Red Flags"   At the end of Phase 1, and as a result of the procedures discussed previously, potential "red flags" may be identified associated with the target company. These are dealt with during Phase 2, and example red flags include:

- Target company or joint venture partner related to a government official.
- Refusal to certify compliance with bribery and corruption laws.

- Excessive use of cash.
- Lack of transparency for particular transactions.
- Unexplained increases in sales or profits in a particular region or business line.
- Payment made from out-of-country sources or payments made to out-of-country bank accounts.
- Excessive use of and/or fees paid to third-party intermediaries dealing with government agencies.
- Travel expenses for customers, particularly government customers, for which there is no legitimate business purpose.
- Charitable contributions to an organization with an affiliation with a government official, customer, or representative.

Phase 2: Anti-Corruption Due Diligence Procedures

Depending on the severity of the red flags identified in Phase I, additional anti-corruption due diligence procedures may be warranted. Such additional procedures could include the following.

Interviews   During the first phase, high-level interviews with key executives were conducted. Though key executives usually have a good view of how the company operates and the policies and procedures at a high level, they usually do not have detailed knowledge on how the procedures are implemented and work on a daily basis in practice, especially at other locations within the country.

This phase should include a more detailed approach in regard to interviews, and during this phase, individuals that are "on the ground" should be interviewed. These individuals may include the finance manager, who reviews and approves payments to third-party intermediaries; the controller, who may know how certain transactions are recorded in the financial systems; or the operations manager, who may have interaction with the customs brokers on a day-to-day basis. In some situations, it may even be beneficial to have an interview with the office secretary or the office clerk who is in charge of going to government entities to obtain permits or licenses.

Transaction Records Analysis   After identifying areas of high risk (e.g., third-party intermediaries, commission payments, success fees, finder's fees, payments to third-party intermediaries, consulting fees, custom brokerage fees, gifts, charitable contributions, or travel and entertainment), the deal team conducts forensic accounting procedures, designed to detect misconduct or potential violations of FCPA or other anti-corruption regulations.

Ideally, the transaction records review is performed in conjunction with employee interviews. Information obtained from interviews can impact the focus of which transaction records to review and vice versa. Examples of suggested and common types of records to review include:

- Customer/vendor files and related transaction activity.
- Business interactions with government entities.
- Interactions with customs, tax, and regulatory officials.
- Cash and petty cash activity.
- Travel, gifts, and entertainment expenses.
- Charitable contributions.
- Controls around cash and disbursements.

Sources of information should not only be limited to accounting support, but should also include other documents, for example, contracts, board minutes, internal audit reports, and so on. The deal team should inquire about the existence of and review external audit reports, internal audit reports, or internal investigation reports for relevant information,

The review of such transactions may bring up additional red flags that may need to be investigated further. For example, during review of petty cash, small, monthly payments to government officials may be identified. These may be explained as facilitating payments: though facilitating payments are allowable under the FCPA, the U.K. Bribery Act does not allow them. In addition, the definition of facilitation payments represents a gray area, which can easily be abused.

Another example of findings as a result of transactions review could be the identification of high expenditures relating to gifts, travel, or entertainment of government officials. Though it is normal business practice to invite a representative of a customer (who can be a representative of a government entity) to visit the company's facilities, utmost attention should be paid to ensure that the customer representative—a government official in this case—does not receive lavish travel or entertainment. Providing accommodations at five-star hotels, meals at expensive restaurants, or golf outings may not justify the purpose of the business trip and may be perceived as having a corrupt intent.

Though identification of such transactions certainly raises red flags, equally important is the way transactions are treated in the books and records of the company. The FCPA's books and records provisions require an SEC registrant make and keep records in accurate detail and in a way that they fairly reflect the nature of the transaction—and this applies to all expenditures, regardless of materiality and the involvement of a government official.

Identification of transactions with no supporting documentation or incorrect recording in the company's accounting system may increase the red flags regarding the internal controls, policies, and the overall culture at the company.

Phase 3: Enhanced Procedures Surrounding Identified Red Flags

Red flags can be identified during any stage of an anti-corruption due diligence. However, it is important to keep in mind that a red flag that was identified during the anti-corruption due diligence procedures does not necessarily mean that the target company has corrupt activity. A red flag is rather an indicator of a potential risk that a corrupt activity may be taking place.

Accordingly, the red flags identified during anti-corruption due diligence procedures need to be resolved prior to proceeding with the contemplated transaction. Resolution of these red flags should be documented properly. This is especially important, as should there be any future problems, the regulators would be interested in finding out about the underlying documentation of the procedures performed, what was discovered, and how the identified potential risks were resolved.

If the acquiring company identifies significant red flags, which it is not able to resolve in a timely manner before the closing of the acquisition, the acquiring company is left with a business decision around whether to proceed with the acquisition. To reiterate, having red flags is not a complete indicator of systematic corruption in the target company; however, each unresolved red flag should be further discussed among the anti-corruption team to address the potential risks to which they may expose the acquiring company.

If the acquiring company decides to go forward with the acquisition, all red flags should be resolved or addressed immediately after closing. In these instances, documentation of the resolution of red flags is key—the acquiring company should make every effort to ensure that the findings and the handling of these findings are appropriately recorded and documented.

Phase 4: Development of Postclosing Compliance Program

Once a deal has closed, the acquiring company should ensure that its anti-corruption compliance program is implemented by the target company in a timely manner. Additionally, as discussed earlier, any red flags identified during due diligence that were not adequately resolved should be fully addressed and the resolution documented.

Key considerations during the postclosing compliance program can include:

- Designating officers responsible for oversight of bribery and corruption monitoring and compliance.
- Reinforcing significant policies, such as documentation standards, travel and entertainment, gift and charitable giving, code of conduct, whistle-blower process, and so on.
- Conducting FCPA and other anti-corruption regulation specific audits on red flags.
- Increase transparency with third-party intermediary dealings.

Anti-corruption training is one of the most effective and important elements of the postclosing compliance program. These training sessions should be conducted with employees based on their risk level (e.g, whether they interact with third parties or government officials/entities) in live training sessions. It is important to provide training sessions customized to the individuals being trained, for example, employees from the finance department should receive detailed training in books and records and internal controls.

Conducting anti-corruption audits is an important element in the monitoring process, through which the effectiveness and the progress of the implementation of postclosing compliance can be documented. As a result of these anti-corruption audits, new risk areas or concerns can also be identified on a timely basis.

The preceding elements of the anti-corruption compliance program are discussed fully in Chapters 4, 5, 6 and 7.

WHAT TO DO WHEN VIOLATIONS ARE FOUND DURING ANTI-CORRUPTION DUE DILIGENCE

An area that the companies need to consider is the steps that the deal team will need to take, when faced with instances of corruption identified at the target company. Accordingly, protocols need to be in place prior to the start of the due diligence activity. Legal counsel should always be included in these findings.

Depending on the nature of the findings, companies can choose to conduct an internal investigation and may consider disclosing the matter to the SEC or DOJ voluntarily. Such a decision is one that will need to be taken by the target company and its counsel, as though the FCPA does not mandate disclosure, cooperation and voluntary disclosure of wrongdoing implies a good-faith effort by the acquiring company to remediate any issues and may partially mitigate any criminal or civil penalties imposed by the SEC or DOJ. The acquiring company may have confidentiality requirements in place that preclude disclosure and legal counsel should be consulted in these situations.

If corrupt activity identified during an acquisition was not disclosed to the government and appropriate steps to deal with this activity was not taken postacquisition, and if this issue is discovered by the government, the consequences and penalties associated with the misconduct may be more severe than if they were voluntarily disclosed initially. Accordingly, voluntary disclosures should be prompt and timely and occur before the regulatory agencies become aware of the FCPA violation through other channels, such as whistle-blowers or the media.

However, if a specific corrupt activity is not identified, and rather instances of lack of internal controls or compliance procedures are noted in the target company, the acquiring company should ensure to implement its own compliance structure on the target company as soon as the acquisition is completed. Among other things, the compliance structure should include training of the employees of the target company in a timely manner in order to raise awareness.

After spending significant amounts of time, resources, and money on conducting a preacquisition due diligence, deciding to walk away from a deal may be one of the toughest decisions. However, this may be the only option available to an acquiring company that has conducted a thorough preacquisition due diligence, only to find that the target company that it is about to acquire was one that was built on corruption.

 SUMMARY

Bribery and corruption risks and issues can be a compelling reason to walk away from a deal. Companies must identify and understand the exposure that an acquisition may bring, and only through robust anti-corruption due diligence procedures can this be done effectively. In some cases, the business reasons may trump the corruption issues, when this is the case performing an investigation postclosing is the critical next step to an effective anti-corruption compliance program.

 NOTES

1. DOJ Opinions 84-02, 03-01, 04-02, 08-01, and 08-02.
2. www.justice.gov/criminal/fraud/fcpa/opinion/2008/0802.pdf.
3. www.justice.gov/criminal/fraud/fcpa/cases/depuy-inc/04-08-11depuy-dpa
.pdf.
4. www.justice.gov/opa/pr/2010/December/10-crm-1428.html.
5. www.justice.gov/criminal/fraud/fcpa/cases/litton-applied/04-03-09latinnode-
govt-sent.pdf.
6. www.sec.gov/litigation/admin/2009/34-60393.pdf.
7. www.sec.gov/litigation/litreleases/2009/lr20896.htm.

CHAPTER NINE

Investigations

THE FINAL PART OF an anti-corruption compliance program is the reactive element, which includes the process for responding to red flags and allegations of bribery and corruption. Refer to Figure 9.1.

The investigation into these issues can be complex and include visits to remote regions of the world where corruption is high and the focus is often getting business without consideration of any other consequences. Investigations are complex and it is possible to devote an entire book to this topic. In fact, you can refer to "The Guide to Investigating Business Fraud" by the professionals of Ernst & Young LLP for further information.

This chapter focuses on the basic elements of an investigation with specific focus on bribery and corruption investigation issues. The basic steps of an investigation are generally consistent across all types of financial investigations. Figure 9.2 shows the key steps of an incident response plan.

A trigger event such as a red flag in a risk assessment or a whistle-blower starts the process. The allegation goes through triage to evaluate its credibility and formulate the initial plan. The allegation is responded to through a series of steps to either prove or refute the allegations. The investigation's

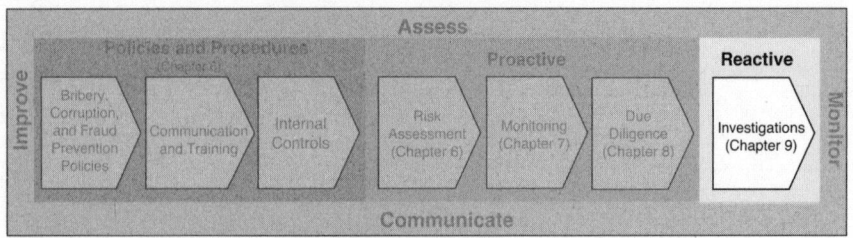

FIGURE 9.1 Anti-Corruption Compliance Program

ultimate goal is to determine if an issue exists and the details of the events. The results of the investigation are ultimately reported on and the resolution of the issue is documented. Depending on the results of the investigation remediation may be required.

 TRIGGER EVENTS

Allegations of fraud and corruption come to light from trigger events in many forms, some of which are more credible than others, for example, a negative internal audit report typically carries more weight than an e-mail from a disgruntled former employee. While trigger events tend to be sudden such as a call to a whistle-blower hotline or a subpoena from the Securities and Exchange Commission (SEC), there are also trigger events that are developed over an extended period of time such as spikes in the level of expenses submitted around bid submission times. Trigger events can also be identified through the functioning of internal controls such as management review of the addition of a new agent to the vendor master file. Following are some of the more common external and internal trigger events:

FIGURE 9.2 Incident Response Plan

	Trigger Event	Summary	Examples
INTERNAL	Whistleblower	Employee reports a potential violation through the whistle-blower process.	Payment being made to a vendor to secure a contract.
	Internal Audit/Corporate Compliance Reports	Through a routine audit, areas of risk can be identified.	T&E abuses: Substantial use of cash with limited supporting documentation.
	Exception reports and data analytics	Violations of internal controls are identified or unusual data patterns.	Someone may exceed an authorization limit or multiple payments to the same vendor on the same day may trigger an exception alert that gets acted upon.
	Management review	Periodic reviews by management may identify potentially problematic areas that require follow-up.	Risk assessment Due diligence Contract review
	Exit interviews	As part of the normal exit interview process an employee may cite a particular practice that requires follow-up.	Reason for departure could be pressure to pay bribes.
	Regular operations	Business practices in different geographies can vary significantly and employees may not be aware that they are involved in a problematic practice.	Rotating employees between locations can help to identify the problematic practices; however, in some cases this can spread the practices.
EXTERNAL	Whistle-blower	Third party reports a potential violation through a company's whistle-blower process.	Competitor who loses contract because they refused to pay a bribe.
	Subpoena/Wells notice/ Information request from regulator	Certain industries are more susceptible than others. Regulators have stepped up investigatory proceedings by issuing subpoenas against U.S. companies and sometimes these have a knock-on effect to various industries and companies.	Regulators have focused on several industries over past few years, including medical devices, freight forwarding, oil services, and the financial services sectors.
	Auditor	Under Section 10A of the Securities Exchange Act an auditor is required to take certain actions when information that indicates that an illegal act, whether or not material to the issuer's financial statements, has or may have occurred.	Identification of kickback scheme.

CASESTUDY: STEEL COMPANY INC.

Continuing the Steel Company Inc. case study, during the risk assessment the forensic accounting team identified an unusual commission payment to an agent in Country D, which was elevated to the attention of general counsel. The commission pertained to the agent's services rendered in connection to identifying a lead and subsequently negotiating a contract with a private prominent investor for a shopping mall renovation project.

The 2009 project entailed the construction of a new wing and modernizing it to surpass the façade and interior of the region's newest shopping center. Steel Company was one of the contractors hired by the investor to design steel structures. Steel Company paid the agent a 25 percent commission based on the value of the contract between Steel Company and the investor. The forensic accounting team learned in follow-up interviews that Steel Company would typically pay agents in Country D commissions ranging from 10 percent to 15 percent of the value of the contract. The forensic accountants appropriately classified the transaction as a "red flag" and alerted the general counsel.

 ## TRIAGE

Triage serves as the filtering process where an allegation is reviewed and the initial response plan is formulated. It is important to consider the seriousness of the allegation and if it should be escalated to the audit committee immediately or if there is time to gain a better understanding. Consideration should also be given to the need for involvement of internal or outside counsel.

How to Respond to an Allegation

The first step to responding to an allegation of improper activity should be for management to conduct an objective assessment of the credibility and seriousness of an allegation. This is effectively a filtering process that management must go through to determine and to effectively triage the company's actions and is an essential step to ensure that the level of the company's response is both appropriate and proportionate. The credibility and seriousness should be continually evaluated as additional facts and circumstances come to light; however, in most cases the company will need to make the initial determinations before all or even most of the facts are known.

If the credibility or seriousness of the allegation is overstated, the company's response will tend to be too heavy handed (e.g., too broad in scope or too detailed). This can significantly increase the costs and time to complete an investigation as resources are dedicated to performing unnecessary tasks and analyses. However, if the credibility or seriousness of an allegation is understated, the company's response is likely to be insufficient, and can result in continued violations by the company with no understanding of the extent of the problem.

The costs to the company of understating the issue could also be significant if the company needs to subsequently restate its financial statements or the level of the company's response becomes a significant factor for the regulators when they are looking to levy fines.

	Examples	
	Too Light	**Too Heavy**
Response	Insufficient resources utilized to investigate matter.	Full investigation without scoping aligned with initial allegation.
	Local management's word taken that there is no issue.	Review of all transactions over an extensive period of time rather than "smarter" review based on analyses of transaction data.
	Investigation team not given appropriate access to information and personnel to assess allegation.	E-mail review performed as a fishing exercise rather than as a controlled and targeted review.
	Issues identified but steps not taken to understand extent of issues.	A look at everything approach rather than following fact patterns.

How to Determine the Credibility of an Allegation of Bribery or Corruption

To determine the credibility of an allegation of bribery or corruption, a company should gather and assess what it knows about the allegation and consider its consistency with known facts. When determining the credibility of the allegation it is good practice to, where possible, revert to the source of the allegation to clarify the company's understanding of the allegation and to seek additional information. As a general rule of thumb, more detailed allegations tend to be more credible. The inverse, however, tends not to be true, as a vague allegation does not necessarily lessen the credibility of the allegation. This is often the case when there are language or cultural differences. For example, a whistle-blower call to a fraud hotline by a Japanese executive is not so common given the social stigma in Japanese culture of being a whistle-blower and as a result the nature of the allegation may be quite vague or distorted.

Given that allegations are not always clearly articulated particularly if the allegation comes from a disgruntled employee or third party, management will need to dissect and aggregate the various points being made to identify the real issue. For example, a call to a whistle-blower hotline from a disgruntled employee could appear to be of a personal nature but stem from jealousy that a colleague is joining government customers on an all expenses paid trip.

When dealing with a whistle-blower claim it is important to make the whistle-blower comfortable that his or her allegations are taken seriously. For example, if they are willing, speak with the whistle-blower and have them confirm the understanding of the allegation. Ambiguous points such as how to spell an unusual name or the relevant timing of a transaction should be clarified. The whistle-blower may also have additional information regarding who was involved or who is likely to have knowledge of the facts or issues and may be able to provide documentation to support the allegation.

The level of credibility would be heightened if the allegation is reasonable, detailed, and consistent with known facts about the business. For example, there would be a high level of credibility associated with an allegation that Ministry of Defense officials were recently given expensive vacations as a *quid pro quo* for signing a new contract if a new contract has recently been signed and there has been an unexplained spike in travel expenses.

Similarly, the credibility of an issue may be lessened if there are known facts that are inconsistent with the actual allegation. For example, there should be a lower level of credibility attributed to an allegation that kickback payments are being made to fictitious vendor, if internal audit has just completed a clean vendor audit of that vendor or if the company ceased doing business with that vendor several years earlier.

However, even if there is only limited credibility attributed to an allegation, some limited steps should be considered to satisfy the company that the allegation is without merit. In this example, the company could review the work conducted by internal audit to ensure that the steps conducted by internal audit would have addressed the allegation and conduct additional procedures as necessary, such as a review of the transaction history with the vendor.

It is important to note that, until the last few years, internal audit has tended to focus more on quantitative transaction analytics and rarely focused on assessing the substance of a transaction. Historically, this has resulted in clean vendor audits being common for agents and other vendors that significantly inflated their invoices provided that they produced all relevant paperwork (e.g., contracts, invoices, and delivery notes).

Who Should Determine the Credibility of an Allegation?

Some companies have developed processes for evaluating fraud allegations as and when they arise. This allows for a consistent approach in the treatment of all allegations. To ensure a consistent approach, these companies should follow their internal fraud protocols to evaluate Foreign Corrupt Practices Act of 1977 (FCPA) allegations provided that the evaluation process has been designed to:

- Include a qualitative assessment of the potential FCPA issue rather than a simple quantitative assessment of a fraud incident.
- Ensure that any materiality considerations do not affect potentially serious matters being elevated appropriately within the company.

Depending on the nature of the allegation, it is likely that several persons or departments within the company may need to be consulted, such as internal audit, finance, human resources, information technology, security, and senior management from the business. It is good practice to have previously socialized fraud protocols within the company and to consult with forensic accountants and outside counsel that have been retained by the company as independent consultants.

The company should designate a person with ultimate responsibility within the company with the necessary professional expertise and authority to be able to conduct an initial evaluation of the allegation and to agree the relevant investigative steps required to address the issue. It is good practice to have the investigative function centrally managed. Given the nature of the FCPA, it is typical for this person to be the general counsel or chief compliance officer or a subject matter specialist within their department. In practice, the head of internal audit or even the CEO/CFO may be responsible.

No matter who is ultimately appointed responsible for the investigative function, it is important that the person and their department are not implicated by the allegation. If this is the case, the company should seek to appoint another person not implicated within the company or a non–executive director or instruct forensic accountants and outside counsel to manage the investigative process with direct reporting to the board of directors or audit committee. For example if the CFO is accused of falsifying records to hide a kickback scheme, the CFO should not be part of the decision making of the investigation or be directly within the line of reporting.

Depending on the severity of the allegation, consideration should be given to involving the audit committee and the company's external auditors. However, this notification would generally take place after the process for preliminarily assessing the credibility of the allegation has taken place.

Initial Determination of the Credibility and Seriousness of an Allegation

If the company determines that the allegation is credible, then it should take immediate steps to preserve relevant data and information and launch an investigation. If, however, having gone through these steps, the company is uncertain or believes that there is very limited credibility of the allegation, the company should take reasonable steps to preserve any relevant data and information and should perform immediate actions to better understand the credibility of an issue. Reasonable steps could include inter alia, a review of transactional data, a review of customer/vendor correspondence, or interviews of key employees.

CASESTUDY: STEEL COMPANY INC.

General counsel first identified and proceeded to gather more information from the key employees involved in the shopping mall renovation project. The employees indicated they had no explanation for the higher commission percentage, the general counsel also instructed internal audit to accumulate all files and documentation to understand the nature of the transaction and in particular, how the commission percentage was determined. Internal audit reviewed the documentation and reported that no support for the commission calculation could be located. Internal audit followed up with the accounts payable manager who had no further information on the calculation but relayed that the commission percentage was higher than usual because this was a special project procured through a new agent.

Given the preliminary interview with the accounts payable manager and the information gathered by internal audit, general counsel recognized a potential FCPA issue and placed a call to Steel Company's external counsel. Under the direction of external counsel, general counsel obtained the due diligence documentation on this agent from the sourcing department. The files indicated that the agent had connections with the municipal council, although they did not make it clear how this relationship affected the negotiation or execution of the contract with the private investor. It seemed that there were a lot of ambiguities and question marks around the transaction, which prompted the company to instruct external counsel to undertake a more extensive investigation. With authorization from general counsel, external counsel retained the forensic accounting firm, previously involved in the FCPA risk assessment, to assist with the investigation.

The issue of whether an allegation actually falls within the remit of the FCPA or the U.K. Bribery Act, for example, whether a government official is involved or if there is a nexus to the United States or United Kingdom, is usually less of a consideration in the early stages of an investigation as management still has a fiduciary obligation to investigate any fraudulent activity. As discussed earlier in the book, the U.S. Department of Justice (DOJ) and Securities and Exchange Commission (SEC) have been very aggressive in asserting the jurisdictional reach of the FCPA and the Serious Fraud Office (SFO) has signaled that they will do the same with the U.K. Bribery Act.

Additionally, if there is fraudulent activity, that activity will likely be recorded incorrectly in the company's books and records and be a violation of the books and records provision and internal controls provision of the FCPA. Consultation with forensic accountants and outside counsel experienced in FCPA matters is critical in the early stages for evaluating the issue and the applicability of the FCPA.

Given that there is no materiality under the FCPA and every transaction is potentially subject to the FCPA, the magnitude of the allegation should not be considered when determining the credibility of the allegation, although it should be considered when assessing the proportionality of the response and setting the investigative scope. For example, an allegation that government officials received gifts when they attended a recent conference may require less of a response if the gifts in question were pens bearing the company's logo that were specifically purchased for the event through a regular and well-controlled procurement process. The allegation may however still be investigated. Refer to Chapter 5, "Policies and Procedures," for further details.

If the company subsequently determines that the allegation is not credible, it is important that the basis for this conclusion is sound and adequately supported. Documenting the initial assessment is an important step to demonstrate to both internal and external stakeholders that the response to the allegation was performed in an adequate and consistent manner. The documentation should clearly indicate the allegation, relevant facts and circumstances considered, individuals consulted, information collected, and conclusion reached and should also include the proposed next steps.

 ## RESPONSE

The response is the most complex and difficult of all reactive elements. Once the allegation has been vetted and further action is required, the key steps are to launch an investigation, preserve and review evidence, perform a forensic accounting review, conduct interviews, and report to the key stakeholders. The following section covers each of these elements in depth to give an understanding of how an investigation might take place and the then needed steps. Each investigation is unique so the facts and circumstances will dictate how most of the procedures within the framework discussed ahead are performed.

Launching an Investigation

When an allegation has been determined to be credible, the company should immediately focus on launching the investigation. Planning is key as it forms the bases of the investigation and the initial planning should include:

- Assemble the investigation team
- Determine the scope of the investigation
- Define the investigative work plan

These steps should be completed swiftly and revisited during the course of the investigation to ensure that they are appropriately aligned with the issues.

Assemble the Investigation Team

When assembling the investigation team consideration should be give to the following:

- Who should lead the investigation?
- Should the investigation be performed under privilege?

- What is the optimal composition of the investigation team?
- Who should the investigation team report to?

A leading practice for the investigations is for the audit committee or special investigation committee to retain independent counsel to lead the investigation team. This provides added protection for all constituents and helps to the extent possible to prevent criticism on the back end of alleged impaired independence. This is also important because this may protect the investigation under attorney-client privilege and the work product doctrine and may assist the company in preserving all of the legal rights associated with such a relationship.

If the audit committee or special investigation committee decides to go forth without independent counsel, then an alternative lead might be appointed. This individual can be internal counsel, the chief internal auditor, or a member of the audit committee. This individual should serve the role to protect independence between management, the audit committee, and the investigation team and to address any concerns or updates between the investigation team and the audit committee.

Depending on the allegation the investigation team could include a number of stakeholders from various departments within the company. The following table sets out who from a company may be involved in the investigation and their potential role:

Department	Potential Role in Investigation
Audit/Special Investigation Committee	Ultimate ownership of investigation and related remediation.
Executive Management	Project sponsorship to encourage cooperation and set proper tone.
Legal/Compliance/ Internal Audit	Review the initial allegation and determine first steps, carry out investigative procedures or support for external members.
Business Unit Management	Encourage cooperation during fieldwork.
Human Resources	Identify employment history of employees implicated in allegation.
Information Technology	Assistance with understanding of IT infrastructure including structured and unstructured data. Assist with data extractions.
Corporate Security	Securing evidence, carry out investigative procedures, or support for external members.

When determining whom to involve in the investigation, the objectivity of certain personnel within the company may be impaired by personal or business interests. Additionally, in-house counsel or others may potentially be involved in the matter or may be friends with and/or report to the "wrongdoers."

External Parties   Retaining outside counsel can provide the specialized legal guidance of a white-collar investigation specialist and also provide attorney-client privilege protections. Additionally, forensic accountants are often engaged to review the financial side of an investigation, which is very often a key part of understanding the allegation and identifying other problematic activity.

Attorneys and forensic accountants should be selected based on their qualifications and also their previous or ongoing interactions with the company and the parties involved. Complications arise when there is lack of independence or transparency between the company, suspected parties, and the attorneys, and accounting firm. Lack of transparency and independence is undoubtedly an area of concern as information exchange and confidentiality might be compromised during the investigation. When the investigation is led by professionals from outside the organization it helps to demonstrate to regulators that the company has taken the allegation seriously and the

COMMUNICATION PROTOCOLS

Communications protocols between the parties are important to the investigation. A formal protocol for communications should be established prior to the investigation so that proper information can be sent to the correct individuals and to not compromise any confidentiality. The audit committee might request updates once a week, which need to be reviewed by its compliance and legal department. Likewise, the audit committee or compliance department might want to use code words and verbiage to mask the sensitive and confidential information. These protocols should be established early on to allow all parties to understand and communicate effectively.

These protocols should also be extended to the investigation team, which could include communication between the forensic accounting team and legal counsel team. Since both teams are working in conjunction, and often on separate areas, the communication between the two teams should follow established protocols. This will keep the teams updated and avoid miscommunication.

investigative parties have greater objectivity. Additionally, by engaging those who work primarily in the area of focus, the investigation will be more likely to identify the issues quickly. Multinational law firms and accounting firms also have resources spread across the world who can quickly access foreign locations and bring with them the knowledge of local business practices.

Determine the Scope of the Investigation

Once the team has been established or after the investigation leader has been identified, establishing the scope for the investigation is the next critical step. Setting the scope provides the team with direction, sets boundaries for the investigation, and helps to control the overall cost of the investigation. Depending on the nature of the allegation, the scope could be very narrow or very broad.

The scope should be based on the allegation and if new information is found during the course of the investigation the scope should be revised as a result. For example, an investigation may start out with an allegation related to one business unit within the company and, as the investigation evolves, it could become clear that the employee who was the ring leader had transferred six months earlier to a similar role in another business unit. In such a case, it may be appropriate to conduct some limited procedures at the employee's new business unit to ensure that the employee is not engaged in similar activity at the new business unit.

When setting the scope, the team needs to consider several key questions which can be thought about at the fundamental level of who, what, where, when, how, and why.

Scoping Questions		Additional Considerations to Limit Scope
Who?	Who may be involved? Who is likely to have relevant knowledge or information? Is management involved?	Can the issues be confined to a business unit, service line or product?
What?	What is the specific allegation? What evidence may exist?	What are the key facts or evidence that can be established, and what are the key facts that require further investigation?
Where?	Where did the allegations take place? Is there reason to suspect that other locations are involved?	Is this an issue related to a specific region, country, or office?

Scoping Questions		Additional Considerations to Limit Scope
When?	When did the events occur? Is the activity ongoing?	Is there any indication of timing from the allegation? For example, has the company only been doing business with the customer over the last two years?
How?	How were the activities conducted? How was the activity concealed?	Has a similar activity occurred previously? If so, how are they similar, and how was it resolved.
Why?	Why did the activity take place? Was an advantage gained?	If the activity involves individual or multiple individuals, understand their background and what they have to gain.

After these questions are answered, a more detailed scope can be established and this will help to determine if the team established has the proper skills to fully respond to the scope. If, as is likely, the answers to some of these questions are not known, the company should set a boundary that is reasonable given the underlying allegation, and then continue to refine the boundaries as the investigation evolves.

There must be a solid, defensible reason for limiting scope. The cost of investigating the allegation is not an acceptable reason; but the fact that there has only been business interaction with a vendor that is the subject of an investigation for the last 18 months is good reason for initially limiting the scope to the past 2 years. If during the course of this investigation, it appears that there has been business interaction with that vendor under another name or using a different vendor to conduct the similar problematic activities during an earlier period then consideration should be made to increase the scope to go further back in time so that it encompasses the problematic activity.

Define the Investigative Work Plan

When the overall scope of the investigation is set, the team needs to build out the detailed procedures that will govern how the investigation will be conducted.

Investigations are not routine and understanding what the information is indicating can lead to important next steps in an investigation. The investigation team must follow the work plan, but must frequently revisit the work plan to ensure that it is focused and current, updating and amending the approach where necessary.

The following table describes a number of areas that would typically be covered in an investigation work plan:

Work Plan Area	Description
Data preservation	The identification and preservation of information relevant to the investigation.
Data collection and processing	Collection focuses on the most effective way to collect relevant data, while processing normalizes the data to make it available to search, analyze, and review.
Analysis of e-mail and electronic documents	The review of the data processed through the use of various technology enablers including analytics and filters.
Forensic accounting review	Focusing on the books and records includes both the review and analysis of electronic accounting information and the investigation into the actual operations to understand transaction flow, documentation, and how this is reflected in the books and records. Overall quantification of the improper activity is also an activity of the forensic accounting review.
Interviews	A key part of the fact gathering process and often takes place throughout the investigation. The focus is to learn or corroborate what happened.
Reporting	Summarizes the work performed and the findings of the investigation.
Remediation	If there have been findings during an investigation, it is most likely due to a failure of one of the elements of the anti-corruption compliance program. Remediation seeks to address this failure.

CASE**STUDY: STEEL COMPANY INC.**

The forensic accountants performed a preliminary review of the supporting documentation available for the commission payment. They noticed that the payment was recorded to two accounts in the general ledger: "Agents Commissions Due" (15 percent of the commission) and "Other Services" (10 percent of the commission). The rationale for the split was not documented in the available support. The vague "Other Services" raised further suspicions.

Working with external counsel, the forensic accountants developed a work plan with initial procedures for data preservation, collection and processing, e-mail review, forensic accounting review, and interviews.

Data Preservation

In the initial stages of identification and collection the investigation team will focus on identifying and preserving a wide range of sources that may be potentially relevant to the matter while collecting a smaller more targeted subset for analysis.

Legal Hold Notices and Management

Legal holds initiate the preservation of reasonably accessible and relevant documents, including that which is electronically stored (ESI) and in hard copy. A sound initial response could incorporate a preliminary analysis and review to determine which archival sources should be considered, which current documents should be preserved, and which custodians will need hold notifications and instructions for future communications. A comprehensive legal hold will include a questionnaire that fleshes out all data sources. By documenting related decisions and the reasoning behind them, legal counsel will generally be able to demonstrate "good faith" hold efforts and avoid later sanctions for failure to participate adequately in the discovery process. This will also create a more realistic and acceptable distinction between documents that can be produced and documents that are truly inaccessible or privileged.

After a legal hold has been initiated, controls should be put in place to ensure that custodians actually execute the procedures as intended. Compliance should be monitored from first notification of the legal hold.

When legal holds affect an international company, complexity is magnified by organizational inconsistencies, conflicting legal regulations, incompatible technical infrastructures, disjointed or undefined records management environments, and other diverse cultural interactions. Business units, processes, and policies may vary vastly from one country to another in order to assimilate with the local economy. Oftentimes, organizations have offices in multiple countries with conflicting national laws affecting legal holds.

The final critical component to the legal hold is that it includes an area for the custodian to certify that they have conducted a reasonable search for documents and preserved, collected, and provided them to counsel.

Identifying Sources of Potentially Relevant Information

During the initial stages of the investigation, data sources are typically identified as containing potentially relevant information after conducting interviews with company information technology (IT). Developing a custodian list can help facilitate this process as the technical team work to identify potentially relevant sources of information and can help with prioritizing preservation. The custodian list should be a fluid list, with additions being made as more is learned during the investigation. Also critical during the identification process is a general understanding of the issues which may include, the general allegation, date range of the investigation, employment dates for relevant custodians, facts regarding how the custodians' computers were handled upon termination, and so on. For example, if the investigation team is concerned about an issue that occurred within the past three years, then e-mail from backup tapes pulled five years ago are not likely to be responsive.

Some companies have created data maps of their infrastructure that document critical systems and their configurations that can be leveraged by the technical team to help understand the company's data sources at the onset of an investigation. These maps typically contain information related to history of the system, who are the primary users, how long data is stored within the system, how the system is backed up, and what tapes/rotation is maintained. If no data maps exist then the company will likely not have a documented backup methodology for high-risk systems that IT and legal can use to determine what archive data exists for those systems.

E-mail is often the key data source for an investigation. E-mail can exist locally on a custodian laptop/desktop, as well as the e-mail server, and on various other locations including offline media (e.g., USB drives). Also important are non-e-mail documents including PDFs, spreadsheets, and the like. We will examine some of the key sources of electronic information in detail in this section.

E-mail/File Servers

Server data can be a very useful source of information during investigations. It is important to determine all data storage servers to which custodians had access, including e-mail servers, private file shares, and group or public file shares. Company servers are typically centralized into a single data center or regional locations, which can have a big impact on the company's ability to transfer the data across international borders. Although it might not be necessary to collect or preserve all of this data, a good understanding of the data universe will help the investigation team to make the best decisions concerning this potentially relevant information. Server-based e-mail is often easy to collect and quick to analyze as an initial pass to ascertain certain facts very early on in the investigation.

E-mail stored on servers often supplements e-mail stored on a custodian's local computer as the configuration and management of e-mail in these locations is different. E-mail server collections can be highly cost effective, as they typically allow you to obtain data for several custodians at one time. Also, if an investigation is highly secretive, an e-mail server collection and review is an easy way to get information without alerting custodians. Key attributes to consider when discussing with the IT department:

- E-mail platform and version (e.g., Microsoft Outlook, Lotus Notes).
- Mailbox size quotas.
- Deleted item rules.
- Automated routines.
- Server migration history.
- Mailbox restoration process.

Private and public file shares are good sources of information that are sometimes overlooked, both by custodians and investigators. The following are some technical points to be considered by the technical team and discussed with a representative from the IT department:

- File share access rules (access control lists).
- File share size quotas.
- Understanding of how the custodians may have used these shares.

Archives and Backup Tapes

Archiving systems for e-mail (e.g., EVault) have become increasingly popular as a means for companies to save space on e-mail servers while still maintaining some level of accessibility to e-mails and attachments. It is generally easier to restore data from e-mail archives than it is to restore data from backup tapes, but the process can take a significant amount of time, depending on the number of custodians and the length of time the e-mail has been archived from the source system.

Backup tapes can be important for filling in gaps in available data or information. It is imperative to understand the backup procedures at the beginning of an investigation so that potentially relevant tapes can be preserved. Most companies have tape rotation policies, which outline specific time periods after which tapes may be reused. If backup tapes are not immediately inventoried at the beginning of an engagement, then it is possible that the most relevant backup data will have been overwritten by the time that gaps are identified.

Custodian PCs

Custodians' computers generally are an excellent source of information as they often times offer the most complete collection of data from each individual. There is a challenge in obtaining information from this source without alerting the custodian under investigation. With recent advances in technology, there are applications that have the ability to collect this information remotely without alerting the custodian. The effectiveness of these technologies is often limited by the company's bandwidth or connectivity options to remote locations.

Computer forensic software, such as EnCase, can be used in conjunction with forensic images to recover deleted files and, if required, conduct a more in-depth analysis of a custodian's computer. For example, computer forensic analysis is often performed to determine if custodians attempted a mass deletion of files during the investigation.

The coordination of the collection activity is usually in place on or near the time the company's legal department issues a notice to preserve documents as part of a legal hold.

Data Collection and Processing

The collection and processing of data is a key step in any investigation. These procedures must be well planned and documented to both keep costs down and to hold up to the scrutiny of regulators or external auditor when evaluating the investigation.

Data Privacy

Significant risks exist around the protection of data. The notion of an employee's personal right to privacy in the work place is dramatically different across geographies, and certain countries have developed aggressive legislation to protect these cultural values.

In October of 1998, the European Union's Data Protection act went into effect as legislation to protect the privacy of information and prohibit the transfer of personal data to non–European Union (EU) countries. Non-EU countries are thought to not "adequately" meet EU standards for privacy protection. Government agencies in the United States take a significantly different approach to privacy and afford little leeway during an investigation when requesting documents from operating entities for U.S.-based companies under investigation.

The U.S. Department of Commerce in consultation with the European Data Privacy Commission has developed a "Safe Harbor" framework to provide a means for U.S. companies to comply with the EU Data Protection act via the U.S. EU Safe Harbor program.[1] In addition to subscribing for safe harbor certification companies have also found it effective to have internal groups and policies that strictly address data privacy and the transmission of electronically stored information across borders.

Data privacy is a legal decision that must be carefully analyzed before collecting or transferring data belonging to employees. It is advisable to seek the advice of local counsel in the specific country to provide guidance on compliance with local regulations and to hire a vendor with experience in dealing with cross border data transfers and subscribes to the Department of Commerce's safe harbor certification process. Additional protection may be afforded by having each custodians sign detailed consent forms with specific information about where their data is going, how it will be filtered to only identify information relevant to the matter, what their data will be used for, and so on.

Types of Collection

As companies look to determine the most effective way to collect data relevant to the investigation, they are often challenged with the sheer volume of data and seek alternative methods such as forensic, targeted, and self-collections to meet their objectives.

Forensic Collection The goal of a forensic collection of electronic information is to preserve the evidence in a manner that is verifiable and admissible in court. A forensic data collection can be done many ways and does not always require the creation of a forensic hard drive image. However, a forensic image of a custodian's computer is still considered the most conservative approach, as it affords the investigative team the most options for the analysis of the evidence downstream.

A forensic image involves making a bit-for-bit "complete" copy of the hard drive. A forensic image preserves the meta data, files, and unallocated clusters on a hard drive. There are specific analysis that can be done only if a forensic image has been created, such as recovery of deleted files.

Targeted Collection A targeted collection is more focused than the process used to create a forensic image. In a targeted collection, the custodian is involved in the identification of what files or documents might be relevant but does not actively participate in the technical aspects of copying or preserving those files. Targeted collections are most common for audit committee or board members who may have interests in multiple companies, or where data privacy rules or other restrictions require this approach.

Self-Collection   Self–collection although similar to targeted collection varies in the fact that the custodian is also responsible for copying/collecting the data. This type of collection is rarely performed during an investigation but can be an effective option depending upon the specifics of the matter. The self-collection process is typically initiated by sending detailed instructions to the custodians involved in the matter with guidance on searching and preserving the documents. The instructions would typically include details on which sources should be checked along with a process to certify that the guidelines have been followed. This type of collection process should be carefully planned and clear, simple guidance provided to help ensure the custodians do not inadvertently alter metadata or miss potentially relevant documents.

Data Processing

After data collection the next phase in the information lifecycle is to normalize the information into a form that makes it available for searching, analysis, and review. This step in the process would include identification and extraction of metadata and document text and creating records containing that information in a relational database. Key considerations during this phase of the process are:

CASESTUDY: STEEL COMPANY INC.

Based on the facts accumulated at that point, external counsel instructed the forensic accountants to collect and process the IT data of certain employees who were privy to the transaction. These employees, or the "custodians," included the three business development employees who led the pursuit, two finance employees who approved the payment and the marketing manager who referred the agent. The forensic accountants collected a forensic image of the custodians' company-issued computers and Blackberry devices.

Deduplication   This is a process whereby duplicate documents are removed from the data set to be reviewed. Duplicates can be identified within custodian or across multiple custodians. Decisions on this process have dramatic effects downstream and need to be carefully considered and discussed with all members of the team.

File-Type Filtering   This is a process wherein files of a specific type are either included or excluded from the review set. Often referred to as "de-NISTing," the process relies on a listing of known file types that are considered to be system or program files and then has the processing software remove files of this type from the data set. Conversely, during this stage of the life cycle, file types can be targeted for inclusion in the process filtering out all others.

Exception Handling   One of the biggest challenges in dealing with un-structured data (e-mail and documents) is that the form can be extremely diverse based on capabilities of the application and the custodian's ability to alter the information. There is no technology that can process 100 percent of all unstructured data types, so it is vitally important that the tool provides you with details on the files it could not properly extract. There may be additional work done on certain file types to make them available for analysis; for example, password-protected files would need to be cracked before document text can be extracted, and unique mailbox formats used in other countries would need to be converted to a format the processing tool can ingest.

Analysis of E-mail and Electronic Documents

Once the data has been normalized or "processed" the next stage of the life cycle requires the development of the review strategy that will be followed to analyze the information to determine the facts of the matter. Over the past several years there has been a significant increase in the capabilities of the tools available to help with the discovery of electronic documents. The volumes of data for analysis have significantly increased as well making it critically important to be extremely focused with respect to the strategy that you employ to filter and identify potentially relevant information.

Understanding the Data Set

Key to effective discovery of information in an investigation is to have a clear understanding of the information that has been collected. Evaluating that information for anomalies to identify potential gaps in the collection or processing errors that can be identified by analyzing document counts among the custodians.

It is also critical that the investigator understands the time period in the data set. Analyzing message counts per month/quarter can help the investigator quickly identify gaps in the collection that may have been created intentionally by the custodian deleting large pockets of documents.

Filtering and E-mail Analytics

Since a large amount of the e-mail collected for an investigation is likely to be irrelevant, it is important to develop appropriate strategies to identify potentially relevant documents. Current forensic technology provides a number of analysis tools to assist with this endeavor.

- **Keyword Search:** The investigative team will frequently develop terms related to the specific allegations or issues, and these keywords are searched across all content, including metadata, available for review. Keyword refinement is a natural part of the search phase as the initial results often demonstrate that some terms are overly broad while others are too narrow. The proposed keyword list can also be submitted to an analytics engine to determine additional terms that it deems are related within the selected data set. Since e-mail review often uncovers new issues that merit new keywords, the process is often iterative. Figure 9.3 is an example of an analytical dashboard that can be used by the investigator to understand the effect the keyword filtering would have on the ultimate document review population by understanding, which custodians in which period display hits for the terms provided. These types of dynamic dashboards are powerful tools for effectively focusing the review effort.

  "Hits" will be identified and the e-mail review team will review the documents to determine their relevance. It is important that the e-mail review team is provided a briefing on the allegation/issue and that they meet and discuss findings regularly during the review as significant information can be learned over a short period. During these meetings criteria should be established as to what should be identified as a "hot document."

  An initial limited review of a sample will reveal the content of the responsive e-mails and this will ensure that these e-mails are on point with the objective. If not, consider revising the search terms or focus on certain custodians or a time period. Updating and revising search terms to reduce

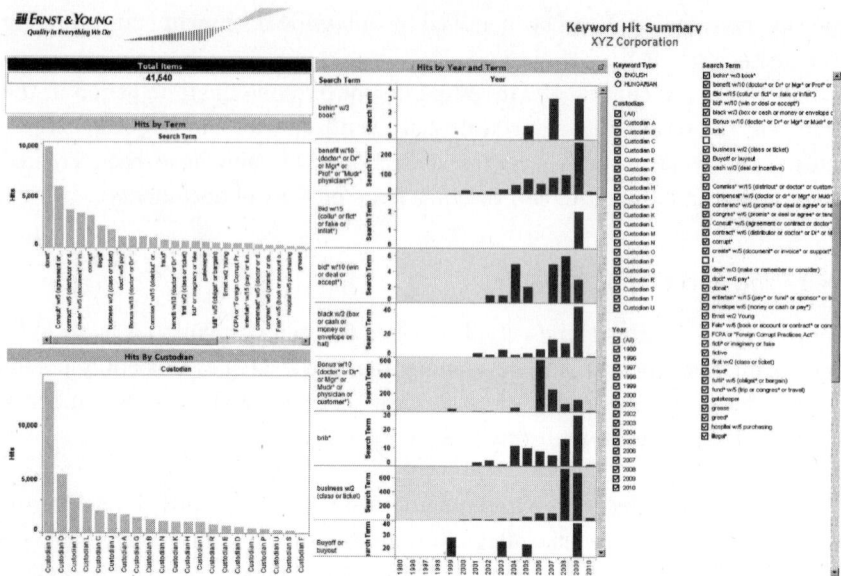

FIGURE 9.3 E-mail Analytics—Keyword Hit Summary

false positives can help orientate the focus of the review to the investigation's scope and objective; it will also eliminate unnecessary time and cost for the reviewers to manually tag and remove the false positives.

Depending on the amount of time that the team has prior to fieldwork and interviews "keywords" should be very focused as an e-mail review can be an incredibly labor intense process if the keywords are too broad and there is a high number of hits.

- **Clusters:** For investigations that merit the additional up-front cost of developing these specific types of indexes, data can be clustered into groups by an engine that analyzes the content of the documents to identify specific concepts or topics being discussed. The process identifies specific topics within the e-mail and attachments and can identify other similar documents that may be discussing the same thing.

- **Custodian Communication Patterns:** A report can be developed to visually display the communication frequency and participants for key custodians. This information can be used to identify key players within the current custodian list or even additional custodians. This type of analysis can lead to findings in communications amongst the custodians that would not necessarily be picked up through keyword searching.

FIGURE 9.4   Fraud Triangle Analytics

- **Text Analytics:** E-mail review is typically expensive and tedious to review given the "false positive" nature of relying on keyword searching to review high-risk documents and because e-mail is personal and its review may pose data privacy risks. By combining the premise of the Fraud Triangle[2] with e-mail communications, research indicates that e-mail communications can be an indicator of an employee's incentive or pressure, opportunity, and rationalization—the three sides of the Fraud Triangle. Instead of performing keyword searches from one random list, the searches are performed using three keyword lists for incentive/pressure, opportunity, and rationalization. Reviewers can then analyze the keyword hit frequency over time to look for areas where all three list of terms might be spiking, indicating the presence of the Fraud Triangle (see Figure 9.4).

    Fraud Triangle Analytics leverages targeted keywords around incentive/pressure, opportunity, and rationalization, supplemented with company-specific and local language jargon, acronyms, and industry-specific terms to track the frequency of those terms in e-mail communications for analysis and comparison to one's peer group. A typical analysis incorporates 25 to 50 employees within a particular region, office, or peer group (e.g., the sales department in a high anti-corruption risk country). E-mail is obtained from the company's live server e-mail system. The results can be provided via a dashboard interface for analysis where individuals can be "scored" and plotted based on their keyword hit frequency based on incentive/pressure, opportunity, and rationalization. For those high-scoring individuals, accountants can "drill-down" on that individuals and look to see where those keywords are appearing over time.

When all three lists spike together over time as demonstrated, that is an indication that the Fraud Triangle might be apparent in that person's e-mail. The keywords driving those spikes are also displayed. The reviewer can further drill in or out into specific high-scoring e-mails, within specific individuals or time frames, for review and issue tagging (e.g., relevant, not relevant, highly relevant, etc.).

■ **Progressive Review:** Document review is a mainstay of corruption investigation, but growing volume and complexity of data to review continues to pose a challenge for investigators who must choose where to invest their time and resources. A successful document review in an investigation isolates the responsive documents (often for production, whether voluntary or under subpoena) and gives the investigators the key facts in the matter. Time is usually limited, even when volume of data to review is far beyond the capacity of a typical human to competently evaluate. Of special concern in many investigations is the identification of privileged or private material, and these challenges often flummox efforts to speed up review without creating risk. The techniques previously outlined—keyword searching, concept clustering, communication pattern analysis, and text analytics—can each progressively contribute valuable insight into aspects of an investigation.

Linguistic classification and contextual analytics go a step farther by leveraging non-obvious connections in the data to pinpoint areas of high value information, and by enabling investigators to consistently apply their interpretation of the review requirements across a data set of any size. The result is increased quality and substantially reduced time frames. Progressive review is built on proven statistical sampling methodologies, implemented through proprietary Ernst & Young technology, and supported by experts in linguistics and legal process.

In short, progressive review leverages computers for the heavy lifting of repetitive comparisons and incorporates the professional judgement of the investigator to reveal the story hidden in the data. In addition, by segmenting documents and building models of relationships among and between actors, documents, and events, progressive review also gives investigators and their counsel tremendous visibility into privilege and privacy considerations early in the process.

This unique approach facilitates early and accurate fact development while simultaneously reducing risk and cost. The end result is a better, faster and cheaper document review that truly reflects the intent of the investigator and provides a clear audit trail that traces every decision back to the judgement of the professional, not an algorithm.

E-mail Review

Often, the most time-intensive and costly phase of the electronic discovery life cycle pertains to the e-mail documents. The objective of the e-mail review should be clear and supplement the objective of the overall investigation.

Strategic decisions that have occurred throughout the process to this point will have a dramatic effect upon determining the eventual population of documents for review. In this section, we focus on key aspects of document review.

E-mail review can be a critical part of any investigation although it has to be used wisely as e-mail reviews are expensive, in terms of both initially acquiring and uploading the data to an e-mail review tool and also the cost of reviewing the responsive e-mails.

The key to a successful e-mail review is fine-tuning the approach before significant review is undertaken. The following approach is recommended:

- Define objective of e-mail review.
- Understand the custodians in the population.
- Understand data population and any anomalies (e.g., gaps or spikes in data); ensure data from suspects and their relevant spheres of influence are included.
- Use concept searching and smart keyword search terms to define initial keyword search terms.
- Tailor the search term list to the investigation.
- Understand initial population of responsive e-mails (e.g., is suspect involved in e-mail, does this provide coverage over the relevant time period?).
- Define tagging taxonomy.
- Conduct limited review and revise search terms (e.g., review a sample of responsive e-mails for each search term to ensure that responsive e-mails are on point with the objective).
- Review and update search terms and amend to reduce false positives; for example, if a significant portion of e-mails responsive to the search term *T-16*, which was thought to be a highly relevant term but generated mostly nonrelevant e-mails, then update search terms to exclude T-16.
- Conduct review of remaining e-mails with regular review.

TRACEABILITY

A key aim for any electronic document review is that each document is traceable. It is important for the investigators to be able to clearly identify the origin of each document and maintain its integrity throughout the electronic discovery life cycle. This becomes critical when documents must be produced to regulatory bodies.

A major objective of the electronic document review is that methodology utilized to identify potentially relevant data is transparent and repeatable. For this reason, documenting the custodian list, overall search process and terms, and the review protocol is imperative. For large-document review teams, training and supervisions of the reviewers will help ensure that the documents are being coded in a consistent manner and review sets are being completed in a timely fashion.

Once the review population is identified the documents are typically divided into manageable batches of documents and assigned to the investigators in a logical manner. These "batches" or "review sets" can be organized by custodian, topic, chronologically, or other categories. This review structure helps to clearly define which documents will be assigned to each reviewer.

Typically, the review will be structured in multiple phases, wherein a group of reviewers will be assigned to look at a set of documents for specific issues as a first pass and make relevance decisions on those documents. A more senior investigator will then typically identify the subset of documents identified as potentially responsive to make a final decision. It is also good practice to review a sample of the documents that have been coded as not responsive to ensure proper relevance decisions are being made by the first pass review team.

Concept Searching and Smart Keyword Initial keyword search terms require careful planning and concept searching can allow the user to understand the key terminology and words, or "concepts" frequently used or applied in the data population. Understanding the frequently used concepts can help fine-tune a list of initial keyword search terms.

Other considerations for "keywords" include foreign language terms of relevance, and depending on the specific scheme in the allegation/issue, generic bribery and corruption terms could be included. Following are examples for certain themes:

Allegation/Issue theme	Potential "keywords"
Payment to government official to secure contract	Kickback Commission to customer Customer advance Bribe
Use of agent to obtain business	Build relationship Commission to customer Side commission
Off-book cash usage for potentially improper activity	Under the table Fund
Excessive entertainment to government official	Customer trip VIP Royal
Avoiding inspection at customs	Expedite Special processing Intervention Facilitate

Tagging Taxonomy   A critical part of the e-mail review is the organization of the reviewed e-mail. This is important so that the documents relevant to each allegation/issue can be quickly associated and the related custodian can be identified. This is critical for interview preparation and ultimate reporting of the overall investigation.

The e-mail review team will establish "tags" in the e-mail review software platform, which will help to organize the hits. This will obviously include a "hot" tag but can be customized for any other number of items. It is important to keep in mind that if an overly complicated tagging structure is developed, it will be difficult to ensure that all reviewers would tag a document in the same manner. The use of these codes will be outlined in the review protocol document for the project, but the codes typically fall into one of the following categories:

- Review progress (i.e., first level review complete, further review required, exported for interview binder, etc.).
- Responsiveness (i.e., hot, relevant, not relevant).
- Issues (specific to each case).
- Privilege/Confidentiality.
- Comments.

The data review phase might be conducted in detail by attorneys and/or forensic accountants. Certain review systems have the capability to automatically update coding decisions or "propagate" to related items, such as duplicates belonging to other custodians, and can be utilized to improve consistency and efficiency.

The tagging conventions should be customized based on the investigation objective, and in many cases, this might include, but is not limited to: relevancy, subcategories and subtopics of the investigation, foreign language (requiring translation), password protected or corrupted files, attorney-client privilege communication, and so on.

Metrics Reporting   Metrics reporting is an important element of an e-mail review, as it allows the team to quickly identify where they stand on the overall process as well as to keep track on the review team.

Metrics reports can be generated daily or weekly to track the progress. As part of an e-mail review, the metrics can identify the number of documents tagged, reviewed, and unreviewed. Tagged documents, such as hot documents, are important to the investigation; these documents should be extracted quickly for further review and to understand how they can be used as supporting documentation for the overall scope and objective of the investigation.

Metrics can be prepared for a number of areas, examples of reports that can be used to monitor the effectiveness and progress of the review are:

- **Reviewer Statistics:** Report that lists the total usage time, total number of document views, and total number of document edits for each reviewer during a specified time period. See Figure 9.5 for an example dashboard.
- **Review Progress:** Report that shows progress of review per review batch. This report can be used to analyze the effectiveness of the reviewers against their peers but must be viewed along with other information regarding the type and complexity of the documents that have been assigned.
- **Annotation Summary:** Report that summarizes the coding decisions being made by the reviewers. This report can be used to shift review resources if during the review a particular custodian is displaying a large amount of relevant information.

Forensic Accounting Review

The forensic accounting review is a key step in the overall investigation as often this review can uncover what actually took place from a flow of funds

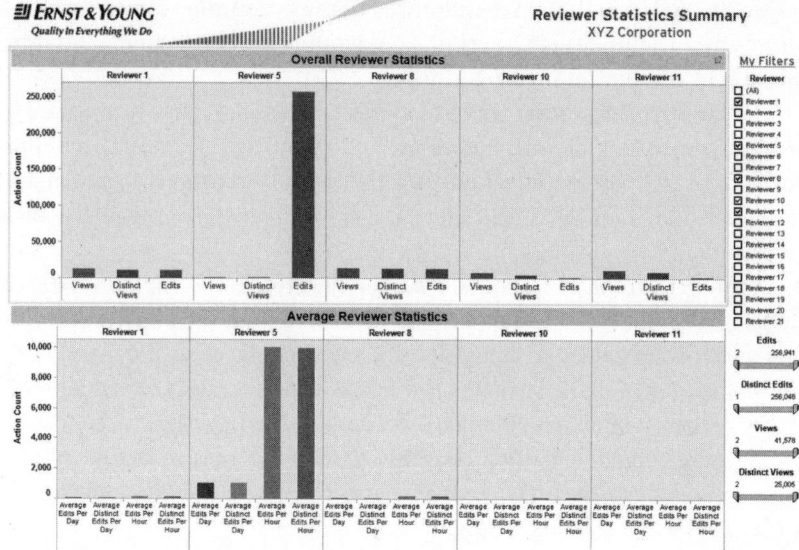

FIGURE 9.5　E-mail Reviewer Statistics Dashboard

CASE STUDY: STEEL COMPANY INC.

With input from external counsel, the forensic accountants developed a listing of key words which were used to search the custodians' data. The results were reviewed by the forensic accountants, who reported their findings to external counsel.

The e-mail review uncovered more facts about the reason for the higher commission. It was revealed that the contemplated mall extension was bordering on government land. In order for the project to be effectuated, a special permit had to be secured from the municipal council. In fact, the success of the project with Steel Company was conditioned on Steel Company's securing this permit on behalf of the investor. To expedite the receipt of the permit, normally a burdensome bureaucratic process, Steel Company made a payment to the municipal council, which was funneled through the agent's commission. The agent also received a kickback. To shy off suspicions by the regional hub in the Far East when reviewing agent's commissions due, the payment to the agent and the bribe were segregated into a separate account. All custodians but one of the finance employees had e-mails implicating their participation and knowledge in the scheme.

perspective and how these were captured in the accounting system. The flow of funds and the underlying accounting detail is crucial to understand in a bribery and corruption investigation.

The forensic accounting review focuses on the books and records. Procedures performed include both the review and analysis of electronic accounting information and the investigation into the actual operations to understand transaction flow and documentation and how this is reflected in the books and records.

Depending on the allegation and scope, the forensic accounting review can be a focused exercise. For example, if all indicators from the e-mail review and other information gained to date point to a very specific issue, the investigation could potentially be limited to a detailed review of one contract or vendor with a cursory review of other activities for the location. The opposite can be true and the allegation could implicate activities that are pervasive across multiple locations and business units and thus the forensic accounting review can also be a robust and time-consuming exercise.

Important sources of information for the accounting review include:

Financial Systems/Reports	Hardcopy Documentation
Chart of accounts	Organizational charts
Annual reports	Accounting approval levels
General ledger	Invoices
Trial balances	Checks
Journal entries	T&E support
Accounting database information	
Accounting transactions	

Perform Analytical Procedures

Companies and business units house large amounts of accounting data and the most effective method to understand and review this data may be through the use of analytical tools. Analytics can be used to search for anomalies or areas of concerns. The investigative team should review the scope and objective of the investigation to determine which accounts and data are relevant and customize the analysis. These analyses can be used to assist the books and records review as well as information used for the interviews.

Examples of analysis include:

- Key accounts: Year-to-year or quarter-to-quarter analysis.
- Vendors: Comparison between vendors duplicate accounts or addresses.
- Sales: Analysis of sales, sales commissions, and credits by month.
- Payroll: Analysis of employee records for government employees or "ghost" employees.
- Duplicative payments: Identify payments made on the same day for the same amount to the same account, to the same or multiple vendors/distributors.
- Cash payments: Stratification of payments made in cash, to whom, over time, business reason—with focus on government expenditures.
- Stratify gift, charity, donation and advertising/promotion expenses by frequency, dollar amounts, and recipients (identify state-owned entities).
- Travel and entertainment: Isolate T&E expenses whose attendees include government officials.

To effectively review and complete the analysis, the investigation team must review the output of the analysis and ensure that the output is reasonable. Additionally, the output of this analysis should be confirmed through a detailed review of transactions in the books and records review. Based on the analyses and findings from the analytic review, the investigation team should review and adjust the scope of books and records review. The findings from data analytics can help the investigation team better identify areas of focus and construct a judgmental sample, which is discussed further later in this chapter. Additionally, after the completion of the books and records review, analytics can be used to assist in the quantification of the potentially improper payments made.

Books and Records Review

The books and records review entails work normally on site to identify and understand the problematic activities and how these are manifested in the accounting system. This process is based on an understanding of the allegation and policies, procedures, and processes at the business unit being investigated. Through the review of the accounting records, discussions with management and detailed testing of transactions greater understanding of the allegation is gained.

Generally, there are four phases to a single location investigation: pre-site preparation, off-site fieldwork, on-site fieldwork, and follow-up.

Pre-Site Preparation   The investigation team should gain an understanding of the business unit being investigated, such as their policies, procedures, processes, operations, management, customers, vendors, and so on. The team should also gain an understanding of cultural practices in the region, industry standards, guidelines, and regulations that are relevant to the company.

Based on discussions with the management, the investigation team will be able to determine if there are corporate or local policies and procedures. Understanding the key elements of the policies and procedures can assist in the identification of areas where controls have been bypassed and further investigation is required. Additionally, weak policies and procedures allow for a location to more easily disguise improper activities.

The investigation scope will help to determine the relevant processes that may have been impacted by the allegation. Through discussions and informational interviews with process owners, a general understanding of the process can be gained.

It is important to understand the approval process with the organization as it can help to identify transactions that may intentionally set below a certain threshold to avoid additional approval. For example, if a company requires approval of any transaction $10,000 or higher by the business unit director, then potentially two $5,000 transactions with the same vendor over a short period of time may have been structured in a way to circumvent this approval.

The organizational structure and operational infrastructure also needs to be reviewed. The investigation team should understand how the company is set up, how its departments are organized, and how individuals and departments report. The team should also confirm the understanding gained during data preservation of its operational infrastructure, which includes accounting infrastructure, the type of accounting system used, data infrastructure, and how its data is housed and stored (via a dedicated central server or online, cloud storage center).

The investigation team should look into any prior work performed at the location, such as previous investigations, consulting work, internal audits, and so on. Prior work can shed additional facts useful for the current investigation and also assist in planning for current investigation.

Off-Site Fieldwork   Given the amount of work to perform during fieldwork, getting a jump on the analysis of information and sampling can save the investigation team a significant amount of time in the field and allow them to focus on understanding the operations and the underlying support for the transactions rather than have to worry about performing analysis and selecting their sample on-site. In some cases, the accounting data is not available in advance so all work must be done on-site.

Accounting Analysis   Accounting analysis can be performed off-site if accounting data has been obtained by the investigation team. Prior to performing this analysis, there should be a conversation between the investigation team and the IT or finance department responsible for gathering and sending this data. The purpose of the conversation is to ensure that the data is sent in the correct format, time period, content and that it is sent via a secure, encrypted method. The second step is to reconcile the accounting data to the general ledger or financial statements to verify the completeness of the data.

Once this has been completed, the investigation team can begin its accounting analysis.

Transaction Review   Transaction review can be commenced off-site, and similar to accounting data, steps should be taken to ensure correct and complete transaction data is sent. The transaction review can include reviewing for proper approval, date and timing of transaction, proper coding, within policy limits, and so on.

Judgmental Sampling   Based on an understanding of the policies, procedures, and processes, as well as the allegation, sampling should be performed on a "judgmental basis." Judgmental sampling differs from statistical sampling generally used in an audit context. The key difference is that in an investigation the focus is a specific allegation(s) and therefore should be able to review the information in the accounting system to more intelligently select your sample; whereas, in an audit context, the objective is to test transactions that are representative of the entire population within an account.

As discussed more fully in Chapter 7, "Monitoring," data analytics can be utilized to help identify anomalies in transactional data and be of critical importance in preparing a judgmental sample during an investigation.

Additional techniques for selecting a judgmental sample include manual reviews of the transactions of an account, focusing on the text fields and the amounts of the transaction. Examples of potential sample items include round sum amounts and transactions with the same vendor over a very short period of time.

Other Analyses   The investigation team may decide to perform other analysis off-site. Depending on the data received and the level of detail, other analyses may include various models and extrapolation, frequency analysis, large dollar amount analysis, concept analysis (on text in data), and so on.

On-Site Fieldwork   Fieldwork is the key to a forensic accounting exercise as the best way to understand how a business operates is to go to the business and observe, discuss, and test the processes and transactions.

When scoping fieldwork, it is important to determine the makeup of the team conducting the fieldwork. While the books and records review is the focus, a significant amount of information is covered, and consideration should be given to ensure that counsel is either present or readily available in case, based on the work performed by the investigation team, someone determines that it is in their best interest to "come clean."

The flow of funds is ultimately the key in a bribery and corruption investigation, and there are many ways to try to figure out where the money went and how it got there.

Potential areas of focus include:

Potential Area of Focus	Specific Procedures	Red Flags
Disbursements (including petty cash)	Identify all bank accounts Identify all petty cash accounts Determine purpose of accounts Determine level of cash transactions Scan disbursements listing for round sum amounts	Off-book cash accounts Lack of control over disbursements High level of cash transactions
Third parties (distributors/agents)	Identify third parties used Review contracts to determine the nature of relationship	"Recommended" agent Excess commission Lack of documentation Refusal of agent to agree to corporate policies
Vendors	Scan vendor master file Review activity by vendor	Vendors located in tax havens

	Review contracts to determine the nature of relationship	Vendors with a small number of large dollar items Lack of due diligence performed on certain vendors
T&E	Review T&E policy Review activity by person Understand key entertainment activities	Lack of required supporting documentation
Consultants' and professionals' services	Identify consultants and professionals used Understand nature of relationships Review activity by vendor	Lack of required supporting documentation Unclear service received
Gifts	Review gift policy Review activity Identify outliers	Lack of documentation
Marketing expenses	Understand marketing activities Review activity Identify outliers	No tangible output related to marketing payment
Facilitation payments	Inquire as to existence of facilitation payments Identify where recorded	Pervasiveness of small unsupported payments
Customers	Indentify government customers Review contracts Review activity Identify anomalies	Pool of funds for various purposes included in contract
Payroll	Obtain list of employees from human resources Obtain payroll file Compare and identify anomalies	Relative of government official Requested to hire someone as a condition for business Lack of documentation Employees with high absence rate
Government interaction	Understand nature of interactions with government Obtain information on payments to government	Lack of justification for interaction with government
Political and charitable contributions	Review policy Review activity Identify anomalies	Donations to charities lead by public officials

Interviews   Interviews are performed on-site with individuals pertinent to the allegation. Interviews are a critical part of the fact-gathering process. It can help confirm findings during fieldwork. Timing on when to interview individuals is also important, depending on the amount of information found in the off-site and on-site fieldwork. Interviews are discussed in greater detail later in this chapter.

Data Preservation   In addition to the overall data preservation discussed above, data preservation is important on-site as companies have various policies on maintaining and destroying information and documentation. If the investigation team deems an item relevant and important, the data should be preserved in a physical or electronic copy. The team should also note the originator, and time and date received. This data could inevitably used in the work papers, which will ultimately support any findings and conclusions.

Document Review   Document review can be performed on-site or off-site. This is dependent on the type of documentation and the volume. Some teams elect to have documents copied and perform the review off-site. In other instances, such as time-sensitive investigations, the investigation team might perform its review on-site to quickly gather as much of the facts and information as possible in a short time. Documents reviewed on-site can include expense reports and support, invoices, checks, contracts, and it is important that the review focuses on original documents.

Process Review   Process review is performed on-site with individuals from the company knowledgeable in their accounting and financial processes and controls. This review requires an in-depth look at how the accounting and financial data is captured and recorded and how that data is ultimately reported in the company's financial statements. The most effective review is to perform a walkthrough with someone at the company to fully understand each step of the process and to identify any areas of concern. Weak internal controls that do not prevent potentially improper activity require remediation. Remediation cannot take place if a full understanding of the issues is not understood.

Follow-up

Additional Targeted Review of Data/Documentation   After the on-site visit and review, the team might find new facts and might need to consider additional data. The team should follow up with a contact at the company to receive the necessary data to continue the investigative work.

Follow up interviews   Once the team has completed the fieldwork and gained an understanding of the facts related to the allegation, follow-up interviews might be needed to clarify topics discussed in prior interviews. The investigation team should identify any statements that do not correlate with the facts and perform follow-up interviews with the individuals to clarify.

Consider Additional Fieldwork   Additional fieldwork might also be necessary, as the initial fieldwork did not yield any conclusive facts. If this is the case, the team might need to perform additional fieldwork, which can include expanding sample size of documents to review, reviewing other processes and controls in the company, performing interviews, and reviewing at a different location where the company has operations, and so on.

Multilocation Considerations   Often, an investigation will require site visits to multiple company locations. Consideration should be given to the approach for visiting the multiple locations. If speed and surprise is a key element of the investigation, then the investigation team will need to be large and cover all locations as quickly as possible. If there is some flexibility in timing, then it is worthwhile to consider performing procedures at one or two locations and incorporating the information learned into the work plan so that the trips to the other locations can be more efficient and effective. When the allegation indicates that the same issue applies to multiple jurisdictions, the work plan should be similar for each jurisdiction to ensure that there is uniformity in the procedures conducted in each jurisdiction. It will reflect poorly on the company if fewer procedures are conducted in one jurisdiction and it subsequently turns out that conducting the additional procedures would have identified more issues. This can translate into the need to conduct significant additional procedures and increased fines being levied against the company.

Quantification   Determining the total amount of improper activity is often a step required for reporting to regulators. This generally cannot be done immediately after the fieldwork portion of forensic accounting review, as there are a lot of details that require confirmation during the final interviews as well as additional analysis of information from the accounting system. Once these additional procedures are performed, the exercise can be simply a manual summation of the activity identified or in situations where corrupt activity is endemic to the location and there is a systematic technique for accomplishing the quantification, it can be performed using predictive modeling.

Statistical Analytics Using Predictive Modeling   Predictive modeling can be very effective in anti-corruption analytics when a known set of transactions has been deemed "high risk" and the auditors wish to "profile" these transactions to identify statistically similar transactions. For example, in a recent FCPA matter, the DOJ alleged that a company had been authorizing "potential improper payments" (PIPs) to government officials through 15 agents in multiple countries. The company was ordered to review over 400,000 transactions with these agents based on source documents. Data analytics were used by the accounting team to review a large sample of the transactions, resulting in identification of a population of PIPs, and eliminating the remaining population as "not PIPs." The accounting team then built a predictive model using the two data sets to profile the PIP population based on payment text description, the payee, the time frames of payment, the location, and so on. The predictive model was then applied to the remaining 398,000 transactions to identify more PIP transactions. The DOJ approved this methodology, which ultimately resulted in significant savings in legal and accounting fees for the company.

CASESTUDY: STEEL COMPANY INC.

With the additional information uncovered during the e-mail review, the forensic accountants revised their work plan to focus on the vendor selection and approval process, agents and the "Other Services" account in the general ledger. The objective of the testing procedures on the Other Services account was to identify if the account contained questionable payments related to other contracts. The three business development employees, whose data was collected and reviewed, were responsible for business leads in Country D and other countries in the Far East, so the forensic accountants expanded their testing to all Far Eastern contracts these employees were in charge of. The accountants also did a comparative analysis of agent commissions by country and within the Far East region and identified two other agents who appeared to have received higher commissions. Based on the review of the vendor selection and approval process, the agents were identified by the same marketing manager, who referred the agent in Country D. The forensic accountants accumulated all available support and shared this information with external counsel.

Interviews

Interviews are a critical part of the fact-gathering process when conducting an investigation. The information gathered during an interview can be the cornerstone of an investigation and can help to confirm findings during fieldwork or point to areas that require further investigation. Do not prematurely interview suspects or terminate persons involved. Management should be prepared to deal with gossip and water cooler talk during the interview process. Despite warnings to employees to keep the discussions confidential, leaks are often inevitable.

Some important things to be aware of when conducting an interview include:

- *The order of interviews is important.* Start at outer edge of a circle and work toward the middle, eventually ending with the key suspect or witness.
- *Be prepared.* Make sure you have reviewed the interviewee's e-mails and documents on the subject you are interviewing him/her on. During the interview, have those materials with you so that you can ask them specific questions about the e-mails or documents.
- *Be alert.* Watch for signals from the interviewee. Body language can be very telling.
- *Take careful notes.* Often you will want to have another person sit in on the interview with the sole responsibility of taking notes.

Interview Selection and Order

During the early stage of the investigation, conduct background information–gathering interviews only of persons who can assist in the initiation of the investigative plan. Figure 9.6 shows the interview escalation chain: as more information is gathered, the interviews move toward those who have potentially greater involvement.

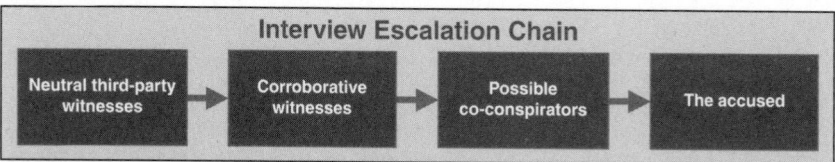

FIGURE 9.6 Interview Escalation Chain

Interview Preparation

Proper preparation includes collecting and analyzing as much information as possible. This allows the interviewer to outline facts and identify "gaps" and "holes," which will provide obvious questions for the interview. Questions should be written in logical order in an interview outline that will be used during the interview. Questions should be grouped into general categories then subdivided into specific questions about that general question.

The e-mail review provides significant background for the interview process. Being well prepared by reviewing the output of the e-mail review make the interview process far more productive and will allow the interviewer to modify the approach based on the path the interview goes. The e-mail review can help to build the outline of a story that the interview process can fill in.

By reading all the "hot" e-mails for a particular custodian an interviewer can develop an interview script and have supporting documentation to formulate questions. When confronted with an e-mail, the path of an interview can completely change and the behavior of the interviewee can move from denial to acceptance. While this is not always the case, reading something from their own e-mail box may make the interviewee realize that it is in their best interest to help the investigation.

INTERVIEW TIPS

- Put yourself at ease:
  - Be well prepared.
  - Do not rush.
  - Take time think about follow-up questions.
  - Have a note taker to reduce burden on interviewer.
- Introduction and interview framing:
  - Clearly identify yourself as a professional to the interviewee.
  - Explain the purpose and process of this investigatory interview.
- Listen:
  - Proper eye contact.
  - Suspend judgment initially.
  - Do not talk too much; let the interviewee speak more.
  - Use feedback checks with interviewee for clarification and understanding of content.

- ▪ Be alert to body language.
- ▪ Stay polite and professional.
- ▪ Distinguish facts from opinions and hearsay:
  - ▪ Distinguish between these types of statements—information gathered is not as useful because if it cannot been verified.
- ▪ Verbal and nonverbal communication:
  - ▪ Verbal indicators which include any auditory signals such as rate of speech, inflection, tone, pitch, and so on.
  - ▪ Verbiage (the actual words, spoken or written) indicators are simply the words someone uses, and doesn't use, in a given situation. For instance, the way an e-mail or text is written or how a person tells a story and the length to which they go, detail they give, and words they typically use, are all examples of understanding and baselining verbiage.
  - ▪ Nonverbal indicators include physical actions, which range from blink rate and pupil dilatation to direction and tapping of the feet.

Conducting the Interview

Generally, an interviewer should be flexible and willing to deviate from the script if the interviewee is providing relevant information and is cooperative. If the interviewee appears to try to lead the interview in a meaningless discussion, the interviewer should take control and move back to the key areas to be covered.

CASESTUDY: STEEL COMPANY INC.

External counsel and the forensic accountants interviewed all custodians about their knowledge of the agent's services, nature of the commission payment and the facts around the transaction. Counsel had at their disposal all documents that had been gathered to date, including "hot" e-mails, other correspondence, sourcing documentation, and general ledger entries to "Other Services," which they showed to the custodians. By paying attention to deviations from their baseline and asking probing follow up questions, the interviewees ultimately admitted their involvement in making or effecting the improper payment to the agent in Country D as well as the two agents in the Far East.

Under the direction of external counsel, the forensic accountants compiled all evidence related to the improper commission payments and documented it. External counsel and general counsel then decided to expand their investigation to the eastern European region, the other non-U.S. market in which Steel Company has operations, with the forensic accountants leading this effort.

The forensic accountants obtained and reviewed documentation for a judgmental sample of agent commissions for the major contracts and proposals in eastern Europe. They also did a comparative analysis of percentage of commissions paid in order to identify outliers. Payments posted to the "Other Services" account were scrutinized. The investigation in eastern Europe did not uncover any problematic payments; however, the accountants observed some internal control weaknesses in the agent due diligence process. The findings from eastern Europe were thoroughly documented.

Reporting

Given the global nature of anti-corruption investigations and the likelihood that transactions or business practices occurred in foreign countries, it is very important to fully understand the laws and rules of the foreign country in which you are operating. Variations in reporting rules can vary greatly from country to country and potentially pose significant challenges. Along with the need to set expectations around how and with whom the report is communicated, decisions regarding what will be in the report need to be addressed.

The report should consider professional and legal requirements such as disclaimers. Confidentiality should also be considered if the report goes to other parties who are not privy to the background and details of the investigation.

A report should provide an executive summary and provide information on the issues investigated and the overall scope of the investigation. The report should be targeted to its recipients; therefore, if the users are not familiar with the background, additional context and explanations should be included. The reports should be factual and all statements be supported with evidence and conclusions should be fully supported and not conjecture or opinions. Any remediation and recommendations should be realistic.

The wording of a report is important especially if it is not subject to attorney-client privilege and could be shared with third parties.

Distribution of Report

Make sure that the distribution of the report is controlled and its further use is restricted. This is important to maintain privilege, ensure that privacy laws are not violated, and make sure that it does not get used against the investigation team.

Format of Reports

Depending on the matter and the needs of the various stakeholders, reporting may take one of several forms; this includes an oral report, summary-level report, or a detailed written report. Reporting may even be rendered jointly with outside counsel.

The decision about whether to produce an oral or written report needs to be taken in consultation with counsel and other stakeholders (board of directors, audit committee, regulators, external auditors). Often, the bigger and more severe the issue, the more likely that interim reports will be oral and final reports will be written or, in some cases, could even be a short PowerPoint presentation.

Final reports, as either written a report or PowerPoint presentation, provide the stakeholders with a set of findings that also include details related to procedures, summary of e-mail review, methodology for data analytics, questions and answers from interviews, and so on. This type of report allows the stakeholder to clearly understand the tasks and steps undertaken throughout the investigation to derive the findings.

Sometimes, reports are quite extensive particularly where law enforcement is involved. When law enforcement or government agency is involved, there might be additional reporting requirements. These reports might be written in conjunction with internal or external counsel.

CASESTUDY: STEEL COMPANY INC.

General counsel, external counsel, and the forensic accountants met to discuss the results from the investigation. External counsel brought up the possibility of self-disclosure to the DOJ in regards to the matter. Also discussed was the overall company's response in terms of personnel actions and preventative measures.

REMEDIATION

Remediation can be needed as soon as the investigation begins. This means that the remediation plan and remediation actions can start at anytime during the investigation. However, depending on the amount of available information, the areas requiring remediation might not be evident until after some work has been performed by the investigation team. Fundamental issues such as the lack of anti-corruption training or the lack of an independent compliance unit might require immediate remediation. The company should bear in mind that any remediation might require discussions with external counsel or government or regulatory agencies before proceeding.

During the course of the investigation it will be important to identify areas for remediation and consider the formulation of a remediation plan. Depending on the allegation/issue and the pervasiveness across the organization, remediation may be needed immediately; alternatively, it may be best for the investigation to be completed prior to remediation. For example, if a company plans to roll out a new anti-corruption policy and training program and the company is in discussions with the government on a potential FCPA violation, it would be advisable to inform the government of the remediation plan prior to implementation.

Disciplinary Measures

Depending on the findings of an investigation, disciplinary measures may be required. This could range from specific training for individuals to termination. These measures will generally be determined by the company with the assistance of outside counsel. If involved, the government generally will expect to be informed of the actions taken on specific employees.

In addition, depending on the level of authority of the individual, the culpability and seriousness of the issue, there might be an impact to the financial reporting for the company as it may affect the auditor's reliance on their sign-off on financial statements. Again, this is a measure the company, with the assistance of outside counsel, should consider before addressing any disciplinary measure. Furthermore, disclosure to the government or regulatory agencies might be necessary depending on the level of authority of the individual and the seriousness.

Training

Anti-Corruption Training

Anti-corruption training can range from individual training to a company-wide training. This type of training can be developed and conducted by the compliance unit, outside counsel, or external third parties. The purpose of the training should reinforce the topic of anti-corruption and FCPA and preventive actions. A record of attendance should be kept for each training session; the company should also decide if this training is required every quarter or every year.

Books and Records Training

Books and records training can range from individual training to department-specific training. This type of training can be developed and conducted by the compliance and internal audit unit, or external third parties. The purpose of the training should reinforce the topic of corporate policies and compliance policies, the need to review and update every quarter or every year, and to maintain proper documentation.

Internal Controls

Depending on the findings of the investigation, remediation of internal controls may be required. This could include the roll out of new controls or improved monitoring of existing controls. The government generally will expect to be informed of the changes to the internal control structure as a result of the investigation. Refer to Chapter 5, "Policies and Procedures," for further details on internal controls.

Corporate Culture

A cornerstone of an effective anti-corruption program is a corporate culture with a "tone from top" that promotes ethical business over the bottom line. If an organization expects to be taken seriously by regulators that it has effectively re-mediated its anti-corruption compliance program then an organization must have clear anti-corruption policies, procedures, and training with ZERO tolerance for violations. Refer to Chapter 4, "Compliance Programs," for further details.

CASESTUDY: STEEL COMPANY INC.

The forensic accountants proposed remediation steps that Steel Company could implement globally to strengthen its processes around retention of new agents, approvals of commission payments and review of activity in the "Other Services" account as well as implementing yearly training on the company's anti-corruption policy for all employees within management, marketing, business development, and finance.

SUMMARY

An incident response plan is the final part of a robust anti-corruption program. Protocols are needed to ensure that red flags and allegations of impropriety are addressed in an appropriate and consistent manner. When investigating bribery and corruption, following the approach discussed throughout this chapter provides a sound basis to demonstrate to regulators that a thorough and complete investigation was performed. Ultimately, remediation is key to the continuous improvement of an anti-corruption compliance program and to reducing the risk that future bribery and corruption issues occur.

NOTES

1. www.export.gov/safeharbor/.
2. The Fraud Triangle illustrates some of the fundamental concepts of fraud deterrence and detection. In the 1950s, criminologist Dr. Donald R. Cressey (one of the co-founders of The Institute for Financial Crime Prevention, the precursor to the Association of Certified Fraud Examiners [ACFE]) developed the Fraud Triangle to explain why people commit fraud. His premise was that all three components—incentive/pressure, opportunity and rationalization—are present where fraud exists.

CHAPTER TEN

Regional Considerations for Bribery and Corruption Risks

T HIS CHAPTER PROVIDES INSIGHTS into the impact of bribery and corruption from a geographic perspective. The regions discussed in this chapter give some perspective on the nuances that can exist doing business internationally. The following regions are presented:

- Asia-Pacific
- Europe
- India and South Asia
- Middle East
- Africa
- Latin America

For each of these regions, we present an overview of bribery and corruption risks, region specific red flags, and greater detail on specific countries.

 ASIA-PACIFIC

For the past decade, the Asia-Pacific region has been the world's most dynamic market, comprising a broad spectrum of economic, political, and cultural systems. Developed and developing economies reside in close prox-imity to each other, as do some of the most open markets in the world with some of the most aggressively protected. When it comes to bribery and corruption risks in the region, diversity is still the operative term—Asia-Pacific countries range from #1 (New Zealand and Singapore) to #176 (Myanmar) out of 178 on Transparency International's (TI) 2010 Corruption Perceptions Index (CPI).

This section offers a general outline around this broad array of countries, highlighting the key differences as well some important similarities to consider when confronting bribery and corruption compliance risk.

General Overview

One will find that despite important distinctions, there are five common themes to managing bribery and corruption risk in the Asia-Pacific region.

1. The *deeply rooted traditional influence* on East Asian business culture, particularly regarding the creation and maintenance of relationships to underpin business interactions, has created tension with anti-corruption requirements. Employees observing centuries-old practices of gift giving and reciprocal benefit and patronage as a virtue in business dealings have frequently been frustrated by the FCPA anti-bribery provision's zero tolerance posture towards *quid pro quo*.
2. The *historic pace and scale of foreign direct investment* in the most rapidly growing economies of the region, particularly in China, has created a flood of capital that local operational managers have been ill equipped to manage. Shortages of skilled managers, especially in the finance and accounting functions, have produced significant weakness in internal controls, which can be abused by prospective bribe payers.
3. *Massive infrastructure spending*—the region is undergoing a physical trans-formation that is unprecedented in its scale and speed. The race to build the foundation of prosperity—airports, hospitals, highways, high-speed rail, utilities, telecommunications—has created unprecedented potential for abuse. For example, China's National Audit Agency (NAA)'s audits of such spending projects from 1996 to 2005 uncovered 1.29 trillion yuan (US$170 billion) in misappropriated and misspent public funds, or about 8 percent of total spending.[1]
4. *Wide reach of the state owned sector.* The region is home to a number of state-led economies, many of which are in the midst of transition from orthodox

communism and/or massive privatization. Companies subject to Foreign Corrupt Practices Act of 1977 (FCPA) requirements and operating in the region are frequently surprised where "foreign officials" can be found— potentially doctors, investment bankers, and factory owners, for example, in addition to a more apparent government bureaucrat.

5. The *pressure to sustain and expand growth* is palpable in the region. One consequence of high single- and double-digit growth in the Asia-Pacific emerging economies is that companies are expected to sustain and expand this growth indefinitely, sometimes with unrealistic targets. The credit crisis and deep recession in the United States, Japan, and European economies has only intensified the pressure on the key growth economies of Asia-Pacific including China, Korea, and the Association of Southeast Asian Nations (ASEAN) member countries to make up for the relative anemia of the developed markets. This intense reliance on Asia-Pacific emerging markets frequently results in a "growth at any cost" culture, which can create both a strong temptation and rationale to cut ethical corners.

While all areas of the economy are susceptible to corruption, certain industries find themselves at the center of these macro-level drivers of corruption risk. Life Sciences, Real Estate and Construction, Extractive Industries, and Telecommunications are just some of the sectors that are managing a multiple-front battle against regulatory, operational, and political complexity.

"Red flags" of corruption are common to Asia as well. The two most prominent corruption risks are:

1. *Cultural practices.* Business travel involving Asian companies typically will involve non business activities. A common practice in China is company-sponsored liaison meetings, which involve international travel and sightseeing. Additionally, in Malaysia it is regular to give gift baskets to visiting associates or businessmen.
2. *Customs officials.* It is considered the "norm" to pay a bribe to custom officers to help avoid customs duties on imported goods, lower tax assessments and expedite imports of goods or sometimes to overlook incomplete and inaccurate documentation.

In the following sections, we present five sample markets—China, Japan, Australia, Korea, and ASEAN, and provide an overview of particularly vulnerable industries as well as local legislation and enforcement trends.

China

In recent years, China has been an area of intense interest for FCPA enforcement. In the past 5 years, China has been a factor in approximately 20 percent of U.S. Department of Justice (DOJ) enforcement cases. The combination of massive public and private investment, a traditional business culture and legal and regulatory unpredictability create particularly acute FCPA compliance risk. Some of the largest recent DOJ cases have focused at least in part on the subject company's activities in the People's Republic of China (PRC).

- **Daimler AG:** Daimler AG's deferred prosecution agreement with the DOJ, which was accompanied by a fine of US$185 million (DOJ and SEC), admitted that employees of DaimlerChrysler China Ltd. (DCCL) made improper payments in the form of commissions, delegation travel, and gifts for the benefit of Chinese government officials in connection with the sale of vehicles to Chinese government customers. As part of its deferred prosecution agreement, Daimler AG was charged with conspiracy to violate the books and records provisions of the FCPA and violating those provisions; while DCCL's deferred prosecution agreement charged it with conspiracy to violating the anti-bribery provisions of the FCPA and violating those provisions.[2]

- **UTStarcom:** According to UTStarcom's nonprosecution agreement, UTStarcom, Inc. is a global telecommunications company that designs, manufactures, and sells network equipment and handsets. The majority of its operations are in China and it operates through its subsidiary UTStarcom China Co. In its 2009 nonprosecution agreement with the DOJ, UTStarcom admitted that between 2002 and 2007 it paid for approximately 225 overseas "training" trips for employees of Chinese government-owned telecommunications companies when no UTStarcom facility was visited and did not conduct training. The destinations included Hawaii, Las Vegas, and New York and the purpose was to obtain and retain customer contracts. Additionally, these trips were improperly recorded as "training" expenses. UTStarcom agreed to pay US$1.5 million in penalties to the both the DOJ and the Securities and Exchange Commission (SEC).[3]

Several other completed FCPA investigations of multinational companies operating in China have focused on similar schemes involving intermediaries, such as travel agencies, to pay for improper travel and entertainment expenses for officials with Chinese government–owned or –controlled customers. Instances of fabricated invoices, improperly documented trips, unapproved sightseeing activities, trips involving little or no business content, and provision of per diem payments and gifts to officials are typical findings. A case concerning fabricated invoices, *fapiao*, occurred in China in 2008. Four men of a Chinese gang produced receipts and invoices valued at 1.05 trillion yuan (US$147 billion). The receipts were produced in different provinces and then shipped to China's larger cities to be sold. The use of fake invoices and receipts is widespread in China. They are used by companies to reduce taxes and individuals use them as fake expense claims.

As for local legislation protecting against bribery and corruption in China, two PRC laws prohibit commercial bribery: (1) Article 8 of the PRC Anti-Unfair Competition Law (AUCL) and (2) Article 164 of the PRC Criminal Law.

Article 8 of the AUCL prohibits a business from "giving bribes in the form of property or other means for the purpose of selling or purchasing products." The person giving the bribe may be held liable for damages under Article 8 of the AUCL. Article 164 of the PRC Criminal Law criminalizes the act of "giving money or property to any employee of a company or enterprise . . . for the purpose of seeking illegitimate benefits." Sentencing guidelines range from less than 3 years to up to 10 years for very large-scale activity. Fines can be levied to both individual and entities under Article 164.

Most recently, another law has been passed to broaden the reach of Chinese anti-bribery legislation, and bring the countries legal regime more in line with its commitments as a signatory to the Organization for Economic Co-operation and Development (OECD) Anti-Bribery Convention. On February 25, 2011, the PRC legislature passed 49 amendments to the PRC Criminal Law. Amendment No. 8 of the PRC Criminal Law criminalizes the payment of bribes to foreign government officials.

The jurisdiction of PRC Criminal Law is similar to that of the FCPA in that it applies to all citizens; all persons located in the PRC, and all institutions (i.e., companies) organized under PRC law. Therefore, joint ventures and subsidiaries of foreign companies would be covered.

For its part, the Chinese government has embarked on a high-profile and sustained anti-corruption drive, and has openly targeted corruption as possibly the largest obstacle to long term social stability and economic growth. Deep Internet penetration and widespread use of social media within China has increased public awareness of official abuses, and high-profile product, food, and drug safety cases have put the risk of corruption to public health and global reputation in stark focus.

On a more granular level, businesses operating in China report a dramatic upswing in local enforcement actions, led by the State Administration for

Industry & Commerce (SAIC), the Public Security Bureau for investigations of the private sector and the Central Commission on Discipline and Inspection, which leads investigations into official corruption. These efforts have been most visible in the health sector, where the former Director of the State Food and Drug Administration, Zheng Xiaoyu, was executed in 2007 for taking approximately US$850,000 in bribes from local and foreign pharmaceutical companies. SAIC investigations into the sales practices of multinational drug and other foreign companies are a common occurrence. Despite the increase in enforcement activity, the consequential risk of corruption remains relatively low. According to the reported disposition of party discipline cases, the odds of a Chinese official going to jail are still less than five percent.[4]

Korea

The Republic of Korea has also been the focus of a number of high-profile FCPA investigations:

- **IBM:** As part of its 2011 civil settlement with the SEC, IBM Corp. acknowledged that from 1998 to 2003, employees of IBM Korea, Inc., an IBM subsidiary, and LG IBM PC Co., Ltd., a joint venture in which IBM held a majority interest, provided cash payments, entertainment, travel, and gifts to officials of several South Korean government entities and computers to officials of additional government entities to secure the sale of product.[5]
- **Control Components Inc.:** A former consultant and former President of Control Components Inc. (CCI)'s South Korea office, Han Yong Kim, is one of six defendants indicted for alleged involvement in CCI's corruption scheme. CCI sold valve and related control solutions for several applications such as power stations and petrochemical facilities. In the related DOJ press release, the DOJ alleged that CCI senior executives approved payments of approximately US$ 4.9 million from 2003 to 2007 to officers and employees of various state-owned customers for the purpose of influencing the award of contracts and project technical specifications. CCI also made corrupt payments to employees of privately owned companies. The company admitted it made over 236 corrupt payments in more than 30 countries from 2003 to 2007, which resulted in approximately US$46.5 million in sales. CCI executives also rewarded customer employees with expensive gifts and extravagant holidays. Due to the violations, CCI was fined US$18.2 million and placed on organizational

probation for three years. The company also needed to create a compliance program and retain an independent compliance monitor for a term of three years.[6]

Bribery issues in Korea are governed by the Criminal Code and the Anti-Corruption Act. The Korean Criminal Code prohibits both official and commercial bribery.

In February 2008, the Anti-Corruption and Civil Rights Commission (ACRC) was created by the integration of the Ombudsman of Korea, the Korea Independent Commission against Corruption, and the Administrative Appeals Commission.

The ACRC formulates national anti-corruption policies to be implemented at every level of government. Also, it discusses and coordinates government-wide measures designed to prevent corruption in the short and long term. ACRC assesses the levels of integrity of public sector organizations each year by surveying citizens who have had firsthand experience with public services. The commission also evaluates the anti-corruption initiatives taken by public organizations on a regular basis. The fundamental objective of these assessments is to encourage public organizations to make voluntary efforts to tackle corruption.[7]

The rise of local anti-corruption enforcement in Korea has also been a notable development in the Asia-Pacific region. Recent inquiries involving foreign companies have been led by the Korea Fair Trade Commission (KFTC), South Korea's regulatory authority for economic competition. The KFTC was established in 1981 within the Economic Planning Board, under the Monopoly Regulation and Fair Trade Act (MRFTA), Law No. 3320, December 31, 1980.

Most recently, the KFTC has been focused on the activities of the pharmaceutical industry. Since 2007, the KFTC has issued approximately KRW 40 billion (roughly US$ 37.4 million) in corrective orders and surcharges against 17 domestic and international pharmaceutical companies, and 11 pharmaceutical investigations were initiated during 2009 and 2010.

Despite significant activity on the local enforcement front in Korea, not all enforcement is conducted in the same manner. Certain cases have illuminated differing perspectives on what normally comprises bribery between Korea and the U.S. of "Christmas money" and "funeral cash" to customers and officials has been treated with relative tolerance by Korean regulators. As such, though enforcement is occurring, the disparity between enforcement standards can create residual FCPA compliance risk.

Japan

As the region's most developed economy, Japan ranks relatively highly on both the Transparency International Corruptions Perceptions and Bribe Payers indices. However, Japan is not immune to FCPA enforcement and corruption risk. One major recent FCPA enforcement case has involved a Japanese company:

- **JGC Corporation:** In April 2011, Japan-based JGC Corporation settled charges with the DOJ in connection with the TSKJ joint venture in Nigeria. Between 1995 and 2004, TSKJ alleged to have bribed Nigerian officials in order to secure engineering, procurement, and construction contracts to build liquefied natural gas facilities on Bonny Island in Nigeria. According to the April 6, 2011 DOJ press release, JGC entered into a two-year deferred prosecution agreement with the DOJ, which included the retention of a compliance consultant to monitor its compliance program and payment of a US$218.8 million criminal fine.[8]

Following its signature to the OECD Convention on combating bribery of foreign officials in International Business Transactions (OECD Anti-bribery Convention) (which is discussed more fully in Chapter 3) in 1997, Japan has taken actions including a revision to the Unfair Competition Prevention Act (UCPA) in September 1998. Other actions include the revision to the Unfair Competition Prevention Law of Japan (UCPL), criminalizing bribery of foreign public officials. Other existing Japanese laws include provisions relevant to other OECD Anti-bribery Convention obligations.

In May 2004, the Japanese government revised the UCPL (enacted on January 1, 2005), which provides that any Japanese national who commits an offense of bribery of foreign public officials outside of Japan may be charged in Japan. This has been subsequently amended to make this bribery punishable even if it is legal where the act occurred.

Enforcement of the law has been limited and the OECD Working Group has been somewhat critical of Japan for the lack of activity. Below are two recent examples of local enforcement:

- **Kyudenko Corp.:** In March 2007, two employees were indicted on charges of bribing Philippine government officials in promoting Kyudenko equipment. During a trip to Japan paid for by Kyudenko in 2004, two representatives of the Philippine National Bureau of Investigation were given sets of golf clubs. The employees were fined ¥700,000 (approximately US$6,000).[9]

■ **Pacific Consultants International (PCI):** During 2009, four former senior executives pled guilty to bribing a Vietnamese official in connection with road construction projects. All four received suspended prison sentences between 18 and 30 months and the company was fined and paid ¥70 million (approximately US$750,000).[10]

While the dollar amount is not significant, Kyudenko was the first use of the UCPL in a foreign bribery and the PCI case was the first UCPL foreign bribery trial. These represent significant enforcement activities by the Japanese authorities and demonstrate that these can be enforced.

In light of the FCPA and UCPL enforcement trend of recent years, it is imperative for Japanese businesses to gain an understanding of those provisions and develop a robust anti-corruption compliance program.

Australia

To date, there has been no FCPA enforcement in Australia. However, in 2005 a government Royal Commission was enacted to investigate the alleged Oil for Food-related payments of US$220 million made in Iraq by the Australian Wheat Board (AWB). A number of civil cases were pending against six AWB executives for alleged breach of director's duties, brought by the Australian Securities and Investments Commission (ASIC) separate from enforcement of the Criminal Code. Only one of these cases proceeded, pending review of whether criminal charges should be brought against the executives. In February 2010, a stay of a second ASIC action was reportedly overturned and on June 3, 2010, it was announced that the criminal aspects had been abandoned and the other five civil cases might be revived. AWB settled a separate civil case brought by shareholders for AUD$39.5 million in February 2010 and the government of Iraq brought an Oil for Food-related civil action against AWB in the US in 2006.[11]

Australia has proscribed bribery and corruption offenses under the Australian Commonwealth Criminal Code Act 1995. Facilitation payments are legal under Australian law.

Division 70 of the Australian Commonwealth Criminal Code Act 1995 prescribes the conduct that will constitute bribery and corruption offenses in Australia. It also states that any company incorporated in Australia, or citizen or persons who live in Australia, can be prosecuted for corrupt conduct that is perpetrated overseas. In early 2010, the Crimes Legislation Amendment Act 2010 (Serious and Organized Crime) (No. 2) increased the penalties for bribery and corruption of Commonwealth or foreign public officials:

■ Individuals—up to 10 years imprisonment and fines of up to AU$1.1 million.
■ Corporations—the higher of AU$11 million or three times the value of the benefit obtained from committing the offense.

If the Court is unable to calculate the value of the benefit, they may assess up to 10 percent of annual turnover derived during the 12 months prior to the offense.

The Australian government continues to make concerted efforts to publicize the need to report foreign bribery, as highlighted by the increase of penalties for violations of applicable legislation in early 2010. By the end of 2011, all of the major states in Australia and the federal government will have standing commissions against corruption ombudsmen's offices with hotlines to receive complaints.

ASEAN

The Association of Southeast Asian Nations (ASEAN) is in many ways a mirror image of the Asia-Pacific region as a whole. The 10 member states of the ASEAN contain the least corrupt country per Transparency International's CPI (Singapore #1) and the second most corrupt country (Myanmar #176). Some of the most liberalized economies in the world sit adjacent to and trade regularly with state-controlled economies. The ASEAN organization has made attempts in recent years to coordinate the efforts of anti-corruption regulators in their member countries. However, these efforts are currently still in early and tentative stages. Below are snapshot views of the anti-corruption environments of selected individual ASEAN member countries:

Indonesia

Corruption continues to be a barrier for investment and business in Indonesia. The Indonesian government has been making an effort to counter this perception. Through the efforts of the Corruption Eradication Commission (known as the KPK), several politicians, legislators, and former ministers have been sentenced on corruption charges under President Yudhoyono, although these efforts have been met with substantial interagency conflict and resistance.

Recent FCPA enforcement activity related to Indonesia includes the *Monsanto, Inc.* matter from 2007. Charles Michael Martin of Monsanto, Inc. settled an action with the SEC that alleged that in 2002 he, as Monsanto's government affairs director for Asia, authorized and directed an Indonesian consulting firm to pay a US$50,000 bribe to a local Indonesian government official in order to induce the repeal of a government decree. In his settlement with the SEC, Martin agreed to pay a fine of US$30,000 and to an injunction not to violate the FCPA.[12] In a January 6, 2005 press release Monsanto announced it had settled this matter with the DOJ and SEC and agreed to a fine totaling US$1.5 million.

Philippines

Today, the Philippines is notable for the intensity of its anti-corruption drive. The government has been working to fast-track and implement a wide range of reform initiatives to rid the country of what has been pervasive corruption. However, despite a serious effort at local enforcement, corruption remains prevalent.

Recent FCPA enforcement activity related to the Philippines includes Emery Transnational. A former subsidiary of Con-way Inc. based in the Philippines, Emery Transnational allegedly made hundreds of small payments totaling at least US$417,000 to Philippines customs officials and to officials of foreign state-owned airlines operating in the Philippines. These payments were made to improperly influence these foreign officials to assist Emery Transnational to obtain or retain business. The company settled the SEC civil case in August 2008 for US$300,000.[13]

Thailand

Corruption is seen locally and by investors as a chronic problem in Thailand. A study by the Office of the Civil Service Commission (OCSC) in 2001, found that 79 percent of businessmen felt that bribery was the norm to get things accomplished. Thailand signed of the United Nations Convention against Corruption in December 2003 and ratified it in March 2011. However, there has been no prosecution of Thai officials and Thai businesses for bribery committed outside Thailand.

There has been a significant amount of FCPA enforcement activity in Thailand and one recent example is Alliance One International Inc. (Alliance One), a global tobacco company. Subsidiaries of Alliance One were accused of paying bribes to Thai government officials to secure contracts with Thailand Tobacco Monopoly (TTM) for the sale of tobacco leaf. In 2010, the subsidiaries admitted to paying kickbacks to certain TTM representatives based on the number of kilograms of tobacco sold to the TTM. Alliance One settled with the SEC to disgorge US$10 million and agreed to pay US$9.5 million to the DOJ.[14]

Vietnam

Vietnam is moving tentatively to tackle corruption with the anti-corruption mechanisms in place unclear and/or inconsistently enforced. As is frequently the case in transitional economies, there is wide gap between legislation and actual practice. The Communist Party of Vietnam passed the country's first Anti-Corruption Law in 2005.

Recent FCPA-related activity from Vietnam includes Nexus Technologies Inc., a privately-held Delaware company, that was indicted for allegedly purchasing a wide variety of equipment and technology, including underwater mapping equipment, bomb containment equipment, helicopter parts, chemical detectors, satellite communication parts, and air tracking systems, for resale to Vietnam. From approximately 1999 through 2008, employees of Nexus engaged in a conspiracy to pay bribes to Vietnamese government officials in exchange for lucrative contracts to supply equipment and technology to Vietnamese government agencies. The employees are alleged to have paid in excess of US$250,000 in bribes to foreign officials in Vietnam. According to a March 16, 2010 DOJ press release, Nexus and a number of employees pleaded guilty to criminal charges conspiracy, money laundering, and violating the FCPA.[15]

Summary

While the frequency and scale of FCPA related activity in Asia Pacific points to a stubbornly high risk environment, local enforcement trends suggest that the region is moving slowly but steadily toward a climate of tighter regulation and transparency.

One should not assume that the powerful drivers of corruption risk as outlined here will diminish or even hold the line in the near term. The "demand" side of the corruption equation appears to be a large factor in this region for the foreseeable future. However, across the board, the countries of the region appear to recognize turning a blind eye to corruption and the effect it has on distorting markets, undermining fairness, and threatening public health, poses great risk to long term stability and prosperity.

EUROPE

Europe has the largest economy in the world but, as with other continents, there is significant variation of wealth. The wealthier countries, as measured by gross domestic product (GDP) per capita, are mostly to the west, and many of the countries in the east of Europe are still emerging from the collapse of communism. They are continuing to transition to fully functioning free market economies.

The European Union (EU), an intergovernmental body composed of 27 European states, comprises the largest single economic area in the world. Accession to the EU is dependent on a number of social and economic tests, which include tackling corruption. Currently, 17 EU countries share the euro as a common currency. Of the major economic powerhouses sharing the euro, the United Kingdom is a notable omission.

The recent global economic recession hit Europe hard, causing rising unemployment and high levels of corporate failures. The downturn has brought the economies of several European countries to the brink of bankruptcy and several, including Ireland, Greece, and Portugal have been forced to apply for financial assistance from the European Union and the International Monetary Fund.

European countries are home to the full spectrum of primary-, secondary-, and tertiary-sector industries. Historically, the most highly regulated industries—the extractive industries, financial services, and pharmaceuticals—are those that have been considered to bear the greatest corruption risk and have therefore come under most scrutiny from the anti-bribery and corruption authorities.

The wide variety of cultural practices within Europe results in a mixed pattern of acceptance and prevalence of corruption as part of everyday life. As a general rule, European countries tend to score above the global average in TI's CPI. The ranks from the 2010 index range from very low in the Scandinavian region (Denmark—rank 1 of 178, Sweden—rank 4 of 178) to very high for Commonwealth of Independent States (CIS) countries including Russia (rank 154 of 178) and Ukraine (rank 134 of 178).When studying the CPI in detail a clear division between the east and west of the regions exists, although there are some notable exceptions, most prominent of which are Italy (rank 67 of 178) and Greece (rank 78 of 178).

As Europe leaves the economic downturn behind some companies are left struggling to achieve organic and ethical growth. The fragile market conditions and economic pressures on individuals and their companies continue to create an environment that is conducive to unethical behavior.

Bribery and corruption has been a hot topic for corporate boards in Europe for a number of years, and with good reason. Even in countries where the local authorities are limited in their appetite for enforcement and capabilities, the increasing willingness of local authorities to support U.S.-led prosecutions heightens the risk. There were more FCPA enforcement actions in 2010 than ever before, with 7 of the largest 10 settlements in the history of the FCPA involving firms headquartered outside the United States.

The scale of the task facing businesses and regulators is striking. In a recent survey by Ernst & Young, two thirds of European respondents stated that bribery and corruption was widespread in their country. This statistic hides significant country variations, with more than 80 percent of the people in emerging European markets reporting that bribery and corruption was widespread, compared with half of that figure in the more mature economic markets. The survey found that one in four respondents believed it was justifiable to give personal gifts to win or retain business while one in five believed that using entertainment was justifiable. Across Europe, an alarming 1 in 25 board directors believed it acceptable to misstate a company's financial records to achieve their aim. And while most companies recognize the business benefits bought by acting with integrity, there remains a high degree of variety to which companies have implemented anti-corruption procedures.[16]

Despite the diverse nature of the countries and cultures within Europe, there are various common "red flags" worthy of comment. These include:

- *Use of intermediaries.* Many Europe-based companies operate in countries outside of Europe with which they are less familiar. Intermediaries are commonly and legitimately used to advance a goal, but in some instances companies turn a blind eye to how the end goal is achieved. The fee paid to the intermediary can be inflated to mask the payment of a bribe by the intermediary.
- *Abuse of off-set agreements.* Relevant to those with interests outside of Europe, some companies make agreements with business partners that involve the support of a charitable or social project such as the building of a school in a developing country. While appearing on the surface to be bona fide, these projects may sometimes be the route for a kick back to be paid or for the business partner to enlarge their personal reputation.
- *Corporate entertainment.* While gift giving is perhaps less prevalent than elsewhere in the world, the use of entertainment as a tool to induce or reward decision makers is commonplace. The line between expenditure designed to promote product or business relationships and expenditure

that may be deemed to be extravagant or lavish is typically difficult for companies and regulators alike to determine. Equally, the context and timing of the entertainment will often give a clearer indication as to the intended nature of the advantage being offered.

There is no common piece of legislation that governs bribery and corruption law across Europe. Some of the leading economies have signed up to the OECD Anti-bribery Convention but there remain many that have not.

For much of the past decade, discussion of bribery and corruption in Europe has been heavily influenced by the extraterritorial reach of the FCPA, but now things are starting to change. The United Kingdom has introduced a much improved legislation in the form of the U.K. Bribery Act, which became effective July 1, 2011. Spain and France have made amendments to their national legislation over the past few years to bring their regimes into line with the standards expected under the OECD Anti-bribery Convention to which they are signatories. And Russia has embarked on a program to improve the perception of its high corruption levels by introducing new laws that increase the penalties for non-compliance.

Each European country maintains its own criminal and civil legislation on bribery and corruption. This section sets out the most noteworthy from a combined viewpoint of their position as a significant global exporter, changes to recent legislation, and its history of enforcement.

United Kingdom

The U.K. Bribery Act received Royal Assent on April 8, 2010, and came into force on July 1, 2011. When the act was passed, the U.K. government heralded it as the "gold standard" of bribery and corruption legislation. However, subsequent guidance from the authorities charged with enforcing it has attracted strong criticism from international observers that it has been weakened.

On paper, the U.K. Bribery Act has a wide remit covering active and passive bribery, bribery of foreign public officials, and business-to-business bribery. It creates a corporate offense of failing to prevent bribery, which provides for unlimited fines and applies extraterritorially to organizations that carry on a business in the United Kingdom.

The offense for failure to prevent bribery has attracted significant attention. The defense available to an organization is proving that "adequate procedures" are in place to prevent bribery. "Adequate procedures" guidance was released by the U.K. government in March 2011.

There are concerns as to whether the appetite for enforcement will match the strident wording of the act. Currently, the Serious Fraud Office (SFO) is set to be the prosecutorial lead. If the wrong decisions are made in regards to enforcement, then the goals set forth within the U.K. Bribery Act could very well be compromised from the beginning.

The U.K. Bribery Act and the adequate procedures guidance are discussed in Chapters 3 and 4, respectively.

The United Kingdom is classified as an "active" enforcer of foreign bribery by TI's 2011 Progress Report on the OECD Anti-Bribery Convention.[17] Enforcement to date has been under legacy bribery legislation and it is expected that enforcement will increase with the U.K. Bribery Act.

Recent enforcement cases have included the following:

- **Balfour Beatty:** A payment of £2.25 million was made for failure to keep accurate records in relation to a joint venture to build the Biblioteca Alexandrina, a library in Egypt. The project was completed in 2001. Balfour Beatty self-reported to the SFO having carried out its own investigation. The settlement was the first to be made under civil recovery powers. An external monitor was appointed following the conclusion of the SFO's investigations.[18]
- **Mabey and Johnson:** Mabey and Johnson is a U.K.-based modular steel bridge supplier who admitted to paying bribes to government representatives in Jamaica, Ghana, and Iraq. Penalties and reparations totaled approximately £6.5m.[19] Two former directors and a sales manager were jailed in the U.K.[20]
- **AMEC:** A settlement of £4.9 million was agreed to after civil proceedings following allegations of books and records offences relating to a public private partnership in which AMEC was a shareholder.[21]
- **BAE Systems:** In the most high profile of bribery cases in the United Kingdom to date, BAE faced allegations that began to be investigated by the SFO in 2004. The allegations centered on a Saudi Arabian defense contract but expanded to include contracts between BAE and other countries including the Czech Republic, Romania and South Africa. In February 2010, BAE settled with the SFO regarding books and records violations relating to a radar system sold to the government of Tanzania and agreed to pay £30 million in fines and voluntary donations.[22] On the same day, BAE admitted conspiring to provide false statements related to its FCPA compliance program to the U.S. government and agreed to pay a US$400 million fine. It was not found guilty of an FCPA violation.[23]

- **Innospec:** Innospec faced investigations by the DOJ, SEC, and U.K. SFO. The U.K. investigation centered on alleged bribes linked to contracts to supply anti-knock petrol additive to the Indonesian government. In total Innospec has agreed to pay US$40 million to settle the claims by the various regulators.[24] In the United Kingdom, the SFO faced judicial criticism for going beyond its powers in its settlement with Innospec.[25]
- **Macmillan Publishing:** The World Bank and SFO initiated parallel corruption investigations into Macmillan Publishers Limited, a U.K. publishing house, education division in East and West Africa. Based on the investigation of the tender process, the SFO noted that "it was plain that the Company may have received revenue that had been derived from unlawful conduct" and levied a penalty of approximately £11 million. The World Bank debarred Macmillian from World Bank funded tenders for at least 3 years.[26]

Germany

Germany has been pursuing a robust anti-corruption enforcement strategy for over a decade. The German anti-corruption legislation, contained within the German Criminal Code (the Strafgesetzbuch or StGB), covers active and passive bribery, public- and private-sector corruption, and has extrajurisdictional reach. Penalties can be levied against companies and their directors, although companies cannot be subject to criminal prosecution.

The current environment compares favorably with the less robust legislative framework of the past. Before the OECD Anti-bribery Convention, German companies were able to deduct any bribes to foreign public officials as business expenses on their tax return. Germany was ranked 15 out of 178 countries in the 2010 Transparency International CPI.[27]

The German Criminal Code sets out that a person is liable to prosecution if they bribe a German public official in return for an act contrary to that official's duty. The bribe may have already taken place or may be planned.

Some auxiliary laws to Germany's national provisions—the EU Anti-Corruption Act (EuBestG) and Act against international corruption (IntBestG)—extend these prohibitions to cover European and foreign public officials. The German public officials themselves may also be prosecuted upon acceptance of the bribe.

It is notable that in Germany only individuals, not the companies involved, are subject to criminal prosecution. Certain activities that many might expect would be caught within the scope of corruption of a public official are not, such as the payment of bribes to members of political parties.

The German Criminal Code also makes it illegal for an employee to bribe to receive improper preferential treatment in relation to the supply of goods or services. In principle, this ban covers both domestic and overseas corruption.

The Administrative Offences Act (the Ordnungswidrigkeitsgesetz or OWiG) sets out that a corporation may be fined where an agent or representative company has committed corruption overseas on the corporate's behalf. Under the same law, companies and their directors may be guilty of an administrative offense if they do not have appropriate controls to prevent bribery by employees of the company. In one case, a compliance officer was found criminally liable for offenses committed by an employee under his supervision.

Facilitation payments are prohibited for domestic bribery, but section 333 of the penal code does not prohibit small foreign facilitation payments.[28]

The fines are dependent on an individual's income. A prison sentence is also possible, dependent on previous criminal record, with a maximum limit of 10 years.

Fines are based on the size of the corporation and the extent of the offenses committed, other penalties include forfeiture and tax sanctions. The fines are limited to €1million. However, the legislation allows for disgorgement of profits so in practice the penalties are much higher.

Germany was classified as an "active" enforcer of foreign bribery by Transparency International's 2011 Progress Report on the OECD Anti-Bribery Convention on the basis of 135 settled cases of foreign bribery and 22 investigations in progress.[29] This makes Germany by far the most active enforcer within Europe. Enforcement activity is largely carried out at the regional level, with the various states establishing specialist prosecution units that have been actively sharing data, experience and best practice models. Recent enforcement has included both domestic bribery by foreign companies and cases of foreign bribery. A selection of the main cases involving global organizations includes:

- **Siemens AG:** The Siemens case still dominates public discussion of anti-bribery enforcement as the company holds the record for largest penalty levied for bribery related offenses. When aggregated, the fines and settlements with the German public prosecutor and SEC and DOJ, comes to US$1.6 billion. This followed the identification of approximately US$1.4 billion of suspicious transactions made by the company between 2001 and 2007.[30]

- **Ferrostaal AG:** Reports indicate that the Munich prosecutor opened a corruption investigation of Ferrostaal related to activities in Africa, Greece and Portugal. Additionally, German prosecutors have charged two former managers of the industrial services group with bribing foreign officials to win contracts in Greece and Portugal.[31]
- **Deutsche Telekom AG:** German authorities have raided the homes and offices of senior executives at the telecom over allegations that its subsidiary, Magyar Telekom, paid roughly €31 million in bribes to consulting companies and lobbying firms in Macedonia and Montenegro.[32]
- **Daimler AG:** The German car and truck making group paid US$185 million in April 2010 to settle charges brought by the DOJ and SEC of paying bribes to foreign officials in at least 22 countries to help secure government contracts.[33] To date no prosecution has been bought by the German authorities.
- **Hewlett-Packard:** German and Russian authorities launched a probe in April 2010 involving several Hewlett-Packard managers from its German operations whom they suspect of paying bribes to win a €35 million contract to supply information technology equipment and software to the Russian prosecutor general's office. Hewlett-Packard has also confirmed that it is under investigation by the SEC in relation to this matter.[34]

France

France, which in 2010 was ranked 25 out of the 178 countries in the Transparency International CPI, has made a number of amendments in recent years to bring its legislation into line with international treaties on corruption. Both domestic and overseas corruption are covered under the French Criminal Code and were revised under the Anti-Corruption Act of 2007.

Although there have been relatively few convictions to date, the actual law is well defined and distinguishes between active and passive corruption, domestic and foreign bribery, as well as bribery in the public and private sectors.

The offenses of active and passive bribery of foreign public officials are defined in the same way as the corresponding domestic offenses. As at domestic level, there are two specific offenses of active and passive bribery of foreign and international judicial personnel (Article 435-7). The Criminal Code prohibits the passive (Article 435-1, Criminal Code) and active (Article 435-3) corruption of foreign public officials. The corruption of private individuals is covered in Article 445-2. The act of proposing the bribery agreement to a private individual or consenting to the individual solicitation is also punishable (Article 445-1).

Under French law, the offense of corruption is a *délit successif,* which means that each individual act is treated as a new offence. Consequently, the limitation period (three years) within which the authorities must take action is triggered by the most recent act. Additionally, French laws have extra-territorial application.

There are no specific provisions or exemptions in French law for facilitation payments.

Under the terms of law, penalties for individuals include up to 10 years imprisonment and a fine of up to €150,000 for the corruption of public officials and five years imprisonment and a fine of €75,000 for private bribery.

Legal entities can face fines of up to five times the maximum fines for individuals as well as additional penalties such as exclusion from government contracts, the prohibition of offering shares to the public or the closure of an establishment for up to five years.

Under French law, only the state prosecutor can initiate proceedings for the offence of bribery. This element of the law has been criticized by international organizations.

A civil party may join a criminal action initiated by the prosecutor or on its own initiate the prosecution by filing a civil party petition. This procedure offers the victim of a criminal offense the possibility of overturning the decision of a state prosecutor who decides not to file charges.

The ability of a civil party to initiate proceedings is a recent development. Historically, civil parties were not admissible to bribery cases, until the French Supreme Court (Cour de Cassation) ruled for the first time in November 2010 that an anti-corruption complaint that was initiated by TI France would be admissible. This ruling has potentially significant implications for enforcement activity in France. In 2011, TI indicated their intention to use this method to launch a complaint relating to the assets owned in France by the former Tunisian president, his family, and close circle of acquaintances.

In TI's 2011 Progress Report on the OECD Anti-Bribery Convention, France was classified as a "moderate" enforcer of foreign bribery, with a total of 19 live judicial and police investigations.[35] All the investigations relate to foreign bribery; there are no known live investigations for domestic bribery. The Progress Report highlighted various perceived inadequacies in the legal framework and enforcement system, including a lack of investigating resources.

In the past few years a number of French companies, their subsidiaries or employees have been the subject of investigations, prosecutions or settlements in foreign jurisdictions, including Alcatel-Lucent, Alstom, Areva, Amaris,

Dumez, EADS, Schneider Electric, Technip, Thales, Total, and Vivendi. Two of the more prominent recent cases included:

- **Alcatel-Lucent:** In December 2010, the telecommunications giant Alcatel-Lucent announced that it had reached settlement with the DOJ and SEC over allegations of widespread improper payments, made through third-party agents, to foreign government officials in Costa Rica, Honduras, Malaysia, and Taiwan. This case was interesting because it was the second time in the history of the FCPA that a company has pleaded guilty to criminal internal controls charges. The combined criminal fine for the parent and three subsidiaries was US$92 million.[36]
- **Technip:** As part of the wider prosecutions relating to the Bonny Island, Nigeria Joint Venture, Technip, the French oil and gas engineering company, made a combined settlement payment to the SEC and DOJ in June 2010 of US$338 million for alleged breaches of the FCPA. Later in 2010, the Nigerian authorities detained Technip staff as part of their investigation into the matter.[37]

Russia

Russia was ranked 154 out of 178 countries in the TI 2010 CPI.[38] In an attempt to address the widely acknowledged historical prevalence of corruption in Russia, the government has, in recent years, taken steps to implement an anti–corruption framework and strategy. This resulted in the approval of a National Anti-Corruption Plan on July 31, 2008 (№Пр-1568). The plan was approved by the Russian president on April 13, 2010 (No. 460). Further evidence that the government was taking the issue seriously came in May 2011 when new legislation was introduced to criminalize bribery and increase the level of fines for companies and individuals who bribe foreign public officials. Russia has recently been invited by the OECD to join its working group on bribery, which is regarded as a first step toward being invited to be a signatory to the OECD'S Anti-bribery Convention.[39]

Russia's anti-corruption laws are set out in the Russian Criminal Code. Russian law prohibits the bribery of public officials and the bribery of responsible officers of private organizations (commercial bribery). This applies to both domestic and foreign corruption.

The Russian Criminal Code prohibits giving or receiving a bribe in the form of money, securities, other assets or benefits in exchange for action, or inaction, by a state or municipal officer or an executive of a state legal entity, or a state corporation.

The Russian Criminal Code prohibits the giving or receiving of bribes of money, securities or assets by a person acting in a management capacity in an organization which results in an action, or inaction, to the benefit of the briber.

The Russian law on bribery applies only to individuals and not to corporate entities. Therefore, in cases of bribery involving a company, the company itself cannot be prosecuted but the officers of a company can be.

The Russian Criminal Code applies to offenses committed outside of Russia in cases where a foreigner or stateless person commits an offense against interests of the Russian Federation or one of its citizens.

Facilitation payments are not permitted in Russia unless they are deemed official and have an official rate. If a payment does not have an official rate, then it may be classed as a bribe.

Under the latest changes to the Criminal Code, introduced in May 2011, the severity of penalties for the giving and accepting of bribes concerning state officials depends on whether an offense is expressly unlawful, for which those involved could expect to incur the higher end penalty, or unqualified, which will incur a lower penalty. The range of penalties which can be incurred for public bribery are a fine of between RUR 100,000 and RUR 500,000 (approximately US$3,400 to US$17,900), the loss of one and a half to three years' worth of salary or other income, or a prison sentence of three to eight years.

The penalty for commercial bribery depends on whether the offense is committed by a group or an individual. For offenses committed by groups, the penalty can be a fine of up to RUR 300,000 (approximately US$10,750), two years' worth of salary or income, limitation of freedoms for up to three years, or a prison sentence of up to four years. For individuals, the penalty is less, with a fine of RUR 200,000 (approximately US$7,200), one and a half years' worth of salary, or imprisonment for up to two years.

Breach of legislation by a corporate can result in fines and seizures with penalties, including the company being prevented from receiving grants, public assistance, or tax or social security benefits. Companies in breach also risk liquidation or suspension. At their most severe, where the bribery is linked to tax evasion, fines can be up to six times the amount evaded.

Prosecutions in relation to corruption in Russia are not commonplace. It is therefore difficult to assess how effectively the law is being enforced. Russia is not part of the OECD Anti-bribery Convention, therefore reporting on the bribery enforcement is less readily available than other European. That said recent examples of Russian authorities launching investigations into allegations of bribery include:

- **Daimler:** There is an ongoing investigation by the Russian authorities into the alleged bribery of Russian officials by Daimler, the German car and truck manufacturing company, who were fined US$185 million by the DOJ and SEC for breaches under the FCPA. The Russian investigation was launched seven months after the Russian division of Daimler pleaded guilty in the United States to charges of bribery. Consequently, the Russian government has come under some criticism for being slow to respond to the allegations.[40]
- **Hewlett-Packard:** In April 2010, it was reported that Russian authorities were cooperating with German prosecutors with regard to an investigation into the involvement of Hewlett-Packard employees in an alleged corrupt business contract in Russia with included potential kickbacks worth US$10.9 million.[41]

Italy

Italy was ranked 67 out of 178 countries in the TI 2010 CPI.[42] A signatory to the OECD Anti-bribery Convention against foreign bribery, Italy is one of the lowest ranked countries that would count itself as part of western Europe. In May 2011, the TI's 2011 Progress Report on the OECD Anti-Bribery Convention noted that the Italian parliament is currently considering revisions to the existing corruption laws to include for the provision of a central supervising body, the role of which will include the compilation and analysis of all corruption in the country.[43]

Domestic and overseas corruption is covered under the Italian Criminal Code and Italian Decree 231/2001 passed in June 2001. By providing liability for companies, Decree 231 encourages corporate governance and compliance structures to mitigate the risk that, employees, and third parties commit crimes.

Legislative decree number 231/2001, promulgated in response to the OECD Anti-bribery Convention, lies behind much of the recent enforcement activity and is now being used to levy criminal sanctions on companies for conduct that elsewhere might generate civil proceedings or regulatory actions.

The Italian parliament has now included new crimes in the law, including fraud against public entities, financial crimes, forgery, terrorist financing, IT violations, market abuse, copyright, and health and safety violations.

Decree 231 extends to any individuals acting in the name of, or on behalf of, the company, such as agents, employees, and distributors. Note that only administrative liability applies to companies not criminal liability.

Crimes committed for the benefit of a company trigger corporate liability and similar to the U.K. Bribery Act, the company has a defense if it can demonstrate adequate measures to prevent the crimes taking place.

Under 231, a defense is allowed if a "vigilance model" of specific controls and systems to prevent inappropriate conduct are in place. Italian companies commonly now have such models and "231 legal audit boards" charged with overseeing the vigilance model, but many multinationals are still not compliant.

Italian prosecutors have very broad powers under other laws, including pre-emptive seizure of corporate assets and documents, "preventive" arrests, and replacing the company's leadership with a judicial administrator.

The legislation can be applied to Italian citizens or corporations operating abroad. Facilitation payments are prohibited by law.

The Italian Criminal Code sets out fines and imprisonment for each relevant criminal offense. The longest jail term that can be imposed for bribery offenses is five years.

The Italian authorities can impose fines of up to €1.5m as well as force the company to disgorge illegally obtained profit, debar it from all public contracts and revoke or suspend operating licenses.

Italian authorities have been active in prosecuting corruption, so that by the end of 2010, 39 entities and individuals had been sanctioned for foreign bribery.[44] However, TI's 2011 Progress Report on the OECD Anti-Bribery Convention noted inadequacies in Italy's anti-corruption legislation including weaknesses in the whistle-blower protection system and in complaint procedures. TI also noted the progression of a number of existing foreign bribery cases but no commencement of new ones in 2010. Ferring Pharmaceuticals and the multinational oil company Total SA were reported to be under investigation for allegations of domestic bribery within Italy.[45] Of the foreign bribery cases, the most prominent involved the ENI SpA group of companies:

- **ENI SpA:** The Italian company ENI SpA and its various subsidiaries (Snamprogetti Netherlands BV and Saipem SpA) have been the subject of various investigations, both home and abroad, in relation to allegations of unethical behavior. In July 2010, ENI and its former Dutch subsidiary Snamprogetti Netherlands BV entered a settlement in the U.S. involving payment of US$365 million in fines in connection with the TSKJ joint venture in Nigeria.[46] A further fine of US$32.5 million was reportedly paid to the Nigerian authorities in relation to the same case in return for an agreement to dismiss all charges against Snamprogetti

Netherlands BV and to renounce any civil claims and criminal charges in its jurisdiction.[47] Another ENI subsidiary, the oil services company Saipem SpA, is reportedly the target of Italian authorities regarding allegations of corrupt activity in Algeria, although no further details have been released to date.[48]

Spain

Spain was ranked 30 out of 178 countries in the TI 2010 CPI.[49] Spain's anti-corruption laws are defined in the 2003 Spanish Criminal Code (the "Code") with laws regarding domestic and overseas corruption set out in articles 419 and 445 of the Code respectively. Largely in response to criticism from the OECD Working Group on Bribery, the Spanish Authorities have recently undertaken various initiatives to strengthen Spanish bribery-related legislation and adapt it to the OECD Anti-bribery Convention to which it is a signatory. In what was considered by some commentators as the most far-reaching reform of criminal law in Spain since the approval of the Criminal Code in 1995, the existing laws were updated in June 2010, with the changes becoming effective from December 2010.

Article 419 of the Code applies to domestic public corruption and prohibits the corruption of Spanish authorities or public servants through promises, presents or offerings with the purpose of obtaining an outcome as a result of an act, or omission of an act, by an authority or public servant. It also prohibits the acceptance of offerings made by Spanish authorities or public servants in exchange of the performance, or omission, of an act and it is illegal for public servants to receive offerings in exchange for duties being performed.

Article 445 of the Code applies to foreign public corruption and prohibits the corruption of foreign authorities or public servants and the acceptance of bribes by foreign authorities and public servants in order to obtain a benefit that may be deemed as irregular.

The Criminal Code does not specifically mention domestic or foreign private corruption but these acts could fall under other offenses within the Code.

Organic Law 5/2010 superseded Law 10/1995 of the Code and became effective on December 23, 2010. This amendment to the law brought about three key changes:

- Under the amended law, companies are now liable for crimes committed in their name or by people who have been authorized to act on their behalf. This can be mitigated by the implementation of controls that prevent bribery and corruption. This amendment is similar to the "Failure of commercial organizations to prevent bribery" offense introduced as part of the U.K. Bribery Act.

■ The offense of private commercial bribery incorporates the EU Framework Directive on corruption within the private sector and so now implicates both the bribe payer and the bribe receiver if an offense is committed.

■ The amended law incorporates criminal liability for companies that bribe foreign government officials so that both companies and individuals can be liable for this offense.

The law regarding domestic public corruption applies to Spanish authorities and public servants or any person based in Spain, whether acting as an individual or on behalf of a company at the time of the offense.

The law regarding foreign corrupt practices applies to a person based in Spain at the time of the offense, whether acting as an individual or on behalf of a company, and to Spanish Nationals committing corruption offenses in countries where corruption is unlawful.

Facilitation payments are prohibited under the Spanish Criminal Code (Article 242.1).

A breach of legislation by a company director can result in imprisonment, fines and disqualifications from between 6 months and 10 years, depending on the seriousness of the offense. Fines are calculated on the basis of the earnings of the director within a range of 10 days to 2 years' worth of earnings or between €2 and €400 per day.

A breach of legislation by a corporation can result in seizures and fines which can include a company being prevented from receiving grants, public assistance or tax or social security benefits. Companies in breach also risk liquidation. Fines can be up to six times the amount evaded when bribery is linked to tax evasion.

TI's 2011 Progress Report on the OECD Anti-Bribery Convention categorized Spain as a "moderate" enforcer, and noted no ongoing domestic or foreign cases or investigations.[50] The prosecution of domestic bribery by foreign companies has historically largely been focused on the fight against organized crime syndicates. In addition, the small number of foreign bribery cases has included:

■ **Instalaciones Inabensa SA:** In 2008, Instalaciones, a subsidiary of Abengoa SA, was charged with bribing the former President of Costa Rica in order obtain an electric contract worth over US$50 million. No further update on the resolution of this case is available.[51]

- **Banco Bilbao Vizcaya Argentaria (BBVA):** In 2002, Spanish authorities investigated and pursued a case involving off-book accounts and bribery in Latin America, which in 2005 resulted in the sentencing of the former president of BBVA on charges of false bookkeeping.[52]

Summary

The effect of the OECD Anti-bribery Convention has been to encourage European countries to strengthen their anti-bribery and corruption laws, even beyond those countries who are signatories. Progress over the past decade has been encouraging with new pieces of legislation and updates to old to reflect robust penalties and, increasingly, extraterritorial reach.

For many European countries a gulf between the legal provisions and the demonstrated appetite to enforce them, particularly against domestic companies exists. The United States continues to take a lead, with enforcement actions to June 2010 outnumbering the sum of all actions in the rest of the world by three to one. As the various European laws, many of which are in their infancy, become more established international commentators will be watching closely to see whether the law's bark is matched by its bite.

INDIA AND SOUTH ASIA

The South Asia region includes countries such as Afghanistan, Bangladesh, Bhutan, India, Maldives, Nepal, Pakistan, and Sri Lanka. South Asia has been experiencing substantial economic growth over the past 20 years, averaging 6 percent a year. With the accelerating economy, the area has seen GDP grow to an estimated 8.7 percent FY2010–11. This high growth is concentrated in certain areas of the region, while poverty remains widespread across most of the South Asia. According to the World Bank, one of the most important aspects of South Asia is its people; 1 million people are expected to join the labor force each month for the next two decades. Therefore, job creation is a key factor contributing to future economic growth. The region lacks integration and investment and trade barriers are high. The lack of integration has hindered growth in transportation, mobility, and scale economies and has led to increased cross-border conflicts. Trade between South Asian countries accounted for less than 2 percent of their combined GDP, whereas in East Asia this figure was 20 percent. The inability of the South Asian regions to cooperate and integrate policies has led to the area's unbalanced growth and lack of inclusive developments.[53]

General Overview

Corruption is part of the social norm and is accepted as a way to avoid administrative delays. Low governmental salaries feed this problem. Major characteristics of corruption in South Asia include:

- *Corruption at the top.* People in positions of power and leadership who are corrupt are rarely investigated and prosecuted.
- *Lack of transparency and inability to access information.* Principles of transparency and an independent, free media are lacking in most countries in South Asia. Access to these tools would help curb corruption.
- *Inefficient governance encourages corruption leading to further poverty.* Effective governance is recognized as a necessary condition to combat poverty and lagging development. Corruption in South Asia leads to uneven development and access to services causing further income inequalities.
- *Weak judicial system.* In South Asia, civil proceedings take many years to reach a resolution. The judicial process can be manipulated with small bribes and these can be used to cause significant delays.

"Red flags" of corruption are common to South Asia as well. The most prominent corruption risks are:

- *Purchase of unnecessary items.* Unnecessary items can be added to purchases due to hidden ownership interests or kickbacks.
- *Connections between bidders or agents.* Recommendations of agents or bidders insisted upon by project or government officials may indicate collusive bidding and kickbacks to the project or government official. A further relatively common type of corruption also involves budget mark-ups, which usually imply some element of collusion at the local level.
- *Pressure to select a certain agent or contractor.* In many situations an agent or contractor is identified by the government official associated with a project and often the connection or relation is not known or disclosed.
- *Questionable invoices.* Invoices that appear to be false, inflated, or duplicated can indicate corruption. These invoices may include improper supporting documentation or terms or conditions that differ from the purchase order or contract.
- *Bribe extortion.* Bribes and informal payments paid by firms in South Asia often arise from red tape, in particular in permits and licenses imposed by local government officials.

South Asian countries have signed the UN Anti-bribery Convention; however, only Bangladesh and the Maldives had ratified the convention. The need to fight corruption is a unifying theme for South Asia. Southern Asian members of parliament (MPs) were initially reluctant to establish a formal network, although after holding a regional seminar, all South Asian countries and their MPs are developing the South Asian Parliamentarians against Corruption (SAPAC) which is a chapter of the Global Organization of Parliamentarians against Corruption (GOPAC). GOPAC is an international network of parliamentarians dedicated to good governance and combating corruption throughout the world.[54]

TI is active in South Asia. The TI chapters help in designing anti-corruption programs with governments, nongovernmental organizations, and media as well as private sector and development partners. The South Asian chapters have emphasized institutional, legal, and policy reform in their work, including efforts to bring greater transparency to government information and to promote the right of a free press to function independently and objectively. Most South Asian countries have yet to enact an access to information law, which is an indispensable foundation for transparency and accountability in governance and for the control and prevention of corruption.

The three sample markets highlighted next—India, Bangladesh, and Pakistan—provide an overview of specific industries exposed to corruption,[55] local anti-corruption laws, and enforcement measures taken to mitigate the risk of corruption within these industries.

India

The Indian economy is growing rapidly, making it very attractive to global businesses. The number of international companies conducting business in India has increased dramatically over the past few years. However, corruption continues to be a serious problem in business operations and in the region. Doing business in India involves facing bribery and corruption-related circumstances from outset. Whether from corporate incorporation to setting up factory, or from importing raw materials to exporting finished products, or from multilocation expansion to obtaining foreign funding, every company that plans to expand has to consider and plan its strategy for the bribery and corruption factor in India.

Some companies appoint compliance officers to deal with government, compliance and anti-bribery matters. These officers develop the company's culture to prevent illegal, unethical, or improper conduct with regard to corruption regulation and enforce the same culture on their employees, suppliers, and intermediaries. Business tycoon Ratan Tata recalled that his group faced tremendous difficulty in establishing a domestic airline in collaboration with Singapore Airlines due to suggestions of bribing a government official to have the deal go through.

Many industries in India have historically been dominated by the state-owned entities. Also, many other industries have the government as their prime/major customer. The regulatory environment in India is also complex enough to influence most of the industries. The industries that directly interact with government for business or regulatory requirements face high risk of bribery and corruption in India.

Recent FCPA cases that have involved India are:

- **Dow Chemical:** DE-Nocil Crop Protection Ltd., a subsidiary of Dow Chemical, headquartered in Mumbai, India, manufactured and marketed pesticides and other products primarily for use in the Indian agriculture industry. DE-Nocil made improper payments to officials in India's Central Insecticides Board to expedite the registration of three DE-Nocil products. Without admitting or denying the allegations in the SEC's complaint, Dow consented to pay a US$325,000 civil penalty.[56]
- **Westinghouse Air Brake Technologies Corporation:** Westinghouse Air Brake Technologies Corporation (Wabtec) agreed to pay approximately US$675,000 and enter into a non-prosecution agreement with the DOJ and consent order with the SEC regarding activities by its Indian subsidiary, Pioneer Friction. Pioneer employees and agents made unlawful payments to officials of the Indian Railway Board (IRB), a government agency that is part of India's Ministry of Railroads. These payments were made to assist Pioneer in obtaining and retaining business with the IRB; to schedule preshipping product inspections; to have certificates of product delivery issued; and to curb excise tax audits.[57]

The FCPA and U.K. Bribery Act have had massive impacts on India, as an emerging market with a significant investments flowing from the United States and United Kingdom. Pressure from foreign companies and those with international operations has also helped to increase pressure to act. Within India an anti-corruption movement is growing and pressure is increasing to pass an updated Lokpal bill to reduce corruption, protect whistle-blowers and give citizens a voice for their grievances. The bill would establish an independent body for investigation of corruption that would not require government approval to investigate corruption and potential violations of existing laws to combat bribery and corruption, such as the Prevention of Corruption Act of 1988 and the Prevention of Money Laundering Act (PMLA) of 2002.

The Prevention of Corruption Act is broader in scope than the FCPA but has an entirely domestic focus. The law prohibits:

1. (a) The acceptance of a bribe or any other gratification by a "public servant" and (b) possession by a public servant of assets "disproportion to his known sources of income." The term *public servant* is broad in scope and includes any person who holds an office or by which such person is required to perform any public duty.
2. A public servant obtaining [any] valuable thing, without consideration from person concerned in proceeding or business transacted by such public servant.

The PMLA in India forms the core of the legal framework put in place by India to combat money laundering. PMLA defines money-laundering offense and provides for the freezing, seizure, and confiscation of the proceeds of crime. The Central Bureau of Investigation is the primary investigation agency in India, which investigates bribery and corruption cases at the central level. The Central Vigilance Commission monitors all vigilance activity under the central government and is free from executive authority.

There has been slow but steady transition in approach toward bribery and corruption. The Securities and Exchange Board of India (SEBI) is considering a proposal to make it mandatory for companies to have a whistle-blower mechanism. Additionally, companies have started emphasizing good business ethics and culture within their own system and dealings with third parties, and with government in particular. There has been an increased focus on setting the tone at the top, strong and zero tolerance policies and procedures, anti-fraud risk assessment, and continuous monitoring and review toward bribery and corruption.

Bangladesh

According to the World Economic Forum Global Competitiveness Report 2009–2010, corruption is one of the major factors that pose major constraints on foreign companies operating in Bangladesh. As such, Bangladesh ranked 134th in TI's 2010 CPI.

Positive initiatives are underway in Bangladesh. According to the International Finance Corporation's "Doing Business" report, Bangladesh was the most active reformer in South Asia in 2010, with key reforms in land, automation, and e-governance.

Some recent FCPA cases that have involved Bangladesh are:

- **Siemens Bangladesh Limited:** Siemens Bangladesh Limited plead guilty to conspiracy to violate the FCPA's anti-bribery and books and records provisions to obtain or retain contracts for a digital cellular mobile telephone network for the Bangladeshi government. Siemens Bangladesh engaged consultants to pay bribes to Bangladeshi officials with corrupt payments totaling more than US$5.3 million which were improperly recorded as "commissions" and "business consulting fees." Siemens Bangladesh agreed to pay a US$500,000 criminal fine.[58]
- **Alcatel-Lucent:** According to a DOJ press release from December 27, 2010, Alcatel-Lucent's and three of its subsidiaries have agreed to pay a combined US$92 million penalty regarding Alcatel-Lucent bribing foreign officials to win business in Costa Rica, Honduras, Malaysia, and Taiwan. The company also admitted it hired agents without proper controls in Kenya, Nigeria, Bangladesh, Ecuador, Nicaragua, Angola, Ivory Coast, Uganda, and Mali. Overall, Alcatel-Lucent admitted making US$48.1 million in profits as a result of the improper payments. The company and three subsidiaries will pay US$45 million in disgorgement to the SEC.[59]

Bangladesh has taken significant steps in fighting money laundering and corruption, by enacting the Money Laundering Prevention Act in 2002. The act defines money laundering as (a) directly or indirectly acquiring assets in an illegal way; and (b) the transfer, conversion, and concealment of assets acquired directly or indirectly in an illegal way.

In 2007, Bangladesh ratified the United Nations Convention against Corruption. Furthermore, Bangladesh enhanced anti-bribery and corruption acts with the Money Laundering Prevention Ordinance (MLPO). The MLPO lists a number of offenses, including corruption and bribery; counterfeiting currency or documents; extortion; fraud; forgery; and illicit trafficking in persons or arms or narcotic drugs and psychotropic substances. In addition, the ordinance also enhances the responsibilities of the central bank, authorizing it to analyze suspicious transaction reports and cash transaction reports and maintain a financial intelligence database and related information.

Another agency instituted in Bangladesh is the Anti-Corruption Commission (ACC). The ACC was established in accordance with the Anti-Corruption Commission Act 2004 to prevent corruption and other corrupt practices in the country and to conduct inquiry and investigation for other specific offences. It ran a year-long awareness campaign against corruption together with Transparency Bangladesh. The ACC is accountable directly to the President and maintains an online list of the number of corruption reports with the overall status.

The high level of corruption has been impeding the process of good governance in Bangladesh. While there are many positive initiatives, anti-corruption measures are still not being enforced in a robust manner.

Pakistan

According to the World Bank, since 2003, Pakistan's economy has grown by more than 6.5 percent per year, with leading industries of textiles, chemicals, food processing, and agriculture. In order to sustain and increase this level of growth, Pakistan needs to invest in and encourage anti-corruption and bribery measures. Bribery and corruption in Pakistan can be found at every level of government from low level interactions up to political authorities. Most of the bribery and corruption can be attributed to the country's political and economic instability. Additionally, the military is involved in virtually all aspects of the economy which makes business subject to preferential treatment. Pakistan is ranked 143rd out of 178 countries in TI's 2010 CPI.

A recent FCPA case that involved Pakistan is:

- **Avery Dennison Corporation:** According to the July 28, 2009 SEC complaint, Avery discovered employees at Paxar Corporation, a publicly traded company Avery acquired in June 2007, had routinely made improper payments to customs and tax officials. During an internal audit review, Avery discovered alleged improper payments to Pakistani customs officials by Paxar's Pakistani subsidiary. Avery agreed to pay approximately US$518,000 in penalties.[60]

Pakistan has established and developed legislation with regard to anti-corruption and bribery and with laws against corruption dating back to 1860. Pakistan's regulatory framework consists of the Pakistan Penal Code of 1860, Prevention of Corruption Act of 1947, and Government Servants Conduct Rules. These rules address active and passive corruption, abuse of office, and usage of public resources for private gain. The Pakistan Penal Code of 1860 defines bribery as:

1. Whoever—(i) gives a gratification to any person with the object of inducing him or any other person to exercise any electoral right or of rewarding any person for having exercised any such right; or (ii) accepts

either for himself or for any other person any gratification as a reward for exercising any such right, or for inducing or attempting to induce any other person to exercise any such right, commit the offense of bribery.

2. A person who offers, or agrees to give, or offers or attempts to procure, a gratification shall be deemed to give a gratification.

3. A person who obtains or agrees to accept or attempts to obtain a gratification shall be deemed to accept a gratification, and a person who accepts a gratification as a motive for doing what he does not intend to do, or as a reward for doing what he has not done, shall be deemed to have accepted the gratification as a reward.[61]

The National Accountability Bureau (NAB) is Pakistan's top anti-corruption organization. NAB is responsible for the elimination of corruption through an approach of awareness, prevention, and enforcement. Most recently, Pakistan developed a National Anti-Corruption Strategy (NACS), which offers a comprehensive plan for tackling corruption. NACS reviews and assesses the causes, nature, extent and impact of corruption in Pakistan as well as develops an integrated framework for tackling corruption with a focus on prevention and enforcement. Additionally, NACS creates and implements action plans for containment of corruption.

NACS has played an important role in incorporating TI's Integrity Pacts in all contracts for goods and services where the estimated cost of the project is over Rupees 5 million for consultancy and over Rupees 50 million for construction contracts. The Integrity Pact is a tool aimed at preventing corruption in public contracting with a formal non-bribery commitment. It stipulates rights and obligations to the effect that neither side will: pay, offer, demand or accept bribes; collude with competitors to obtain the contract; or engage in such abuses while executing the contract.[62]

The lack of political leadership combined with the absence of a legitimate political process for anti-corruption policies are still major obstacles in the fight against corruption.

Summary

Although countries in South Asia are taking measures to prevent bribery and corruption both are still quite prevalent in most areas. As most of the countries are strengthening their laws and lowering the barriers to entry in order to welcome foreign investment, businesses should be aware of the risks of entering these markets.

 **MIDDLE EAST**

The economy of the Middle East is increasingly diverse, although dominated by the oil and gas industry, which contributes much of the wealth in the region. The political infrastructure of many countries in the region have authoritarian characteristics that allow for limited public participation in government, albeit the events in the spring of 2011 may lead to significant changes in the coming years.

TI's 2010 CPI indicates that one group of Middle Eastern countries (comprising Jordan and the Gulf Cooperation Council countries[63]) ranks above the world median but many other Middle Eastern countries, including Egypt, Yemen and Syria, fall below it. The implementation of anti-corruption policies throughout the region has proved difficult due partly to a lack of belief and recognition by the wider population that their own adherence to these policies will be beneficial, especially in poorer countries and those where the use of influence is seen as the way to make things happen. There has been a significant amount of FCPA enforcement related to the oil and gas, pharmaceutical, automotive, defense contract, health care, and industrial goods sectors in the Middle East.

This section highlights general prevention of corruption mechanisms in the Middle East, FCPA cases involving the region, and an overview of some of the local legislation to combat the risk of corruption.

The United Nations Convention against Corruption (UNCAC) is the only international convention applicable to the Middle East. This convention has been signed and ratified by all Middle Eastern countries except Oman (Saudi Arabia and Syria are signatories but have not yet ratified it). However, the implementation of the actual policies continues to pose a challenge. The ultimate goal of the convention is the prevention, detection, and sanctioning of corruption. The UNCAC lays out a series of anti-corruption policies that promote global cooperation and accountability. Chapter 3 provides further details regarding the UNCAC.

Middle Eastern countries share the following characteristics that lead to an increased susceptibility to bribery and corruption risks:

- Political infrastructure with authoritarian characteristics which allows for limited public participation, low transparency, little accountability for reform and uncertain commitment to enacting new anti-corruption laws.
- Judicial systems that are not always equipped to deal with fraud and corruption, particularly in complex cases.

- Reliance on increased foreign direct investment as many nations continue to rely on oil exports and foreign investment in oil and gas infrastructure as their main source of revenues.
- In some of the poorer countries, increasing income inequality has led to an even greater concentration of power and wealth around a few elite individuals.

In the Middle East, the providing of gifts is customary, the settlement of debts in cash is common, and there is a significant amount of trading with related parties. Historically, trading in goods has been a cornerstone of business and, perhaps because of this, corruption is not necessarily seen as being a pernicious crime to the extent that it is in other parts of the world.

The following "red flags" may be indicative of corruption in the Middle East:

- The provision of *gifts and kickbacks* can be common in business dealings and is viewed as a normal business practice.
- *Conflicts of interest* can lead to abuses such as awarding contracts to connected companies or improper commission or discount arrangements.
- Little or no *due diligence* on suppliers and agents (even though there is limited information available in the public domain).
- *Lack of clear guidance* within organizations on acceptable and unacceptable business practices and the requirement to disclose and manage conflicts of interest situations.
- *Facilitation type payments*, especially in relation to issues like obtaining visas for employees where there is a high level of bureaucracy which can cause delays.

Highlighted next are five sample markets—Saudi Arabia, the United Arab Emirates, Iraq, Kuwait, and Egypt—to provide an overview of specific industries exposed to corruption, local anti-corruption laws, and enforcement measures taken to mitigate the risks of corruption.

Saudi Arabia

Saudi Arabia offers one of the largest markets in the Middle East and is relatively stable in terms of politics and economy. Saudi Arabia has increased trade among its neighbors, which has had a positive effect on foreign direct investment. The government, controlled by the royal al-Saud family, has shown efforts to fight corruption by implementing a national strategy to combat corruption in 2007 and forming a National Committee to Combat Corruption (NCCC) in 2011.

There have been a number of FCPA cases relating to Saudi Arabia including the following:

- **HealthSouth:** The DOJ alleged that while trying to secure a staffing and management services contract for a hospital in Saudi Arabia, which is overseen by a Saudi Arabian foundation, HealthSouth was solicited by the director general of this foundation for US$1 million. HealthSouth agreed to pay US$500,000 per year for five years through a bogus consulting agreement between the director general and an Australian HealthSouth affiliate.[64]

Saudi Arabia's Law for Combating Bribery criminalizes various aspects of corruption, including abuse of authority and office for personal interest, as well as active and passive bribery.

The law sets out that:

- Every public employee who, for himself or others, accepts a promise or offer to perform, neglect, or cease to perform his duties or alleged duties shall be considered an offender and be punished by imprisonment of no more than 10 years and fined by no more than a million Saudi riyal.
- Every public employee who accepts an offer to use a real or alleged authority to obtain from any public authority a labor, order, decision, commitment, authorization, import agreement, job, service or any kind of advantage shall be considered an offender and be punishable by law.
- Every public employee who requests, accepts, or acquires a promise or an offer because of his job to follow up a transaction in any government department shall be punished by no more than two years of imprisonment and fined no more than 50,000 Saudi riyal.[65]

The Saudi Arabian Monetary Agency has also issued the Law of Combating Money Laundering in order to reduce corrupt activity. Article two of this law sets out that anyone who commits any of the following actions shall be deemed a perpetrator of a money laundering crime:

- Conducting any transaction involving property or proceeds with the knowledge that such property or proceeds came as a result of a criminal activity or from an illegal or illegitimate source.

- Carrying, earning, using, keeping, receiving or transferring any property or proceeds with the knowledge that such property or proceeds came as a result of a criminal activity or from an illegal or illegitimate source.
- Concealing or camouflaging the nature, movement, source, ownership, or place and method of disposition with property or proceeds while knowing that such property or proceeds came as a result of a criminal activity or from an illegal or illegitimate source.
- Financing terrorism, terrorist acts, and terrorist organizations.
- Participating by way of agreement, assistance, incitement, advice, counsel, facilitation, collaboration, covering, or attempt in committing a crime listed hereunder.[66]

Saudi Arabia has also passed the Basic Law of Governance, which states that all state revenue, expenditure, assets, and institutions are subject to audits to ensure proper use performance, and management. There are no laws holding public officials accountable for financial disclosure or that allow for access to government information.

To improve anti-corruption laws in 2007, the Council of Ministers approved the National Strategy to Protect Integrity and Combat Corruption. This was followed by a Royal Decree in March 2011 requiring the establishment of the NCCC within three months. The NCCC is a government department that will oversee all other government departments and report directly to His Majesty King Abdullah bin Abdul Aziz and thus its creation will enhance anti-corruption regulations already in place. Saudi Arabia has also set up a Prosecution and Investigation Commission (PIC) to investigate corruption cases and report them to the Council of Ministers. While many steps have been taken to fight corruption, the royal family and many high-ranking officials still have little or no public accountability, resulting in a lack of the transparency necessary to achieve a corruption free society.

United Arab Emirates

Foreign direct investment has been steadily increasing in the UAE as the country has begun to diversify its economy away from a reliance on oil production. There have been some high profile corruption cases related to the collapse in the real estate market in 2008 (especially in the emirate of Dubai[67]). This has resulted in a greater focus by government on the issue of corruption and the need for enhanced government transparency. In addition to oil and gas, the financial services and real estate sectors, dominate the market and have weathered a number of fraudulent schemes reportedly totaling several billions of dollars.

The UAE enacted Federal Law No. 1 of 2004 on Combating Terror Crimes and Federal Law No. 2 of 2006 on Cybercrimes, which contains articles dealing with bribery, embezzlement, money laundering and terrorist financing.

Article 62 of the UAE Constitution prohibits government ministers from performing in financial, professional or commercial work as well as prohibits participation in commercial transactions with the government. The UAE Central Bank's Anti-Money Laundering and Suspicious Case Unit (AMLSCU) functions as a financial intelligence unit to deal with anti–money laundering tasks, such as blacklisting bank accounts and identifying attempted money laundering.

Iraq

The economy of Iraq is largely dominated by the oil sector, which accounts for approximately 90 percent of the country's revenues. Due to the increase in foreign direct investment in the country, other sectors, including construction and services, have grown significantly. The war-torn country's economy is continuing to rebound through agreements with the International Monetary Fund and World Bank as well as improvements in the oil sector; however, corruption is still prevalent throughout the country as the government continues to pursue and implement strategies for the reform and restructuring of struggling industries.

The United Nation's Oil for Food scandal is a high profile example of the widespread corruption in Iraq. Security Council Resolution 986, adopted by the UN, allowed the Iraqi government to sell oil in order to purchase humanitarian supplies. In order to win contracts, oil purchasers and humanitarian goods suppliers provided kickbacks to the government under the guise of a falsely increased contract price.

The following FCPA cases are from Iraq:

- **ABB Ltd.:** According to a DOJ press release dated September 29, 2010, ABB Ltd.–Jordan paid more than US$300,000 in kickbacks to the former Iraqi government in exchange for 11 purchase orders for electrical equipment and services worth more than US$5.9 million under the UN Oil for Food Program. Additionally, in a SEC press release on the same day, it was alleged that these kickbacks were improperly recorded as "after sales service", "consultation costs" and "commission." in its books and records.

- **AB Volvo:** Per a March 20, 2008 DOJ press release, two subsidiaries of AB Volvo paid approximately US$6 million to the Iraqi government in kickbacks in return for contracts for trucks and equipment.
- **Fiat:** According to a December 22, 2008 DOJ press release, subsidiaries of Fiat S.p.A., paid approximately US$4.4 million to the Iraqi government in kickbacks to obtain industrial equipment contracts.

While there are no specific anti-corruption laws in Iraq, the Iraqi Penal Code criminalizes corruption in Iraq as a punishable offense.

The Penal Code sets out in paragraph 307:

- Any public official or agent who seeks or accepts for himself or for another a gift, benefit, honor, or promise thereof to carry out any duty of his employment or to refrain from doing so or to contravene such duty is punishable by a term of imprisonment not exceeding 10 years or by detention plus a fine which should not be less than the amount he sought, was given, or was promised but should not, under any circumstances, exceed 500 dinars.
- The penalty will be a term of imprisonment not exceeding 7 years or detention if such request, acceptance or receipt occurs with intent to receive remuneration after such duty is or is not carried out or following the contravention of such duty.[68]

Paragraph 308 goes on to state that:

- Any public official or agent who seeks or receives for himself or for another a gift, benefit, privilege, or promise thereof to carry out or refrain from carrying out an act that does not fall within the duties of his office but he claims or considers that such act was carried out in error is punishable by a term of imprisonment not exceeding 7 years or by detention plus a fine of not less than the amount he sought, was given or was promised. The fine should not, under any circumstances, exceed 500 dinars.[69]

Iraq created the Commission on Public Integrity in 2004, as an independent commission under the oversight of the legislature in the Iraqi Constitution, to enforce anti-corruption laws and transparency. The Commission on Public Integrity is supported by the Board of Supreme Audit (BSA) and the Inspector General's Office (IGO) within each Ministry.

In 2007 the Iraqi Foundation launched an anti-corruption campaign called The Provincial Accountability and Governance Project. The goal of the campaign is to enhance transparency and accountability within the government. The project was implemented in 15 provinces across the country in order to enhance the country's ability to implement anti-corruptive practices at the provincial level. The project set up provincial-based Integrity Monitoring Groups to oversee and enhance anti-corruptive strategies and engage civic groups to carry out good governance and ethical practices.

Kuwait

Kuwait accounts for nearly nine percent of the world's oil supply and continues to be one of the fastest-growing economies in the region due to its oil production. Although Kuwait has a parliament, much of the real power resides with the Emir and the ruling Al-Sabah family.

The Kuwait Penal Law 31/1970 criminalizes corruption in Kuwait. The Law includes passive and active bribery, attempted corruption, extortion, and use of public resources for personal gain; however, it does not cover bribing a foreign official. Specific anti-corruption laws have yet to be passed by government.

Kuwait adopted a National Anti-Corruption Strategy in 2008 to fight corruption and in 2011, further activities are underway to aid in anti-corruption efforts. Kuwait's National Anti-Corruption Strategy has created an independent oversight body to fight corruption, enhance transparency, and protect whistle-blowers; however, there are currently no whistle-blower laws in place to protect members of the public or the private sector.

Egypt

Egypt remains one of the most populous countries in the region. Up until the events of early 2011, which led to a change in the regime, its economy (which relies heavily on tourism and oil and gas exports) was growing, as it is a country that is rich in natural resources and agricultural products. A reduction in taxes and tariffs had expanded the private sector and assisted Egypt's recent economic recovery, but this has also led to increased corruption in the country.

The following FCPA cases relate to activities in Egypt:

- **United Industrial Corporation:** In 2009, United Industrial Corporation (UIC) agreed to a cease-and-desist order for violating the FCPA.

According to the SEC, UIC through its subsidiary ACL Technologies (ACL) made payments to an agent (a retired Egyptian Air Force (EAF) general) related to an airport depot project. Thomas Wurzel, ACL's former president, continued to authorize payments with the knowledge that the agent would transfer funds to EAF officials in order to secure business for UIC. UIC paid US$337,679 in disgorgement and prejudgment interest in regards to the SEC's order.[70]

- **Lockheed Corp.:** According to a January 27, 1995 DOJ press release, a consultant for the company was an elected government official in Egypt and used political influence to secure business for the company. Lockheed agreed to make monthly payments to the member of parliament (MP) and was awarded aircraft contracts. The DOJ fined Lockheed and Lockheed agreed to pay total penalties of US$24.8 million.

Egypt has no specific anti-corruption laws in place, but does address active and passive bribery of government officials, abuse of office, and embezzlement as criminal acts in its Penal Code; however bribery of foreign public officials is not covered. In 2002, President Mubarak passed Law No. 80 of 2002 promulgating the Anti-Money Laundering Law and its Amendments to address issues related to money laundering throughout the country.

The law prohibits the laundering and trafficking of funds generated from illegal drug related activities.

The law further establishes an independent unit to combat money laundering, and sets out anti-money laundering rules that entities, individuals, and financial institutions must follow along with the applicable fines and custodial sentences for breaches of the law.

Due to the Lotus Revolution in January of 2011, the status of anti-corruption and bribery laws throughout Egypt have been of high importance and an issue of much political debate. Still, much needs to be done throughout the region in order to establish a strong commitment to anti-corruption regulation.

Summary

While anti-corruption efforts in many countries in the Middle East are on the rise, fraud and corruption are still quite prevalent, as shown by the numerous FCPA cases involving conduct in the region. The effects of the global financial crisis (particularly for the real estate market in Dubai) and the more recent political unrest in some countries have led many of these nations to attempt to strengthen their anti-corruption laws and practices. However, progress has been slow given the lack of transparency in some political systems and mixed attitudes towards the issue of corruption. Companies should therefore continue to be acutely aware of corruption and the risks it imposes while doing business throughout the region.

 ## AFRICA

Africa has one of the fastest growing economies in the world primarily driven by the oil and extractive industries. The increased risk of corruption that comes with this substantial growth translates, according to the African Union, to an estimated US$140 billion being stolen from Africa each year due to corruption.[71] Many of the corruption risks in Africa are heightened due to unsophisticated (many business processes), poor control environments and local political and cultural sensitivities that are common in unstable legal, political and business environments.

There has been a significant amount of FCPA enforcement in Africa covering a broad range of activities that includes oil and gas, telecommunications, pharmaceuticals, infrastructure, financial services, and defense contracts, among others. Given the extent of this enforcement and the media attention associated with it, it is not surprising that Africa is considered to have a higher risk of corruption with the majority of its countries being ranked higher than 100 in the TI CPI. Countries range from Botswana, 33 out of 178 on the CPI, to Somalia, which is 178 and considered to be the most corrupt country on the index.

This section highlights general prevention of corruption in Africa, FCPA cases from the region, and an overview of some of the local legislation to combat the risk of corruption.

On July 11, 2003, the African Union (AU) Convention on Preventing and Combating Corruption was adopted. The AU convention is a regional agreement setting the framework for the prevention of corruption in Africa. Refer to Chapter 3 for further details on the AU convention.

African countries share the following characteristics that lead to an increased susceptibility to bribery and corruption risk:

- Increasing levels of foreign direct investment primarily in the extractive industries combined with rising commodity prices and rapid development of Africa's industrial and service sectors.

- Infrastructure spending accounts for more than half of Africa's recent growth. This trend is expected to continue in the future. Ernst & Young's Africa Attractiveness Survey 2011 estimated that new foreign direct investment projects will amount to US$ 150 billion in 2015.[72]
- Wide reach of the state-owned sector stemming from infrastructure spending.
- The pressure to sustain and expand growth from the moderate recovery Africa has faced in the past few years due to a volatile trade sector, high interest rates compared to other regions, and a struggle to keep up with the global financial architecture.

The most common corruption risks in Africa are as follows:

- *Pressure to select a certain supplier or contractor.* In many situations an agent or contractor is identified by the government official associated with a project and often the connection or relation is not known or disclosed.
- *Questionable invoices.* Invoices that include improper or insufficient additional supporting documentation are strong indicators of corruption.
- *Informal payments.* Improper payments by businesses in Africa often arise from the significant levels of "red tape" in the region particularly related to business permits and licenses, the import of goods and traffic violations.
- *Use of intermediaries.* The unnecessary use of agents, brokers and facilitators to "assist" with negotiations is widespread. The fees paid to these intermediaries are often non-distinct and might be used to pay bribes.
- It is not uncommon for *petty corruption* to be found in areas like identification books, marriage and birth certificates, and driving licenses.

Highlighted next are four sample markets—Nigeria, South Africa, Angola, and Kenya—to provide an overview of specific industries exposed to corruption, local anti-corruption laws, and enforcement measures taken to mitigate the risk of corruption.

Nigeria

In recent years, Nigeria has been an area of intense focus for FCPA enforcement and, towards the end of 2010, it was estimated that there were 15 pending investigations by the SEC and DOJ. Some of the largest FCPA cases have involved Nigeria. One of the leading reasons is that Nigeria has become important exporter of oil and gas to the United States.

The following are FCPA cases relate to activities in Nigeria:

- **Siemens:** The SEC alleged that Siemens COM made approximately US$12.7 million in suspicious payments, including at least US$4.5 million of bribes, in connection with four government telecommunications projects in Nigeria. Payments were allegedly made to government officials. Due to coordinated enforcement actions by the DOJ, SEC, and German authorities, Siemens paid US$1.6 billion in penalties, fines, and disgorgement to resolve its corruption cases in the U.S. and Germany.[73]
- **TSKJ:** Formed in 1990, TSKJ was a four-company joint venture whose purpose was bidding on and later providing engineering, procurement, and construction services to design and build a government-controlled liquefied natural gas plant on Bonny Island, Nigeria. The partners included JGC Corporation, Kellogg Brown & Root Inc., Technip S.A., and Snamprogetti Netherlands B.V. TSKJ authorized, and paid bribes to Nigerian government officials, employees state owned and controlled entities related to the Bonny Island contracts. To facilitate and conceal the bribes, the joint venture used an individual and a Japanese trading company. The four partners and several individuals have been held accountable either through deferred prosecution agreements or guilty pleas and have paid approximately US$1.5 billion in penalties.[74]

The majority of the other FCPA prosecutions of multinational companies operating in Nigeria are related to oil and gas. However, there were various other investigations related to military and law enforcement as well as industrial goods.

Bribery issues in Nigeria are governed by the Corrupt Practices and other Related Offences Act of 2000 and local enforcement is not uncommon. Under the Corrupt Practices and other Related Offences Act, a person is guilty of corruption if he:

a. asks for, receives or obtains any property or benefit of any kind for himself or for any other person; or
b. agrees or attempts to receive or obtain any property; or
c. benefits of any kind for himself or for any other person, on account of:
   i. anything already done or omitted to be done, or for any favor or disfavor already shown to any person by himself in the discharge of his official duties or in relation to any matter connected with the functions, affairs

or business of a Government department, or corporate body or other organization or institution in which he is serving as an official, or

ii. anything to be afterwards done or omitted to be done or favor or disfavor to be afterwards shown to any person, by himself in the discharge of his official duties or in relation to any such matter as aforesaid is guilty of an offence of Official corruption and is liable to imprisonment for seven (7) years.[75]

Local enforcement is handled by the Economic and Financial Crimes Commission (EFCC). The EFCC has been active in performing local investigations of multinationals including raiding offices and arresting employees particularly after the DOJ or other enforcement body reaches a settlement for corrupt activity in Nigeria.

Overall, Nigeria has become a major investment destination for multinational companies. Due to the high instances of corruption in Nigeria, there has been an increase in FCPA enforcement as well as enforcement by local authorities.

South Africa

South Africa is the second most populous nation and one of the most diversified economies in Africa. As one of the more developed countries, it is the third least corrupt country in Africa and ranked as number 54 of 178 on the CPI.

In South Africa, the National Council of Provinces passed the Prevention and Combating of Corrupt Activities Act of 2004 that replaced the Corruption Act of 1992 aimed at combating corruption throughout the country. The Act states:

A person is guilty of corruption if he or she directly or indirectly:

- Accepts, agrees, or offers to accept any gratification from any other person whether for the benefit of himself or herself or for the benefit of another person; or
- Gives or agrees or offers to give to any other person any gratification for the benefit of that other person or for the benefit of another person.[76]

In order to influence another person to act in an illegal manner or act in a way which leads to the abuse of power or violation of law in order to achieve an unjustified result.

Not only does the act create the general offence of corruption but it also creates a number of specific offenses pertaining to auctions, contracts, procurement, dealings with foreign public officials, and public officials. The act applies to both public and private entities and individuals and not just as it relates to dealings with the public sector but also to dealings within entities and individuals within the private sector.

Like the FCPA, the act provides for extraterritorial jurisdiction, and the sanctions for noncompliance can range from penalties to long terms of imprisonment, as well as being listed in the defaulters register. The act is similar to the U.K. Bribery Act in that it prohibits any type of facilitation payment (unlike the FCPA).

In addition, Section 34 of the act sets out that any person who holds a position of authority in an organization has a duty to report corruption and other offences such as fraud and theft over R100,000.

The Act was a result of South Africa's Public Service Anti-Corruption Strategy, which also led to the formation of the National Anti-Corruption Coordinating Committee and the National Anti-Corruption Forum designed to coordinate and aid the government in anti-corruption policies and enforcement.

While there has been no FCPA enforcement activity in South Africa, high profile corruption issues exist including a recent admission by Saab that payments for a "consulting contract in South Africa" were made surrounding a contract for military aircraft.[77]

Angola

Angola's economy has undergone a period of great change over the last decade. The economy is recovering from many years of civil war to being one of the fastest growing economies in the world. Angola's economy is primarily driven by its oil and diamond exports as well as infrastructure spending. Angola is also a member state of the SADC. The following are FCPA cases from Angola:

- **Pride International:** In its 2008 Annual Report, Pride disclosed that during the period from 2001 through 2006, payments were allegedly made to government officials in Saudi Arabia, Kazakhstan, Brazil, Nigeria, Libya, Angola, and the Republic of Congo. These were made in order expedite rigs or equipment though customs, as well as resolve outstanding issues with customs, immigration, tax, licensing or merchant marine authorities in those countries.
- **ABB Ltd.:** According to the SEC's July 2004 complaint, from 1998 through 2003, ABB's US and foreign-based subsidiaries doing business in Nigeria, Angola, and Kazakhstan, offered and made illicit payments

totaling over US$1.1 million to government officials in those countries in order to obtain and retain business. In Angola, ABB's subsidiary made improper payments as part of three training trips to the Angolan state-owned oil company's engineers to win contracts. ABB settled with the SEC and agreed to disgorge US$5.9 million in profits and paid a US$10.5 million fine to the DOJ in a related matter.[78]

▪ **Baker Hughes:** The SEC alleged, that between 1998 and 2003, Baker Hughes paid over US$10.3 million to an agent and recorded these payments as "commissions". Baker Hughes failed to take measures to assure itself that the agent making improper payments to officials at Angola's state-owned oil company. Baker Hughes inherited the relationship with the agent through its acquisition of Western Atlas Corporation in 1998.

Additionally, the SEC alleged that between 1999 and 2002, Baker Hughes made US$1.2 million in payments to another Angolan agent, without conducting due diligence on this agent. When the agent was identified as the brother of a senior-level employee of a state-owned entity the arrangement was terminated; however a severance payment of US$500,000 was paid. Baker Hughes settled with the SEC and DOJ and paid approximately US$44 million in penalties and fines.[79]

Recently, the Angolan government has adopted a zero tolerance approach and the Angolan parliament has approved the Public Administration Probity law that regulates activities of public agents and consolidates several other anti-corruption laws that were in place since 1989. The new law prohibits public servants from asking or taking payments or gifts that would diminish their credibility or independence. Additionally, in 2010 Angola made a high level commitment with the Financial Action Task Force (FATF) to address weaknesses with its anti-money laundering/combat the financing of terrorism measures.

Kenya

Kenya has one of the larger economies in East and Central Africa and has made a name for itself as one of Africa's leading technology and communications centers for IT professionals. Kenya has also been expanding its tourism and agriculture industries. However, Kenya continues to be a focus area for FCPA enforcement.

The following are FCPA cases from Kenya:

- **Alcatel Lucent:** Alcatel's subsidiaries allegedly used consultants who performed little or no legitimate work to funnel bribes to government officials in order to obtain or retain lucrative telecommunications contracts and other contracts.[80]
- **Gautam Sengupta and Ramendra Basu:** World Bank employees, the defendants conspired with a Swedish consultant and steered World Bank contracts to certain Swedish companies in exchange for kickbacks amounting to US$127,000. A Kenyan government official received payments through an account controlled by the Swedish consultant. Both pleaded guilty to violating the FCPA and received prison sentences.[81]

Kenya has the following local bribery and corruption related legislation:

- **Public Officers Ethics Act: Section 11(3):** Public officer may accept a gift given to him in his official capacity but, unless the gift is a non-monetary gift that does not exceed value prescribed by regulation, such gift shall be deemed to be a gift to the public officer's organization.
- **Public Officers Ethics Act: Section 11(2):** Public officer shall not accept or request gifts or favors from a person who:
  - Has an interest that may be affected by carrying out, or not carrying out, of the public officer's duties.
  - Carries on regulated activities with respect to which the public officer's organization has a role.
  - Has a contractual or similar relationship with the public officer's organization.[82]
- **Anti-Corruption and Economic Crimes Act of 2003:** A person is guilty of an offense if he or she:
  - Corruptly receives or solicits, or corruptly agrees to receive or solicit, certain benefits.
  - Corruptly gives or offers, or corruptly agrees to give or offer, certain benefits.[83]

The Kenya Anti-Corruption Commission is required to enforce these acts and to provide reports on the current status of investigations relating to the Anti-Corruption and Economic Crimes Act.

As one of East and Central Africa's larger economies, Kenya is significant to many businesses in the sub-region. Due to the high instances of corruption, it continues to be a focus of FCPA enforcement.

Summary

While the level of anti-corruption measures in many countries in Africa is on the rise, fraud and corruption are still prevalent, as demonstrated by the numerous FCPA cases involving activities in the region. Pressure from increases in foreign direct investment and political unrest have led many of these nations to attempt to strengthen their anti-corruption laws and practices. Inefficient and far from transparent political systems have made these changes slowly and enforcement remains low. Companies should continue to be acutely aware of corruption and the risks it imposes while doing business throughout the region.

 LATIN AMERICA

Latin America has a diverse, growing economy with several countries whose GDP per capita rivals that of more developed nations. The agriculture, manufacturing, oil and gas, and transportation industries are the main contributors to revenue throughout the region. Poverty and unemployment, however, are the region's biggest challenges as income inequality continues to widen between the poorest and richest countries in the area as well as within countries themselves. This inequality hinders economic development, causes political unrest and drives widespread fraud throughout the region. Corruption throughout Latin America stems from political instability, poverty, and rampant drug-related crimes. Pressure to sustain and expand growth through trade and foreign direct investments has also led to widespread corruption. FCPA-related cases are prevalent in the telecommunications, energy, financial services, consumer goods, and transportation industries, with the majority of cases stemming from the oil and gas sector. According to TI's 2010 CPI, many Latin American countries rank well below the world median, including Mexico (#98) and Venezuela (#164).

During 1996, several countries within the Organization of American States (OAS) developed the Inter-American Convention against Corruption (IACAC) as a mechanism that encourages cooperation among states to combat corruption. This was one of the first of its kind, and was implemented in early 1997.

The IACAC promotes adherence to a comprehensive system of anti-corruptive measures along with interstate monitoring and compliance of these measures to prevent and detect fraudulent acts. Chapter 3 has further information on the IACAC.

Many Latin American nations have the following common characteristics, which allow for an increased susceptibility to various bribery and corruption risks:

- Governments with low accountability and transparency, which lead to abuses of power and legal systems that contributes to the increased discretionary power of public officials. This is coupled with judicial systems that lack appropriate measures to punish corrupt officials, amplifying the problem.
- Increases in drug trafficking and drug-related crimes throughout the region.
- High unemployment rates, which lead to a disproportionate distribution of wealth and pressures to create jobs to boost local economies.
- An increased desire to sustain and boost economic growth, especially in the form of foreign direct investments related to the mining and oil and gas industries.

In Latin America, common "red flag" issues tend to be overlooked and tolerated. These can include:

- *Land development and appropriation.* The exchange of gifts and benefits is common in these arrangements. Additionally, related party relationships are undisclosed.
- *Complex bureaucratic procedures and regulations.* To obtain permits, licenses, registration for businesses, and investments in Latin America, there are numerous regulations that make it challenging to establish business activities. It is not uncommon for petty corruption to be found in other areas as well such as identification cards, birth certificates, and driving licenses.
- *Use of intermediaries.* Unnecessary use of an agent, broker, or facilitator to "assist" with negotiations. The fee paid to the local agent is non-distinct and often used to pay bribes.

Presented below are several example countries—Mexico, Brazil, Argentina, Colombia, Venezuela, and Peru—and these provide an overview of particularly exposed industries as well as local legislation and enforcement trends.

Mexico

Mexico's free market economy, which in 2010 was approximately US$1.56 trillion,[83] has made it an attractive target for foreign investment over the years. Well-developed infrastructure and a liberal regulatory environment have sustained this trend. After a significant fall in GDP in 2009, Mexico was able to achieve growth in the manufacturing, telecommunications, energy, and mining sectors, and has experienced positive GDP growth over the past year due to increased exports to the United States. However, disproportionate distribution of wealth, high unemployment, high level of corruption and drug-related crime continue to plague the country. In some economic sectors, corruption is said to have taken on heightened organizational prowess and local governments, municipalities, and law enforcement are often accused of being involved in acts of corruption and collaboration with drug cartels, particularly in the northern parts of Mexico.

The following are FCPA cases involving Mexico:

- **Pride International Inc.:** The SEC and DOJ alleged that Pride used a Mexican marketing agent to facilitate US$10,000 in funds to Mexican officials with the intent to avoid fines and penalties for customs violations in Mexico. The SEC alleged Bobby Benton, a former employee of Pride International, was involved in bribing a Mexican customs official. According to the SEC litigation release on November 4, 2010, Benton consented to pay a civil penalty in the amount of US$40,000, but has not admitted or denied the SEC's allegations. According to a Pride press release dated December 7, 2010, the combined DOJ and SEC settlements for Pride International and an international subsidiary totalled a sum of US$56.2 million.
- **Lindsey Manufacturing:** According to a DOJ press release dated May 10, 2011, Lindsey Manufacturing and two executives were found guilty in a scheme that paid bribes to Mexican officials and a state electric company, Comisión Federal de Electricidad (CFE). The DOJ alleged that Lindsey hired Enrique Anguilar to make sales to CFE, and in return would pay 30 percent commission on all contracts obtained with CFE. However, part

of this commission was knowingly used to bribe Mexican officials. Additionally, Lindsey Manufacturing wired US$5.9 million to the Grupo Internacional de Asesores S.A. to pay bribes in exchange for the award of CFE contract. Grupo purchased gifts for officials on Lindsey's behalf, including a US$297,500 Ferrari Spyder and a US$1.8 million yacht. The parties involved were found guilty of FCPA conspiracy, laundering, and bribery charges. Sentencing for Lindsey Manufacturing is scheduled for September 2011; however, due to prosecutorial misconduct there is a chance that the convictions will be dismissed.

Locally, the Mexican Penal Code (*Código Penal Federal*) makes bribery and corruption illegal. Mexico's National Agreement for Transparency further expands on punitive actions for the items noted within the Mexican Penal Code, including an average of 5 to 10 years of imprisonment for many corruption violations.

President Calderon's administration has put in place the Manifesto of Anti-Corruption Efforts, comprised of six focal areas:

1. Accounting and fiscal reform
2. Educational content
3. Regulatory simplification
4. Promotion of transparency
5. Institutional accountability
6. Professionalization of public service[84]

This initiative, along with the implementation of the Federal Competition Commission and new tax reforms, has led Mexico in the right direction towards combating corruption; however, it is still seen as a widespread problem throughout the region.

The most recent step taken against corruption was the approval by the Mexican Senate of the Anti-corruption Law in May 2011. The new legislation establishes who is accountable as well as penalties for individuals and legal entities that are noncompliant during transactions involving federal government contracts or international commercial transactions. Non-compliance is subject to penalties if the accountable party is paying illegal gratuities to a government official in order for the official to perform or not perform a duty related to his normal course of business or carry out a duty that would cause the accountable party to gain an unfair benefit or advantage in obtaining a federal government contract. For those held accountable, penalties may be in the form of fines and debarment from government contracts.

Another significant piece of legislation being considered in Mexico is the Anti-Money Laundering Bill, currently awaiting approval in Congress. The bill strengthens criminal penalties and imposes additional reporting requirements on nonbank institutions in Mexico. It mandates penalties for institutions and employees who fail to notify the government of specified suspicious activities. It also restricts cash purchases for items such as jewelry, vehicles, and real estate.

While Mexico is thought to have a strong legal foundation and framework to fight corruption it is not known for strict enforcement of these laws. According to TI's 2011 Progress Report, Mexico has not actively enforced the OECD Anti-bribery Convention, nor does it have many ongoing investigations dealing with foreign bribery.[84] The main reasons for lack of enforcement are an inefficient judicial system and little accountability of high-ranking officials.

Brazil

Brazil's massive market size and potential for growth make it one of the world's leading destinations for global businesses and investments. The emerging market's stronghold in the agricultural, mining, manufacturing, and service sectors drives its economy. Despite a well-developed business environment, corruption still poses a major problem with doing business in Brazil. It was ranked 69th out of 178 countries in TI's 2010 CPI, 48 places below Chile.

Corruption stems from dealing with local-level governments and a wide-range of regulatory agencies in order to do business, increasing the likelihood of bribery. The complexity of Brazil's tax structure is a risk factor for corruption. And although surveys from international agencies such as the World Bank indicate that few companies expect to offer bribes in exchange for contracts, there remains a serious problem with corruption in the award of contracts for public works.

The following are FCPA cases involving Brazil:

- **Nature's Sunshine Products (NSP):** NSP manufactures and sells nutritional and personal care products. The SEC alleged that a subsidiary of NSP in Brazil made cash payments to illegally import certain vitamins, herbal products, and nutritional supplements into Brazil that were not registered as "medicines." Subsequently, the SEC alleged that the subsidiary altered their financial records to hide the cash payments. The cash payments occurred in 2000 and 2001. According to the SEC litigation release on July 31, 2009, NSP consented to pay a civil penalty in the amount of US$600,000, but has not admitted or denied the SEC's allegations.

■ **Sitel Corp.:** Sitel Corp. is a U.S.-based company that serves as a call center outsourcing provider. Sitel voluntarily contacted the SEC regarding accounting errors and failures to remit municipal taxes for their Brazil subsidiary. According to Sitel Corp.'s 2006 10-K, they contacted the SEC and provided the results of their own investigation and are responding to the SEC's requests for further information.

Locally, the Brazilian penal code criminalizes corruption and addresses other areas including embezzlement and graft. Specifically, law 10.467 of the penal code addresses anti-money laundering legislation, while Article 337-B defines active bribery as a promising, offering, or giving any improper advantage to a foreign public official.[87]

Furthermore, Law # 9613 pertains specifically to money laundering and concealment of assets. Chapter 1 Article 1 of the law states:

Concealment of dissimulation of the nature, origin, location, availability, handling, or ownership of assets, rights or valuables directly or indirectly originated from criminal activities as follows:

1. Illicit trafficking of narcotic substances or related drugs.
2. Terrorism.
3. Smuggling or trafficking of weaponry, ammunition or materials intended for the production thereof.
4. Kidnapping for ransom.
5. Acts detrimental to the government authorities, including by demanding any advantage, for itself or third parties, as a condition or price for the performance or nonperformance of administrative acts.
6. Acts detrimental to the Brazilian financial system.[88]

Further steps are also being taken in Brazil to combat corruption. For example, in 2010 a draft bill was sent to Congress that would create direct legal liability for individuals and other entities caught committing acts of corruption and bribery against public officials. Also in 2010, Congress approved the Ficha Limpa Law, which prohibits public officials from running for office for eight years if they have pending criminal charges against them, have been previously convicted of a serious crime, or resigned from political office to avoid impeachment.

While impressive steps have been taken to fight corruption, according to TI's 2011 Progress Report, Brazil has not implemented regulations for the protection of whistle-blowers. Also, Brazil does not have many ongoing investigations dealing with foreign bribery.[89] These inefficiencies are mainly due to the decentralization within the government and the ineffectiveness of the judicial system to stabilize anti-corruption efforts.

Argentina

Argentina's economy is rich in natural resources with an abundance of agricultural exports and a large diverse group of industrial sectors. Continuing to climb out of a recession from a decade ago, Argentina has achieved an impressive growth rate and a stable political environment. Investor confidence has been on the rise as domestic and foreign investors are investing more over the past decade. However, the lack of regulation and enforcement of property acquisitions and property rights is a big risk factor in Argentina. Furthermore, procurement contracts in the provinces and customs along the borders are easily subject to bribery and worry remains over improper tax collections.

The following FCPA cases involve Argentina:

- **Helmerich & Payne (H&P):** H&P engages in contract drilling of oil and gas wells for exploration and production companies. According to an SEC litigation release on July 30, 2009, from 2003 to 2008 there were approximately US$185,673 (approximately US$166,000 for Argentina and US$19,673 for Venezuela) of improper payments made by subsidiaries of H&P in Venezuela and Argentina to foreign customs officials. The payments were made to avoid the normal delays that occur in the transport of drilling equipment internationally. The SEC ordered that H&P pay back illegal profits of US$320,604 and interest of US$55,077 to the United States Treasury. According to a DOJ press release on July 30, 2009, H&P forced to pay an additional penalty of US$1 million and to implement additional internal controls.
- **Ball Corp.:** Ball Corp. is provider of metal packaging for beverages, foods, and household products. Ball Corp. voluntarily contacted the SEC regarding bribes of at least US$106,749 made in 2006 and 2007 by its Argentine subsidiary, Formametal. The bribes were made to ensure

that prohibited machinery would be imported into Argentina and that certain raw materials would leave the country with a reduced tax rate. According to the related SEC litigation release on March 24, 2011, a penalty of US$300,000 was ordered for the repeated bribes.

■ **BJ Services Co.:** The SEC alleged that in 2001, the Argentine subsidiary of BJ Services Co., made bribes to Argentine customs officials in the amount of 65,000 pesos. These payments were made in order for customs officials to neglect previous importation violations made by the company. According to a SEC litigation release on March 10, 2004, BJ Services has agreed to cease and desist from committing or causing violations of the provisions of the FCPA.

■ **IBM-Argentina:** According to a SEC litigation release on December 21, 2000, an IBM subsidiary made illicit payments to Argentine officials during 1994. IBM did not admit or deny the charges, but agreed to cease and desist from committing or causing any future violation as well as pay a civil fine of US$300,000.

The Argentinean Criminal Code ". . . criminalizes attempted corruption, extortion, active and passive bribery, bribery of foreign officials, private sector corruption and money laundering."[90] Sentences can carry a term of up to six years in prison and/or removal from office. Argentina has been proactive with anti-corruption involvement in the United Nations Convention against Corruption's Conference of State Parties as well as the Mechanism for Follow-Up on the Implementation of the Inter-American Convention against Corruption.

Established in 1999, an agency known as the Oficina Anticorrupción (Anti-Corruption Office) was created to combat political corruption through investigation and prosecution. This agency is run by the Ministry of Justice and Human Rights. According to the United Nations Office on Drugs and Crime 2010 Country Report, the agency has investigated between 400 and 500 cases since 2000 primarily stemming from fraud and other noncompliance related matters. However, bribery is not among the leading types of cases that have been investigated.[91]

On February 15, 2011, Resolution No. 39/11 was issued by the Financial Information Unit (UIF) and published in the Official Bulletin. The resolution regulates the duties of importers, exporters, customs brokers, and customs transportation agents and establishes measures and procedures to be observed by the abovementioned liable parties with respect to money laundering and terrorism financing crimes.

The main requirements set forth in UIF Resolution No. 39/11 are as follows:

- Setting an anti-money laundering and anti-terrorism financing policy.
- Setting a training plan for personnel regarding money laundering and terrorism financing.
- Appointing an enforcement officer before the UIF.

The law states that, in the event of non-compliance with any of the reporting obligations with the UIF, fines from 1 to 10 times the total value of the goods or transaction to which the infringement refers shall be imposed, provided that the act did not constitute a more serious offense.

In June 2011, Argentina passed an Anti-Money Laundering bill, which most importantly, makes money laundering a criminal action. This bill will allow the prosecution of Argentineans who commit a money-laundering act in any country and will allow for the government to seize or freeze property and other assets related to the act.[92]

President Kirchner has taken several regulatory measures to combat corruption, however, despite the regulatory activity noted above, Argentina's anti-corruption enforcement still has many inefficiencies and not yet capable to provide checks and balances. Manuel Garrido, Argentinás former chief prosecutor for corruption cases, resigned at the beginning of 2011 due to the ineffectiveness of the government to award any convictions in five years and over 100 cases. The U.S. embassy stated, "Argentina's corruption scandals frequently make a big splash at the outset, only to dissipate into oblivion due to the languid pace of the 'investigations' and the endless juridical pingpong to which they are submitted."[93]

Colombia

The Colombian economy is primarily driven by the oil and gas industry, with important contributions from agriculture, infrastructure, and housing. Economic reforms in the oil and gas industry have fueled Colombia's economy in recent years. Infrastructure, drug trafficking, unemployment, and poverty continue to be the biggest issues hindering the economy. Corruption throughout the region stems from narcotics trafficking, and a corrupt political system fueled by a weak infrastructure, all of which continue to pose a threat to new and existing businesses.

In 2001, Chiquita Brands International Inc was found to have made payments to foreign customs officials by their wholly owned foreign subsidiary of Chiquita. According to an SEC litigation release on October 3, 2001, Banadex, Chiquita's subsidiary, paid US$30,000 to local customs officials in Columbia in order to secure a renewal of its license at its Turbo, Colombia, port facility. The payments were made between 1996 and 1997 and were incorrectly classified in the accounting records. The employee's involved were terminated and Chiquita paid US$100,000 in a civil penalty after the item was found during an internal investigation.

In May 2011, an Anti-Corruption Statute proposed to Congress by President Santos was passed. With this statute in place, any cash advances from the state related to public works projects will be managed by a third party financial institution instead of the contractor. The appointed financial institution will act as a trustee and is aimed to alleviate favoritism towards contractors who were large campaign supporters and to hinder these advances being used to pay fines for campaign supporters for other crimes committed against the state. While anti-bribery initiatives are taking place in Colombia, the lack of enforcement is still prevalent.

Venezuela

The Venezuelan economy boasts a wealth of natural resources, mainly oil, which accounts for 95 percent of the country's export earnings and 55 percent of its total budget revenues.[94] The economy has recently been fueled by increasing oil prices, increased government and consumer spending due to easier access to credit. Corruption, however, is prevalent at most levels of society and has negatively affected the desire to obtain government contracts and licenses.

The following FCPA cases involve Venezuela:

- **Oil States International:** – Oil States International is a manufacturer of capital equipment for deepwater production facilities and a service provider to the oil and gas industry. The SEC alleged that Oil States paid US$348,350 in improper payments to the Venezuelan governments, which were hidden as payments for consulting services. According to the SEC's related release on April 27, 2006, Oil States International was ordered to cease and desist from violations in the future.
- **Joey Summers:** Between 2003 and 2005 the SEC alleged that Summers, Pride International's country manager, authorized as well as allowed payments of US$384,000 to various third-party companies in an effort that those payments would ultimately be given to an official at Petroleos de Venezuela S.A. (Venezuela's state owned oil company). This was done

with the hope of gaining three new drilling contracts. It is also alleged that US$30,000 was given to an employee of Petroleos de Venezuela S.A. from another third party, in order for Summers to obtain payment of receivables. According to the SEC litigation Release on August 5, 2010, Summers consented to pay a civil penalty in the amount of US$25,000, but has not admitted or denied the SEC's allegations.

Venezuela's Anti-Corruption Law of 2003 sets forth several guidelines to combat corruption. These include:

- Criminalizing passive and active corruption, extortion, and money laundering.
- Requiring public officials to present a sworn statement of personal assets within the first 30 days of entering and leaving office.
- Requiring the state to make the account of public goods and expense information public three times annually.
- Prohibiting public officials from having hidden foreign bank accounts.[95]

President Chavez has declared a zero tolerance policy toward corruption, which has translated into the developing and implementing of legislative guidance and agencies to help combat corruption and enforce anti-bribery initiatives. Venezuela has also implemented the Zero Tax Evasion and Zero Contraband initiatives, to reduce tax evasion and improve customs, respectively. The country has a good set of regulations on public procurement as well as a well-developed system of e-governance. In May 2011, the Venezuela National Assembly discussed a bill for anti-corruption designed to increase penalties for state officials, organizations, and entities that receive illegal funds from the government. The goal is to increase the abilities of the judicial system to prevent and fight corruption.

Nevertheless, enforcement of these laws and initiatives is still weak and the centralization of power within the government has reduced accountability and left corruption quite prevalent throughout the country. Furthermore, the OAS Inter-American Convention against Corruption's Third Round Implementation Report 2010 determined Venezuela's anti-corruption efforts has deficiencies. Areas of deficiency include transnational bribery, embezzlement, and the bribery of domestic and foreign officials. Still common today are requests for facilitation payments to decrease processing time or obtain favorable treatment. Government contracts remain vulnerable to corruption because of a lack of transparency in the tender processes.

Peru

Peru's economy is driven by the mining, natural resources, and fishing industries and is steadily growing at over 6 percent each year.[96] Government spending and private investment have contributed to growth as the country has successfully weathered the global recession. A growing middle class and improved infrastructure is helping to expand the country's internal markets, as well as diversifying its exports portfolio. For almost 20 years, Peru's economy has been supported by an open market economic model, which provides identical rights to national and foreign investment. Bribery and corruption remain a major issue for competitiveness, due to weak governmental procurement controls and transactions transparency, and the licenses needed to establish and operate a business. Despite government anti-corruption efforts, some public officers acting individually pressure executives of companies operating in Peru.

Decree No. 635 of the Peruvian Penal Code criminalizes ". . . covers attempted corruption, extortion, passive and active bribery and money laundering."[97] To further combat corruption and in response to major corruption scandals that have plagued the country in the past including one that led to the President's impeachment in 2000 and eventual guilty plea for bribery, Peru created the Law on the Public Service Code of Ethics. The law provides the ethical standards that public officials need to abide by while holding their positions. The government has also increased the punishment for those found guilty of corruption. The prison sentences for illicit enrichment have increased from a 2- to 4-year range seen from prior governments to an 8- to 18-year range for senior officials in today's government. Over the past decade there has been an increase in officials charged with corruption related charges. Primarily, the charges related to embezzlement and misappropriation of assets.

As one of four pilot countries, Peru was a leader in implementing the G8 Anti-Corruption and Transparency Initiative, which has aided in increasing accountability and transparency throughout the judicial system. The Peruvian government also created the Iniciativa Nacional Anticorrupción (INA) whose purpose is to study the causes of corruption in Peru along with creating the guidelines for the anti-corruption strategy. The government moved to an electronic government contracting platform for procurement of contracts and subsequently created a system called Sistema Electronico de Contratciones del Estado (SEACE).

In spite of these and other actions, the Peruvian anti-corruption framework is still the subject of complaints among companies due to its lack of clarity, excessive red tape, and extended bribery to win public contracts, particularly in concessions for the extraction of natural resources. However, there has not been any FCPA enforcement due to activities in Peru.

Summary

Many Latin American countries have developed strong foundations and conceptual frameworks to fight corruption, and for the most part, embarked on adopting enhanced anti-corruption legislation. However, centralization within most governments in the region has led to decreased accountability and transparency and severe inefficiencies in carrying out many of the laws and regulations that have been put in place. The multitude of public anti-corruption agencies, while good in theory, has become largely ineffective at dealing with the widespread corruption throughout the region. Pressures to encourage foreign direct investment, as well as a widespread problem with narcotics trafficking, unemployment and poverty, have further spread the risk of corruption throughout the region. Companies need to be prepared to address these risks when doing business in the region.

 NOTES

1. Minxin Pei, "Corruption Threatens China's Future." Carnegie Endowment Policy Brief No. 55, October 2007.
2. www.justice.gov/opa/pr/2010/April/10-crm-360.html.
3. www.justice.gov/opa/pr/2009/December/09-crm-1390.html.
4. Minxin Pei, "Corruption Threatens China's Future." Carnegie Endowment Policy Brief No. 55, October 2007.
5. www.sec.gov/litigation/litreleases/2011/lr21889.htm.
6. Department of Justice Press Release, July 31, 2009; case information filed July 22, 2009. www.justice.gov/opa/pr/2009/July/09-crm-754.html
7. www.acrc.go.kr/eng/board.do?command=searchDetail&method=searchList &menuId=020301.
8. www.justice.gov/opa/pr/2011/April/11-crm-431.htm
9. "Kyudenko employees face summary charges over bribery in Philippines." *Kyodo News* March 16, 2007 "Transparency International Progress Report 2010: Enforcement of the OECD Anti-Bribery Convention" *Transparency International* 3rd Edition page 41.
10. "Ex-PCI execs found guilty of bribery." *The Daily Yomiuri* January 30, 2009 "Japanese exec avoids jail in Vietnam graft case." *Agence France Presse* March 24, 2009 "Transparency International Progress Report 2010:

Enforcement of the OECD Anti-Bribery Convention" *Transparency International* page 42.

11. "Progress Report 2010: Enforcement of the OECD Anti-Bribery Convention." Transparency International. www.transparency.org/publications/publications/conventions/oecd_report_2010, p19

12. www.sec.gov/litigation/litreleases/2007/lr20029.htm

13. "Alliance One International Inc. And Universal Corporation Resolve Related Fcpa Matters Involving Bribes Paid To Foreign Government Officials," DOJ, January 1, 2011, www.sec.gov/litigation/litreleases/2008/lr20690.htm; www.sec.gov/litigation/complaints/2008/comp20690.pdf

14. www.justice.gov/opa/pr/2010/August/10-crm-903.html

15. www.justice.gov/opa/pr/2010/March/10-crm-270.html

16. Ernst & Young, European Fraud Survey 2011.

17. "Progress Report 2011: Enforcement of the OECD Anti-Bribery Convention." Transparency International. www.transparency.org/content/download/61106/978536://, page 66.

18. "Serious Fraud Office successfully obtains first ever Civil Recovery Order involving major plc," SFO, October 6, 2008, www.sfo.gov.uk/press-room/latest-press-releases/press-releases-2008/balfour-beatty-plc.aspx.

19. "Mabey & Johnson Ltd appeared at Southwark Crown Court today for sentence in relation to admitted offences of overseas corruption and breaching UN sanctions. The company is to pay £6.6M. This is the first prosecution brought in the UK against a company for these offences," SFO, September 25, 2009, www.sfo.gov.uk/press-room/latest-press-releases/press-releases-2009/mabey--johnson-ltd-sentencing-.aspx.

20. "Mabey & Johnson Ltd: Former executives jailed for helping finance Saddam Hussein's government," SFO, February 23, 2011, http://www.sfo.gov.uk/press-room/latest-press-releases/press-releases-2011/mabey--johnson-ltd-former-executives-jailed-for-helping-finance-saddam-hussein's-government.aspx.

21. "The Serious Fraud Office has today obtained a Civil Recovery Order of almost £5 million against AMEC plc, an international engineering and project management firm," SFO, October 26, 2009, www.sfo.gov.uk/press-room/latest-press-releases/press-releases-2009/sfo-obtains-civil-recovery-order-against-amec-plc.aspx.

22. www.sfo.gov.uk/press-room/latest-press-releases/press-releases-2010/bae-fined-in-tanzania-defence-contract-case.aspx.

23. www.justice.gov/opa/pr/2010/March/10-crm-209.html.

24. "Innospec Limited prosecuted for corruption by the SFO," SFO, March 18, 2010, www.sfo.gov.uk/press-room/latest-press-releases/press-releases-2010/innospec-limited-prosecuted-for-corruption-by-the-sfo.aspx.

25. "Innospec chemicals firm fined $12.7m in bribery case," BBC News, March 26, 2010, http://news.bbc.co.uk/1/hi/8589398.stm.
26. www.sfo.gov.uk/press-room/latest-press-releases/press-releases-2011/action-on-macmillan-publishers-limited.aspx
27. http://transparency.org/policy_research/surveys_indices/cpi/2010.
28. "Progress Report 2011: Enforcement of the OECD Anti-Bribery Convention." Transparency International. www.transparency.org/content/download/61106/978536://, page 38.
29. "Progress Report 2011: Enforcement of the OECD Anti-Bribery Convention." Transparency International. www.transparency.org/content/download/61106/978536://, page 35.
30. www.justice.gov/opa/pr/2008/December/08-crm-1105.html
31. "Progress Report 2011: Enforcement of the OECD Anti-Bribery Convention." Transparency International. www.transparency.org/content/download/61106/978536://, page 36.
32. Kevin J. O'Brien, "Deutsche Telekom Is Focus of Corruption Investigation," New York Times article, September 15, 2010, www.nytimes.com/2010/09/16/technology/16telekom.html.
33. "Daimler AG and Three Subsidiaries Resolve Foreign Corrupt Practices Act Investigation and Agree to Pay $93.6 Million in Criminal Penalties," DOJ, April 1, 2010, www.justice.gov/opa/pr/2010/April/10-crm-360.html.
34. Daniel Schäfer in Frankfurt and Richard Waters in San Francisco, "HP raided in Moscow over €35m bribes probe," FT.com article, April 15, 2010, www.ft.com/intl/cms/s/2/470fbf00-482a-11df-b998-00144feab49a.html#axzz1OGHk2cuB.
35. "Progress Report 2011: Enforcement of the OECD Anti-Bribery Convention." Transparency International. www.transparency.org/content/download/61106/978536://, page 33.
36. "Alcatel-Lucent S.A. and Three Subsidiaries Agree to Pay $92 Million to Resolve Foreign Corrupt Practices Act Investigation" DOJ, December 27, 2010, www.justice.gov/opa/pr/2010/December/10-crm-1481.html.
37. "Technip S.A. Resolves Foreign Corrupt Practices Act Investigation and Agrees to Pay $240 Million Criminal Penalty," DOJ, June 28, 2010, www.justice.gov/opa/pr/2010/June/10-crm-751.html.
38. http://transparency.org/policy_research/surveys_indices/cpi/2010/results.
39. OECD, May 25, 2011, www.oecd.org/document/24/0,3746,en_21571361_44315115_47983768_1_1_1_1,00.html.
40. www.ft.com/cms/s/0/9eee745a-ee9c-11df-9db0-00144feab49a.html#axzz1NwxE5JpU.
41. www.reuters.com/article/2010/04/15/us-hp-russia-idUSTRE63E2ZR20100415.
42. http://transparency.org/policy_research/surveys_indices/cpi/2010.

43. "Progress Report 2011: Enforcement of the OECD Anti-Bribery Convention." Transparency International. www.transparency.org/content/download/61106/ 978536://, page 45.
44. OECD, "Data on Enforcement of the Anti-Bribery Convention" April 20, 2011.
45. "Progress Report 2011: Enforcement of the OECD Anti-Bribery Convention." Transparency International. www.transparency.org/content/download/61106/ 978536://, page 45.
46. "Securities and Exchange Commission v. ENI, S.p.A. and Snamprogetti Netherlands, B.V., Case No. 4:10-cv-02414, S.D. Tex. (Houston)," U.S. SEC Litigation Release 21588, July 7, 2010, www.sec.gov/litigation/litreleases/2010/ lr21588.htm.
47. www.transparency.hu/files/p/685/9481630348.pdf.
48. "UPDATE 1-Italy magistrates open Saipem probe – sources" Reuters article, March 31, 2011, http://af.reuters.com/article/commoditiesNews/ idAFN3116752120110331.
49. http://transparency.org/policy_research/surveys_indices/cpi/2010/results.
50. "Progress Report 2011: Enforcement of the OECD Anti-Bribery Convention." Transparency International. www.transparency.org/content/download/61106/ 978536://, page 60.
51. "Progress Report 2010: Enforcement of the OECD Anti-Bribery Convention." Transparency International. www.transparency.org/publications/publications/ conventions/oecd_report_2010, page 56.
52. Id. and Socolovsky, Jerome. "Bank scandal shakes government, sends shock waves through Spanish boardrooms." *Associated Press Newswires*, May 31, 2002.
53. "South Asia - Regional Strategy Update 2011" and "South Asia - Regional Brief 2011" The World Bank http://siteresources.worldbank.org/SOUTH ASIAEXT/Resources/223546-1296680097256/7707437-1300119933024/ SAR_Strategy_2011.pdf, http://go.worldbank.org/4VDAYM8NIO.
54. www.gopacnetwork.org/
55. www.transparency.org./regional_pages/asia_pacific
56. "SEC Files Settled Enforcement Action Against The Dow Chemical Company for Foreign Corrupt Practices Act Violations." SEC. February 13, 2007. www.sec .gov/litigation/litreleases/2007/lr20000.htm
57. DOJ, February 14, 2008, www.justice.gov/opa/pr/2008/February/08_crm_ 116.html
58. "Siemens AG and Three Subsidiaries Plead Guilty to Foreign Corrupt Practices Act Violations and Agree to Pay USD 450 Million in Combined Criminal Fines." DOJ, December 15, 2008. www.justice.gov/opa/pr/2008/December/08-crm-1105.html and www.justice.gov/criminal/fraud/fcpa/cases/siemens/12-15-08siemensbangla-statement.pdf

59. "Alcatel-Lucent S.A. and Three Subsidiaries Agree to Pay $92 Million to Resolve Foreign Corrupt Practices Act Investigation" DOJ, December 27, 2010, www.justice.gov/opa/pr/2010/December/10-crm-1481.html

60. www.sec.gov/litigation/complaints/2009/comp21156.pdf

61. *Pakistan Penal Code, 1860* [Pakistan], Act XLV of 1860, 6 October 1860, available at: www.unhcr.org/refworld/docid/485231942.html

62. www.transparency.org/global_priorities/public_contracting/integrity_pacts

63. An association of six Gulf countries (Saudi Arabia, Kuwait, the United Arab Emirates, Qatar, Bahrain, and Oman), founded on Islamic beliefs, working together towards common political and economic objectives

64. "Former Healthsouth Officers Indicted in Connection with Bribery Involving Saudi Hospital," DOJ, July 1, 2004 www.justice.gov/criminal/pr/2004/07/ 2004_3692_FORMER_HEALTHSOUTH_ O.htm

65. Alharbi Ali Khalaf S, "An Overview of the Saudi Arabian Criminal Justice Procedures Against Corruption in the Public Secto," www.unafei.or.jp/eng lish/pdf/RS_No77/No77_14PA_Khalaf.pdf; Page 124-125 under bribery law.

66. Article 2 of the Anti Money Laundering (AML) law; www.sama.gov.sa/sites/ samaen/MoneyLaundry/Documents/anti_money_laundering_(aml)_law_ar_ en.pdf.62

67. The UAE is made up of seven emirates: Abu Dhabi, Dubai, Sharjah, Ras Al Khaimah, Fujairah, Umm Al Qawain, and Ajman.

68. http://law.case.edu/saddamtrial/documents/Iraqi_Penal_Code_1969.pdf; Paragraph 307

69. http://law.case.edu/saddamtrial/documents/Iraqi_Penal_Code_1969.pdf; Paragraph 308.

70. www.sec.gov/litigation/admin/2009/34-60005.pdf

71. Hamm, Steve "Africa's Anti-Corruption Hero" *Bloomberg Businessweek*, www .businessweek.com/technology/content/jun2009/tc20090612_591279.htm.

72. Ernst & Young "It's time for Africa: Ernst & Young's 2011 Africa attractiveness survery"

73. http://www.justice.gov/opa/pr/2008/December/08-crm-1105.html; www .sec.gov/litigation/complaints/2008/comp20829.pdf

74. "JGC Corporation Resolves Foreign Corrupt Practices Act Investigation and Agrees to Pay a $218.8 Million Criminal Penalty," DOJ, April 6, 2011, www .justice.gov/opa/pr/2011/April/11-crm-431.html]

75. www.nigeria-law.org/Corrupt%20Practices%20and%20other%20Related% 20Offences%20Act%202000.htm.

76. www.info.gov.za/acts/2004/a12-04/a12-04a.pdf.

77. www.saabgroup.com/About-Saab/Newsroom/Press-releases–News/2011—6/ Saab-completes-internal-investigation-regarding-consultant-contract-in- South-Africa/

78. www.sec.gov/litigation/litreleases/lr18775.htm

79. www.sec.gov/litigation/complaints/2007/comp20094.pdf; "SEC Charges Baker Hughes With Foreign Bribery and With Violating 2001 Commission Cease-and-Desist Order," SEC, April 26, 2007, www.sec.gov/news/press/2007/2007-77.htm

80. "SEC Charges Alcatel-Lucent with FCPA Violations." SEC, December 27, 2010.

81. "Former World Bank Employee Sentenced for Taking Kickbacks and Assisting in the Bribery of a Foreign Official," DOJ, April 25, 2008, www.justice.gov/opa/pr/2008/April/08-crm-341.html

82. *Laws of Kenya: The Public Officer Ethics Act* www.kacc.go.ke/docs/legal/poe.pdf

83. Laws of Kenya, The Anti-CorrupTion And eConomiC Crimes ACT, Chapter 65, 2003, www.kacc.go.ke/docs/legal/aceca.pdf.

84. Based on 2010 and 2009 estimates, respectively GDP according to The CIA World Fact Book, www.cia.gov/library/publications/the-world-factbook/geos/mx.html.

85. "Anti-corruption profile - Mexico." *Thomson Reuters Foundation Homepage—Trust.org.* www.trust.org/trustlaw/country-profiles/good-governance.dot?id=d68d7eae-74c4-4518-815a-7c2cbfa037db.

86. "Progress Report 2011: Enforcement of the OECD Anti-Bribery Convention." *Transparency International.*www.transparency.org/content/download/61106/978536://, p. 52.

87. "Brazilian Penal Code Law No. 10.467" Unofficial Translation by *Organization for Economic Co-operation and Development* www.oecd.org/dataoecd/43/26/33783624.pdf.

88. "Brazilian Law No. 9.613" *Presidência da República Casa Civil* Unofficial translation, www.planalto.gov.br/ccivil_03/Leis/L9613.htm.

89. "Progress Report 2011: Enforcement of the OECD Anti-Bribery Convention." *Transparency International.*www.transparency.org/content/download/61106/978536://, pp. 23.

90. "Anti-corruption profile - Argentina." *Thomson Reuters Foundation Homepage—Trust.org.* http://www.trust.org/trustlaw/country-profiles/good-governance.dot?id=03878ca0-07fe-42c1-8f1a-2c8cdc202b23.

91. Pilot Review Programme: Argentina, United Nations Office of Drug And Crime. *Argentina Country Report.*www.anticorrupcion.gov.ar/documentos/Argentina,%20country%20repor.pdf.

92. "Argentine money laundering bill passes Senate." *Business & Financial News, Breaking US & International News | Reuters.com.*www.reuters.com/article/2011/06/01/argentina-moneylaundering-idUSN0117759220110601.

93. "US Embassy: Corruption unpunished in Argentina—Yahoo! Finance." Associated Press, February 9, 2011. http://finance.yahoo.com/news/US-Embassy-Corruption-apf-4128696917.html?x=0.

94. "CIA The World Factbook—Venezuela." *CIA The World Factbook.*www.cia.gov/library/publications/the-world-factbook/geos/ve.html.

95. "Anti-corruption profile - Venezuela." *Thomson Reuters Foundation Homepage – Trust.org.* www.trust.org/trustlaw/country-profiles/good-governance.dot?id= e20c0ed5-1692-4066-83c2-2ef83da252a3.
96. "CIA The World FactbookPeru." *CIA The World Factbook.*www.cia.gov/library/publications/the-world-factbook/geos/pe.html.
97. "Anti-corruption profile - Peru." *Thomson Reuters Foundation Homepage – Trust.org.* http://www.trust.org/trustlaw/country-profiles/good-governance.dot?id=52a71879-ba03-4428-b7f8-c6597735542a.

 ## CONTRIBUTORS

This section was written with contributions from the following Ernst & Young professionals:

Asia Pacific

John Auerbach: FIDS Partner in Shanghai, China
Roger Darvall-Stevens: FIDS Partner in Melbourne, Australia
Hee Dong Yoo: FIDS Director in Seoul, Korea

Europe

Jonathan Middup: FIDS Partner in Birmingham, United Kingdom
Stefan Heissner: FIDS Partner in Dusseldorf, Germany
Paolo Marcon: FIDS Partner in Milan, Italy
Philippe Hontarrede: FIDS Partner in Paris, France
Ivan Ryutov: FIDS Partner in Moscow, Russia
Ricardo Noreña Herra: FIDS Partner in Madrid, Spain
Mark Goff: FIDS Senior Manager in London, United Kingdom

India and South Asia

Arpinder Singh: FIDS Partner in Mumbai, India
Shariq Zaidi: FIDS Partner in Karachi, Pakistan
Vinay Garodiya: FIDS Senior Manager in Mumbai, India

Middle East and Africa

Bob Chandler: FIDS Partner in Manama, Bahrain
Sharon Van Rooyen: FIDS Partner in Johannesburg, South Africa
Richard Thomas: FIDS Principal in New York City, United States

Joe da Silva: FIDS Partner in Johannesburg, South Africa
Hannes Van Der Walt: FIDS Senior Manager in Pretoria, South Africa
JD Minotti: FIDS Senior Manager in Chicago, United States

Latin America

Jose Francisco Compagno: FIDS Partner in Sao Paulo, Brazil
Jose Trevino: FIDS Partner in Mexico City, Mexico
Andrea Rey: FIDS Partner in Buenos Aires, Argentina
Rafael Huamán: FIDS Partner in Lima, Perú

CHAPTER ELEVEN

Industry Considerations for Bribery and Corruption Risks

T HIS CHAPTER PROVIDES INSIGHTS into the impact of bribery and corruption from an industry perspective. Some industries have been focused on having a robust anti-corruption compliance program for many years, while others have given little consideration to their potential risks. The following industries are presented:

Aerospace and Defense
Automotive
Construction and Real Estate
Consumer Products
Diversified Industrial
Energy
Financial Services
Life Sciences
Media and Entertainment
Mining and Metals
Retail and Wholesale
Technology
Transportation

For each of these industries, this chapter presents an overview of bribery and corruption risks and trends and areas for consideration in reducing the overall risk and strengthening anti-corruption compliance programs.

 AEROSPACE AND DEFENSE

Aerospace and defense is a global industry with hundreds of billions of dollars in annual revenue that is largely comprised of the production, sale, and service of military weapons and systems along with the commercial and general aircraft market. While the United States continues to be the largest spender in the world on aerospace and defense equipment, the economic downturn has decreased U.S. spending on airliners as well as the availability of government money for defense spending. With less growth opportunities at home, aerospace and defense contractors are pursuing customers and relationships in new markets that will drive sales growth over the next few decades. As a result, the industry is experiencing accelerating growth in globalization. The emergence of new high-growth markets, accumulation of wealth in developing economies, and continual evolution of military alliances provides market access that the industry has not experienced in the past. Also adding to the globalization of the industry is a broader supply chain to capitalize on low-cost manufacturing as well as access to investing in top research and development projects, the lifeblood of the industry.

There are a number of common challenges companies meet by expanding into international markets. Among them are the different standards of business ethics across cultures including different interpretations and tolerations of bribery and corruption practices.

Specific Risk Factors

Companies in the aerospace and defense industry face heightened corruption and bribery risks compared to other industries due to opportunity and incentive. The high level of interaction with government officials inherent to an industry dealing with militaries around the world creates opportunity; the fact that their products are sold through contracts that may be worth billions of dollars creates incentive. Paying a nominal bribe to a government official in order to secure a billion-dollar contract makes sense from a purely quantitative stand point. When ethical and legal ramifications are factored in, the cost of participating in corrupt activity outweighs the perceived benefit. To define potential consequences, the U.S. Department of Justice (DOJ) and Securities and Exchange Commission (SEC) have focused significant Foreign Corrupt Practices Act (FCPA) enforcement actions against industry giants such as BAE Systems and Lockheed Martin. As a result of the government's scrutiny, aerospace and defense contractors need to be especially sensitive to both the intent and appearance of their interactions with any foreign government official. Such a notion is not new to defense contractors who are subject to International Traffic in Arms Regulations (ITAR) which regulates the export and import of defense articles and services to non-U.S. persons.

Following are the significant risk areas that aerospace and defense companies face, each of which is discussed in greater detail:

- Foreign government customers
- Consultants, representatives, and other third parties
- Partnering and joint ventures
- Political and charitable contributions
- Promotional expenses
- Books and records treatment of contract expenses

Foreign Government Customers

Aerospace and defense contractors enter into contracts with foreign governments and militaries to sell their products and services. Negotiations with high-ranking government officials are a textbook situation for corruption. Factors that affect the risk when dealing with government customers include (1) type of government contract; (2) scope of services; (3) contract concessions; and (4) offset obligations.

Programs with a foreign government are classified as either Foreign Military Sales (FMS) or Direct Commercial Sale (DCS). FMS contracts include the company, foreign government, and the U.S. government as parties to the contract. Under FMS, the U.S. government procures defense products and services on behalf of the foreign government customer, and the U.S. government serves as an intermediary between the company and the ultimate customer. Under DCS contracts, the company directly negotiates with foreign customers, thereby increasing the interaction with foreign officials and associated corruption risk.

The scope of contract also impacts the potential risk of corruption. Providing services as opposed to tangible goods is more susceptible to corruption because often services have less defined deliverables and include sustained interface with foreign government personnel. Also, contracts may include ancillary costs, called other direct costs (ODC). Without enough clarification in the contract to define the ODC components, the foreign customer may request ancillary monies be used or substituted for activities outside the scope of the contract, which may provide personal benefits to government personnel.

Certain contract concessions, especially nonroutine negotiations, increase corruption risk. Examples include contractual disputes and contract deobligations (deobligation is the process in which the customer has paid excess funds over the value of the goods/services the company has delivered). During these nonroutine concessions, the foreign customer may attempt to redirect funds toward other activities, which may again, provide personal benefits or advantages to government personnel.

Offset obligations are common in defense contracts with foreign governments. An offset is an obligation in which the company performs certain services that are for the general well-being or development of the local economy as a condition of the contract with the foreign government. Offset obligations may be direct or indirect. Direct offsets relate to the underlying transaction, such as the requirement for the company to purchase components from local manufacturers. Indirect offsets are not related to the defense contract and may include building schools or hospitals in the foreign country or providing foreign investment in a certain technology or industry. Offsets carry a number of corruption risks, which include (1) offset boards and officials; (2) sole-source third parties; and (3) offset service providers/consultants. Foreign offset programs generally have local offset laws or policies, which are overseen by governing bodies. If a company is attempting to receive offset credit for certain activities to reduce their offset obligations, there is a threat of providing bribes in order to influence local offset officials. Companies need to be wary of direct offset agreements that require sole sourcing or exclusivity with a subcontractor or manufacturer in the local economy. The third party may have those exclusivity rights because of familial or other ties to government officials. In addition, indirect offsets may be completely unrelated to the company's line of business. Performing activities outside of the company's business acumen may require significant use of offset service providers and consultants, which also exposes the company to corruption risks.

Consultants, Representatives, and Other Third Parties

In foreign markets, there is pervasive use of third parties such as consultants and representatives. Often, local governments will accept meetings only through relationships, and so consultants may be engaged for their connections. Many consultants have personal or political relationships with higher-ranking officials and are retired military officers themselves. Companies need to be cautious that any relationships with government decision makers are not of a family nature. Consultants or representatives may also be used as a conduit to pass along bribery payments on the company's behalf. Using a third-party intermediary for corrupt activity is strictly prohibited by the FCPA and the U.K. Bribery Act. In the same regard, companies use local subcontractors, offset service providers, and other local professionals that carry this risk of corruption. The company has a responsibility to know the actions of its third parties, who are acting as agents of the company and may be engaging with government agencies.

Partnering and Joint Ventures

Often, aerospace and defense companies will partner with a local company when doing business in foreign locations. For example, local laws may require foreign programs and representative offices to have a local sponsor. The sponsor is often an individual who receives fees or commissions from the company. As a result, it's important to understand the political relations of sponsors so that sponsorship fees cannot be viewed as a pretense for bribery payments.

Also, aerospace and defense contractors often partner with other foreign and local companies, forming joint ventures or consortiums, in order to produce the various components and services that are involved with complex defense articles and aerospace technologies. Significant business relationships increase the risk of corruption because the company could be liable for the actions of its business partners. Even in situations where the company had no direct involvement in the corrupt act, if the company does not take measures to prevent unethical activity in its enterprises and the corrupt behavior of its partners benefit the company, the company may face FCPA ramifications.

Political and Charitable Contributions

Because of its obvious ties to the government sector, aerospace and defense companies may participate in foreign political campaigns or lobbying activities. Historically, this area has a very high risk of abuse and corruption. Also, because company funds are being used to influence a decision or outcome, the bribery and corruption risk associated with political contributions and lobbying is greater and requires the highest level of controls within the company.

Charitable contributions and donations are often made to foreign organizations for seemingly benign purposes. However, often overlooked is the organization's affiliation with high-ranking officials or royal families. In more clever bribery schemes, a non-for-profit organization is a sham company that flows directly back into the pockets of an official.

Promotional Expenses

Many cultures have local customs and traditions that foreign businesses may be expected to participate in. A common custom that may conflict with the American view of ethics is gift giving. Foreign businesses typically give significant customers and vendors small gifts around holidays. In some cultures, the giving of cash is appropriate. While participating in local customs is not prohibited by the FCPA, it's important that such customs are not abused as a mechanism to provide lavish gifts to government affiliated individuals.

Because aerospace and defense contracts usually range in the millions of dollars, it's common for the customer to attend multiple demonstrations, meetings, and inspections. The company may pay for such ordinary business travel for government customers under the FCPA, as long as such travel is not extravagant. In addition, trips should be to the company's offices or facilities, as opposed to more desirable or vacation destinations.

Books and Records Treatment of Contract Expenses

The aerospace and defense industry, due to the nature of its business, has unique factors that may impact its compliance with the books and records provision of the FCPA. Companies in the industry commonly use the Financial Accounting Standards Board (FASB) Accounting Standards Codification (ASC) Topic 605-35 (formerly known as AICPA Statement of Position 81-1, Accounting for Performance of Construction-Type and Certain Production-Type Contracts). The guidance outlines acceptable approaches for recognizing revenue on contracts that span multiple reporting periods, such as the percentage of completion method. Under this method, the company may recognize revenue over the life of the contract based on the degree of completion as measured by costs incurred.

Most often, corrupt payments are accounted for as an expense. If a bribe is recorded as a contract-related expense, the amount will be factored into the percentage of completion calculation and thereby cause revenue to be recognized. In essence, corrupt expenses may increase the amount of revenue recognition, which perpetuates the violation. To further complicate the matter, costs associated with construction contracts are accumulated on the balance sheet in a construction in process (CIP) account. Often, the CIP account lacks adequate transparency into the underlying nature of the expenses (i.e., there are not enough subaccounts within CIP to accurately reflect the classes of transactions). The lack of detail surrounding the costs in CIP increases the probability of including potentially corrupt payments in this account without awareness by accounting management.

In addition to the risks highlighted previously, the aerospace and defense industry faces corruption risks similar to those of other industries. Local bank accounts and petty cash provide sources to pay bribes or facilitation payments. The movement of personnel and equipment, which requires interaction with foreign immigration and customs departments, may create the occasion in which a small, under-the-table fee will get the people and goods to where they need to be on time. Other routine interactions with regulatory bodies may include business permits, licenses, and taxes.

Bribery and Corruption Issues Impacting the Aerospace and Defense Industry

The aerospace and defense industry has felt the force of the vigorous enforcement of the FCPA by both the DOJ and SEC. In total, the industry has paid over US$500 million in fines and disgorgement under the act.

The use of sales representatives and consultants is a common trend in the majority of FCPA-related cases involving defense contractors. These individuals act as agents of a company and are typically used to conceal payments and the relationship with government officials. Some examples include:

- **BAE Systems:** BAE Systems plc pleaded guilty in 2010 and agreed to pay a penalty of US$400 million for conspiring to defraud the United States and for violating the Arms Export Control Act and the International Traffic in Arms Regulations. According to the DOJ, BAE used offshore shell companies to make payments to intermediaries known as "marketing advisers" with the knowledge that there was a "high probability" that these payments were being used to secure defense contracts.[1]
- **Titan Corporation:** In 2005, Titan Corporation pleaded guilty to multiple counts of violating the FCPA and agreed to pay a criminal fine of US$ 13 million and civil disgorgement of US$15.4 million. Titan Corporation allegedly transferred more than US$2 million through an agent in the African nation of Benin, specifically for the reelection campaign of Benin's incumbent president. The company apparently was involved with a telecommunications project within the country. In addition, the

payments were falsely recorded as "consulting" services in the company's books and records.[2]

■ **Lockheed Martin:** According to a January 27, 1995 DOJ press release, Lockheed Martin pled guilty for the conspiracy to violate the FCPA and paid US$21.8 million with a US$3 million civil fine. A consultant for the company in Egypt was an elected official and used political influence to secure business for the company.

■ **United Industrial Corporation:** In 2009, UIC (United Industrial Corporation) agreed to a cease-and-desist order for violating the FCPA. According to the SEC, UIC through its subsidiary ACL (ACL Technologies) made payments to an agent (retired Egyptian Air Force general) related to an airport depot project. Thomas Wurzel, ACL's former president, continued to authorize payments with the knowledge that the agent would transfer funds to EAF officials in order to secure business for UIC. UIC paid US$337,679 in disgorgement and prejudgment interest in regards to the SEC's order.[3]

In the past few years, the DOJ and SEC have increased the number of criminal prosecutions of individuals under the FCPA and the aerospace and defense contractors have been subject to monetary fines in the tens of thousands of dollars as well as imprisonment. However, this is not new for the industry. In the mid-1990s, Suleiman Nassar, a regional vice president of Lockheed, was sentenced to 18 months in prison due to his involvement in corrupt payments to an Egyptian consultant (U.S. v. Nassar). Similarly, in 1991, Richard Liebo, former vice president at NAPCO, was sentenced to 18 months with three years of probation for purchasing airplane tickets for a Nigerian government official although the sentence was later reduced in a retrial, Liebo did serve two months in prison (U.S. v. Liebo). Other individuals from the industry prosecuted under the FCPA have been subject to civil fines, probation, and community service.

What Should Aerospace and Defense Companies Be Doing

Due to the significant risks inherent in the industry and the threat of enforcement action by the DOJ and SEC, aerospace and defense contractors must set the gold standard when it comes to an anti-corruption infrastructure. A robust anti-corruption compliance program includes a comprehensive risk assessment to identify the higher-risk contracts, programs, and activities. Chapters 4 and 6 describe this in detail. When performing a risk assessment, the company needs to focus on where the customer is ultimately located, not just the location of the company's foreign offices.

Effort and resources commensurate with the level of risks should be dedicated to mitigating the company's corruption risks through the use of employee awareness programs, third-party due diligence, financial controls and processing, and ongoing monitoring activities.

To specifically identify and guard against the risks noted, below is a table of common red flags and risk mitigation techniques for the common corruption risks faced by the aerospace and defense industry:

Aerospace and Defense Corruption Risks	Common Red Flags	Risk Mitigation Techniques
Foreign government customers	Large number of modifications or other agreements after contract finalization Large amount of surplus funding upon contract completion Providing services or materials not directly related to the contract scope	Clear and specific contract language with foreign governments Provide training for employees responsible for negotiations and ongoing customer interface
Consultants/Reps/Other third parties	Excessive commissions given the product and/or territory involved Substantial expense reimbursement such as out-of-pocket charges Requesting payment outside of territory where services were rendered or where third party resides Lack of transparency in third-party documentation such as statement of work, invoices, and so on	Thorough due diligence of prospective third parties Emphasis toward third-party training and certifications Measures to provide anti-corruption contract provisions and audit rights
Partnering and joint ventures	Lack of management involvement in operations Partner is specified by foreign government or contract Partner does not appear to add value commensurate with their share of profits	Implementation of company's anti-corruption program at joint venture/partners Transactional-based due diligence (Merger and Acquisition (M&A)) with certifications

		Measures to provide anti-corruption contract provisions and audit rights
Political and charitable contributions	Large contributions authorized and paid locally with little supporting documentation and transparency to home office Payments to individuals instead of entities Contributions recorded as "other" or "misc" instead of appropriate accounts where contributions/donations are typically recorded	Due diligence of organizations and individuals receiving contributions Recording contributions in segregated account Development of a clear internal approval process for all contributions/donations
Promotional expenses	Demonstrations or program meetings involving desirable or vacation locations Significant cash advances or reimbursements lacking detail Prevalent use of petty cash locally without receipts	Clear policies and approval process for the solicitation of promotion expenses Employee training over acceptable and unacceptable business development practices Maintaining a gift log for tracking and reporting purposes

 ## AUTOMOTIVE

The automotive industry has gone through significant change and a financially difficult period in the last several years. During the economic downturn, automotive companies and suppliers focused on cutting costs in an effort to preserve profit margins. The reduction in consumer spending impacted sales in both the original equipment manufacturer (OEM) and aftermarkets. In 2010, with an improving economy, consumer spending began to recover and most automotive related businesses began to see improved results.

With continued slow growth in demand in most home markets of the automotive industry including North America, Europe, and Japan, and increased competition across the globe, many automotive OEM's and suppliers are moving to new markets for growth and to seek cheaper sourcing alternatives in order to remain competitive. For many companies this means increased emphasis on investments outside of familiar geographies and into markets where companies have less experience and are subject to higher risks for bribery and corruption.

Traditionally, the automotive industry has not been a primary focus of regulatory enforcement, in part based on the markets in which they historically had operations. Many companies are venturing into certain markets, such as China, India, Brazil, Indonesia, and Mexico, which, according to Transparency International[4] have a high susceptibility toward bribery and corruption. These markets are previously untapped and may require companies to do business with governments or local conditions that have a history of corruption. In other cases, companies may be doing business with new or previously unknown partners, suppliers and other third parties to access the local market. Additionally, these third parties may not be fully aware of the requirements of the FCPA or may operate with the view that they are not subject to the requirements of the act.

Specific Risk Factors

Companies in the automotive industry face bribery and corruption risks similar to those faced by other industries. The following table shows various risks that automotive companies may face across the sectors of the industry:

	OEMs	Suppliers	Dealers	Aftermarket Services	Retail Parts
Government customers	√	√	√	√	
Government-related joint ventures	√	√			
Use of third parties	√	√			√
Licenses	√	√	√	√	√
Permits - Production - Import/Export	√	√	√	√	√
Movement of personnel and equipment - Visas - Customs-clearance	√	√		√	√
Local bank accounts and petty cash	√	√	√	√	√
Sales incentives	√		√		

The automotive industry can have many touch points with governments. In industries such as military sales and fleet sales, government is the key customer. In Africa, the Middle East, and parts of Asia, governments often control access to markets and the process to issue licenses for sales in developing markets. Governments also control the customs process for delivering supplies and the movement of finished products throughout these markets. Often, when interacting with governments in the developing world, third-party intermediaries are used to assist in this process. The risks around government interaction and use of third parties and ways to address these risks have been covered in depth in other sections of this book.

Certain risk areas specific to the automotive industry are worth highlighting. Next, the risks related to overseas production and sales, which include the use of third parties and customs clearance, are highlighted.

Overseas Sales

Automotive sales are an area of intense risk to companies as the markets include many government touch points including civil and military customers. The risks can include a number of areas including:

- Gifts and donations.
- Travel and entertainment (T&E) expenses paid for government officials.
- Inflated invoices on sales transactions.
- Kickbacks paid to government officials.

Payments can also be made directly or through a "commission" to secure larger sales of military or fleet size transactions.

In developing markets, many transactions are done through third parties and may not be properly controlled under the processes and compliance programs in place at automotive companies. Additionally, there have been cases where the violations that occurred were directly recorded in the books of these companies. These risks and the potential impact of violations increase the need for additional procedures related to FCPA compliance in developing countries. Procedures to review expense reimbursements, payments to third parties and analysis of sales activities are necessary to balance the potential risks in these areas. Internal audit and investigative teams need to be trained on bribery and corruption so they can understand the company's policy, the laws, and the impact of any violation.

Customs Clearance

The customs clearance process is another area that is subject to increased risk. Each country has its own laws and regulations that can be onerous to navigate, and many government employees and outside agents may be involved in managing the process. It is important that companies understand the nature of the work of their customs clearance agents and brokers to limit its bribery and corruption exposure.

Automotive companies must also be aware of local laws and behaviors. For instance, relatively minor documentation discrepancies may result in significant customs clearance delays. This provides the customs clearance officials with potential leverage for obtaining a bribe. With the importance of "just-in-time" logistics of the automotive industry, where the delivery of materials is especially time-sensitive, customs and other government officials may gain leverage. For example, the delay in receiving parts from a supplier could lead to losses of millions of dollars per day due to lost production.

In some cases, a customs clearance entity may offer expedited clearance. It is important to clearly understand the nature and components of this service offering. In some countries, there is the potential that the customs clearance entity may be making illegal payments in order to expedite the shipment. If a third-party supplier is responsible for customs clearance, the direct risks may be reduced. However, if a company becomes aware of a supplier's potential improper activity, then it may have the risk of breaching anti-corruption laws, particularly if the company directly or indirectly funds those activities.

Bribery and Corruption Issues Impacting the Automotive Industry

Historically, the automotive industry has not received major attention from the DOJ related to FCPA enforcement. However, this changed with the 2010 Daimler AG matter discussed below.

Recent Case

In early 2010, Daimler AG and three of its subsidiaries resolved charges related to an FCPA investigation into the company's worldwide sales practices. According to court documents as well as a DOJ press release dated April 1, 2010, Daimler AG

[. . .] engaged in a long-standing practice of paying bribes to foreign government officials through a variety of mechanisms, including the use of corporate ledger accounts known internally as "third-party accounts" or "TPAs," corporate "cash desks," offshore bank accounts, deceptive pricing arrangements and third-party intermediaries. Daimler AG and its subsidiaries made hundreds of improper payments worth tens of millions of dollars to foreign officials in at least 22 countries—including China, Croatia, Egypt, Greece, Hungary, Indonesia, Iraq, Ivory Coast, Latvia, Nigeria, Russia, Serbia and Montenegro, Thailand, Turkey, Turkmenistan, Uzbekistan, Vietnam, and others—to assist in securing contracts with government customers for the purchase of Daimler vehicles. The contracts were valued at hundreds of millions of dollars. In some cases, Daimler AG or its subsidiaries wire transferred these improper payments to U.S. bank accounts or to the foreign bank accounts of U.S. shell companies, in order for those entities to pass on the bribes. Within Daimler AG and its subsidiaries, bribe payments were often identified and recorded as "commissions," "special discounts," and/or "nützliche Aufwendungen" or "N.A." payments, which translates to "useful payment" or "necessary payment," and was understood by certain Daimler employees to mean "official bribe." Also, certain corrupt payments continued as late as January 2008, after the DOJ had begun its investigation. In all cases, Daimler AG improperly recorded these corrupt payments in its corporate books and records. Daimler AG admitted that it earned more than $50 million in profits from transactions. Daimler AG also admitted that it agreed to pay kickbacks to the former Iraqi government in connection with contracts to sell vehicles to Iraq under the UN's Oil for Food program [. . .]

[. . .] Daimler AG entered into a deferred prosecution agreement and agreed to the filing of criminal information charging that company with one count of conspiracy to violate the books and records provisions of the FCPA and one count of violating those provisions. Daimler AG's Chinese subsidiary also entered into a deferred prosecution agreement and agreed to the filing, charging it with one count of conspiracy to violate the anti-bribery provisions of the FCPA and one count of violating those provisions. In total, Daimler AG and its subsidiaries paid $93.6 million in criminal fines and penalties [. . .][and in] a related civil complaint filed by the [SEC]. Daimler AG agreed to pay $91.4 million in disgorgement of profits related to those violations. [. . .][Also] Daimler AG agreed to retain an independent compliance monitor for a three-year period to oversee the company's continued implementation and maintenance of an FCPA compliance program, and to make reports to the company and the [DOJ].[5]

What Should Automotive Companies Be Doing?

There is a developing trend of automotive companies to upgrade their anti-bribery and anti-corruption programs as part of their global expansion. While many automotive companies have established anti-bribery and anti-corruption programs, the movement into new markets and the increased complexity associated with foreign investment in the sector will both broaden the geographic scope of bribery and corruption risk and test the strength of existing programs.

Existing anti-bribery and anti-corruption programs, training, and employee confirmation of awareness, and compliance with these programs may not provide enough comfort as companies expand their markets. A number of practices should be considered to help address the increased risks that exist. Some of the examples include:

- Periodic and scheduled anti-bribery and anti-corruption risk assessments that consider country risk, historical events, third-party interaction, and includes consideration of existing policies and controls.
- Transaction testing in certain countries or associated with certain business relationships on a proactive basis to consider any "red flags" that may emerge as a result of items noted during the risk assessment.
- Detailed anti-bribery and anti-corruption training for impacted employees and third-party business partners including agents and joint venture partners.
- Training and work step consideration for internal audit departments as part of their recurring audit process.
- Development and implementation of a defined anti-bribery and anti-corruption due diligence program as part of any merger, acquisition, or other joint venture activities.

Special consideration should be given to:

- *Third parties.* Third parties operate on a company's behalf and can create vicarious liability for the company. Therefore, it is important to know where third parties are used, which third parties are used, why they are used, what they are actually doing for the company, and what compliance and monitoring provisions are included in contracts with those parties. While automotive companies traditionally have relationships with global suppliers that have compliance programs, there are typically local suppliers that may not operate with the same level of awareness and controls related to FCPA. All agreements should be written and the underlying business relationship and purpose should be included in the contract. A red flag to look for are payments or commissions that fall outside of the normal range for this service. Another red flag is services provided by import/export agents that are not properly supported or documented. With "just-in-time" logistics as a key performance indicator for the industry, the movement of product is critical. Companies may not be exempt from liability if a third party commits a violation on their behalf. Reviewing invoices for expedited charges, clearance fees and other costs outside of the traditional costs should be considered.

- *Gifts/Entertainment policy.* Policies should not be developed in isolation at the company-wide level and generically pushed down to every location in which the company operates. These policies should remain flexible enough to accommodate more stringent local laws and allow for exceptions approved with documented approval from legal, compliance, and other related parties. For example, it is common for automotive companies to have officials visit their plants as part of the sales process. The expenses associated with these visits should be reasonable, preapproved, properly documented, and within appropriate guidelines of corporate policies.
- *Mergers and acquisitions.* As automotive companies look for ways to expand their business globally, the company should consider development of a formal policy with specific procedures for anti-corruption due diligence in any contemplated merger, acquisition, or joint venture. There have been cases where a company has either terminated or substantially discounted the value of acquisitions based on gaining an understanding of the existing business and sales process and the underlying risks associated with FCPA. Conducting anti-corruption due diligence and postacquisition assessments are key elements assessed by regulators should an issue arise. The risks include:
  - Becoming liable for continuing corrupt activities that failed to be identified and stopped.
  - Overpaying for a business that was built on corruption.

- Inheriting corrupt employees from the acquired company.
- Becoming saddled with significant increased compliance costs required to change the new business that were not anticipated.

The amount of anti-corruption due diligence that can be performed in the context of a merger or acquisition is subject to negotiation between the buyer and the seller and is often conducted under intense time constraints. If the situation permits, anti-corruption due diligence should include some or all of the following activities:

- Background investigation and public database searches of key executives.
- Sales analysis and understanding of the underlying business development practices of the acquisition target.
- Interviews of key executives relating to corruption risks and any past issues.
- Review of documents related to acquired company's anti-corruption compliance program, past incidents of corruption and risks of corruption in the business.
- Forensic accounting and transaction testing procedures related to high-corruption-risk transactions.

Statements accurately disclosing any past corrupt actions or violations of any anti-corruption regulations should also be included in the seller's representations and warranties related to the transaction or as part of the merger or joint venture contract. The contract also should address future compliance with the applicable anti-corruption laws. Following the closing of the transaction, automotive companies should put anti-corruption compliance high on their integration plan priorities and conduct further risk assessment procedures as necessary to address the corruption risks posed by the any new business relationships or acquisitions.

 ## CONSTRUCTION AND REAL ESTATE

The construction and real estate industry by its nature is considered a medium to high risk in relation to the FCPA and other anti-bribery legislation. While there have been very few cases prosecuted in this area in relation to FCPA, there have been many scandals and investigations at a local level. As companies compete for projects internationally, it opens up the possibility that companies may encounter more serious FCPA and other anti-corruption compliance issues.

The industry factors that make the construction industry vulnerable to potential corruption issues include:

Risk	Description of Risk
Attitude toward fraud and corruption	The perception is that fraud is endemic in the industry. The industry is always combating theft and other fraudulent practices such as ghost employees and bad workmanship.
Government-funded projects	Infrastructure projects are often either government funded or funded through public/private partnerships. Therefore, the government is a large purchaser of services, as a result there can be many touch points with government officials.
Planning/Zoning process	The planning/zoning process in many countries is quite lengthy and can be open to abuse by corrupt officials.
Use of subcontractors and third parties	There is a high level of use of subcontractors and consultants/agents. This offers the opportunity for the use of third parties to make or solicit bribes.
Large contracts	The size of the contracts involved can be significant, and as a result political power can be concentrated in the hands of a number of political appointees.

Specific Risk Factors of Industry

Companies in the construction and real estate industry face bribery and corruption risks similar to those faced by other industries, but also industry-specific risks. The risks include:

- Use of joint venture partners.
- Obtaining licenses and planning permission.
- High use of subcontractors and consultants/agents.
- Disposition of contingent amounts in contracts.
- Negotiation on additions to the specifications and cost overruns.
- Ghost employees.
- Donations to political parties/local community organization.
- T&E expenses.
- Books and records treatment of contract expenses.

Certain risk areas specific to the construction and real estate industry are worth highlighting. A number of these risks are discussed below.

Joint Venture Partners

In some jurisdictions, it is necessary to have a local partner either as a result of legal requirements or from a commercial point of view. It is important to understand the identity of the local partner and their relationships with the local authorities. This is recommended so that the company can ensure that the selection of a local partner is not seen as a de-facto bribery mechanism and is in fact a true commercial relationship.

It is important to ensure that local partners have the required corruption training so they are aware of the risks involved. It is important that joint venture partners do not involve themselves in bribes or corrupt payments, which at a very minimum will have a significant commercial impact on the joint venture. It may lead to legal consequences for the individuals in the joint venture. These problems often also have consequences for the parent company and potentially its directors and officers.

The company should also ensure that it has sufficient rights of access to the books and records of the joint venture. The company needs to include in its internal audit testing plan the audit of joint ventures, with particular focus on testing for corruption issues.

Obtaining Planning Permission/Zoning Changes

Obtaining of planning permission may involve the change of the use of the land, meeting environmental and other local regulations. It can be a lengthy process that involves dealing with multiple government officials/departments, local councils/committees, and state/federal authorities as required. There may be significant delays and roadblocks in the process. This can result in opportunities for corrupt officials to solicit bribes.

In many cases, companies employ local consultants to help them through the process. It is vitally important that a formal agreement is put in place to help ensure that the local consultant is not exposing the organization to legal risk. Also, the payments to local consultants should be scrutinized to ensure that the payments are in line with the service being provided and that no illegal payments are being funded through these payments.

The company should consider making all license payments/application fees directly or provide a company check or bank draft to the consultant for lodging with the relevant authorities and insist on an official receipt for the payment.

Use of Subcontractors and Consultants/Agents

Due to the nature of the construction industry, there is a high use of subcontractors, often with many layers of subcontractors. Also, there can be the use of consultants and agents particularly in the contract procurement process. This increases the risk of fraud, including corruption risk. To combat that risk, the company should have a written contract with all the key subcontractors that clearly discusses the work expected and rates, and also should include fraud and anti-corruption language.

Cost overruns or nonstandard expenses or charges by subcontractors should be examined either using an independent third party (LC architect or engineer) or by the appropriate project manager to try and ensure that there are no potential corruption issues.

Consultant/Agent fees should be examined to ensure that they are appropriate to the work being performed, and all out-of-pocket expenses should have adequate supporting documentation.

All subcontractors and consultants/agents should have an appropriate level of due diligence performed on them. The services or work done by the third parties should determine the level of due diligence required.

Contingent Amounts

Many construction contracts often include contingent amounts for cost overruns or additional items that arise during the construction process. It is an area that can be open to abuse if not properly controlled and as in other industries been an area of concern in relation to anti-corruption.

In particular, the issue of cash refunds to related companies or the completion of work for related parties has been used in other industries to make corrupt payments. Sufficient controls around cash refunds or work for related parties need to be implemented to help prevent these types of payments.

Negotiation of Cost Overruns/Add-ons

One of the critical factors in determining the ultimate profitability of a contract can be the outcome of the negotiation of cost overruns and/or payment on additional job requests. This can offer opportunities for consultants or clients to attempt to leverage payments or other benefits as part of the negotiations.

This is particularly problematic in the situation where the customer is a government entity or involves consultants representing government entities.

Also, as a result of the U.K. Bribery Act, commercial bribery is an offense, so this will increase the risk with nongovernmental entities also.

Ghost Employees

Ghost employees are a significant problem with the construction industry and have been a mechanism for making corrupt payments in the industry. They have been used as a mechanism for bribery by paying nonexistent employees or relatives/friends of government officials.

This is a drain on the profitability of projects that all construction companies attempt to mitigate. The payment of a government employee or his close relations in this manner can result in fines to the company and potential disgorgement of profits on the contract.

Another area of concern is the employment of off-duty government security personnel to conduct security. While this is legal in some countries and may be the best option, controls need to be implemented to ensure that off-duty governmental officials are being paid the market rate for the hours that they actually work.

Donations to Political Parties/Local Community Organizations

The construction industry has been a relatively easy target by political parties/ local community organizations to gain donations both at local, state, and federal levels. This is particularly prevalent in the planning process stage and in the awarding of contracts.

Proper controls and processes need to be put into place to ensure that all donations are properly authorized and recorded. Also, due diligence should be performed to ensure that the donation is for the purposes of the organization as a whole and is not benefiting specific individuals. All donations above a certain amount should be authorized by the appropriate level of senior management (outside the country of operation if possible).

Travel and Entertainment Expenses

It is very important to have clear guidelines for T&E. All members of management and the appropriate levels of staff need to be trained on those guidelines. T&E that involves paying airfares or accommodation of third parties should be preapproved. Any entertainment of a third party over a certain threshold should require preapproval. This can help reduce the risk of improper entertainment of clients that may be considered de-facto bribery.

Also, the giving of gifts should be discouraged. In particular, gifts of cash should be prohibited.

Books and Records Treatment of Contract Expenses

Due to the nature of its business, the construction industry, due to the nature of its business, has unique factors that may impact its compliance with the books and records provision of the FCPA. Companies in the industry commonly use the FASB ASC Topic 605-35 (formerly known as AICPA Statement of Position 81-1, Accounting for Performance of Construction-Type and Certain Production-Type Contracts). The guidance outlines acceptable approaches for recognizing revenue on contracts that span multiple reporting periods, such as the percentage-of-completion method. Under this method, the company may recognize revenue over the life of the contract based on the degree of completion as measured by costs incurred.

Most often, corrupt payments are accounted for as an expense. If a bribe is recorded as a contract-related expense, the amount will be factored into the percentage-of-completion calculation and thereby cause revenue to be recognized. In essence, corrupt expenses may increase the amount of revenue recognition, which perpetuates the violation. To further complicate the matter, costs associated with construction contracts are accumulated on the balance sheet in a CIP account. Often, the CIP account lacks adequate transparency into the underlying nature of the expenses (i.e., there are not enough subaccounts within CIP to accurately reflect the classes of transactions). The lack of detail surrounding the costs in CIP increases the probability of including potentially corrupt payments in this account without awareness by accounting management.

Bribery and Corruption Issues Impacting Construction and Real Estate

While the construction industry has not been the target of the DOJ when it comes to FCPA enforcement, there have been a number of cases pursued by the DOJ against construction companies and suppliers of services and equipment to construction companies related to the oil and gas industry.

One of the most significant bribery and corruption investigations and enforcement actions relates to a joint venture formed to bid on and provide engineering, procurement, and construction services to design and build a government controlled liquefied natural gas plant on Bonny Island, Nigeria.

Formed in 1990, TSKJ was a four company joint venture whose partners included JGC Corporation, Kellogg Brown & Root Inc., Technip S.A., and Snamprogetti Netherlands B.V. TSKJ authorized and paid bribes to Nigerian government officials and employees of state owned and controlled entities related to the Bonny Island contracts. To facilitate and conceal the bribes, the joint venture used an individual and a Japanese trading company. The four partners and several individuals have been held accountable either through deferred prosecution agreements or guilty pleas and have paid approximately US$1.5 billion in penalties. The amount of these penalties and the related investigations significantly exceeds the profits generated by the joint-venture. In addition to the actions of the U.S. Government, the Nigerian authorities have also investigated these activities.[6]

What Should Construction and Real Estate Companies Be Doing?

Bribery and corruption has always been a challenge for construction companies due to the nature of the industry. The area of particular concern in corruption cases has been in the awarding of contracts and the obtaining of planning permission/permits. This is the case for both domestic and international projects. Many of the cases in the public arena focus in these areas.

To address the bribery and corruption risks that construction companies face, the risks need to be identified and understood. A comprehensive bribery and corruption risk assessment should be undertaken. Chapter 6 describes this in detail. Once the risk assessment has been completed, the overall anti-corruption compliance program should be reviewed to determine if it is sufficient to mitigate the risks identified. Additionally, review the communication and training programs to ensure that they adequately convey the corporate message to remote and risky locations.

Special consideration should be given to:

- Use of consultants or agents in obtaining business or advising on a bid process or used for lobbying purposes. Due diligence should be done on the background of these consultants or agents. Also, there should be a clear contract with these consultants that sets out the services to be provided and the anti-corruption stance of the organization. The payments of these consultants should be reviewed and approved at a senior level of the organization. In particular, payment of any expenses should be fully supported.
- Training—the construction industry has a poor reputation in regards to corruption and fraud. Domestic corruption can cause losses and potential litigation. The monetary impact of corruption in regards to the FCPA in terms of legal costs, fines, and potential costs of ongoing monitorship can be significant to an organization. Also, it brings the potential for

disbarment from government contracts. It is therefore critical that the appropriate training is done at all levels so that the company can instill the proper corporate culture regarding corruption.

 ## CONSUMER PRODUCTS

The consumer products industry is comprised of a variety of products that can be grouped into subsectors: beverage, food, household and personal care, and tobacco.

Today, many competing companies produce products that are very similar in terms of price, quality, and packaging; therefore, competition is strong. To succeed against the competition it is paramount for companies to create a brand name that consumers recognize, aspire to, and trust. Brand recognition or differentiation is a major barrier for new firms and products entering and being successful in new markets.

To provide an idea of the size of the sector, consumer spending in the United States accounts for about 70 percent of gross domestic product (GDP).[7] The global consumer products sector is expected to continue to grow with the rise of emerging markets such as Brazil, Russia, India, and China (BRIC). One billion people will enter the middle class by 2020, and 66 percent of them will live in emerging markets.[8] Their spending power creates a huge commercial opportunity. In short, the growth expected in emerging markets is the biggest opportunity for consumer products companies for years to come and will certainly be a big factor that will distinguish the winners and losers of tomorrow.

While there are obvious benefits of capturing a slice of the emerging markets, there are also several risks involved with selling and producing products internationally. Emerging economies often play by different rules than developed ones, operating with corrupt governments that impede market dynamics and profitability.

Specific Risk Factors

Bribery and corruption risks can generally be grouped into three categories:

1. *Sales channel/route to market.* Paying bribes to regulators to obtain trading and product licenses; paying bribes to customers to win or retain business or sales contracts.
2. *Operations and production.* Paying bribes to government departments that regulate manufacturing and/or production operations. This risk also applies

to construction or other capital projects that require specific licenses and permits. Examples of regulation include operational and construction licenses and permits, labor laws and conditions, health and safety requirements, pollution control, and emergency services (police, fire).

3. *Movement of products.* This area includes paying bribes to customs officials to assist in facilitating the movement of products across border or movement of product within an area that is known for corruption. This could include bribes sought by local police who impound cars in an attempt to collect a bribe or to resolve disputes with local police in the normal course of operations.

Sales Channel/Route to Market

The end customer for consumer products is usually an individual buying from a retailer outlet. In most countries, retail chains and distributors and wholesalers that supply retailers are predominantly privately owned and managed. Therefore, commercial bribery laws in countries of operation and from a global perspective the U.K. Bribery Act will be a key concern.

- *Advertising and promotion (A&P).* A&P budgets in the consumer products sector are used to support brand investment and brand promotion which are designed to promote and improve sales. A&P budgets can be significant. A&P budgets are typically used for the following:
  - Price support (discounts)
  - Promotions (e.g., two for one)
  - Advertising
  - Samples

  Consumer products companies often rely on third-party distributors to supply products in a particular territory and control the local A&P spending. Monitoring how distributors utilize A&P budgets and establishing proof of performance and effectiveness of the A&P spending often is a key control utilized by consumer products companies. Not implementing controls and investing the time to monitor A&P spending can lead to a lack of transparency and control over the actions of the distributors. This lack of oversight may lead to the A&P budget being used improperly. Another key control is monitoring of the A&P budget in conjunction with other incentives such as pricing and free goods. A control that reviews the total incentive program as an independent function has been seen as effective in detecting improper business relationships.

- *Product placement.* Placement of product is essential to driving sales in many consumer product markets. For example, the placement of products at eye level in a retail store or behind a bar is essential to grabbing the attention of consumers. Therefore, there is an incentive to influence how and where store managers display products. This can lead to risks that improper payments are made to individuals to influence how products are placed in retail outlets. These inducements are often smaller in value and lower in frequency on an individual basis but can be deployed in a systematic way by distributors who deal with multiple retail outlets and store managers.
- *Free samples.* Free samples are often provided via new product launches and can also be utilized as promotions. Free samples of product is standard in consumer products but also can be a source of risk if the free samples are not properly controlled. This risk is similar to some of the problems in the medical device and pharmaceutical industries. Certain segments like alcohol and tobacco companies also have increased risk due to the intrinsic demand for the product. Key risks to be aware of include kickback schemes for free goods, use of the actual product as an inducement to gain an advantage, and selling free samples to create a slush fund to be utilized for other "off the books" purposes.
- *Trading licenses.* Again, beverage and tobacco companies are exposed to greater corruption risk when trying to obtain trading licenses. This is due to the supply of liquor and tobacco being heavily regulated. Therefore, the issue of a trading license can be extremely valuable and subject to regulatory approval.
- *Product licenses.* Individual product licenses or certifications are required by regulators throughout the world before a product can be sold in a country or region. Regulation around food, liquor, and tobacco is particularly strong. This regulation presents companies with a barrier to the market and creates risk when dealing with government officials to obtain the necessary licenses and certifications before a product can be sold. Licenses and permits for trademarks and other intellectual property can also be a source of government regulation.

Consumer products companies face similar bribery and corruption risks as other industries relative to the "operational" corruption risks and risks inherent in product logistics including supply chain. However, these issues may be more severe in certain consumer product companies in the food industry, as there are the risks of manufacturing combined with product distribution where the product could be perishable and susceptible to heat or humidity in order to maintain the product quality. These unique characteristics may put a "bull's eye" on trucks if the "bribee" knows that the product would be in danger if not moved quickly. In addition, in certain countries, beverage and tobacco companies have unique risks in their dealing with government due to specific legislation regulating these products.

Bribery and Corruption Issues Impacting the Consumer Product Industry

The consumer products sector has experienced some notable FCPA investigations and prosecutions but certainly not on the scale of the other industries such as the aerospace and defense industry.

Some examples include:

- **Alliance One International Inc.:** According to the complaint filed by the SEC, Alliance One, which at one time was Dimon, Inc. and Standard Commercial Corporation before combining, made bribes in excess of US$1.2 million to TTM (Thailand Tobacco Monopoly) to get more than US$18 million in sales contracts, as well as made improper payments in the Republic of Kyrgyzstan, China, Greece, and Indonesia. It was alleged that the nature of the payments was not properly recorded in their accounting records. Furthermore, it was alleged that a Dimon subsidiary paid more than US$3 million to Kyrgyzstan officials to buy tobacco for eventual resale to Dimon's customers. Also, there were alleged payments made to tax officials in Kyrgyzstan, Indonesia, and Greece. Standard is alleged to have made an improper payment to a political candidate and provided gifts, T&E, to foreign officials in Asia. Total disgorgement, fines, and penalties amounted to approximately US$19.45 million.[9]
- **Chiquita Brands International:** In 2001, Chiquita Brands International Inc. was found to have made payments to foreign customs officials by their wholly owned foreign subsidiary of Chiquita. Banadex, Chiquita's subsidiary, paid US$30,000 to local customs officials in Colombia to secure a renewal of its license at its Turbo, Colombia, port facility. The payments were made between 1996 and 1997 and were incorrectly classified in the accounting records. The employees involved were terminated and Chiquita paid US$100,000 in a civil penalty after the item was found during an internal investigation.[10]
- **Avon:** In 2008, Avon, the beauty products company, voluntarily disclosed that it was conducting an internal investigation of its China

operations, focusing on being compliant with the FCPA. The company, under the oversight of the audit committee, commenced the investigation in June 2008 after Avon received an allegation that certain T&E, and other expenses may have been improperly incurred in connection with the company's China operations. The company voluntarily contacted the SEC and the DOJ to advise both agencies that an internal investigation was being performed. The company is currently complying with all requests from the agencies with respect to this matter. This investigation was still ongoing as of March 2011 and has been expanded to additional countries.[11]

▪ **Kraft Foods Inc.:** In its 2010 10-K, Kraft disclosed that they received a subpoena from the SEC. The subpoena, issued in connection with an investigation under the FCPA, primarily relates to a facility located in India that was acquired in the Cadbury acquisition. The request seeks information regarding dealings with Indian governmental agencies and officials to obtain approvals related to the operation of the Cadbury facility.[12]

What Should Consumer Products Companies Be Doing?

The anti-corruption focus for a consumer products company is not materially different from other industries. Clear anti-corruption focus on the tone at the top with an emphasis on ethics is foundational toward waging an anti-corruption campaign. This includes making sure that key corporate and local leaders are visible in discussing the organizations views on ethics generally and corruption specifically. In the emerging markets, the local leadership will be important in making sure the message does not get lost and there is consistency between objectives of the local team and the compliance messages. For example, if the CEO addresses the company yearly and starts with a strong ethical message and the local team communicates the importance of hitting the sales numbers, the message may be lost.

Relative to financial controls for corruption risks, controls over cash are very important in certain emerging markets. In some markets, consumer products companies are paid in cash by retailers and/or distributors, so tight controls are required from a fraud and bribery perspective to ensure that cash is properly recorded and reconciled. Furthermore, cash can be used in promotional and brand-building events, which necessitates strong controls to ensure that the cash is not used for improper payments and supporting documentation is maintained.

Having the other pieces of the anti-corruption program as described in Chapter 5 also apply to consumer products. Consumer product companies may be more susceptible to operational risks than other companies, especially in the transportation area for certain segments of the market. Many of these products are manufactured and distributed locally, which opens up regulation from local regulators, especially in the food and beverage industries. Distribution also opens a company up to different tax schemes where product is distributed across geographies that have different local tax benefits.

 ## DIVERSIFIED INDUSTRIAL

Diversified industrial products companies manufacture and deliver a range of products, systems, and solutions to industry and to end customers. These range from products that are ready for use, such as a piece of equipment like a metal press or lathe; components that are incorporated into other products, such as a motor or alternator to be built into a standby electrical generator; or turnkey solutions where the manufacturer provides a product that is incorporated into an overall system or solution that is also installed, tested, and commissioned.

Industrial manufacturers have been at the forefront of the drive to locate manufacturing activities in emerging overseas markets. They have taken advantage of lower manufacturing costs and are implementing strategies to locate their manufacturing facilities closer to the emerging market customer base.

Moving into new areas increases the risks associated with bribery and corruption and other international trade compliance concerns. Unfortunately, many of the fastest-growing economies are plagued by traditionally weak governance structures and associated problems with bribery and corruption.

Specific Risk Factors Relating to the Industry

Industrial products companies are exposed to many transactions and activities that carry typical risks associated with the FCPA and other anti-bribery statutes. These include:

- Significant exposure to government customers and end customers.
- Significant exposure to high risk industries such as oil and gas or mining.
- Routine interactions with government related to certifying and licensing products.

- Routine interactions with government related to permitting and licensing their facilities.
- Interactions with government related to the movement of their people, visas, and work permits.
- Interactions with government related to the movement of goods, imports, and exports.

There are, however, several features of industrial manufacturers that result in variations and, in certain instances, unique exposures to these risks.

When sales are made directly to government customers or state-owned enterprises (SOEs) the risks and exposures associated with these government customers are relatively easy to identify and evaluate. However, many industrial products sales are made to contractors who incorporate the products into other solutions for an end-user customer. Examples would be equipment sold to a contactor constructing a government building (such as an airport, theatre, or stadium) or equipment sold to a shipyard constructing a naval vessel for a military customer. This means that these sales may not be flagged as a government and may not be subject to the same degree of scrutiny as an easily identifiable direct sale to a government customer.

In many instances, the end-user customer has a significant say in the design of the solution and may be prone to persuasion regarding the individual components. Accordingly, many of these companies split their time and effort between influencing customers to buy their products and encouraging end users to specify their products. In the preceding shipping example, the industrial manufacturer would seek to encourage the shipyard to buy their product to install in the vessel; at the same time they would try to encourage the navy to specify their product (or create a set of specifications that favor their product). As there is often no direct contractual relationship between the company and the end user, these activities can be difficult to identify and monitor.

Industrial products companies are exposed to other high-risk industries that are subject to intense regulatory scrutiny. They sell to customers in industries like oil and gas, mining, telecommunications, and utilities, as well as organizations that build or upgrade government infrastructure. These manufacturers are regularly exposed to the risks associated with bribery and corruption prevalent in these industries and can also be implicated during investigations conducted into the activities of their customers and end users.

Many manufacturers of specialized products are exposed to risks associated with export. They pursue sales opportunities outside of their geographic areas and, if they have no local subsidiary in the territory, are forced to rely on local distributors and agents. It is difficult to control the activities of these sales intermediaries. This increases the risks of their making inappropriate payments on behalf of their principal.

Liability for the conduct of distributors and agents can be complex to manage. Many organizations assume that a straight "buy/sell" arrangement with their distributor network will insulate them from all risks. For routine sales of inventory items, this may be the case; however, for large or unusual orders where the distributor may facilitate a discussion directly between the customer and the manufacturer, the lines become more blurred. Furthermore, in many instances with larger or more complex orders, placed through a local distributor, the customer may insist on being invoiced directly by the manufacturer.

Sales of industrial products often involve services related to installation and commissioning with local subcontractors supplying smaller components and various engineering services. These vendors are increasingly being used to facilitate inappropriate payments, and they are much harder to detect than the highly scrutinized payments to sales agents and other sales intermediaries. Potentially troubling situations can arise when customers or end users insist that the manufacturer subcontract certain work to preferred local vendors.

Industrial products are complex, and there is often a need for training customer employees. This typically takes place near the head office of the parent company. There can also be a need for occasional factory visits and other customer travel to inspect progress or to participate in testing. These trips can be used to facilitate inappropriate T&E that could fall outside of safe harbors for reasonable customer T&E. Additionally, the products and solutions these companies deliver are complex and can require high levels of customization and integration. It is not uncommon for engineering specialists to spend significant time at end-user locations both during the sales process and during implementation. This results in high levels of travel and lodging expenditures in the ordinary course of business. Again these expenses can be used to facilitate inappropriate T&E that could fall outside of the legislative safe harbors.

Industrial manufacturers have many touch points with government. Their manufacturing facilities are subject to various licensing and permitting requirements for their operations. Their products are also complex and subject to various permits and certifications. As the emerging economies become more sophisticated, the standards they apply become more onerous and more aligned with the more developed economies. Witness the increased focus on workplace safety and environmental standards. Many of these licenses, permits, and certifications can be difficult to obtain without specialized local knowledge. In certain markets characterized by legacy bureaucracies, like China, India, or Russia, these are practically impossible to obtain without the services of a local consultant familiar with the workings of the various government departments. This clearly presents the risk that the local consultant makes inappropriate payments in order to secure the required documentation.

Bribery and Corruption Issues Impacting Industrial Products Companies

Enforcement trends relating to industrial products companies reflect clear risks when these companies sell products and services into high-risk geographies and high-risk industries. A significant proportion of the recent enforcement actions related to Iraq, have their origins in the various "Oil for Food" investigations.

Control Components Inc. (CCI) is one of the more well-known examples of enforcement actions involving an industrial products company. CCI sold valve and related control solutions for severe applications such as power stations and petrochemical facilities. Based on the related DOJ press release, CCI senior executives approved payments of approximately US$4.9 million from 2003 to 2007 to officers and employees of various state-owned customers for the purpose of influencing the award of contracts and project technical specifications. CCI also made corrupt payments to employees of privately owned companies. The company admitted it made over 236 corrupt payments in more than 30 countries from 2003 to 2007, which resulted in approximately US$46.5 million in sales. CCI executives also rewarded customer employees with expensive gifts and extravagant holidays. Due to the violations, CCI was fined US$18.2 million and placed on organizational probation for three years. The company also needed to create a compliance program and retain an independent compliance monitor for a term of three years. The DOJ indicted six former CCI executives in April 2009 related to the same conduct and two other former employees pled guilty to related charges.[13]

What Should Industrial Products Companies Be Doing?

Due to the risks facing industrial manufacturers, special consideration should be given to (1) identifying specific corruption risks; (2) identifying the red flags

associated with these risks, where applicable; and (3) establishing processes
and procedures to mitigate these risks.

Typical Corruption Risks	Common Red Flags (if Applicable)	Risk Mitigation
Distributors and representatives, third-party intermediaries, agents, and consultants	Unclear and varying wording of distributor contracts; lack of contract Numerous intermediaries, agents, and consultants High expenditures on third parties and subcontractors Fixed fee or fixed percentage contracts with unclear scope and deliverables Lack of clear explanations regarding the services Agent recommended or required by the customer or end user Payments in third-party locations, tax havens, etc.	Clear and consistent contract terms for distributors Anti-bribery wording and certification Train distributors on applicable legislation Legal oversight over variations to typical contract terms Clear and consistent contract terms for third parties Third-party due diligence process Document the rationale for engaging the intermediary Maintain a list of declined vendors
Legacy corruption risk in acquisitions	No forensic due diligence before acquisition Acquired business processes and procedures still immature Lack of awareness of corruption risks	Conduct forensic due diligence as part of transaction due diligence Roll out policies, procedures, and training rapidly Conduct a follow-up assessment shortly after rollout
Failure to identify end-user customer and end-user geographic location	End-user customers not known; information about end users sparse	Clear identification of customer as well as end user Base risk assessment on end-user customer and end-user geographic risk
Travel, entertainment, gifts, and customer travel	High levels of travel, entertainment, and gifts Occurrences of customer	Establish clear policies around travel, entertainment, gifts, and

| | travel and training visits
Poor supporting documentation, no clear business purpose, attendees not identified, etc. | customer travel
Establish clear policies and norms around customer travel and training visits
Preapproval required for significant expenditures |
| Controls can be circumvented | No anti-corruption monitoring program; complete reliance on processes and controls functioning properly
Poor monitoring program, such as a few steps added to the internal audit program | Establish a robust anti-corruption monitoring program
Follow up exceptions and improve processes to correct identified weaknesses |

 ## ENERGY

The oil and gas, chemicals, and utilities (energy) industry is a cornerstone of the global economy. Developed and developing nations require large amounts of petroleum-based fuels, chemical products, and electricity. Compounded with heavy current demand, studies have shown that the global energy demand will grow 45 percent by 2035.[14] From power and petrochemicals to natural gas and minerals processing, the energy industry is an important part of the infrastructure and maintenance of society in almost all countries.

The energy industry will see a renewed and expanded focus on regulatory compliance. Governments and consumers are increasingly concerned with the effect carbon dioxide (CO_2) emissions and other greenhouse gases have on the climate. At the top of the risk radar in Ernst & Young's Business Risk Report 2010 for the oil and gas industry was "uncertain energy policy." However, this uncertainty cannot prevent companies from establishing robust compliance programs to maximize accountability and begin to reduce corruption. The industry must remain vigilant with respect to the risks posed by bribery and corruption.

Specific Risk Factors

Companies in the energy industry are particularly susceptible to bribery and corruption risks because of their global operations. The locations of oil and gas reserves dictate where operations must be centered, regardless of the area's aptitude for corruption. Transparency International, annually publishes their Corruption Perception Index (CPI), which is useful in identifying and analyzing a particular country's corruption risk. The 2010 CPI indicated that nearly three quarters of the 178 countries in the index scored below 5 on a scale from 10 (highly clean) to 0 (highly corrupt). For instance, Iran, Iraq, Venezuela, and Nigeria hold many of the world's proven oil reserves, yet all of these countries rank very low on the 2010 CPI (146, 175, 164, and 134 out of 178, respectively). Countries rich in natural resources that lack governmental enforcement of anti-corruption policies expose oil and gas companies to a myriad of FCPA, U.K. Bribery Act, and other bribery and corruption risks. Risks to the oil and gas industry include (but are not limited to):

- Operations in high-risk countries where bribery is common.
- Use of intermediaries, consultants, and/or agents.
- Interaction with governmental agencies or employees.
- Stringent regulatory environments.
- Lack of proper due diligence in mergers and acquisitions.
- Weak internal controls that are not designed to prevent the concealment of bribery.
- Weak tone at the top.
- Decentralized decision-making functions.
- Lack of communication and emphasis on employee responsibilities.
- Lack of codified policies including those for gifts, hospitality, entertainment, expenses, travel, customs and permits, political contribution, charitable donations, facilitating payments, solicitation, and extortion.
- Lack of anti-corruption training.
- Lack of a reporting channel (hotline) and investigation procedures.

Unsurprisingly, bribery and corruption risk is highest in countries where there is a high degree and history of corruption. These risks are further elevated for industries that have a high degree of interaction with governments or SOEs whose employees are deemed to be government officials under the FCPA. Industries that involve significant regulation like the energy industries normally are required to have this increased interaction with governmental officials and agents of the government, and therefore face increased risks for bribery and corruption.

Additionally, a significant portion of the world's petroleum reserves are located in regions such as the Middle East, South America, and Africa. Transparency International's 2010 CPI shows that certain regions that tend to have a greater amount of petroleum generally fall toward the higher end of being potentially more corrupt.

Global regulators expect companies to maintain effective anti-corruption compliance programs. These compliance programs must address the risks mentioned earlier and also should employ a chief compliance officer to oversee the continual evaluation of the program and implement solutions to prevent, detect, and report violations of global anti-bribery and anti-corruption laws. Although implementation of a compliance program can be costly, the lack of one can be even more detrimental. The consequences of an underdeveloped or poorly implemented compliance program can be seen with the increased enforcement of the FCPA and the U.K. Bribery Act. Global regulators are imposing extensive fines and other remediation requirements to liable companies, which can often amount to millions of dollars. It remains in the best interest of energy companies to not only be aware of the potential corruption and bribery risks the industry faces, but also to use this knowledge to design and implement a robust anti-corruption program.

Bribery and Corruption Issues Impacting the Energy Industry

For several years, U.S. regulators have increased their focus on industry-wide prosecutions of companies and individuals. Investigations typically begin with one company and spread to others within the same industry or service offering type. This trend is exemplified in the much publicized Panalpina deferred prosecution agreements. Stemming from the actions of freight forwarder Panalpina, seven energy companies paid a combined US$237 million in fines and disgorgements of profits. Of the top 10 FCPA-related monetary settlements in history, five were issued to companies within the energy industry:

1. KBR/Halliburton—US$579 million (2009)
2. Snamprogetti Netherlands B.V./ENI S.p.a—US$365 million (2010)
3. Technip S.A.—US$338 million (2010)
4. JGC Corporation—US$219 million (2011)
5. Panalpina—US$82 million (2010)
   Source: Related DOJ and/or SEC settlements

As shown above, FCPA penalty "top 10" lists were significantly revised in 2010, as that year brought numerous enforcement actions related to bribery and corruption against energy companies.

Finally, the Association of Certified Fraud Examiner's Report to the Nation indicates the top three regions of corruption cases are Asia, Europe, and Africa, respectively—all important regions for energy companies.

What Should Energy Companies Be Doing?

Energy companies must be cognizant of increased anti-bribery and anti-corruption enforcement and take a proactive approach to risk and compliance. Merger-and-acquisition due diligence has become especially important because acquiring companies may assume successor liability for potential corrupt actions of the acquired company.

In June 2008, the DOJ issued Opinion 08-02 to Halliburton in response to an inquiry from the company regarding its liability related to a U.K.-based acquisition target. Because U.K. law limited Halliburton's ability to conduct extensive due diligence prior to closing, it wanted the DOJ to determine: if not completing the due diligence prior to the acquisition would result in Halliburton assuming responsibility for any of target's FCPA liabilities stemming from preacquisition conduct and whether Halliburton would be held criminally liable for any unlawful conduct committed by the target during postacquisition but before Halliburton's due diligence procedures are completed. The DOJ determined that a 180-day postclosing period was a reasonable time frame for Halliburton to complete its due diligence. During this time period, Halliburton would not be liable for prior illegal activity of its acquisition, provided it took appropriate action to stop those activities, put in place proper controls, and ensure that no violations occurred on its watch. This decision applied only to Halliburton, but it clearly demonstrates the need for companies in the energy sectors making global acquisitions to have a robust anti-corruption due diligence process. Refer to Chapter 8 "Anti-Corruption Due Diligence" for further details.

The activities of third-party agents in foreign countries can have significant consequences for the energy companies for whom they act. Companies must incorporate strong due diligence and monitoring procedures for their relationships with third parties, including consultants, joint venture partners, distributors, and subcontractors. Contracts with third parties should include specific language referencing the third party's responsibilities and compliance with respect to anti-bribery and anti-corruption laws. Other contractual mechanisms include the right to review the third parties' books and records, the right to terminate the contract based on corrupt acts by third parties, and annual certifications of compliance with the anti-bribery and anti-corruption contract provisions.

Finally, it is imperative that energy companies maintain robust anti-corruption compliance programs that include conducting compliance assessments at high-risk locations.

Monitoring

Many energy companies are monitoring their business units' compliance with company policies and procedures. Companies select the specific business units to assess through a risk-based approach. While some companies in other industries conduct assessments in six to eight countries annually, many energy companies may conduct upwards of 25 to 30 assessments. These assessments usually require in-country fieldwork, though desk audits and business-unit self-assessments may suffice depending on the risk assessment. Chapter 7, "Monitoring," discusses these activities in further detail.

Other Areas to Consider

Secondment and Management Rotation in High-Risk Countries   Some countries have a culture of corruption. When doing business in such countries, bringing in expatriates as country managers where legally allowed may help break the impact of the local culture. Using a system of rotating management also reduces corruption risk because local operations would be subjected to review by two different managers, making it harder for corrupt practices to escape notice.

Government Security   Many energy-rich nations are subject to civil uncertainty, and it is common for energy companies to hire security to escort workers and merchandise in transit or to guard facilities. In some countries, legally permitted security forces are themselves government entities that are paid for the services they provide. These entities may also be, or be instrumentalities of, foreign governments.

Royalty, Tribal Ownership, and Special Considerations Regarding Land in Certain Countries   Some jurisdictions feature tribal or feudal organizations. Royalty or tribal elders may also be considered foreign officials. Enhanced or modified controls and due diligence may be appropriate in such countries, particularly with respect to land right grants and joint venture partners.

To specifically identify and guard against the risks noted, the following table lists common red flags for potential risks and risk mitigation techniques for the common corruption risks faced by the energy industry:

Energy Corruption Risks	Common Red Flags	Risk Mitigation Techniques
Joint ventures and nonoperated joint ventures	Non-U.S. company, as operator, lacks existing or robust anti-corruption program Partner is specified by foreign government or contract U.S. company, as nonoperator, may not have rights to know how funds are spent	Thorough due diligence of business partners Implementation of company's anti-corruption program at joint venture/partners, including nonoperated joint ventures Transactional-based due diligence (M&A) with certifications Measures to provide anti-corruption contract provisions and execute audit rights Educate management representatives to be aware of potentially corrupt behavior
Foreign government customers	Large number of modifications or other agreements after contract finalization Withholding earned payments Requests to use specific third-party vendors or service providers	Clear and specific contract language with foreign governments Provide training for employees responsible for negotiations and ongoing customer interface Thorough due diligence of vendors and service providers
Agents/Consultants/ Reps/Other third parties	Excessive commissions given the services provided and/or territory involved Substantial expense reimbursement such as out-of-pocket charges Requesting payment outside of territory where services were rendered or where third party resides Lack of transparency in third-party documentation such as statement of work, invoices, etc.	Thorough due diligence of prospective third parties Emphasis toward third-party training and certifications Measures to provide anti-corruption contract provisions, audit rights, and termination clauses Implementation of a reporting system (e.g., hotline) where stakeholders can report possible violations Proper monitoring, approval, and coding of the "facilitation

	Long waits to attain licenses/ permits and/or regulatory examinations	payments" account if necessary
Political and charitable contributions	Large contributions authorized and paid locally with little supporting documentation and transparency to home office Payments to individuals instead of entities Contributions recorded as "other" or "misc" instead of appropriate accounts where contributions/donations are typically recorded	Due diligence of organizations and individuals receiving contributions Recording and thorough monitoring of contributions in segregated account Development of a clear internal approval process for all contributions/donations
Promotional expenses	Significant cash advances or reimbursements lacking detail Prevalent use of petty cash locally without receipts Requested reimbursements for upgraded travel or travel including family members	Clear policies and approval process for the solicitation of promotion expenses Employee training over acceptable and unacceptable business development practices Maintaining a gift log for tracking and reporting purposes
Workforce/Unions	Request of hiring and/or promotion of specific individuals due to governmental association Requests for union dues/ donations Unusually long waits/issues with the attainment of work permits/ visas for employees	Due diligence of individuals being hired and full disclosure of governmental relationships Implementation of a system where hiring and/or promotions are based on objective measurements Clear policies and monitoring and approval process for the these expenses
Travel, meals, and expenses for foreign government officials	Expense reports lacking valid business purpose Expense reports lacking list of names of individuals benefiting from expenses Expense reports lacking receipts/supporting documentation	Clear policies and approvals for interacting with foreign government officials Clearly defined approval process for obtaining management approval prior to engaging in activity Employee training on who qualifies as a foreign government official and acceptable business practices for interacting with said officials

FINANCIAL SERVICES

Coming off the heels of the financial markets collapse in the United States and abroad, it is no surprise that the financial services industry is under intense regulatory scrutiny. The timing of increased regulatory oversight resulting from the collapse of financial markets has combined with continuing concerns over the facilitation of the financing of terrorism and illicit drug trade along with the maturation of various bribery and corruption regulations that impact financial services. With bribery and corruption costing the world economy about US$1 trillion, regulators have shifted focus to financial services firms that do business with foreign governments, foreign officials, SOEs and other parties who present bribery and corruption risk.

Significant regulatory reform in the United States, most notably the Dodd-Frank Financial Reform Act of 2010, and public pressures for increased transparency and accountability have upped the ante for those firms that do business abroad. This is in an attempt to rebuild credit markets, reestablish consumer confidence, and promote regulatory compliance.

Beginning in late 2008, and driven by the then-evolving credit crisis, FCPA regulators and law enforcement shifted their focus toward the financial services industry. Mark Mendelsohn, former deputy chief of the DOJ's Fraud Section, spearheaded a call to arms for regulators tasked with FCPA oversight of the financial services industry. The SEC and other regulatory agencies, including the Financial Industry Regulatory Authority (FINRA), followed suit, and FCPA investigations against financial services firms have been increasing ever since. In January 2011, and in their first broad stroke toward industry-wide enforcement, the SEC sent letters to large banks and private equity firms regarding their dealings with sovereign wealth funds (SWFs). The SEC considers SWF employees as "foreign officials," and therefore within the scope of the FCPA. Accordingly, the SEC focus is assessing financial services firms' compliance (or lack thereof) with the FCPA in their efforts to obtain, maintain, and build new business with SWFs.

Further, recent regulatory actions taken abroad, namely the 2010 U.K. Bribery Act, add to the pressures placed on global financial services institutions around anti-bribery and corruption. The U.K. Bribery Act extends violative actions to include commercial bribery and other measures that are not otherwise violative of the FCPA. It is therefore critical that financial services institutions assess and account for risks driven by the FCPA and other local regulations, depending on their geographic footprint.

Specific Risk Factors of Industry

The financial services industry, as any other industry, is not immune to bribery and corruption. The following table highlights those risks most commonly faced across the various sectors of the financial industry (black, high risk; gray, medium risk):

Top FCPA Risk Areas	Asset Management	Banking and Capital Markets	Insurance
Conducting business with agents			
Mergers and acquisitions			
Joint ventures			
Gifts and entertainment			
Charitable and social contributions			
Vendor approval			
Business with government and government-controlled entities			
Real estate and energy investing			

The financial services industry presents many unique bribery and corruption risks, as discussed next. While many of these risks are thematically consistent with other industries, the manner in which these risks manifest themselves can be difficult to detect and monitor, and often leave firms in difficult positions. Investments in emerging markets, integration of financial markets, and industry consolidation have all contributed to heightened bribery and corruption risks in the financial services industry.

Asset Management Sector Specific Risks

As described earlier, asset management firms have recently been the focus of the SEC and DOJ scrutiny, most notably with the January 2011 SEC letters of inquiry into asset manager and private equity firm dealings with SWFs. U.S. regulators view SWF employees as foreign government officials. This distinction is often not fully appreciated by those in a position to procure new business with SWFs. Effective and verifiable compliance policies and procedures around business development expenditures, including gifts, meals, travel, entertainment, and other costs incurred in acquiring or maintaining client relationships should implemented firm-wide. Asset management firms should assess their full range of counterparties, clients, and other business relationships, which may fall within the ever-expanding definition of government officials or affiliates. For those firms that have or seek to expand their presence in emerging markets and other regions known for extensive government involvement in financial markets, these bribery and corruption risks are that much more relevant.

Private equity (PE) firms and hedge funds that invest in international markets and corporations are presented with significant bribery and corruption risks. Most notably, PE firms can find themselves in a dangerous and costly position if violations or issues are present at the portfolio company level. PE firms must consider and address bribery and corruption risk across their organization as the parent company or firm can be held liable for FCPA violations for companies in which it has an ownership or control position. Acquirers should perform anti-corruption due diligence procedures in order to assess bribery and corruption risks and develop a plan to monitor and mitigate those risks.

Wealth management firms who operate or have clients in foreign countries must also address risks associated with this sector. For example, in countries such as Russia, which has extensive government ownership of local businesses, asset management firms should be able to distinguish clients employed by these businesses, as they are viewed by U.S. regulators as foreign government officials. The same holds true for SWF employees, trustees, and other affiliates. Effective identification and continuous monitoring of these relationships is a key element toward achieving compliance. Ongoing anti-bribery and -corruption monitoring is largely underappreciated by financial services firms, including asset managers. Simply assessing these risks when on-boarding a new client, for example, may not alleviate all bribery and corruption risk. For those firms operating in emerging markets and jurisdictions with extensive government ownership of local businesses, firms should reassess the impact of nationalization, ownership changes, and other business transactions which may have an impact on the bribery and corruption risk profile of clients and other business relationships or institutions.

Banking and Capital Markets Sector Specific Risks

The rapid pace of consolidation and globalization of banking and capital markets firms, coupled with increased regulatory focus on the financial services industry, provides for an environment ripe with FCPA risk.

As the global economy recovers from the recent recession, M&A volume has steadily increased. Corporations and governments have also increased spending levels in investments abroad. Investment banks and underwriters involved in global dealings must be keenly aware of the risks associated with transacting abroad. Given the rapid pace of most M&A transactions, banks are faced with the difficult task of assessing, evaluating, and reacting to potential bribery and corruption risk in a short time frame. Banks must have a clear understanding of all parties involved in the underlying transaction, how those relationships were formed, and whether those relationships pose bribery and corruption risk.

Similarly, banks that either participate or underwrite securities offerings for governments, SOEs, or other affiliated entities must tread carefully. Amounts spent on gifts, entertainment, travel, and other deal-related expenses all pose bribery and corruption risk for the firm. Similar to M&A activity, these transactions are often conducted at a fast pace and may not leave a significant amount of time to evaluate and monitor risk. Building timely and effective FCPA monitoring, reporting, and record-keeping protocols is a key success factor in promoting FCPA compliance. It is critical to identify and understand the roles of all parties involved in the transaction, and whether those roles are FCPA compliant both in form and substance.

Personal and commercial retail banking is one of the most heavily regulated components of the banking and capital markets sector. While most of the regulatory activity in this area relates to anti-money laundering and Bank Secrecy Act issues, banks must take note of the heightened bribery and corruption risks associated with banking relationships with individuals and corporates. Traditional customer and transaction due diligence often does not consider bribery and corruption risks. Banks that service foreign governments, SOEs, and government officials must assess how those relationships were built, and rigorously monitor amounts spent on gifts, travel, entertainment, and other expenditures involvement these clients. In addition, correspondent bank accounts pose risks for banking firms. Accounts held at commercial correspondent banks to service the cash clearing, liquidity management, and investment needs of a smaller institution can be a means of facilitating transfers of corrupt payments. The SEC and DOJ continue to claim that they possess territorial jurisdiction over foreign corporations based on overseas financial transactions involving U.S. dollars.

Insurance Sector Specific Risks

Insurance companies with operations abroad are generally required to obtain government licenses prior to writing policies. The process by which business licenses are obtained in developed markets can be a relatively mechanical process, and one which poses little bribery and corruption risk. However, companies that do business in emerging markets and other high-risk countries may find themselves in situations where foreign governments or government officials seek payments or other items of value in order to facilitate the licensing process. While this risk is not unique to the insurance industry, it is nonetheless heightened by the strict regulations associated with marketing and writing insurance products globally.

The widespread use of and reliance on agents in the insurance industry underscores the need for companies to establish and implement FCPA compliance programs designed to promote awareness, identification, and reporting of FCPA issues. The risk of rogue agents offering incentives to foreign governments, officials, and other affiliates in a position to direct business to the insurance company is ever present.

Bribery and Corruption Issues Impacting the Financial Services Industry

Investigations and enforcement activity in the financial services industry, like most others, is on the rise in recent years.

- **Aon Ltd.:** On January 8, 2009, the United Kingdom's Financial Services Authority (FSA) fined Aon Ltd. £5.25 million (approximately US$8 million) for failing to maintain an effective system of controls to counter bribery and corruption risks. The FSA alleged that from January 2005 to September 2007 Aon Ltd. failed to properly assess and prevent illegal payments from being made to third parties who helped the company obtain business overseas, especially in countries considered high risk for corruption. As a result of this failure, Aon's employees made approximately US$7 million in suspicious payments.[15]
- **CB Richard Ellis:** In an October 2010 SEC filing, the global real estate investment firm CB Richard Ellis (CBRE) disclosed possible FCPA violations in China. CBRE conducted an internal investigation and identified payments to local government officials for non-business entertainment and gifts. The company also disclosed an additional internal investigation. This investigation was still ongoing as of the disclosure and relates to the use of an agent in China for an investment property for one of the company's funds in 2008. Per CBRE's 2010 annual report, the investigation had been concluded by the company as well as the SEC and DOJ.[16]
- **Morgan Stanley:** On February 9, 2009, Morgan Stanley disclosed in a filing that it has discovered actions initiated by an employee in China

that could potentially be in violation of the FCPA. It explains that in early 2003, the investment bank started investing billions in various real estate deals in Shanghai. The now terminated employee was one of Morgan Stanley's top property dealers in China, which focused on various SOEs. The investigation is still ongoing according to public reports.[17]

The recent SEC inquiry into SWFs is seen as the first step in what is likely to be a broad-based sweep of the financial services industry. This would follow a similar pattern to the investigative approach taken in the oil and gas industry and pharmaceutical and medical devices industries.

What Should Financial Services Companies Be Doing?

Financial services companies need to understand and manage the risks related to bribery and corruption in order to stay ahead of ever-increasing regulatory and enforcement focus. In order to mitigate these risks, the following factors should be considered:

- *Culture and environment.* Fighting corruption should start by addressing the institution's own culture and environment. PE firms in particular must promote compliance across their organization, as well as their portfolio companies. Banks and asset managers should establish clear policies and procedures for those in a position to procure, develop, maintain, and build client relationships. Finally, insurance companies should assess the impact of agent risk and promote compliance with company policy across the agent population.
- *Risk management.* Financial services firms have many risks that are unique to the industry and may not have a full appreciation for how bribery and corruption risks arise within their own operating environments. The fluidity with which investment banking, M&A and other transactions occur presents considerable risk that companies are not fully informed and aware of the parties involved in these dealings. PE firms are also responsible for FCPA compliance at the portfolio company and should take steps to ensure that relevant risks are identified and factored into appropriate bribery and corruption risk assessment and compliance programs.
- *Monitoring.* Continuous, ongoing monitoring of potential FCPA violations is particularly challenging for financial services firms given the volume and pace of business, use of agents and intermediaries, and the sheer

number of business relationships for banks, asset managers, and insurance companies. Vendor, agent, client, and transaction due diligence is the first step in mitigating bribery and corruption risk. However, companies should also develop monitoring practices to identify changes in the risk profile of business relationships, unusual or potentially inappropriate activity, and other drivers of bribery and corruption risk. The primary challenge for multinational firms is to deploy these practices on a consistent basis across geographies and business lines.

 ## LIFE SCIENCES

The life sciences industry is a dynamic one wrought with regulatory requirements and continuous public scrutiny, yet one that is expanding with more investments and initiatives than ever before. For purposes of this section, the life sciences industry includes the following sectors: pharmaceuticals; biotechnology; and medical devices, technology, and equipment.

In this ever-changing and highly regulated environment, the consequences of failure can have devastating and lasting repercussions. Whether the failure is caused by innocent mistakes, negligence, or wrongdoing, the damage can be considerable or irreparable, including patient death. Companies are being forced to identify, investigate, and mitigate these risks with more vigilance than ever before. This section explores the specific bribery and corruption risks facing this industry and different ways to address them.

Specific Risk Factors

Recent corruption cases have covered a variety of industries, but there are particular factors present within the life sciences industry that increase the risk of corruption.

Expansion into Emerging Markets

Most life science companies operate on a global basis and are expanding in emerging markets.

Problems leading to noncompliance often are caused by local cultural issues—including bribery, corruption, and quid pro quo arrangements that may have historically been accepted practices—as well as by employees' lack of understanding of the principles of the FCPA or its applicability to activities in their respective countries.

Internationally, many healthcare systems are government owned and operated, this significantly elevates bribery and corruption risk. Therefore, during the course of business, interactions with individuals considered to be government officials, such as many health care professionals (HCPs) or hospital administrators, can be frequent.[18] Given the frequency of interaction between life sciences sales and marketing representatives and those HCPs, companies must take precautions to ensure that the interactions are focused on exchange of scientific information to improve patient health and outcomes rather than to improperly influence HCPs in using or prescribing a particular product.

In some markets, government-employed HCPs have relatively low levels of salary compared to those in private practice. As a result, even small gifts, meals, or entertainment that might be considered de minimis in many countries may be perceived as attempts to improperly influence HCPs and other decision makers, requiring carefully considered policies, training, and monitoring.[19]

Use of Third Parties

The significant use of third parties, particularly in emerging markets with the attendant risks described earlier, to sell or distribute products often results in interactions with HCPs and other government officials by individuals not under the direct control of the life science company.

Life science companies entering new geographic markets often use third parties such as distributors or contract sales forces because they do not have sufficient resources with language and business fluency, business networks, or supply chains to sell directly. Use of third parties may also appear to be a lower-cost way to determine whether there is a market for the company's products in those markets. Further, in some cases, only local companies may submit tender bids to hospital or other health care organizations so third parties are a necessity.

Under the FCPA, the U.K. Bribery Act, and most Organization for Economic Co-operation and Development (OECD)-related legislation, companies can be liable for corrupt payments or other benefits provided to government officials by those third parties. Exercising control over promotional activities of a disparate network of wholesalers and distributors is a significant challenge. Enforcement actions, particularly in the United States, nevertheless indicate a trend to hold parent companies responsible for the unethical or illegal behavior of their agents and intermediaries.

Payments to Health Care Professionals

Frequently, within the normal course of business, life sciences companies make payments to HCPs and/or health care organizations.

The life science industry conducts global activities related to both HCPs and health care institutions such as continuing medical education and other scientific/medical research like conducting clinical trials and postmarket studies. International, regional, and national health care compliance codes have been adopted by many life science companies to oversee such activities, but these standards may be at odds with business practices in the emerging markets that have not yet adopted similar codes. Employees in emerging markets subject to healthcare compliance codes of the parent company may feel that, by not participating in such HCP sponsorship activities, they are at a significant competitive disadvantage compared to other local companies that are not subject to the same guidelines and may be tempted to work around the codes.

▪ Fee-for-service payments to HCPs

It is common practice for life sciences companies to contract HCPs to perform services related to their field of expertise, such as speaking at medical conferences and participating in research and postmarket studies. However, these legitimate programs can also be used as a means to provide benefits to HCPs in return for sales. Further, the value of fees paid to HCPs for such services may not be individually large, but inclusion of related travel, lodging, and entertainment expenses may aggregate to significant values. And even small payments can be violations of anti-corruption laws. Similar reimbursement issues may also apply when companies sponsor individual HCPs to attend conferences, where such sponsorship is permissible under local law.

▪ Event grants and sponsorships

Life science companies recognize the value of medical events where scientific information is exchanged. Accordingly, they support the participation of HCPs to events convened by hospitals and medical associations. In most circumstances, sponsorships for HCP participation are vetted by the company's medical department for their relevant scientific value.

These activities, however, can create corruption risk when they are led by the sales and marketing functions and are directly linked to specific sales targets or customers (e.g., through sponsorships of specific HCPs with purchasing authority or historic or potential high-volume usage of the company's products).

Identifying the extent of a company's involvement in, and direct influence over, an event may be difficult. In some countries, such as China, medical events may be organized by a third-party vendor (usually a travel agent) rather than the convener. In many markets, medical societies or health care institutions convening a conference simply do not have the internal resources and expertise to organize large events and thus require assistance from an outside party. However, these third-party organizers (whose actual ownership is often undisclosed) have also been used as a means to pool sponsorship funds from various donors and redistribute them in sometimes questionable directions, such as payments to HCPs and/or kickbacks to employees of the sponsoring company. Further, these third parties rarely provide itemized details regarding the actual expenses incurred in connection with the event, making it difficult to defend the propriety or business purpose of the expenditures in the event of an investigation.

▪ Donations

Life science companies often provide donations to charitable and other organizations, particularly those focused on medical research or health-related issues. The line between these donations and an attempt to influence individuals or institutions can be blurry. For example, in emerging markets, funding may be lacking for the most basic of hospital needs, yet donations to a state-run hospital may create the appearance of an attempt to influence government entities or officials.

Additionally, care must be taken to determine the ownership, control, and purpose of charitable organizations to determine whether they are bona fide charitable organizations and are unrelated to individual HCPs or individuals with an ability to influence purchasing decisions at government entities. Donations to organizations supported by prominent HCPs, their family members, or government officials may raise questions about the true intent of the donations.

Bribery and Corruption Issues Impacting the Life Sciences Industry

Laws addressing bribery and corruption are certainly not new, yet the related business risks and potential penalties for bribery and corruption within the life science industry has gained greater prominence in recent years. The DOJ has brought several actions against a variety of medical device companies (such as Biomet Inc., DePuy, Inc., Stryker Corp., Zimmer Holdings Inc., Smith & Nephew plc, Medtronic Inc., and Wright Medical Technology, Inc., who all disclosed FCPA investigations that started in 2007 and 2008) and several international pharmaceutical companies (such as Eli Lilly, Johnson & Johnson, Pfizer, Bristol-Myers Squibb, AstraZeneca, and Novartis) have had FCPA investigations or settlements in recent years.

The DOJ is taking a more proactive approach to looking into the sales practices of global pharmaceutical companies. In a 2009 keynote address to the Tenth Annual Pharmaceutical Regulatory and Compliance Congress and Best Practices Forum, Lanny A. Breuer, assistant attorney general, Criminal Division stated,

> . . . one area of criminal enforcement that will be a focus for the Criminal Division . . . [is] the FCPA to the pharmaceutical industry. . . . Our FCPA unit and our health care fraud unit are already beginning to work together to investigate FCPA violations in the pharmaceutical and device industries in an effort to maximize our ability to effectively enforce the law in this area. Moreover, we will continue to work closely with our partners at the SEC to ensure that the full range of the federal government's enforcement tools and remedies are utilized. Our focus and resolve in the FCPA area will not abate, and we will be intensely focused on rooting out foreign bribery in your industry.[20]

In 2010, there were numerous pharmaceutical and medical device industry settlements in the United States for allegations ranging from off-label promotion,[21] quality control issues,[22] false claims,[23] kickbacks to physicians,[24] unauthorized use for medical devices in clinical trials,[25] and manufacturing and distribution of adulterated drugs.[26]

There were also numerous prosecutions of individuals in 2010, such as:

- **InterMune:** Former CEO convicted of wire fraud.[27]
- **Purdue:** Three former executives pled guilty to conspiracy charges to misbrand.[28]
- **Pfizer:** Former district manager found guilty of obstruction of justice.[29]
- **GlaxoSmithKline:** Alleged obstruction of justice and false statements made by former attorney.[30]
- **KV Pharmaceutical:** Former chairman banned from federal healthcare.[31]
- **Stryker:** Former president charged with wire fraud, aiding and abetting, conspiracy, and false statements.[32]
- **Bristol-Myers Squibb:** Two former executives settle for alleged inflation of profits.[33]
- **Spectranetics:** Former CEO indicted on 12 counts including conspiracy to defraud the government.[34]

Given the heightened focus on the life science industry by the DOJ, the recent federal settlements and personal liability cases brought to light, life sciences companies should actively review and refresh their anti-bribery and corruption efforts.

What Should Health Sciences Companies Be Doing?

Understand Local Laws and Industry Guidance

Knowledge of the local laws in each of the countries in which the company's products are sold is key as they may be more or less restrictive than other international laws and guidance. Knowing the strength of the local laws may impact the formation of policies developed at a company-wide level or may require additional local policies. Also, more relaxed local laws may suggest that business practices may be more amenable to allowing payments to government officials and thus may require additional training of employees and monitoring of activity.

In addition to local laws, local industry codes of practice may govern the promotional activities of the life sciences company. For example, the European Federation of Pharmaceutical Industries and Associations (EFPIA) represents the pharmaceutical industry operating in Europe and its code outlines specific standards relating to focus areas which are meant to ensure the highest possible standards in the promotion and advertising of medicines[35] in the region. Diverse life science companies may also be subject to multiple industry codes if they have both pharmaceutical and medical device products, for example. It is important for companies to not only understand these larger regional codes but also those codes of practice specific to the country where business is conducted. The separate country codes often adopt the standards of the regional code and supplement clauses that take into account the nuances of the nation's culture, as well as specific limits on promotional activities that may exist.[36] Understanding the content of the codes is important when identifying potential bribery and corruption risks that may exist within a particular market or region.

Develop Practical Policies

Policies should not be developed in isolation at the company-wide level and generically pushed down to every location in which the company's products are sold. These policies should be informed by the culture of the company, elaborate on the company's code of conduct to the extent necessary to address the primary legal requirements, and remain flexible enough to accommodate more stringent local laws and allow for exceptions approved at high executive levels. Compliance principles should drive policies and behavior, but allow for some local variation with documented approval from legal, compliance, and other related parties.

Another key objective of policies for life science companies is to set clear definitions of both a health care professional (who that includes) and a government official (what defines the classification) in that country. The definitions are the building block to establishing policies around the interactions with these high-risk third parties and the risk factors identified in the preceding section.

Develop and Deliver Effective Training

Most life science companies have developed training regarding their policies or codes of conduct. However, findings from compliance assessments often indicate that the policies and the spirit in which they were created are often not understood by individuals in local markets.

The training should be extended not only to sales professionals, but also members of management and administration who may interact with local government officials for business permits or other issues, including manufacturing and research-and-development (R&D) site employees. Finance and accounting professionals responsible for recording transactions in the books and records should also receive training. It may also be necessary to develop training materials for, or to present training to, third parties to ensure that they understand their obligations when working on behalf of the company.

Monitor and Assess the Program

The best policies on paper may not translate into effective programs in the field, particularly when working in emerging markets where a full complement of personnel and a robust control structure may not yet exist. Using a combination of risk assessments, tools like Transparency International's CPI, internal audit findings, hotline calls, and other inputs, companies should select both high-risk and a certain number of other operations at random to assess the effectiveness of the programs.

Due to the relationships and interactions with HCPs, who are also considered government officials, and the increased enforcement pressure, there are many risks that are inherent within the life sciences industry. The points laid out here can assist in both mitigating and managing those risks and effectively responding to potential compliance issues when they arise. Chapters 4, 5, 6, and 7 provide guidance on the areas highlighted in this section.

MEDIA AND ENTERTAINMENT

Industry Overview

The media and entertainment (M&E) industry is comprised of a broad range of businesses, including publishing (books, magazines, and newspapers), advertising, broadcasting and cable networks, cable and satellite operators, film and television production, music, sports, interactive media, and video games.

The industry continues to undergo significant transformation as customers explore new ways of receiving digital media and content, such as the Internet, portable digital devices (e.g., the iPod) and video-on-demand services. This paradigm shift, in conjunction with the recent economic downturn, has placed tremendous pressure on operating margins. Many M&E companies have established profitable digital businesses to respond to the increase in online activity by consumers. During the economic downturn, M&E companies, like those in many other industries, focused on cost cutting to offset the reduction in their revenues. (For example, the auto, real estate, and financial services companies were significantly impacted by the recession.) In turn, M&E companies experienced a reduction in advertising revenues due to their customers' cost-cutting efforts. Additionally, M&E companies experienced a decline in music, DVD, video game, and subscription revenues due to the reduction in consumer spending. As the economy began to improve in 2010, M&E companies' financial results improved with to an increase in advertising and consumer spending.

Future revenue growth will be driven by expansion into new international markets. Significant opportunities exist with the growing middle class and the increase in literacy levels in emerging markets, such as the BRIC countries. This increase in wealth provides additional purchasing power for broadband, movies, music, and video games; the increased literacy rates drive demand for newspapers, magazines, and books. However, this new revenue also brings new risks, such as piracy, bribery, and corruption.

Specific Risk Factors

While companies in the M&E industry have bribery and corruption risks similar to those in other industries, including oil and gas, pharmaceuticals, and medical devices, their risk profile is not as high as in these other industries. The following table illustrates the areas in which M&E companies may experience corruption risk by sector within the industry.

	Publishing	Advertising	Broadcasting and Cable Networks	Cable and Satellite Operators	Filmed Entertainment	Music	Sports and Other
Government customers	✓	✓	✓				
Government media outlets	✓	✓				✓	
Use of third parties	✓	✓	✓	✓	✓	✓	✓
Licenses	✓		✓	✓	✓	✓	
Permits - *Production* - *Ad space*	✓	✓	✓	✓	✓	✓	✓
Movement of personnel and equipment - Visas - Customs clearance - Local crews	✓		✓		✓	✓	✓
Local bank accounts and petty cash	✓	✓	✓	✓	✓	✓	✓
Sources	✓		✓				

The M&E industry may interact with government officials in many capacities. In certain nations, the government procures the textbooks for the entire country. In Africa, the Middle East, and parts of Asia, the government may control or own all the media outlets, including newspapers, television, and radio. Certain governments control the licensing of cable and satellite networks, as well as radio and television broadcasting. In many cases, M&E companies will interact with government officials during their day-to-day operations in areas such as production permits or transporting equipment to international locations.

There are several specific risks to the M&E industry. Companies may use third-party intermediaries to facilitate government interactions, especially with developing or third world countries. Another section of this book addresses bribery and corruption risks and mitigating controls associated with government interaction and the use of third parties.

The following is a discussion of the specific risks associated with international film and television production, as well as music touring.

International Film and Television Production

For many years, film and television production has thrived in international settings due to the numerous benefits associated with foreign locations, such as lower production costs, inexpensive labor, favorable exchange rates, and unique filming locations.

Production costs range from less than a US$1 million for independent pictures to over US$100 million for blockbuster movies. Production activities include obtaining permits for the set locations, construction of elaborate sets, hiring of local crews to assist with production, working with local officials for disruptive activities (e.g., a car chase or the use of pyrotechnics) and moving expensive equipment and personnel. Due to the nature of the payments and production locations, the production assistant generally carries a significant amount of cash. For example, local crews are traditionally paid in cash.

Although significant amounts of cash are required to pay for local expenses, such as crews and set construction, cash transactions increase the risk of corruption. There is significant pressure to maintain the production schedule, and cash can typically solve production problems. Due to the location and individuals involved, effective cash controls may not be in place or individuals may not be aware of corporate policies. An article in the *Los Angeles Times* on April 15, 2007, discusses the movie *Sahara,* filmed in Morocco. The movie budget included US$237,386 of "courtesy payments," "gratuities," and "local bribes" to expedite filming in Morocco for items including removal of palm trees from an old French Fort. Additionally, according to the Los Angeles Times there was a US$40,688 payment to stop a river improvement project that would have interrupted filming, along with a US$23,250 payment for "Political/Mayoral support."

This scenario is only one of many that could occur with international production. To mitigate these risks, a company should minimize the cash on hand and review the detailed descriptions and support for cash disbursements. Additionally, employees must receive training to ensure that they understand their company's bribery and corruption policies, the laws and the impact of a violation. Another section of this book addresses the topics of bribery and corruption risks, mitigating controls associated with cash transactions, and training and awareness of employees.

Music Touring

M&E companies have experienced an overall decrease in music revenues since the increase in digital music sales has not offset the decline in CD sales. To counteract the impact of this lost revenue, many current record deals have become "360-degree" deals where the record company or promoter shares in all revenues that an artist generates. This revenue covers all of the artist activities in the entertainment industry including activities outside of music. The music-related revenues include use of the artist product in a number of digital media as well as merchandising and touring. Music touring is a lucrative but complex business. Tours, especially for major artists, often include securing numerous venues, transporting expensive and complex stages, and setting up and breaking down the venues on very tight timetables as a tour travels throughout the world—not to mention managing high-profile stars in the spotlight. This scenario creates a high-risk environment for bribery and corruption.

The venue is a key component to a tour. In certain countries, the government may own the venues. This creates the risk of a potentially improper payment, gift, or lavish entertainment to secure a particular venue. Many companies use third-party promoters to secure a venue. To mitigate the associated risk, it is important to know who the third party is, to understand the nature of the service the promoter is providing, and to determine if the fees are appropriate. It is also important to perform a check to see if a third party has had any previous corruption allegations and to be certain that the contractual documentation includes language to ensure compliance with local laws, as well as with the FCPA and the U.K. Bribery Act.

The transportation logistics associated with the movement of a stage and equipment between countries can be very challenging. All these items must pass through customs, a complex process in which complete and accurate documentation is required for timely processing. Music tours are under significant time pressures. A minor customs documentation error can cause equipment to be so delayed that it would not arrive at the next venue on time for the performance. These types of scenarios create an environment ripe for corruption. For example, a customs official may request a payment to "expedite" the stage and equipment through customs or a payment to overlook customs documentation issues to allow the stage and equipment to clear customs expeditiously. Companies should train their employees to understand that these types of payments are not permitted.

High-profile artists and their entourages could draw attention wherever they go, they might not obey the local laws and may get themselves into trouble with the local authorities who may expect payments to "look the other way" regarding an artist's conduct. Certain artists may expect that someone from the company will handle these situations, but a company should not be responsible for or facilitate these types of payments. Expense reimbursements should be reviewed in detail and the amount of cash on hand should be limited. Additionally, employees must receive training to ensure that they understand the company's bribery and corruption policy, along with the laws and the impact of a violation.

These risks apply to all the M&E industry sectors which include touring.

Bribery and Corruption Issues Impacting Media and Entertainment

To date, the M&E industry has not been a focus of the DOJ's enforcement actions. However, the Green case has received a significant amount of publicity. In 2009, Gerald and Patricia Green were convicted for bribes related to the Bangkok International Film Festival. With the DOJ's increase in prosecutions and the international cooperation occurring between agencies, the M&E industry should be prepared to receive additional attention from the regulators.

According to the DOJ's September 14, 2009 press release From 2002 to 2007, the Greens paid approximately US$1.8 million in bribes to influence the former governor of the Tourism Authority of Thailand to steer contracts for them to operate the annual film festival. The payments were characterized as "sales commissions" and were channeled to overseas accounts in the name of the former governor's daughter and a friend.

Jerome Mooney, who represented Gerald Green, said that he thought the case was pursued in part as a warning by the government to the entertainment industry as to how it should interact with foreign countries as production increasingly takes place around the world.[37]

The Greens were also found guilty of money laundering and were ultimately sentenced to six months of prison time.

Internationally there has been enforcement activity in the industry. Macmillan Publishers Limited, a U.K. publishing house, faced scrutiny for their operations in Africa. The World Bank and U.K. Serious Fraud Office (SFO) initiated parallel corruption investigations into the company's education division in East and West Africa. Based on the investigation of the tender process, the SFO noted that "it was plain that the Company may have received revenue that had been derived from unlawful conduct" and levied a penalty of approximately £11 million. The World Bank debarred Macmillian from World Bank funded tenders for at least 3 years.[38]

What Should Media and Entertainment Companies Be Doing?

M&E companies have not historically focused on their anti-corruption compliance programs. To address these risks appropriately, a company should perform a comprehensive risk assessment to identify the actual risks posed by the nature of its operations, the degree of its business with government entities, its use of agents and third-party intermediaries, the countries where it does business, and the regulatory environment. Chapter 6 describes this process in detail. Once the risk assessment has been completed, the overall bribery and corruption compliance program should be reviewed to determine if it is sufficient to mitigate the identified risks. Specifically, attention should be paid to the overall policy, training programs, and associated communications to ensure the message is clear and understood in all locations, especially the high-risk ones.

Special consideration should be given to:

- *Third parties.* Third parties operate on a company's behalf and can create vicarious liability for a company. Therefore, it is important to know where the third parties are being used, which third parties are being used, why they are being used, what they are actually doing for the company, and what compliance and monitoring provisions are included in contracts with these parties. All agreements should be expressed in writing, and the underlying business relationship and purpose should be included in the contract. Red flags to look for are payments or commissions that fall outside the normal range for a service.

- *Gifts/Entertainment policy.* Policies should not be developed in isolation at the company-wide level and generically pushed down to every location in which a company operates. These policies should be remain flexible enough to accommodate more stringent local laws and should allow for exceptions when documented approval is obtained from legal, compliance, and other related parties.

 ## MINING AND METALS

The mining and metals industry continues to grow with more exploration and production projects being developed annually. These projects provide the raw materials needed for all aspects of society ranging from the manufacturing, chemical, energy and construction industries to the precious metals that form a value based investment and store of value through unpredictable economic times.

The mining and metals industry is at the root of many significant and influential events in history and has helped define economic and infrastructure development. The industry continues to be on the forefront of the current global economy. The recent economic environment has been favorable to the mining community as commodity prices, equity markets, and transaction values have remained strong. The recent increase in market activity and investment valuations is in direct response to global demand for resources and the willingness for global capital markets to provide financing. Commodities have remained in the limelight, as precious metals such as gold and silver have continued their role as both a flight to safety and a hedge against inflation. With high commodity prices come cash flows enabling companies to fund growth and expansion.

Companies around the world have invested in and reactivated capital projects and exploration activities, increasingly located in frontier regions as known reserves in developed economies become depleted and as emerging economies look to fuel their economic growth. Large amounts of money are being spent in these frontier regions and with internal controls either not yet operating effectively or streamlined during the financial crisis; the result is a heightened risk of bribery and corruption.

Specific Risk Factors

Company management and boards of directors have an interest in understanding and mitigating the risks that may negatively impact stock price.

Shareholders have expectations around company growth and the return on their investment, but an illegal act, such as bribery and corruption, could have significant consequences in a highly regulated environment. Permits and licenses can be suspended, key contracts terminated, community support lost, and the resource itself could be lost to the company.

The mining and metals sector is more vulnerable than many other industries to fraud, bribery, and corruption. Experience shows that stock prices are sensitive to fraud risk; an association with fraud can have a disproportionate effect on stock prices because investors worry about the consequences beyond the disclosed misrepresentation. Investors begin to focus on critical questions, such as: What else remains to be discovered? And this in turn leads to questions about what the impact will be on the organization's ability to operate—not just its profitability, but also its social license to operate, its ability to access new projects, and its relationships with stakeholders, such as local regulators.

With competition for assets increasing in a market where the lifespan of established mines continue to wane, companies are driven to take on greater risk by exploring options in new countries with political situations that are relatively less mature or even unstable. Many companies have ventured into politically risky regions, where security of tenure remains fluid and changes in regulations, mining taxes, and royalty regimes may happen with minimal notice.

Some characteristics unique to the mining and metals sector provide specific risk exposures for consideration.

Operational Risks in Remote Locations

The risk of operating in remote locations can lead to a heightened risk of fraud, bribery, and corruption. As noted earlier, as the global appetite for commodities grows and known reserves are depleted, there is a willingness by companies to explore, develop, and operate further afield in remote geographies that previously were unexplored or deemed too risky. The economic cost-benefit analysis that previously may have restricted entry to particular countries and regions has been tipped in favor of rapid development in order to access deposits.

New remote locations pose unique challenges. For example, the segregation of duties can be significantly less effective where relationships with the local team are close-knit and may be stronger than relationships with a distant head office. Internal controls and systems may be new or evolving, rather than "tried and tested," and policies and procedures may not adequately deal with local business customs and practices, or even be known or understood by the mine—even if translated into the local language. This distance from the head office may result in decisions being made, which is rationalized as being for the good of the local project, when the result is a violation of explicit guidelines and legislation related to bribery and corruption.

High Levels of Government Regulation

The mining and metals sector is one of the most highly regulated sectors due to the health, safety, and environmental impacts as well as the relative importance of the sector to many emerging market economies. Licenses, permits, and approvals require frequent interactions with government officials. Similarly, government officials may also control access to the utilities and infrastructure such as the ports and railways systems that are integral to establishing and maintaining the lifeblood of an operation.

The compensation of these government officials may be low relative to the economic consequence of their decisions. The combination of many opportunities, pressure to complete and rationalizations make for a significant exposure to corruption or extortion.

Many countries have refreshed their anti-corruption regulations and renewed their enforcement commitments. A number of countries have established specialist law enforcement bodies to deal with domestic corruption. In addition, many countries have either been more aggressive in enforcing their extraterritorial corruption legislation, such as the FCPA, or have expanded legislation, such as the U.K. Bribery Act, which includes a failure to prevent bribes as a criminal offense, or the Dodd-Frank Act, which includes potentially significant financial incentives to whistle-blowers.

The large capital expenditures required represent a significant opportunity for some individuals in a position of power and influence. Despite the efforts of governments to tackle the issues of corruption head-on, some individual government officials may abuse their powers to delay or divert approvals to extort personal financial benefits. Their ability to extort the corrupt payments remains high, as the mining industry is constrained by the location of the resource. Companies that do not have the option of readily moving away from the geographic location of the resource rarely have sufficient diversity to be able to economically survive the loss of the resource.

This ability to control the operating capacity of the project heightens the risk that mining companies are exposed to various levels of government officials who may have the power to block, delay, or frustrate a project.

Expenditures in Remote Locations

Operating in remote locations can result in environments where communication and physical access remains a challenge, banking systems are poor and antiquated, supply routes remain insecure, and business is conducted in a primarily cash-based economy. The relative abundance of assets within and available to the mine site contrasts starkly with the lack of resources available to nearby residents and communities, these factors can translate to a heightened risk of the misappropriation of assets from the site. The misappropriation of cash and valuable near-cash assets from the mine site could include items such as food, stores, fuel, petty cash, and expense reimbursements. Even private use of vehicles and specialized equipment has a tangible financial cost and direct impact to company profitability.

In some cases, the local community is affected by preexisting illegal activities, such as organized crime or drugs. Mine assets can become lucrative targets or useful facilities for criminal elements—from growing narcotics on mine property to using mine facilities such as airfields for distribution of product.

While the misappropriation of assets may be individually immaterial, a culture of tolerance of petty theft or wrongdoing can easily allow a culture of entitlement to take hold, with a cumulative significant impact. In addition, tolerance of theft can lead to a tolerance of other illegal acts, such as petty corruption.

Procurement

The requirements associated with maintaining a mining operation naturally make procurement an area of heightened fraud risk. The size and frequency of local purchases make the operation a significant, if not primary target for vendors in the local business community. Even where competitive procurement practices are possible, unscrupulous vendors may seek to circumvent them.

These frauds can include sole-source scams, bid rigging, purchasing goods at inflated prices, paying for goods that they never received, receiving inferior goods, extending contracts without authorization, or adjusting contract terms without approval. The risk exists that these fictitious vendors may be used to channel funds to shell companies set up with the sole purpose of making corrupt payments.

Local Compensation and Contract Awards

Weak governance over local contract awards has the potential to taint the company with the perception that they are supporting the exploitation of the local community by a privileged few.

The mining industry is heavily regulated and companies are often required to make payments to the benefit of the local community. These may include payments to parties impacted by project developments, social services, such as clinics or schools, or to contribute in other ways to the development of not only the resource but also to the local community. These parties can range from landowners to the users of infrastructure that is being diverted for the project. The risk exists that the company is making good-faith payments, but that these funds are being diverted away to unscrupulous middle men and pockets of community members, which can result in reputational damage for the company and an inability to continue operations.

A similar risk exists when local vendors are given preference in contracts in compliance with regulatory agreements. The principle is sound in that these goods and services are often best suited to local suppliers, for example, transportation, security, and canteen facilities. That said, lack of effective competition together with long-standing community relationships between employees and local vendors can elevate the risks of bribery and corruption if these contracts are employed as a scheme to pay inflated amounts to influential individuals, such as government officials.

Bribery and Corruption Issues Impacting the Mining and Metals Industry

There are several recent examples within the mining and metals industry of the repercussions of violating the FCPA, including:

- **Control Components Inc. (CCI):** CCI, a company that designs and manufactures service control valves for use in the extractive industry, pled guilty to violating the anti-bribery provisions of the FCPA. The scheme involved bribing foreign officials and employees of various foreign state-owned companies to secure contracts in more than 30 countries. Due to the violations, CCI was fined US$18.2 million and placed on organizational probation for three years. The company also needed to create a compliance program and retain an independent compliance monitor for a term of three years. The DOJ indicted six former CCI executives in April 2009 related to the same conduct and two other former employees pled guilty to related charges.[39]
- **BHP Billiton:** In April 2010, BHP Billiton, one of the world's largest mining companies, disclosed that it was the target of a U.S. SEC investigation for potential violations of the FCPA. Further details have yet to be

disclosed, but the company stated that the investigation related to minerals exploration projects and involved possible violations of applicable anti-corruption laws when interacting with government officials.

Realistic Alternatives to Tolerating the Risk of Bribery and Corruption

Corruption is inherently inefficient and drives costs up. The costs can accumulate if ignored and allowed to become systemic.

The fraud, bribery, and corruption risk exposures highlighted earlier can be managed by taking a risk-based approach. One of the better ways to mitigate the exposures is to recognize and manage them, rather than accepting them as costs of doing business in the sector. Companies can proactively address exposures by implementing practical solutions such as targeted policies and procedures, awareness training, management rotation, specific due diligence on acquisitions, and risk-oriented site audits.

What Should Mining and Metals Companies Be Doing?

Mining and metals companies are constrained by the geographic location of ore bodies and assets, and do not have the relocation flexibility that may be available in other industries. A realistic approach to mitigating risk in geographically diverse environments is the development of a robust anti-corruption compliance program, including a comprehensive risk assessment to identify the higher-risk contracts, activities, and geographical locations. Effort and resources commensurate with the level of risks should be dedicated to mitigating the company's corruption risks through the use of employee awareness programs, third-party due diligence, financial controls and processing, and ongoing monitoring activities.

A robust anti-corruption compliance program is tailored to the fact pattern of a particular company and their circumstances, but as a starting point the following table lists common red flags and risk mitigation techniques for the common corruption risks faced by the mining and metals industry:

Mining and Metals Corruption Risks	Common Red Flags	Risk Mitigation Techniques
Joint venture arrangements	Due to the capital requirements of large international mining projects a joint venture arrangement is often a solution achieved to access ore bodies	Develop a structure to monitor the venture prior to entering the contract, this includes negotiation of monitoring/audit mechanisms

globally. These arrangements can expose a company if the joint venture partner's diligence associated with FCPA risks is not aligned. Risks can be exacerbated if:

prior to entering the arrangement.
Implement the company's anti-corruption program at joint venture/
partners.

	- The JV partner is specified by foreign government or contract. - The company is not actively involved in management of the JV. - Partner does not appear to add value commensurate with their share of profits.	- Transactional based due diligence (M&A) with certifications. - Measures to provide anti-corruption contract provisions and audit rights.
Consultants/Reps/ Other third parties	- Excessive commissions and payments to local consultants and handlers charged with "negotiating" with government entities. - Substantial expense reimbursement such as out-of-pocket charges. - Requesting payments to be made outside of the country where services were rendered or where third party resides. - Lack of transparency in third-party documentation such as statement of work, invoices that define the services as "consulting" with no other details, etc.	- Thorough due diligence of prospective third parties. - Emphasis toward third-party training and certifications. - Measures to provide anti-corruption contract provisions and audit rights.
Political and charitable contributions	- Large contributions authorized and paid locally with little supporting documentation and transparency to home office. - Payments to individuals instead of entities. - Contributions recorded as "other" or "misc" instead of appropriate accounts	- Due diligence of organizations and individuals receiving contributions. - Recording contributions in segregated account. - Development of a clear internal approval process for all contributions/donations.

| | where contributions/donations are typically recorded. | |
| Promotional expenses | - Meetings with government officials at locations outside of the country or at other desirable destinations or vacation locations.
- Significant cash advances or reimbursements lacking detail.
- Prevalent use of petty cash locally without receipts. | - Clear policies and approval process for the solicitation of promotion expenses.
- Employee training over acceptable and unacceptable business development practices.
- Maintaining a gift log for tracking and reporting purposes. |

 ## RETAIL AND WHOLESALE

The retail and wholesale industry appears to have a low risk in relation to the FCPA and other anti-bribery legislation. However, in recent decades its exposure has increased as a greater proportion of consumer products are being sourced from outside the United States. Also, as retail and wholesale companies expand their operations into international locations through direct investment or acquisition, they run the risk of operating in more high-risk locations from a corruption perspective. In particular, retail and wholesale companies are targeting the BRIC countries for expansion due to the size of the markets and the growing standard of living in those locations. Also, with the U.K. Bribery Act, commercial bribery is an offense and retail and wholesale companies need to ensure their controls also prevent commercial bribery.

Specific Risk Factors

Companies in the retail and wholesale industry face bribery and corruption risks similar to those faced by other industries. The risks include:

- Investing in new markets with joint venture partners.
- Obtaining licenses and planning permission for new sites.
- Acquisition of existing business.
- Dealing with government officials (ongoing basis).
- T&E expenses.
- Purchasing from government-controlled or -owned enterprises.

- Bribes accepted by representatives of the organization.
- Security.
- Free samples/counterfeiting of goods.
- Customs clearance.

The retail and wholesale industry can have many touch points with governments. One of the most difficult areas for any organization to understand is the ultimate ownership of an entity and whether a company is government owned or controlled and as a result that the company is effectively dealing with government officials which may increase the compliance risk. The company should institute due diligence procedures to ensure that they know whom they are doing business with and understand any resulting risk factors.

Certain other risk areas specific to the retail and wholesale industry are worth highlighting. The risks related to investing in new markets, day-to-day interactions with government officials, and T&E are addressed in detail next.

Investing in New Markets

Joint Venture Partners   In some jurisdictions, it is necessary to have a local partner either as a result of legal requirements or from a commercial point of view. It is important to understand the identity of the local partner and their relationships with the local authorities. This is recommended so that the company can ensure that the selection of a local partner is not seen as a de-facto bribery mechanism and is in fact a true commercial relationship.

It is important to ensure that local partners have the required corruption training so they are aware of the risks involved. It is important that a joint venture partner does not involve themselves in the payment of bribes or corrupt payments, which at a very minimum will have a significant commercial impact on the joint venture. It may lead to legal consequences for the individuals in the joint venture. These problems often also have consequences for the parent company and potentially its directors and officers.

The company should also ensure it has sufficient rights of access to the books and records of the joint venture. The company needs to include in its internal audit testing plan the audit of joint ventures, with particular focus on testing for corruption issues.

Construction of New Stores/Warehouses   Obtaining of planning permission may involve the change of the use of the land, meeting environmental and other local regulations. It can be a lengthy process that involves dealing with multiple government officials/departments, local councils/committees, and state/federal authorities as required. There may be significant delays and roadblocks in the process. This can result in opportunities for corrupt officials to solicit bribes.

In many cases, companies employ local consultants to help them through the process. It is vitally important that a formal agreement is put in place to help ensure that the local consultant is not exposing the organization to legal risk. Also, the payments to local consultants should be scrutinized to ensure that payments are in line with the service being provided and that no illegal payments are being funded.

The company should consider making all license payments/application fees directly or provide a company check or bank draft to the consultant for lodging with the relevant authorities and insist on an official receipt for the payment.

During the construction phase, there may be many dealings with various government inspectors or departments (including utilities which may be government owned). Appropriate controls should be put in place to avoid the payment of bribes to these inspectors/government officials. Construction company/project managers should also be made fully aware of the company's policies and procedures.

Acquisition of Existing Business Companies may also expand by purchasing an existing local company. When buying an indigenous operation, it is probable that they have had a limited focus on corruption issues. It is important that the anti-corruption due-diligence process is tailored as a result. Postacquisition it may be advisable to do a more formal risk assessment and roll out the parent companies policies, ethos, and procedures. Training of management and certain staff levels should be performed.

Day-to-Day Interactions with Government Officials

Retail and wholesale organizations sell a diverse range of products. As a result, there may be multiple ongoing interactions with a range of government officials and departments. Examples include food safety inspectors, health department regulators (if selling medicines), environmental inspectors, health and safety inspectors, and tax and regulatory authorities.

Appropriate controls need to be implemented to ensure that no corrupt payments are made. Appropriate reporting of interactions with government officials is maintained including a mechanism for reporting and dealing with requests for bribes.

Also, all entertaining of government officials should be authorized in advance to ensure it is compliant with the company's anti-corruption policies. Gifts to government officials should be prohibited unless there are special circumstances.

Travel and Entertainment Expenses

It is very important to have clear guidelines for T&E. In the fashion industry this is particularly important due to the number of trade shows and fashion shows that are held annually. There can be substantial amounts paid to entertain third parties, including but not limited to suppliers, customers, and media personnel. It is important to address this subject clearly in the T&E expense policy.

All management and the appropriate levels of staff need to be trained on those guidelines. Any T&E that involves paying airfares or accommodation of third parties should be preapproved. Also, any entertainment of a third party over a certain threshold should require preapproval. This can help reduce the risk of improper entertainment of clients that may be considered de-facto bribery. This is particularly important in light of the U.K. Bribery Act.

An associated risk with trade shows and fashion shows is the risk of corruption in relation to obtaining the necessary licenses and approvals from the local government departments and the booking of the venues/accommodation. It is important that those risks are addressed in the T&E guidelines or in separate guidelines in relation to trade shows/fashion shows.

Other Potential Risk Areas

Bribes Accepted by Representatives of Retail and Wholesale Organizations   Retail and wholesale organizations can have significant buying power. It may offer opportunities for employees in these organizations to try and solicit corrupt payments. It is important that an organization have the appropriate controls and guidelines to manage this risk. Ultimately, if not controlled, the organization will suffer from a monetary perspective and a reputational perspective, and the increased focus on commercial bribery may lead to additional legal cost and problems.

Security   In some jurisdictions, it is illegal to employ off-duty law enforcement officials to carry out security. In countries where it is allowed, care should be taken to ensure that payments are for legitimate security services and not a mechanism for making corrupt payments.

Customs Clearance   Customs clearance has become a focus of regulators in recent years in relation to corrupt payments. Retail or wholesale companies that are involved in the customs clearance process in countries with a higher risk profile have a higher risk profile as a result. Controls and procedures need to be implemented to address this risk area. In particular if a third-party clearing agent is being used, particular attention needs to be paid to the amounts being paid to the third-party agent and in particular any out-of-pocket expenses.

Also, all customs payments should be paid directly where possible and the official receipt should be demanded for all custom payments.

Free Samples/Counterfeit Goods Free samples are often provided via new product launches and can also be utilized as promotions. Key risks to be aware of include kickback schemes for free goods, use of the actual product as an inducement to gain an advantage and selling free samples to create a slush fund to be utilized for other "off-the-books" purposes.

Another related risk is the overproduction or counterfeiting of product or ignoring of the company's controls around counterfeiting of product (e.g., deliberate noninvestigation of counterfeit claims). These counterfeit/overproduction excesses can be used for direct bribes or to create a slush fund at the supplier level for off-the-books purposes.

Bribery and Corruption Issues Impacting the Retail and Wholesale Industry

While the retail and wholesale industry has not been in the crosshairs of the DOJ when it comes to FCPA enforcement, in 2008 Avon, the beauty products company, voluntarily disclosed that it was conducting an internal investigation of its China operations, focusing on being compliant with the FCPA. The company, under the oversight of the audit committee, commenced the investigation in June 2008 after Avon received an allegation that certain travel, entertainment, and other expenses may have been improperly incurred in connection with the company's China operations.[40] The company voluntarily contacted the SEC and DOJ to advise both agencies that an internal investigation was being performed. This investigation was still ongoing as of March 2011 and has been expanded to additional countries.[41]

It is not unusual if the SEC or DOJ identify any industry-specific practices that were problematic for them to make inquiries of companies that they think may face similar issues. So any issues identified in the Avon investigation may result in the SEC or DOJ sending inquiry letters to other retailers.

What Should Retail and Wholesale Companies Be Doing?

Retail and wholesale companies have some of the most complex supply chains of all industries. They often source product from many companies that operate in high-risk locations from a corruption perspective. The increase in focus in anti-corruption by the DOJ and the passing of new laws such as the U.K. Bribery Act is resulting in further responsibility being placed on companies to ensure that they can sufficiently prove that they have done sufficient due-diligence on their counterparties to ensure they are corruption free. A risk-based approach is critical where a company has a large number of suppliers and agents.

To address the bribery and corruption risk that retail and wholesale companies face, the risks need to be identified and understood. A comprehensive bribery and corruption risk assessment should be undertaken. Chapter 6 describes this in detail. Once the risk assessment has been completed, the overall bribery and corruption compliance program should be reviewed to determine if it is sufficient to mitigate the risks identified. Additionally, review the communication and training programs to ensure that they convey the corporate message to remote and risky locations.

Special consideration should be given to the following items:

- *Designing an anti-corruption due-diligence process for all current and future agents, consultants, and major suppliers.* The approach needs to be risk based. It is recommended that it be controlled centrally by the compliance or legal department; some of the tasks can be distributed to the regions subject to the policies of the company. Depending on the initial assessment, further, more detailed steps may need to be considered. Independence from the business operations for the final decisions needs to be carefully considered.
- *T&E policy.* The retail and wholesale industry has many touch points with outside clients and government officials. In recent years, *government official* has been widely defined in some of the cases settled by the DOJ. As a result, it is important that there are clear T&E policies. Consideration of proactive monitoring such as the use of data analytics should be considered. Also, preapproval for certain forms of expenditure should be considered.
- *Sample/Counterfeit goods.* It is important that the company have clear guidelines around both sample goods and counterfeit goods. It is in a company's financial interest that there are strict controls over sample goods and it has strong anti-counterfeit policies. Anti-bribery legislation also applies to nonmonetary bribery mechanisms and the use of third parties to pay bribes. So it is important to implement strong policies and monitor them aggressively in this area.

 TECHNOLOGY

The technology industry includes communications equipment; computer, peripherals and electronics; Internet and social media; IT services; semiconductors; software, clean tech, and telecommunications companies.

The technology industry is dynamic and characterized by rapid product evolution, short product life cycles, coupled with intense competition, and need to introduce new products and services to the market. Growth is fueled by global expansion. Many companies use third-party sales intermediaries such as distributors, resellers, agents, and/or consultants to quickly create a presence in new or emerging markets. In particular, the industry has seen expansion of and investment in emerging markets such as the BRIC countries and other international locations as government-owned enterprises continue to be privatized. With these increased opportunities comes added bribery and corruption risks as companies and their agents race to seize competitive advantage.

The technology industry is currently seeing many disruptive innovation trends, triggering aggressive expansion and investment strategies by many technology firms. This is evidenced by the increasing prevalence of cross-industry mergers or acquisitions as the lines between media and entertainment, consumer goods and technology industry become less clear. Additionally, cloud computing represents a fundamental paradigm shift in IT software and services that can improve business agility for all industries and increase business and consumer access to computing, storage and communications power. International Data Corporation calls cloud computing the foundation for the technology industry's next 20 years of growth. One can already begin to see the impact in the industry with the introduction of tablet technology such as the iPad. Additionally, communication and distribution of data continues to evolve from wired, voice-driven products to mobile networks and Internet products.

Changes in technology have placed pressure on companies to adapt to new market opportunities and to develop new products and services in order to compete in an ever-changing market. This evolving market landscape shapes and re-shapes how companies do business at a pace unique to the technology sector.

Specific Risk Factors of Industry

Some of the same bribery and corruption risks overlap and are found in all industries. Other risks are either more dominant in certain industry sectors and/or are magnified in certain sectors due to the nature of their business models, their go-to-market strategies, the geographies in which they operate, and the pace of competition.

The following table shows various risks that technology and telecommunication companies may face across various sectors of the industry:

	Communications Equipment	Computers, Peripherals & Electronics	Internet and Social Media	IT and Computer Services	Semiconductors	Software	CleanTech	Telecom
Use of third parties	✓	✓	✓	✓	✓	✓		✓
Government customers	✓	✓	✓	✓		✓		✓
State-owned enterprises							✓	✓
Pricing mechanisms		✓		✓	✓	✓		
Local laws and regulations - Licenses - Permits - Taxing authorities	✓	✓	✓	✓	✓	✓	✓	✓
Movement of product - Third-party logistics - Customs clearance - Export controls	✓	✓			✓		✓	✓
M&A activity	✓	✓		✓	✓			✓

There are several areas of risk specific to the technology industry. The use of third-party sales intermediaries, sales to government-affiliated enterprises, common pricing mechanisms, offshore manufacturing, and gifts and entertainment are of particular concern in the technology sector.

Use of Third Parties

Third parties such as distributors, resellers, agents, or consultants are used to quickly create a presence in or access to new or emerging markets. Sometimes they are the initial foothold in establishing a sales presence prior to an actual sales office or subsidiary being established. In other instances, it is their knowledge of the local business community and their relationships that make them effective business partners. That said, while third parties are retained to operate on a company's behalf, their actions are not always as transparent or controllable as those of a company's own employees. Accordingly, these third-party arrangements can create exposure to additional bribery and corruption risks.

Third-party intermediaries include not only those used in the sales channel, but also as part of a company's overall business operations and strategy. This may include joint venture partners, logistics providers, customs agents, marketing consultants and other service providers and vendors. In many enforcement actions, improper payments were made through the use of third parties. Refer to Chapter 5, "Policies and Procedures," for more information on the risk associated with the use of third parties.

Sales to Government-Affiliated Enterprises

While some prospective customers are obviously government-affiliated, it is not clear in all instances, particularly for a company's sales force. For example, in some countries, such as China, much of the economy is comprised of SOEs. In various enforcement actions, the U.S. government has often treated such enterprises as "foreign officials" under the FCPA thereby triggering potential liability under the statute. Yet many companies, their employees and their third-party intermediaries do not always recognize this as a compliance risk.

For the technology sector, relevant examples include companies that sell electronics into the defense industry, computer hardware to government agencies, software to public education systems, and communications equipment and services into state-owned telecommunications companies.

Common Pricing Mechanisms

Contractual arrangements with distributors and resellers often include provisions for special discounts, rebates, price protection and volume discounts. Additionally, it is not uncommon for a sale to be a "bundled" package of products and services delivered by a combination of the company, its distributor, and other service providers, including leasing and financing agents. These types of transactions add complexity to the overall pricing arrangements and can obscure the underlying margins earned by each party to the transaction, complicating a company's ability to understand the funds flow and identify potential improper payments and other risk attributes.

Offshore Manufacturing

In an effort to increase cost efficiencies, many U.S.-based technology companies, particularly semiconductor companies, have shifted their production offshore to facilities located in lower-cost geographies, such as Asia and Latin America. These arrangements may be achieved through various mechanisms, such as establishing a local subsidiary, entering into a joint venture, or using a third-party contract manufacturer. Each scenario produces its own set of bribery and corruption risks. Companies may have direct or indirect interactions with government officials in order to secure preferential tax treatments, business permits, branding or IP registration, or construction licenses. The ability to secure, or expedite, these permits and licenses is critical to the successful launch of a new enterprise or the continued operation of in-country business activities.

Gifts and Entertainment

Competition for business internationally can be very intense as these countries continue to develop their infrastructure and technological capabilities. In many cases, a country will choose one vendor to provide services to the country. Multiple providers vying for these lucrative contracts in which the winner takes all creates a significant corruption risk. Companies use cash, lavish gifts, and entertainment to influence these decisions. This behavior is seen in the IBM settlement in which improper payments in the form of cash, gifts, travel and entertainment were made to South Korean officials.[42] Additionally, improper T&E expenses were paid for Chinese officials, such as trips with unapproved sightseeing itineraries or with little or no business content. In this case, employees created slush funds with the travel agency to pay for these trips, which were described as training sessions. More than 100 IBM employees were involved which highlights the cultural acceptance of certain behaviors.[43]

Similar behavior was also exhibited in the UTStarcom case in which the company paid for more than 200 overseas "training" trips for employees of Chinese government-owned telecommunications companies; however, these trips were entirely or primarily for sightseeing. Additionally, the SEC alleged that UTStarcom made improper payments to consultants in China and Mongolia while knowing that they would pay bribes to foreign government officials.[44]

Bribery and Corruption Issues Impacting the Technology Industry

Siemens, the electronics and industrial products giant who used to manufacture communications networks, set the bar for the imposition of fines and penalties arising from FCPA violations. In December 2008, Siemens pled guilty to violating the internal controls and books and records provisions of the FCPA, resulting in the largest combined total of fines and penalties yet, totaling US$1.6 billion, as well as significant investigation costs.

The SEC continues to demonstrate its intent to actively enforce the FCPA, In August 2009, the SEC announced the creation of a specialized FCPA unit to focus on new and proactive approaches to identifying FCPA violations. In May 2010, the SEC opened a unit in San Francisco dedicated to FCPA enforcement. The assistant regional director leading the unit, Tracy L. Davis, at the time stated that "[t]he fact that we have a significant presence of companies in Silicon Valley who do business internationally, specifically in Asia, makes us well-suited for addressing these kinds of issues. That's one of the reasons why San Francisco is a particularly good location for an FCPA unit."[45]

Shortly after the office was opened, Veraz Networks, Inc. settled SEC charges with a fine of US$300,000. Veraz, a San Jose, California–based telecommunications company, was charged with violating the books and records and internal controls provisions by making improper payments to government officials in China and Vietnam.[46] The settlement highlights two points. First, it reinforced the government's message when it opened the FCPA regional unit in San Francisco that it would focus on Silicon Valley companies operating in Asia. Second, it once again highlighted that there is no materiality threshold for FCPA violations. In the Veraz SEC complaint, it was alleged that a third party provided gifts and entertainment totaling approximately US$4,500. The SEC fined Veraz US$300,000 and Veraz spent approximately US$2.5 million in defending the matter. It is clear that the SEC will not hesitate to investigate or take enforcement action against a company, regardless of the magnitude of alleged violation.

In December 2010, Alcatel-Lucent entered into a deferred prosecution agreement with the DOJ. Alcatel-Lucent, in an unprecedented move, agreed to stop using third-party sales agents worldwide.[47] Although the government did highlight that this move was unsolicited by the government, it does highlight some of the extreme measures companies are willing to make when faced with FCPA prosecution.

In addition to Veraz and Alcatel-Lucent, in the past two years alone IBM, Maxwell Technologies, UTStarcom, and Comverse Technology, among others, all entered into settlement agreements relating to FCPA violations. The list of technology companies facing FCPA-related issues is expanding every year.

What Should Technology Companies Be Doing

It is clear the technology industry will continue to be a focus of FCPA investigations given the government's investments in staffing, commitment to cooperating with international regulators and recent history of high-profile settlements. Despite the recent financial crisis, the SEC continues to emphasize that corporate cost cutting-measures should be balanced against the need to maintain an adequate compliance program along with an effective system of internal financial controls.

Technology companies should continue to evaluate their anti-corruption compliance programs. Special consideration should be given to the following risk areas:

- *Third-party due diligence.* Third-party intermediaries engaging in improper activity while working on a company's behalf can create exposure to additional bribery and corruption risks and prosecution under the FCPA. Therefore, it is important to know which third parties are being used, why they are being used, what they are actually doing for the company, where the third parties are being used, and what compliance and monitoring provisions are included in contracts with these parties. Arrangements should be evidenced by a written agreement that documents, among other things, the underlying business relationship between the parties, its purpose and the basis for the economic consideration.
- *Sales to government-affiliated entities.* Know the customers. Many companies have stumbled into potential FCPA violations by not recognizing that some of their customers are affiliated with the local government and could be deemed a "foreign official" under the FCPA. As with third party

intermediaries, it is useful for companies to consider what level of added due diligence may be warranted as part of their processes for qualifying new and existing customers.

■ *Common pricing mechanisms.* Know the distribution system. In addition to vetting third parties, perform a distributor/agent review that incorporates testing for FCPA risks. This may include reviewing contractual provisions, confirming that appropriate approvals were obtained prior to retaining an intermediary, performing sample transactional testing, and developing data analytics to evaluate trends and possible anomalies for further inquiry.

■ *Gifts/Entertainment policy.* Travel and expense policies should not be developed in isolation at the company-wide level and unilaterally pushed down to every location in which a company operates without regard for local business practices. These policies should remain flexible enough to accommodate local laws and customs and potentially allow for exceptions when documented approval is obtained from legal, compliance and other relevant parties. Some level of testing and proactive monitoring of expense activity may also be useful, especially when considering that supporting expense receipt documentation in some geographies sometimes varies as to its accuracy and authenticity.

■ *Cash.* Policies should be developed to prevent the use of large sums of cash. This will require payments to be made through an established accounts payable process, the procedures and controls for which will aid in managing anti-corruption risks.

Policies, procedures, and training for all of the above considerations are, of course, a key part of an overall anti-corruption compliance program.

 TRANSPORTATION

Every industry, every company—from the centuries old durable goods manufacturer to the biotech start-up—relies on commercial transportation. Increases in consumers' web-based ordering and tracking and producers'/retailers' desire to exchange inventory build up for just-in-time product delivery have increased emphasis on speed of shipment. Shipments that a generation ago would have taken weeks or months and tremendous expense to deliver are now in the hands of their recipients in days or overnight. The commercial transportation industry has been heavily influenced by digital advances but remains focused on the physical—moving raw materials, product parts, and finished goods throughout the supply chain.

The commercial transportation industry includes sectors that move goods via land, air and sea or a combination thereof. Industry participants, for sake of this discussion, do one of two things: (1) transport physical materials from one point to another or (2) coordinate materials transport utilizing a network of transporters external to the company.

Many commercial transportation companies are expanding offerings to become more comprehensive service providers for their customers. This expansion has come via intermodal carrier shipments (e.g., ship from China to the United States, via ground freight within the United States) and adding routes in locations critical to customer operations. For example, resulting from increased demand for Asian shipments, UPS began operations of an intra-Asia air hub in Shenzhen, China in 2010.

The increased level of cross-border transactions and emphasis on timely shipment creates a challenging business environment with significant risks of bribery and corruption.

Specific Risk Factors

Although specific interactions differ, bribery and corruption risks for companies operating in the commercial transportation industry can generally be viewed as driven by the same sorts of factors—whether the transport is via land, sea or air. Shipping companies need to secure docks at heavily trafficked ports, airlines landing slots, and any carrier unloading product may encounter handlers. Depending on location, each of these necessary actions may involve interaction with a SOE. Airports and shipping ports are frequently historically government owned. A number of airlines are state-owned or partially state-owned. Most shipping ports are government owned or operated by government employees.

As a result of the centrality of government interests in daily operations of transport companies, interactions with officials are part of daily activities for these companies. The most frequent government interactions for transport companies are with customs personnel, however personnel employed in other functions (e.g., product loading/unloading) may also present corruption risks.

Operating within a country prone to a high degree of corruption presents a higher level of bribery risk in certain routine activities—to obtain necessary business permits and licenses, to pay tariffs, customs duties and taxes, and so on—and transport companies, as is the case with companies in any other industry, are subject to these enhanced risks. Transport companies face additional risks more pertinent in their industry—as product passes through intrastate checkpoints, crosses borders, and so on—due to the frequency of direct interaction with government functions.

Presented below are a few key drivers that tend to increase the corruption risk to commercial transportation.

Geographic Areas of Operation

Companies that transport product within or between more corrupt areas of the world face a higher risk of violative conduct. The degree to which companies operate in highly corrupt and bureaucratic areas of the world is directly proportionate to operating risk. Cross-border transactions in free-trade zones will be of lower risk than those elsewhere, as there will be fewer government touch points and relatively little scrutiny. Intrastate shipments in certain low CPI score countries will be of particular risk as check points are frequent, regulations are strict, vehicle impound is a distinct possibility, and governmental decision makers have a history of corrupt activity.

Customs Clearance

As a result of direct involvement in cross-border shipments, commercial transportation companies will have a high level of direct or indirect interaction with customs officials. Many of these dealings with customs officials may relate to routine tasks such as obtaining an import permit for a properly documented shipment with no specific import restrictions. There is an increased risk of corrupt activity when the customs official possesses the ability to exercise discretion regarding whether the shipment will enter the country and what tariffs/fees will be assessed on the shipment. A specific example where commercial transportation companies and their customers face problems relates to temporary importation. Customs officials may have the authority to grant a shipment's contents temporary import status, which can serve to reduce the amount of import duty assessed. Transocean noted issues with obtaining temporary importation permits in its September 17, 2010 SEC 424B5 filing:

> Our current investigations include a review of amounts paid to and by customs brokers in connection with the obtaining of permits for the temporary importation of vessels and the clearance of goods and materials. These permits and clearances are necessary in order for

us to operate our vessels in certain jurisdictions. There is a risk that we may not be able to obtain import permits or renew temporary importation permits in West African countries, including Nigeria, in a manner that complies with the FCPA. As a result, we may not have the means to renew temporary importation permits for rigs located in the relevant jurisdictions as they expire or to send goods and equipment into those jurisdictions, in which event we may be forced to terminate the pending drilling contracts and relocate the rigs or leave the rigs in these countries and risk permanent importation issues, either of which could have an adverse effect on our financial results. In addition, termination of drilling contracts could result in damage claims by customers. Following the completion of existing investigations, we will continue to be subject to the FCPA and these risks.

Type of Product Transported

Customs officials are tasked with evaluation of a product's attributes to determine if it is suitable (and legal) for import/export and to assess applicable taxes based on these attributes. Local laws and regulations will set forth these parameters and the documentation required for clearance. Commercial transport companies that frequently deal with products that are heavily taxed or regulated will often be faced with strict documentation standards and/or substantial tax levies. Customs officials, as gatekeepers have the responsibility to enforce these rules. Commercial transport companies dealing with more heavily regulated products are most incented to influence customs officials. In Argentina, for example, import of used products is prohibited. The recent Ball Corporation case illustrates this point, as payments were allegedly made to circumvent these laws.[48]

The type of product transported also dictates the amount of tariff to be charged for import/export. The Ball case also illustrates this issue as the enforcement action also results from improper payments paid to reduce tariffs on raw materials export—copper scrap metal in this instance.[49]

Emphasis on Timing

Timely delivery of products is frequently critical. If production is halted in the destination country and the product to be delivered is a part critical to resuming production, delays may be costing company hundreds of thousands of dollars or more each day. Oil and gas and motor vehicles are two examples of industries where specialized parts are critical to production—and a halt in production means sizable financial loss. In such situations, a shipping company (or its customs clearance agent) may be faced with a tremendous amount of pressure to expedite the shipment through customs.

Other urgent delivery may be more consistent to the industry. In industries where the product has a short-term expiration date, such as temperature-controlled transport of consumables, an entire shipment may be rendered worthless if unexpected delays occur. Shipments subject to time pressures or special handling may present increased risks of corrupt payments.

Seasonality

During certain periods of the year (e.g., during the U.S. holidays), demand increases for commercial transportation services. Carriers frequently hit capacity during periods, and space allocation becomes a challenge for freight forwarders and logistics intermediaries. In areas of the world where airlines, railways or other carriers are SOEs, the negotiation to get allocated space may directly involve a government official. These circumstances frequently result in improper payments to the government officials deciding freight allocation in order to secure first rights on limited space.

Transporter's Role in Improper Activity

A key issue in determining complicity for improper payments relates to who directed such payments and who was aware of such payments. This may not be the entity that funds the payment. A particular shipment's clearance may be visible to personnel from the company requesting shipment, the carrier and an intermediary such as a freight forwarder. Other subcontractors or agents may also be employed; for example, freight forwarders often employ third parties specifically tasked with managing customs clearance. Customs brokers present additional risks as these entities can often be used to mask funds used for improper payments to government officials. Monitoring and detection of customs brokers' activities is particularly challenging as they separated by degrees from the ultimate customer and the services they render may include commingled legitimate customs clearance services and illicit bribes.

Varying Incoterms may further blur visibility as to who controls decisions pertaining to government officials after product sale. If product is shipped ex works, for example, the customer will take ownership and pay for shipping costs from the seller's facility. The seller, however, may coordinate shipping on behalf of the customer and make all decision up to the delivery of product at the customer's facility. In situations like this, the customer may have funded a bribe without knowing such a bribe took place.

Bribery and Corruption Issues Impacting the Commercial Transportation Industry

The commercial transportation sector has been subjected to FCPA investigations and enforcement actions for many years. Companies have seen enforcement actions relating not only to interactions with customs officials, but also employees of state-owned transportation providers. Customers of these transportation companies have also been impacted by enforcement actions.

Some relevant matters for the commercial transportation industry have been referenced earlier; other examples include:

- **Panalpina:** The DOJ described the Panalpina matter as follows in its related November 4, 2010 press release:

  In documents filed in US District Court for the Southern District of Texas, Panalpina World Transport (Holding) Ltd., a global freight forwarding and logistics services firm based in Basel, Switzerland, and its US-based subsidiary, Panalpina Inc., admitted that the companies, through subsidiaries and affiliates (collectively "Panalpina"), engaged in a scheme to pay bribes to numerous foreign officials on behalf of many of its customers in the oil and gas industry. They did so in order to circumvent local rules and regulations relating to the import of goods and materials into numerous foreign jurisdictions. Panalpina admitted that between 2002 and 2007, it paid thousands of bribes totaling at least $27 million to foreign officials in at least seven countries, including Angola, Azerbaijan, Brazil, Kazakhstan, Nigeria, Russia and Turkmenistan. Also today, Panalpina's customers, including Shell Nigeria Exploration and Production Company Ltd. (SNEPCO), Transocean Inc. and Tidewater Marine International Inc., admitted that the companies approved of or condoned the payment of bribes on their behalf in Nigeria and falsely recorded the bribe payments made on their behalf as legitimate business expenses in their corporate books, records and accounts.

  As part of the agreed resolution, the department today filed a criminal information charging Panalpina World Transport with conspiring to violate and violating the anti-bribery provisions of the FCPA. The department and Panalpina World Transport agreed to resolve the charges by entering into a deferred prosecution agreement. The department also filed a criminal information charging Panalpina Inc. with conspiring to violate the books and records provisions of the FCPA and with aiding and abetting certain customers in violating the books and records provisions of the FCPA. Panalpina Inc. has agreed to plead guilty to the charges. The agreements require the payment of a $70.56 million criminal penalty.

■ **Con-way, Inc.:** – The SEC described the Con-way matter in its related August 27, 2008, litigation release as follows:

The Securities and Exchange Commission today filed a settled civil action in the United States District Court for the District of Columbia charging Conway Inc. ("Con-way"), a San Mateo, California international freight transportation company, with violations of the books and records and internal controls provisions of the Foreign Corrupt Practices Act. According to the complaint, a Philippines-based firm controlled by Con-way made approximately $417,000 in improper payments to numerous foreign government officials between 2000 and 2003. Without admitting or denying the allegations in the commission's complaint, Con-way agreed to pay a $300,000 civil penalty.

The complaint alleges that Emery Transnational, a Manila, Philippines-based firm engaged in shipping and freight operations in the Philippines, was controlled by a wholly owned, U.S.-based subsidiary of Con-way. The complaint further alleges that between 2000 and 2003, Emery Transnational made approximately $244,000 in improper payments to foreign officials at the Philippines Bureau of Customs and the Philippine Economic Zone Area. The complaint alleges that these payments were made to induce these foreign officials to violate customs regulations, settle customs disputes, and reduce or not enforce otherwise legitimate fines for administrative violations.

The complaint also alleges that, during this period, Emery Transnational made approximately $173,000 in improper payments to foreign officials at fourteen state-owned airlines that conducted business in the Philippines. The complaint alleges that these payments were made to induce airline officials to improperly reserve space for Emery Transnational on the airplanes, to falsely underweigh shipments, and to improperly consolidate multiple shipments into a single shipment, resulting in lower shipping charges.

According to the complaint, none of the improper payments made by Emery Transnational were accurately reflected in Con-way's books and records, and Con-way knowingly failed to implement a system of internal accounting controls concerning Emery Transnational that would both ensure that Emery Transnational complied with the FCPA and require that the payments it made to foreign officials were accurately reflected on its books and records.

What Should Commercial Transportation Companies Be Doing?

Companies operating in the commercial transportation industry, while party to all of the systemic anti-bribery risks companies face, have an elevated risk in areas dealing with customs clearance. Commercial transportation companies must establish clear policies to identify how personnel deal with customs or other government personnel on a location-specific basis. Local practices and regulations will vary greatly not only by country, but also considering other factors such as the mode of transportation and the variety of products transported.

The hub and spoke set up of many transportation companies creates a decentralized structure that emphasizes the need to have consistently implemented controls and anti-bribery training of all employees with direct interaction with government officials. Commercial transportation companies need to consider not just employees at office locations, but personnel at remote warehouse locations and other sites in their supply chain. Anti-bribery training should extend to local leaders, who in turn should play a role in providing training to subordinates, thus setting the tone at the top of the local entity.

Due to the frequent use of third-party intermediaries to provide customs clearance services, companies should implement vendor due diligence procedures to identify corruption risks with existing and potential business partners. Contracts with customs-clearance and other third party intermediaries should contain anti-bribery language and strong audit rights that clearly identify the company's ability to review all documentation in support of transactions entered into on behalf of the company. These considerations should extend to subagents or other contractors utilized by company vendors. As with key company employees, anti-bribery training should extend to third parties acting on the company's behalf.

Having the other elements of an anti-corruption compliance program as described in Chapter 4 also apply to commercial transportation companies. As many commercial transportation companies and their affiliates regularly interact with government officials in legitimate activities, these companies must also be mindful to specifically address the proper recording of transactions to provide employees the ability to identify expenses outside of the normal course.

Commercial transport companies may have frequent cash transactions, for example, payment for expediting customs clearance, flight landing fees, and fuel charges. Companies should tightly control and monitor these transactions and carefully evaluate the necessity for cash transactions against inherent risk while exploring feasibility of noncash alternatives.

NOTES

1. "BAE Systems PLC Pleads Guilty and Ordered to Pay $400 Million Criminal Fine," DOJ, March 1, 2010, www.justice.gov/opa/pr/2010/March/10-crm-209.html
2. DOJ News Release, March 1, 2005, www.justice.gov/criminal/fraud/fcpa/cases/titan-corp/03-01-05titan-pr-plea.pdf
3. www.sec.gov/litigation/admin/2009/34-60005.pdf
4. Transparency International is a nonprofit group focused on global anti-corruption efforts; www.transparency.org.
5. "Daimler AG and Three Subsidiaries Resolve Foreign Corrupt Practices Act Investigation and Agree to Pay $93.6 Million in Criminal Penalties," U.S. DOJ press release dated April 1, 2010. www.justice.gov/opa/pr/2010/April/10-crm-360.html
6. "JGC Corporation Resolves Foreign Corrupt Practices Act Investigation and Agrees to Pay a $218.8 Million Criminal Penalty." DOJ, April 6, 2011, www.justice.gov/opa/pr/2011/April/11-crm-431.html
7. "Consumer Spending Looks Firmer in March," *Wall Street Journal*, April 29, 2011.
8. Ernst & Young, "Tracking Global Trends: How Six Key Developments are Shaping the Business World."
9. SEC Litigation Release No. 21618 August 6, 2010. www.sec.gov/litigation/litreleases/2010/lr21618.htm
10. "SEC Settles Case against Chiquita Brands International, Inc.," SEC, October 3, 2001. www.sec.gov/litigation/litreleases/lr17169.htm
11. Avon press release, October 20, 2008; Avon's 2010 annual report, Avon press release, May 3, 2011.
12. Kraft 10-K filed February 28, 2011.
13. "Control Components Inc. Pleads Guilty to Foreign Bribery Charges and Agrees to Pay $18.2 Million Criminal Fine," U.S. DOJ press release, July 31, 2009; case information filed July 22, 2009. www.justice.gov/opa/pr/2009/July/09-crm-754.html
14. Source: IEA, *World Energy Outlook*, May 2010.

15. "FSA Fines Aon Limited £5.25m for Failings in Its Anti-Bribery and Corruption Systems and Controls." FSA press release, January 8, 2009.

16. 8-K filed by CBRE, October 2010; 10-K filed by CBRE, March 2011.

17. 8-K filed by Morgan Stanley, February 2009; 10-Q filed by Morgan Stanley, March, 2009; 10-K filed by Morgan Stanley, December 2010.

18. Gregory Crouse and Thomas Gregory, "Risky Business: What Life Sciences Need to Know About the US Foreign Corrupt Practices Act Before an Acquisition." Reprinted from the October 2009 issue of *Pharmaceutical Commerce.*

19. Ernst & Young, "Managing Bribery and Corruption Risk in Life Science." 2009, EYG no. DQ0025.

20. Lanny A. Breuer Assistant Attorney General Criminal Division, speech, November, 12, 2009 www.ehcca.com/presentations/pharmacongress10/breuer_2.pdf.

21. AtriCure, Estech, AstraZeneca, Ortho-McNeil, Novartis, Forest Laboratories, Inc., Kos, Elan.

22. Genzyme.

23. Schwarz Pharma, Allergan, Abbott, Braun, Dey.

24. Wright Medical, Ela Medical, Exactech.

25. Synthes.

26. GlaxoSmithKline.

27. Jim Edwards, "InterMune CEO Faces 20 Years in Prison for Writing a Press Release," bnet.com, September 30, 2009, www.bnet.com/blog/drug-business/intermune-ceo-faces-20-years-in-prison-for-writing-a-press-release/3060.

28. Anique Gonzalez, "OxyContin Manufacturer, Executives Plead Guilty to Drug Misbranding," GeneralCounselConsulting.com, www.gcconsulting.com/articles/120181/73/OxyContin-Manufacturer-Executives-Plead-Guilty-to-Drug-Misbranding.

29. Jim Edwards, "Pfizer District Sales Manager Guilty of Altering Off-Label Celebrex Documents," bnet.com, March 19, 2009, www.bnet.com/blog/drug-business/pfizer-district-sales-manager-guilty-of-altering-off-label-celebrex-documents/956.

30. Legal News, "Former Glaxo lawyer indicted again over drug probe," insidecounsel.com, April 15, 2011, www.insidecounsel.com/News/2011/4/Pages/Former-Glaxo-lawyer-indicted-again-over-drug-probe.aspx.

31. Jaimie Oh, "Former Chairman of KV Pharmaceutical First Exec to be Banned From Healthcare Programs," beckersasc.com, November 22, 2010, www.beckersasc.com/stark-act-and-fraud-abuse-issues/former-chairman-of-kv-pharmaceutical-first-exec-to-be-banned-from-healthcare-programs.html.

32. Ros Krasny, "UPDATE 4-Stryker unit indicted in marketing scheme: DOJ," Reuters.com, October 28, 2009, www.reuters.com/article/2009/10/28/stryker-idUSN2832038020091028.

33. "Bristol-Myers in $300m settlement," BBC News, June 16, 2005, news.bbc.co.uk/2/hi/business/4098416.stm.

34. Wayne Heilman, "Three former Spectranetics executives indicted," The Gazette, August 31, 2010, www.gazette.com/articles/medical-103831-office-fda.html.

35. EFPIA web site, www.efpia.org/content/default.asp?PageID=615.

36. See note 17.

37. Ben Fritz, "Producers Found Guilty in Thai Film Festival Bribery Case." *Los Angeles Times*, September 14, 2009.

38. www.sfo.gov.uk/press-room/latest-press-releases/press-releases-2011/action-on-macmillan-publishers-limited.aspx

39. "Control Components Inc. Pleads Guilty to Foreign Bribery Charges and Agrees to Pay $18.2 Million Criminal Fine," DOJ, July 31, 2009, www.justice.gov/opa/pr/2009/July/09-crm-754.html

40. Avon press release, October 20, 2008.

41. Avon press release, May 3, 2011.

42. "IBM to Pay $10 Million in Settled FCPA Enforcement Action," U.S. SEC. Litigation Release No. 21889, filed March 18, 2011 www.sec.gov/litigation/litreleases/2011/lr21889.htm.

43. www.sec.gov/litigation/complaints/2011/comp21889.pdf

44. "UTStarcom, Inc. Non-prosecution agreement," DOJ, December 31, 2009, www.justice.gov/criminal/pr/documents/12-31-09UTSI-%20NPA-Agreement .pdf, www.sec.gov/litigation/litreleases/2009/lr21357.htm

45. U.S. Securities and Exchange Commission, speech by SEC staff. Remarks before the New York City Bar: "My First 100 Days as Director of Enforcement," August 5, 2009, Robert Khuzami, Director, SEC Division of Enforcement; www.sewc.gov/news/speech/2009/spch080509rk.htm.

46. "SEC Charges California Telecommunications Company with FCPA Violations," U.S. SEC, Litigation Release No. 21581, June 29, 2010); www.sec.gov/litigation/litreleases/2010/lr21581.htm.

47. United States Southern District of Florida Court, *United States of America v. Alcatel-Lucent, S.A.*, Deferred Prosecution Agreement, Case No. 10-20907, December 20, 2010.

48. www.sec.gov/litigation/admin/2011/34-64123.pdf

49. Id.

 ## CONTRIBUTORS

This section was written with contributions from the following Ernst & Young professionals:

Aerospace and Defense

Richard Thomas: FIDS Principal in New York City, USA

Katie Duggan: FIDS Senior Manager in New York City, USA

Automotive

Brian Jarzynski: FIDS Senior Manager in Detroit, USA

Construction and Real Estate

Brian Browne: FIDS Senior Manager in New York City, USA

Consumer Products

Jonathan Feig: FIDS Partner in Chicago, USA
Miles Ripley: FIDS Senior Manager in Chicago, USA

Diversified Industrial

Michael Stravidis: FIDS Partner in Chicago, USA

Energy

Douglas Tymkiw: FIDS Partner in New Orleans, USA
Warren Breaux: FIDS Manager in New Orleans, USA

Financial Services

Bradley Massam: FIDS Partner in New York City, USA
Christopher Sercy: FIDS Principal in New York City, USA
Stephen Ross: FIDS Senior Manager in New York City, USA
Walid Raad: FIDS Senior Manager in New York City, USA

Life Sciences

Ted Acosta: FIDS Principal in New York City, USA
SanDee Priser: FIDS Partner in Frankfurt, Germany
Casey Horton: FIDS Senior Manager in Chicago, USA

Media and Entertainment

Carol Palmer Winig: FIDS Partner in Boston, USA
Amanda Massucci: FIDS Partner in Los Angeles, USA
Tom Pannell: FIDS Senior Manager in New York City, USA

Metals and Mining

Mike Savage: FIDS Partner in Toronto, Canada
Zain Raheel: FIDS Senior Manager in Toronto, Canada

Retail and Wholesale

Brian Browne: FIDS Senior Manager in New York City, USA

Technology

Catherine Madrid: FIDS Partner in San Francisco, USA
Carol Palmer Winig: FIDS Partner in Boston, USA
Randy Joshi: FIDS Senior Manager in San Francisco, USA

Transportation

Jeffrey Budzynski: FIDS Senior Manager in Chicago, USA

Acknowledgments

The authors and contributors would like to thank these individuals for their invaluable contributions to the book:

Mark Amoroso
Natasha Andrews-Noel
Sara Brandfon
Aaron Brehove
Tamara Bretan
Brian Browne
Jake Chun
Rich Corgel
Chris Costa
Winnie Dang
Bill Foale
Emilie Herman
Heidi Hueseman
Desi Ivanova
Kyle Koehler
Ed Luo
Andrea Mackiewicz
Patrick O'Connor
Mark O'Mara
Lorynn Riley
Todd Roif
Roman Shapiro
Andy Senich

Alexandra Stern
Jeff Taylor
Melanie Trinidad
Ernst & Young SCORE team
Eloise Wagner
Wiley Corporate F&A team

About the Authors

Brian Loughman is the Americas Leader of Ernst & Young LLP's Fraud Investigation & Dispute Services (FIDS) practice, which helps organizations address complex issues related to fraud, regulatory compliance, and business disputes. The firm works with diverse global clients including some of the world's largest companies and law firms, helping them conduct internal investigations, identify and investigate corruption and white-collar crime, assess fraud and compliance risk, calculate damages in disputes, and provide expert witness testimony.

He has extensive experience leading complex global investigations and remediation efforts. He has worked with many multinational organizations on a wide variety of investigative matters relating to anti-bribery and corruption, accounting fraud, corporate internal investigations, as well as internal controls assessment, remediation, and compliance matters. He frequently presents investigative findings to regulators, including the Securities and Exchange Commission and the Department of Justice. (brian.loughman@ey.com)

Richard Sibery is the Americas Leader for Fraud and Investigations with Ernst & Young LLP's FIDS practice. Richard has almost 20 years of experience advising clients and their outside counsel on a wide-range of accounting matters, including bribery and corruption, fraud, corporate internal investigations and compliance matters. He has led a large number of international bribery and corruption projects, both investigative and preventative, across a wide range of industries. In addition to experience presenting his findings to the Department of Justice and the Securities and Exchange Commission, he has also written and spoken extensively on bribery and corruption.

Richard earned his BS in Economics from The Wharton School of the University of Pennsylvania, has a MS in Taxation from the Fordham University Graduate School of Business and a JD from Fordham Law School. He is a certified public accountant and a member of the Executive Committee of the American Institute of Certified Public Accountants' (AICPA) Forensic and Valuation Services Section. (richard.sibery@ey.com)

About the Contributors

 CHAPTER CONTRIBUTORS

Tom Pannell is the lead contributing author and is a Fraud Investigation & Dispute Services (FIDS) Senior Manager with Ernst & Young LLP in New York. He primarily works on fraud and forensic investigations with a focus on bribery and corruption. Tom has spent his entire career with Ernst & Young. He has experience within Assurance, Advisory Services and FIDS and has served clients in a number of different industries. Tom has significant international experience, including in the Americas, Europe, Asia, and Africa. (tom.pannell@ey.com)

Virginia Adams is a FIDS Senior Manager in the New York office of Ernst & Young LLP. Virginia has substantial experience in forensic accounting and corruption investigations, financial statement audits, and various litigation matters. She focuses on bribery and corruption-related matters, including investigations and compliance reviews across various industries. Virginia has led global investigation teams and has extensive experience in Asia, Europe, and South America. (virginia.adams@ey.com)

Bill Henderson is a FIDS Partner in the New York office of Ernst & Young LLP. Bill's practice is focused on business investigations, forensic accounting, corporate fraud prevention, and compliance risk management. Bill is a CPA, attorney, and former federal prosecutor with more than 20 years of experience investigating complex financial matters and providing critical information and solutions to clients. He has conducted investigations both in the United States and overseas involving alleged bribery and foreign corrupt practices, earnings management, money laundering, securities fraud, employee fraud and dishonesty, and commercial disputes. Bill has extensive experience in fraud prevention and the design of organizational compliance and business ethics programs. (william.henderson@ey.com)

Carlos Singh is a FIDS Senior Manager in the San Francisco office of Ernst & Young LLP. He specializes in corporate compliance and ethics. Before joining Ernst & Young, Carlos worked as a federal prosecutor with the U.S. Department of Justice, serving as a member of the department's Money Laundering Section. He also previously worked as a trial lawyer in the Civil Division, handling complex civil litigation. Carlos provides insight on how prosecutors or regulators may evaluate a compliance program, which in turn permits strategic assessment and improvement of a program in order to be better able to detect and prevent noncompliance, promote an ethical culture, and enhance business performance. (carlos.singh@ey.com)

Melda Tanyeri is a FIDS Senior Manager with Ernst & Young et Associés in Paris. Melda has significant experience in a wide range of domestic and international fraud and forensic investigations, in a variety of industries, including financial services, healthcare, telecommunications, and oil and gas industries. She has had significant international experience in Europe, South America, Asia, and Africa. (melda.tanyeri@fr.ey.com)

Richard Thomas is a FIDS Principal with Ernst & Young LLP in New York. He has extensive experience in corporate investigations and restructurings with a strong international focus. He has worked closely with companies and their legal advisors on issues surrounding bribery and corruption, internal investigations, and regulatory and other fraud-related matters. He led the investigative practice of the Ernst & Young member firm in the Cayman Islands, managing international investigations, regulatory engagements, cross-border restructurings, and insolvencies. He has significant international experience in the Americas, Europe, Africa, Asia, Middle East, and the Caribbean. (richard.thomas2@ey.com)

Greg Wolski is a FIDS Partner with Ernst & Young LLP in Chicago. His focus areas include anti-corruption due diligence, litigation, auditing, and advisory services. Greg has extensive experience as a technical consultant and independent partner on accounting and financial reporting, due diligence, litigation, and advisory issues for over 150 mergers and acquisitions. He specializes in inventory, contract accounting and pricing, environmental costs and expenses, project management, purchase price disputes, and financial statement accounting practice and procedures. (gregory.wolski@ey.com)

ADDITIONAL CONTRIBUTORS

Amy Hawkes is a FIDS Partner in the Los Angeles office of Ernst & Young LLP. Amy focuses her practice in the areas of forensic accounting, bribery and corruption, financial fraud investigations, accounting malpractice, and litigation support matters. She also has extensive experience conducting interviews and testimonies of accounting professionals, corporate directors, and company executives. Amy spent several years with the U.S. Securities and Exchange Commission's division of enforcement where she was responsible for the performance of investigations for securities violations primarily related to financial fraud and insider trading. (amy.hawkes@ey.com)

Steve Kuzma is a FIDS Partner in the Atlanta office of Ernst & Young LLP. He is the Americas Leader for the Corporate Compliance Advisory Services group. He helps companies identify and prioritize compliance risks related to legal, regulatory or business requirements. He assists with the design and implementation of compliance programs and helps make sure those programs are integrated into the company's processes and controls. He also helps to measure the effectiveness of existing compliance programs and makes recommendations for improvements. (steven.kuzma@ey.com)

Catherine Madrid is a FIDS Partner with Ernst & Young LLP in San Francisco. Catherine focuses on corporate internal investigations, bribery and corruption, financial fraud investigations, U.S. Securities and Exchange Commission enforcement matters, compliance reviews, and financial damages assessments relating to complex commercial disputes. She has conducted investigations for public and private companies and led numerous investigations on behalf of audit and special committees. Catherine has extensive experience in contract and policy compliance reviews and due diligence reviews. (catherine.madrid@ey.com)

David Rogers is a FIDS Senior Manager in the Dallas office of Ernst & Young LLP. He is an information technology professional with extensive experience in providing services to address complex legal technology and business problems. Dave has a concentration in investigation and litigation consulting, with an emphasis on computer forensics and electronic discovery. He has worked with numerous multinational corporations, helping them navigate the complexities of the electronic discovery life cycle and implement procedures to comply with preservation notices and legal holds in a cost-effective manner. (dave.rogers@ey.com)

Bryan Schillinger is an Executive Director with Ernst & Young LLP in Houston with the Customs and International Trade practice. Bryan has extensive experience assisting exporters and importers with export controls, economic sanctions, anti-boycott, and customs laws. His background includes prior legal practice and previous service as international trade counsel for a global Fortune 500 oilfield service company, where he advised on trade matters regarding some of the most challenging countries in the world. (bryan .schillinger@ey.com)

Daniel Torpey is a FIDS Partner with Ernst & Young LLP in Dallas. He is a CPA and former auditor with over 25 years of public accounting experience. Dan leads the Forensic Data Analytics practice in the Americas with a focus on helping companies with their overall corporate compliance programs as they relate to anti-fraud and business conduct efforts. Dan has testified in state, federal and international proceedings in the area of forensic accounting, investigations and compliance issues and was a designated forensic accounting expert on the insurance losses from the World Trade Center. Dan is also the co-author of "Business Interruption: Coverage, Claims and Recovery" published by National Underwriter. (daniel.torpey@ey.com)

Vincent Walden is a FIDS Partner with Ernst & Young LLP in New York. He specializes in text analytics, forensic data mining, and electronic discovery services. He is experienced with providing clients substantial anti-fraud-based innovation, research, and analytics, including link analysis, text data mining, metadata analysis, entity extraction, and cluster analysis. Vincent leads teams to help clients discover patterns and anomalies in huge sets of disparate data, with a focus on unstructured, text-based data sources such as e-mail and corporate file share networks. (vincent.walden@ey.com)

Index